MANAGING
CLASSROOM
BEHAVIOR

AN ECOLOGICAL
APPROACH TO
ACADEMIC AND
SOCIAL LEARNING

JOEL MACHT
UNIVERSITY OF DENVER

Longman
New York & London

Managing Classroom Behavior:
An Ecological Approach to Academic and Social Learning

For Nancy, Lee, and C

Longman, 95 Church Street, White Plains, N.Y. 10601

Associated companies:
Longman Group Ltd., London
Longman Cheshire Pty., Melbourne
Longman Paul Pty., Auckland
Copp Clark Pitman, Toronto

Executive editor: Raymond T. O'Connell
Development editor: Elsa van Bergen
Production editor: Ann P. Kearns
Text design: Jill Francis Wood
Cover design: Jill Francis Wood
Production supervisor: Kathleen M. Ryan

Library of Congress Cataloging-in-Publication Data

Macht, Joel, 1938-
    Managing classroom behavior: an ecological approach to academic and social
learning / Joel Macht.

        p.   cm.
    Bibliography: p.
    Includes index.
    ISBN 0-8013-0429-6
    1. Special education.   2. Developmentally disabled children—
Education.   3. Behavior modification.   I. Title.
LC3965.M23 1990
371.9—dc20   89-34262
                                                                  CIP

ABCDEFGHIJ-ML-99   98   97   96   95   94   93   92   91   90

CONTENTS

CONTENTS

CONTENTS

CONTENTS

CONTENTS

CONTENTS

CONTENTS

CONTENTS

CONTENTS

CONTENTS

CONTENTS

INTRODUCTION

The purpose of this book is to help you work with the individuals for whom you have accepted responsibility. Its intended audience is students and those who seek my consulting services during my working days: teachers, parents, physicians, therapists, and educational administrators. It will focus on problems of everyday living and schooling—problems presented not only by children whose genetic endowments and developmental experiences have provided them with sound bodies and keen minds, but also those youngsters who labor under the burden of physical disabilities.

Any book that attempts to help you with the problems individuals exhibit faces the dilemma of what issues to cover. No one effort could ever speak to all the subtleties and difficulties that are a part of daily life and schooling: The individuals we work with are sufficiently different from one another to make such a goal impossible. Consultants, without first-hand knowledge of many particulars unique to an individual, place themselves in an untenable position if they choose to offer advice as though that individual and his or her personal, surrounding environment were representative of others. They could of course do so, but the outcome would likely not be very productive or accurate. Instead of looking at specific problems teachers and care-givers face daily, I have chosen, through various topics, to discuss a *process* that will help you discover your own solutions to the problems presented by the individuals with whom you work. It is a process with some application to developmentally disabled adults as well; the focus is on helping people for whom daily living is a difficult task.

You will find the text practical and free of jargon, offering the "hands-on" suggestions most commonly requested by my colleagues who work daily with their targeted populations. If its style of delivery seems relaxed, as though coming in the form of a workshop, as though peppered with pages from my notebook, that is as intended, for the content has been taken from lectures, inservices, previous writings, and the many cases I've been involved with over the past twenty years. As such, it will focus less on theory and documented research, and more on *well-researched ideas* that can help us achieve some of the goals that occupy our time, energy, and caring. I have tried to discuss important topics using nontechnical language that is comfortable to me personally and familiar to many teachers and therapists. I do, however, provide a brief glossary of a few commonly employed technical terms that I have chosen either not to use within the body of this text, or have used sparingly. This will show how the technical and nontechnical terms fit together and should serve to demystify certain words frequently used in specific professional circles.

I have tried to reflect, as closely as possible, the actual process I and other professionals follow when involved with an individual client. My hope is that you will sense that we are conversing with one another. To that end, a fictional teacher, parent, therapist, or "friendly" iconoclast will join us from time to time throughout this project and will interject issues and ask questions that perhaps will be similar to those you might raise. The resulting "conversations" and stepwise sequencing of the actual process used on an everyday basis are intended to make the content more animated and easier to identify with. Since, however, you and I are not seated across from one another, and since it is likely you will want to know the rationale or justification for a proposed suggestion, I will often include my own rationale, along with differing points of view offered by other professionals, regarding the basis for, and controversies over, a particular course of action. I will present my biases knowing full well that mine and yours may not mesh. If, however, I provide you with "food for thought" and ideas to discuss with other professionals, then I will have achieved a large part of what I intended.

Occasions will arise where I will ask you to spend some private time by yourself or group time within your classroom thinking about or discussing some of the "food for thought" issues that may contain some elements of controversy. Further, I may suggest you try an exercise or two that will either help you better understand certain points, or assist you in dissecting the potential controversy within those points. On these occasions, you will find in the margin, across from material set in boldface type, a box with a number printed within its borders:

$$\boxed{\ \ \mathbf{1.1}\ \ }$$

A corresponding numbered box will appear in an "end-of-chapter summary" where I will review certain issues as well as indicate some of what will be forthcoming, and where I may ask you some questions, ask you to try some exercises or consider some assertions or suggestions. As you will see, this Introduction contains a sample of a marginal box keyed to a question at the end of the discussion. (Note: The issues and exercises make great short-answer test questions, so be on your toes!)

A final thought on format: the book is purposely casual. I'd like you to relax with it. While there are, I hope, points worth remembering, I don't want you to look on this book as one that requires hours of rote practice to prepare you for hours of test "regurgitation." I'd much prefer you and your friends talk, debate, analyze, and scrutinize the material. Think about the stories, the characters, the content provided. At this point in our profession's growth, we need good thinkers, doubters, and debaters, not dutiful regurgitators. We have enough of the latter. All professionals who work with children and developmentally disabled adults know that we are still debating our issues. There remains considerable room for well-thought-out disagreement.

TOPICS TO BE DISCUSSED

The manuscript's topics were not chosen whimsically. They represent issues that persistently surface when I and other professionals discuss ways of helping individuals achieve success, regardless of problems presented or locations where the problems are observed. The issues are equally at home with teachers in a classroom, therapists in a hospital, and care-givers in a foster placement or group home. I believe, regardless of your chosen professional endeavors, you will recognize the issues and benefit from their discussion. The following represents a sample of the topics.

DISCIPLINE/BEHAVIOR MANAGEMENT

By far, the most frequently requested topic of inservices and professional queries I receive deals with the issues of discipline and behavior management. Rarely a day passes where I am not on the phone talking with some party who is experiencing difficulty with the behavior of a student or client. While I am accommodating the requests, the focus of the conversation, as is true of this book, shifts as quickly as possible toward looking at relationships between activities and the troubling, undesired behaviors.

DISCIPLINARY PROGRAMS AS THEY RELATE TO ACADEMIC AND NONACADEMIC ACTIVITIES

You will discover shortly how important it is to recognize that undesired behaviors never occur in isolation, that social/emotional problems and learning problems invariably go hand in hand, and that perceiving them as separate from each other may be akin to seeing nothing. Taking behavior out of its associative academic and home context—working with it as though it were unrelated to its surroundings—will rarely produce lasting, meaningful results for any of us. Thus, you will be asked to view an individual's actions, along with his or her accompanying uniquenesses, as they occur and interact within a variety of settings where the individual develops, studies, and pursues the ends the individual sees as having importance. You will be asked to see the individual's behaviors as being only a small part of the total picture that warrants your attention and concern: What the individual is doing, or is being asked to do, or perceives and interprets as relevant—all are of equal significance. You will be asked to see behaviors as interrelated components of the tasks presently being assigned or required, be the tasks academic, social/emotional, work related, or life sustaining.

INDIVIDUALITY: ASSESSMENT AND REMEDIATION

I will urge you to see all the individuals with whom you work, first and foremost, as being themselves with their own strengths and frailties; see them as being at a particular position along a developmental scale that may or may not be similar to that of others. I will ask you to be less concerned with what labeled group they might be identified with, or what characteristics they might have in common with those who share classrooms or other locations, and envision each apart from others, as individuals with their own special selves, trying to achieve what is *individually valued*, doing what they can to find personal meaning and worth.

A NONCATEGORICAL POPULATION

Because I will implore you to see each individual as a separate entity, regardless of strengths and frailties, **you will notice that I do not describe or accept the description of individuals as being "disabled,"** "underachievers," "retarded," or "disturbed." Terms such as "typical," "mildly-" or "moderately-involved" are equally without benefit. New phrases, such as "attention-deficit-disorders" or "gifted-handicapped" represent little more than the jargon of the day; like others, they, too, will eventually disappear for lack of worth. This material will speak to all individuals in schools and special settings, regardless of which convenient label or category has been employed. While certainly recognizing and appreciating the variability that exists among individuals, I hope you will join me in my conclusion that such labels do not provide us with any useful information about what individuals do, what they are like, or what we can do to help them.

EDUCATION'S CATEGORICAL APPROACH TO DIFFERENCES: "DRAGONS OF CONVENIENCE"

Moreover, I hope you will see that labels and names that have become a familiar, constant, and increasingly suspicious aspect of educational thought—names that I have termed "Dragons of Convenience"—have moved us away from providing services on the basis of individual variability and need; labels actually hide an individual's unique needs from us. I will introduce you to the "dragons" in Chapter 11, and, perhaps with more passion than eloquence, I will try to show you how the "dragons" have long outlived their usefulness, how they are presently placing a burden on students who are burdened enough by a system often insensitive to the whole individual.

AN ECOLOGICAL/DEVELOPMENTAL MODEL

I will offer you a view where the "dragons" are programmatically unnecessary. Without them, you will be able to concentrate more fully on where students are in relation to their developmental experiences and skills, and where they are in relation to their total environment—what I will term "life space," a system that both surrounds and impacts on them. The offered view will be "ecological" in that what they do affects their environment, and what their environment does influences them. They can no more be separated from their environment than their environment can be separated from them. The view, additionally, is developmental in that what they are presently doing is intimately involved with previous experiences, personal perceptions, and acquired skills. What new experiences, perceptions, and skills they are prepared to understand and master are, in part, related to those past acquisitions, both academic and nonacademic in nature.

INTRODUCTION

THE INDIVIDUAL'S PRESENT PERFORMANCE LEVEL

You will be urged, as you go about your student teaching, field experience, practicum, or professional endeavors to constantly see individuals from the ecological/developmental perspective; to see how their efforts in reading, writing, and math, efforts with thinking, creating, and problem solving, fit within their educational and noneducational "life space;" to see them not only in terms of what they are doing, but to see them as a developing, functioning being in relation to all that is happening outside themselves, as well as what is happening within. You will be asked to interpret the above in terms of "Present Performance Level," a measure that will provide you with specific information about individuals' uniqueness, where they are *now* in relationship to where you would like them to be; a measure that ultimately takes precedence over where someone else suggests they should be, or where someone else hopes they would be; a measure that will help you determine where your remediation, your teaching efforts must begin.

BEYOND AGE, GRADE LEVEL, AND INTELLECTUAL CAPACITY

The "Present Performance Level" will assist you in going beyond the traditional and often weak barometers of age, grade level, and estimates of "intelligence" used to determine instructional placements and interventions. In their place, you will have first-hand evidence of an individual's developmental level as it relates to cognitive, conceptual, motoric, and social/emotional strengths. You will be able to see individuals, not solely as compared with others who sit in nearby desks, but compared with themselves: where they are *today* in relation to where they were yesterday. As such, you will lessen the chances that they will be asked to become involved in tasks for which they lack the necessary prerequisite skills, as well as lessen the chances that they will be asked to do something they have long since accomplished.

RELEVANCE AND SUCCESS

You will be able to help individuals see the relevance of what they are being asked to do; be able to challenge without overwhelming; be able to provide them with a taste of success without having them experience the frustration that can come with constant disappointment and failure.

THE RELATIONSHIP BETWEEN
—————————— BEHAVIOR AND ACADEMICS ——————————

As the above topics may indicate, the book is not intended as one solely devoted to the management of behavior found in a classroom or special setting, *or* one devoted solely to the delivery of task-oriented materials geared toward students or individuals with or without special needs. Rather, the book will look at many of the issues involved with both social behavior and academic pursuits. It is intended as one in a series of readings designed for educators and other professionals who have accepted the challenge to help people whose developmental progress would benefit from a guiding hand.

I wish I could tell you that what we will discuss will be easy to put into practice. Such, I must admit, is most often not the case. The material will require careful consideration as you read, and much practice as you attempt to replicate the process. It will also require that you work closely with your colleagues and perhaps your own consultant as you search for ways to better the lives of those for whom you have accepted responsibility. Many times throughout the text, the word "magic" will be found. What you will discover quickly is that there is *no* magic to what we do. If you have been in the field for any length of time, you have already discovered that. If you are preparing, through your college studies, to enter the field, you will discover this the moment you set eyes on the first individual who is in need of your assistance.

—————————————— SUMMARY ——————————————

Let's practice with the first marginal box and its boldface material. There's something about that highlighted text I'd like you to consider.

Labeling

 Evidently, I'm not fond of labels, names, and categories as they are used to describe children, students, and adults. Try the following question. Discuss it with your classmates, colleagues, or just think about it yourself.

Question: What problems, if any, may arise when professionals use various labels, such as learning disabled or emotionally disturbed, to describe a student?

Notice that no answer to the question will be provided at the time the box is presented. (I may provide you with some hints or things to consider, but an answer will *not* be offered.) Rather than simply read an answer, I'd prefer you play with the issue to whatever degree you (and your professor) may wish. One thing is certain: Before you finish this book, you will have my view. If you'd like, you can then compare your ideas with mine.

1

THE MEANING
OF BEHAVIOR

The phone call can come from any number of sources. The described problems can approach the unimaginable, often surpass understanding: a 3-month-old who stops eating; a 60-year-old who begins self-abusing; a fourth grader who continues to struggle with his academics and his own well-being. The subject of the call is always behavior—what someone is doing or not doing. The characterization of the behavior is always that it is undesired. Implicitly or explicitly, the caller's words indicate that the behavior needs to be altered and replaced by another behavior or set of behaviors that are deemed healthier, more appropriate, more desirable, or easier for others to work or live with. Regardless of professional theory, an individual's behavior, seen within the context of his or her environment, becomes the impetus for inquiry. It has been that way since time immemorial. It is not likely to change.

THE FIX-IT APPROACH

Logically, it would seem that if a behavior was not "right," if it did not fit within someone's perceived scope of desirability, then it simply should be fixed—somewhat akin to a TV set that goes on the blink or a car that stubbornly refuses to turn over on a cold winter morning. The precedent for such thinking goes far beyond modern-day mechanical devices: A novice skier breaks a bone in his leg while bouncing through a field of moguls on an expert slope—the break is fixed by an orthopedic surgeon; an energetic, youthful first-grader is having difficulty remaining in her seat and attending to her teacher's confusing lessons—the "attention-deficit" and unacceptable work is "fixed" by a five-day-a-week regimen of pills.

―――――――――――――――― "FIXING" IN ISOLATION ―――――――――――――――

While the "let's-fix-it" logic holds true for cars and TV's, it's at best questionable when human behavior enters the arena. Such thinking often fails to consider the relationship the behavior holds with other variables related to the individual's past and present environment—other variables that might help us understand why the behavior is occurring. Granted the skier's leg was fixed, but someone needs to tell him about "bunny" slopes, and lessons, and self-preservation—otherwise, the next item in a cast may be his neck! Too, the first-grader, now medicated, *may* be slowed down as a result of her altered brain chemistry, she *may* attend more to what has been presented, but someone should loudly raise some pointed questions to her teacher and educational system about what *they* are doing to fit the educational program to the child's uniqueness. Otherwise the child may lose more than her appetite and, perhaps, a few inches of growth.

> *Associated Press: October 21, 1988:* At least 750,000 U.S. children are taking stimulant medications to curb their overactivity or inattentiveness, but researchers said . . . it is not known if they are getting the drugs appropriately. "Medication treatment for hyperactive children in the United States has emerged from its minor treatment role in the 1960s to become dominant child mental health intervention in the late 1980s," the researchers said.
>
> "A national estimate of 750,000 youth receiving (stimulant) medication in 1987 can be viewed as a conservative one," they wrote in today's Journal of the American Medical Association . . . A furor has arisen over giving a child stimulants such as Ritalin, Dexedrine and Cylert. They once were prescribed mainly to stem hyperactivity, but now also are given to non-hyperactive children who have trouble paying attention, the researchers said . . . "If the present trends continue, over 1 million U.S. children will be receiving stimulant medication by the early 1990s. . . ."

The article quoted above suggested that the use of medication "is appropriate if a youngster has a problem that meets the strict psychiatric definition of 'hyperactivity' or 'attention-deficit.'"

First, there are no "strict" definitions available that provide clear-cut parameters for what the terms "hyperactivity" or "attention-deficit" behaviors represent. Notice, for example, the "essential" features that are viewed by some professionals as signs of "inappropriate" inattention and impulsivity.[1]

Please look carefully at each word and phrase. Besides the fact that the characterizations could easily fit a sizeable portion of any student population (including graduate students), the phrases are filled with ambiguities that cannot help but lead to confusion and differing opinions.

Inattention

1. Often fails to finish things he or she starts
2. Often doesn't seem to listen
3. Is easily distracted
4. Has difficulty concentrating on school work or other tasks requiring sustained attention
5. Has difficulty sticking to a play activity

Impulsivity

1. Often acts before thinking
2. Shifts excessively from one activity to another
3. Has difficulty organizing work (this not being due to cognitive impairment)
4. Needs lots of supervision
5. Frequently calls out in class
6. Has difficulty awaiting turns in games or group sessions

More often than not, the determination of "hyperactivity" or "attention-deficits" is a judgment call (opinion) made or offered *prior* to an in-depth investigation of the children's activities in relation to what they are being asked to do in classrooms. It is quite common for two teachers to maintain totally different opinions regarding the presence of the purported "conditions." Second, physicians prescribe the medication, more often than not, only after being pressured to do so by teachers or parents. The physicians are not likely to spend the needed time within a classroom to observe the children's behaviors as they relate to assignments, teacher methodology, and class structure. Third, stimulant medication, if it is to be tried at all, should be a *last* option, not a *first* choice. This "rule" must hold true even if a student manifests *all* of the above stated characterizations. Fourth, it is readily apparent that professionals who opt for medication first are often unaware of any alternative approaches, much less alternative ways of viewing the messages within the student's behaviors. For them, medication becomes the easy solution.

PROBLEMS DO NOT BEGIN OVERNIGHT

Human behavior, with the rarest of exceptions, does not suddenly break down or fail one morning to start. Problems that reach a consultant's ear generally progress inconspicuously, building strength as each day passes. Equally inconspicuous factors continually influence the behavior making it increasingly resistant to change. Then, at some point, often guided by a painful level of frustration or concern, the call for assistance is made. As opposed to cars and TV sets, it is not merely a matter of replacing simple tubes and batteries. "Fixing" an individual is not something that comes easily, for the behavior in question has found a *place* and *purpose*.

THE THEORETICAL WINDOW

Fortunately, human behavior provides us with more than just a picture of its actions in isolation. It affords us a window through which we can see much more than movements of bones and muscles as they traverse a field of snow, more than the perceived disruptive or unacceptable activities of a fledgling first-grader who is trying to find his or her way through the rules and regulations that are imposed within the confines of an educational facility. Human behavior tells us something about behaving individuals, something about the way their heads work, something about their values and developmental level, about who and what they are, about environment and experience, past and present. Above all, the behavior tells us that "fixing" in isolation, without consideration for the uniqueness of the individual or his or her surrounding environment, may settle the waters momentarily, but do little for future waves that are likely to occur.

DIVERSE VIEWS OF BEHAVIOR

The meaning of behavior as seen through the window varies dramatically across theories. For some professionals, the skiier's speeding behavior will reflect a "death wish"; others will see it as indicating simple carelessness. Someone might suggest a bravado that is intended to cover an inadequacy of self; someone else, a romantic perhaps, might offer an interpretation that speaks to a need or desire to impress a partner of the opposite gender. The meaning behind the young student's behavior could be viewed with equal variability: a disordered brain, a disturbed psyche, inadequate maturity, inadequate security, a tired teacher, a wide-awake child, outlandish expectations on the part of a system, or the typical behavior of a developing 6-year-old.

Understand that a debate over the meaning behind behavior is not just an academic exercise undertaken by "ivory tower" philosophers. The determination of meaning often sets the stage for professional remediation. Logically, we would assume that medication was prescribed for the first-grader because her behavior was seen as indicating a disorder of physiology. In today's parlance, the child would be viewed as *having* an "attention-deficit-disorder." Logically, "fix it"—quiet the kid down so she doesn't fidget so much, so she attends more. On the other hand, medication certainly would not have been prescribed (for the child!) had the picture seen through the window been interpreted as a reflection of an insensitive teacher or an antiquated educational system. Under the latter circumstances, "treatment" would have involved inservicing the teacher or changing the system. Meaning is very important; its determination can produce interesting differences with regard to suggestions for treatment.

Many years ago I watched on television a noted comedian who had temporarily replaced an equally admired talk show host who was on vacation. The comedian had expressed to his audience his inordinate fear of flying and had scheduled several guest "experts" to discuss this problem behavior. Three of the guests were professionals (one psychiatrist, two psychologists). The fourth guest, an actor, was a friend of the comedian. The first psychologist said that fear of flying was reflective of a poor self-concept. He suggested therapy to enhance the comedian's sense of personal worth. The psychiatrist, a true iconoclast, said that he had no idea why the comedian was afraid of winged vehicles, but a few joint visits would certainly solve the problem.

The second psychologist, to the utter delight of the audience, said the flying problem was reflective of the comedian's experience with masturbation. In true comedic style, the host, upon hearing the speaker's view, feigned a dead-fall to the floor. After the host laboriously struggled to his seat, the professional, with a straight face, asked the man if he recalled feeling a physical "let-down" shortly after masturbating. Laughing uncontrollably, and unable to speak, the gentleman vigorously nodded "yes." The expressed phrase "physical let-down" quickly changed to "fall-down," and the professional, impervious to the merriment, pointed out, as though he were lecturing to a group of naive first-year medical students, that the comedian was unconsciously unable to discriminate between the "fall-down" from masturbating and the "fall-down" from a diving airplane—or something to that effect. He suggested therapy to work through the sexual problems.

The actor-friend walked on the stage laughing hysterically. The infectious laughter quickly spread to everyone in the building—cameramen included: the TV picture shimmered like a bowl of Jello. Fifteen minutes transpired before the host and guest could even speak to one another. The guest, eventually with a straight face that had come from years of studying acting, calmly stated: "I think you're afraid to die!" After more laughter, he suggested the comedian take a train! Considerable difference between meaning and treatment!

MY VIEW THROUGH THE WINDOW

Professionals' views and biases are determined to a large extent by their training and experiences. One doesn't come up with an association between fear of flying and masturbation for kicks. Such an interpretation has to be educated into a professional's repertoire. My training, education, and experience would preclude such an idea from ever being considered, much less expressed. Likewise, I have difficulty with the following position suggested by K.F. Tift to the readers of an article entitled "The Disturbed Child in the Classroom."

> You will become increasingly aware that the behavior which angers you is a signal of illness, just as red spots are a signal of measles . . .[2]

My view through the window doesn't show me that. Neither does it allow me to accept the following.

> A commonly observed symptom of tension in many young children is between-meal . . . nibbling. This . . . child usually demands sweets . . . cookies, candy, cake, ice cream, and desserts of various kinds. He is ordinarily not hungry at mealtime and nibbles and picks at his food . . . Such eating habits usually indicate an emotionally disturbed state.[3]

> Paul cannot sit still in class. He is intelligent, but he cannot concentrate or learn. His work is poor and erratic; he attacks an assignment aggressively but soon gives it up; he is loud, often disruptive and impulsive and is apt to create chaotic situations about him. At home, Paul is prone to frequent temper tantrums . . . He tells lies. He is excitable, aggressive, exceptionally clumsy, and he has trouble sleeping. In short, he is a problem for both his parents and teachers. On the surface Paul may appear to be a troublemaker or a bad boy, but in fact he is a troubled youngster. . . . Like nearly seven hundred thousand other youngsters, predominately boys, Paul suffers from a behavior disorder known as hyperactivity, or attention deficit disorder.[4]

The above views are too pat, too easy. They take prodigious issues involved with human behavior and reduce them to physiological, educational/psychological diseases and conditions. They ring of the distant past when plagues were thought to be due to the wrath of evil spirits, when a man's "aberrant" behavior was said to reflect "disordered motions of his nervous tissue," when an individual's unacceptable social behavior was said to be caused by congested blood that could be rectified by a handful of leeches. They ignore the complexities of the environment, the influence the environment can have on the individual's life space. They turn away from all we know about the adaptability of the human organism—both young and old. They picture man and boy, woman and girl as weak creatures, incapable of finding their own way, given their own uniquenesses, to achieve what they value. They take behavior and see it as a sign of illness. They have abandoned the concept of health. Expediency has become the byword. They have looked through the smallest frame of an immensely large window.

ADAPTIVE, PURPOSIVE, FUNCTIONAL BEHAVIOR

Twenty years of working with a vastly heterogeneous population has taught me what some of my colleagues have failed to consider: Regardless of manifested behavior, no matter how distasteful, disturbing, annoying, or unsettling the behavior might be to *someone else*, the individual manifesting the behavior *is doing the best he or she can to satisfy needs, to obtain what is valued and perceived as important.* Behavior, no matter its own flavor, no matter which words are used to characterize its color, is nevertheless *adaptive, purposive,* and *functional:* It is adaptive in that it has been acquired through lessons learned from the individual's surrounding environment; it is purposive in that there is a desired goal that the individual is struggling to reach; it is functional in that it works—it brings the individual what is desired through the behaviors that have been learned.

Neither you nor I have to accept the notion that the child's behavior that angers us is a sign of illness; that nibbling between meals, eating sweets rather than brussels sprouts, is a sign of a disturbed state of mind; that Paul's behavior, admittedly a problem for his parents and teachers, is a sign that his physiological attention system is deficient or disordered. It is equally plausible, and likely more accurate, to conclude that each child, each adult (parent and teacher), given his or her strengths and weaknesses, is doing the best he or she can within the given circumstances. All are adapting and adjusting to what I call their "natural environment." The natural environment exists on the other side of the window. It represents a ubiquitous and powerful system, capable of influencing a multitude of difficulties affecting both child and adult. **Concluding that an individual's behavior is solely a function of a deficiency attributed to the individual denies the existence of the world within which the individual lives.** It is a conclusion more suitable for an ostrich than an inquiring mind.

1.1

NOTES

1. Kirk, S.A., & Chalfant, J.C. (1984). *Academic and developmental learning disabilities* (p. 77). Denver: Love Publishing.
2. Tift, K.F. (1968). The disturbed child in the classroom. *NEA Journal, 57,* 12–14.
3. Thorpe, L.P., Katz, B., & Lewis, R.T. (1961). *The psychology of abnormal behavior.* New York: Ronald Press.
4. Gardner, H. (1982). *Developmental psychology* (p. 486). Boston: Little, Brown.

SUMMARY

KEEP IN MIND

1. An individual's behavior is always being influenced by the many aspects and features of his or her own unique environment. If you see the behavior isolated from that environment, you will often gain a distorted, narrow view of both the individual and what he or she is presently doing.
2. Isolated views increase the chances we will attempt to "fix" in isolation; such views further increase the likelihood we will overlook how the behavior fits within the individual's environment, and what meaning the behavior may be conveying. The behavior of a difficult child is a function of many factors. The behavior must be seen in relation to those factors.
3. Diverse views as to a behavior's meaning are common. Depending on academic training and personal bias, any two of us may view the same behavior quite differently. While it is important to accept the existence of these diverse views, it is essential that you train yourself to be open and objective when observing individuals' actions. Be careful about accepting too narrow a view of the meaning behind them. Be particularly cautious about assuming that behaviors are reflective of some educational, psychological, or physiological pathology that exists *within* an individual.
4. There may (read: will) come a time when a youngster is going to behave in such a way as to make it difficult for you to appreciate his or her actions. You will find the behavior annoying, grating, or downright repugnant. You may become very concerned over the behavior. Regardless of your personal reaction, and difficult as it may be, try to

remember that behavior, no matter its flavor or apparent intent, is, nevertheless:

a. adaptive
b. purposive
c. functional

The behavior has found a place within the individual's environment. It has meaning, and it has value. To work with the behavior, you will need to find its purpose, meaning, and value; you will need to discover where and how the behavior fits within the youngster's environment.

Your View through the Window

| 1.1 | A friend of yours has a 16-month-old baby. The friend reports that, of late, the baby has been crying more frequently at various times throughout the day. She would like your opinion as to what the crying behavior might mean (or signify). Once you have offered several possible answers as to the meaning of the child's behavior, compare your answers with a colleague. See which one of you developed the most alternative views for the child's behavior. Were you able to come up with some "meanings" that did *not* indicate anything was wrong with the child? (Hint: Remember that behavior has purpose; it may produce an outcome the child might value.)

CONSIDER AS WE LOOK AHEAD

1. We know that behavior is adaptive: It comes about, in part, as a result of experiences with the environment. We know that behavior serves some purpose; behavior provides an individual with the means to gain access to personal goals and momentary values. But the concept of behavior, as it occurs in classrooms, homes, and special settings, is more complex than often considered. A closer look at the concept of behavior will demonstrate that:
   a. Behaviors occur in pairs: those deemed desired; those deemed undesired.
   b. More often than not, we respond to the undesired behaviors, often neglecting the desired counterparts.
   c. By responding mainly to an individual's undesired behavior, we may be making the situation more difficult for everyone.
2. One of the very first steps we need to take in order to assist individuals is to determine precisely what they are doing, as well as what we would prefer them to do. Said differently, we need to establish "behavior-pairs," the topic of the next chapter.

2

BEHAVIOR-PAIRS

Someone once suggested that little in life is guaranteed other than death and taxes. We can, quite comfortably, add another guarantee to that limited list of assurances: Bring children together, children and adults together, and you will have the needed ingredients to produce a kaleidoscopic representation of behavior, ranging from the familiar to the near shocking. Add an element of structure to the scene, and the colors of the behaviors will change. Add requirements, and more change is likely. With the increased changes in activities, their levels, frequency, intensity, and character, another guarantee will surface: One of the children, somewhere within the crowd, is going to do something that is not going to be appreciated by either another child, an adult, or both; one child, with perhaps all the innocence of a baby's first smile, is going to step into (and onto) someone else's territory. The child will exercise his or her own oats, heritage, and "biosocial" acquisitions and is going to upset someone's applecart, guaranteed. So, too, is the fact that the "undesired" behavior will be seen.

It is not surprising that undesired behaviors initially, and often quickly, draw our attention. By all observations, parents, teachers, and therapists prefer their daily activities and responsibilities to run smoothly. Undesired behaviors not only tell us that something within the natural environment needs investigation, they do upset the daily applecart; they interfere with our personal and academic goals and plans. If we put aside the resulting unsettled emotions that can be produced by such behaviors, changes in schedules, routines, and methods are often required to deal with the unexpected diversions from what is preferred. When my assistance is sought, I eventually ask: "Tell me what the individual is doing." Without exception, what follows is a varied list of perceived undesired actions: "He defies my requests; his aggressiveness toward his peers has increased; he is unwilling to attend to his school work; he rarely shows any responsibility; he won't eat any solid foods." Undesired behaviors are on the tip of our tongue. They represent what we would prefer the individual not do.

"That's human nature, isn't it? Even with my own children, I'm more tuned into the behaviors that upset me than those that are pleasing," the teacher conceded.

"I'm not certain that such represents human nature, but it certainly is common. Watch many of us as we work with our students or clients and you will see that **when an individual is doing precisely what we want, when everything is running smoothly, we often do not notice what is actually happening.** Then watch how quickly our attention is drawn to the individual when something he does runs counter to what we desire. Ask us to describe the individual's behavior and we're likely to recall with ease the undesired actions."

| 2.1 |

"It is obvious we must attend to more than just undesired behaviors," the teacher reflected.

"We certainly have to be aware that more than the 'undesired' is happening," I suggested. "I worked recently with a 20-year-old male in a special classroom. His teacher's assigned task incorporated the familiar pegboard, and he had been asked to sort and place the pegs in the board's holes by color. After a few minutes of correct sorting, the young man left the table and meandered around the room. His teacher took him by the arm and directed him back to his seat. 'He never does anything right,' the teacher flatly stated to me *while* the man once again began to sort the pegs. I directed the teacher's attention toward the man, pointing to him as he worked on the activity the teacher had assigned. She replied with some embarrassment, 'Well, almost never.'"

"The man was doing what the teacher wanted."

"Absolutely yes. Granted, it was not occurring as often, as regularly as the teacher preferred, but it was happening. What we sometimes do not realize is that undesired behaviors *always* have a more desired counterpart, a counterpart that represents a behavior we would prefer the individual do. **Unless we teach ourselves to look for this counterpart, it may go unnoticed.**"

| 2.2 |

"It sounds like you're saying that behaviors come in pairs."

"Precisely. Together, the two behaviors, the one that is seen as desired along with its undesired counterpart, are referred to as 'behavior-pairs.'[1] The accurate determination and recognition of behavior-pairs is our first step toward helping the subject achieve success with his studies and social actions."

BEHAVIOR-PAIRS: WHAT MUST BE SEEN

Behavior-pairs represent two incompatible behaviors that cannot occur at the same time. From your perspective, one behavior will be desirable; the other undesirable. (As you will discover shortly, the student's perception of the desirability and undesirability of behavior may be the opposite of yours!) Let's look at the "undesired" behaviors mentioned above that were brought to my attention over one week.

Undesired Behaviors

1. Being defiant
2. Being aggressive toward peers
3. Refusing to attend to school work
4. Being irresponsible
5. Not eating any solids

Because all undesired behaviors have desired alternatives, the behavior-pairs might loosely appear as follows:

Desired Behaviors	Undesired Behaviors
1. Being cooperative	1. Being defiant
2. Not being aggressive	2. Being aggressive toward peers
3. Completing school work	3. Refusing to attend to school work
4. Not being irresponsible	4. Being irresponsible
5. Eating solid foods	5. Not eating any solids

Barring some unusual exceptions, you will want the desired behaviors to replace those designated as undesired.

THE PURPOSE OF BEHAVIOR-PAIRS

Regardless of the professional setting where you will (or presently do) find yourself, regardless of the types of individuals you're working with, be they described as multiply-handicapped, mildly or moderately involved, gifted, typical, regular, normal, atypical, irregular, or (heaven forbid) abnormal, there are many reasons why it will be helpful for you to view individuals' behaviors as occurring in incompatible pairs. Enhanced communication is an obvious advantage—they help you clarify and focus on presenting problems.

GUIDELINES

Further, *behavior-pairs serve as guidelines.* They specify limits and help students whose actions have required attention to recognize the expectations you hold for them. These guidelines remove some of the confusion that can exist within their environment.

CONSISTENCY

Behavior-pairs improve chances for consistency. They provide a forum for teachers and parents and therapists to share biases and preferences, and increase the chances that everyone involved with the individual will have similar expectations, as well as improving the chances that everyone will respond to the behaviors in a similar way.

FEWER REACTIONS TO UNDESIRED BEHAVIORS

Behavior-pairs will help you avoid reacting to only one side of the pair—most often the undesired side. It is common for us to be upset by, and react to, whatever a youngster is doing that is not desired. Conversely, it is equally common to neglect responding to what is viewed as desirable. The concept of behavior-pairs can remind you that every undesired behavior has a desired counterpart.

MORE EFFECTIVE PROGRAMS

Behavior-pairs increase the chances that your educational programs will be effective. Without attention to the pairs, most of your programs will fall short of what you have in mind. Dealing with only one side of the pair may be a futile exercise. The individual may learn what not to do, without knowing what to do. He or she may learn what to do without knowing what to avoid doing. Neither situation will provide optimum benefits.

THE QUALITY OF BEING OBSERVABLE

2.3

For the behavior-pairs to accomplish the above they need to be written and discussed in a manner that enhances communication rather than impedes it. For this to occur, **the behaviors within the pairs will have to be observable.** There must be several good reasons why all fields of science require that the objects of their investigations be observable and definable. Wouldn't it be easier and less time consuming if clear definitions weren't required? We could say whatever we wished, experiment with whatever we wanted, and go about our business. Unfortunately, if we chose to do this few others would know what we were saying or doing. And then there's a chance *we* wouldn't know precisely what we were doing or saying either. Think for a moment of what difficulties might arise if someone spoke to you about a student whose "aggressive" and "irresponsible" behavior had increased without telling you what those "behaviors" represented.

CONFUSING CONCLUSIONS

"You might not know what the caller was talking about, what behaviors were being referred to. You might think the student was doing something that he wasn't doing," the parent who had joined the teacher suggested. "Two people could use the same word and be talking about something totally different."

"Would that be less time consuming?"

"I don't think so," the teacher answered. "In fact, you could end up wasting a lot of time."

"Anything else?"

"You might begin treating something that wasn't an issue while missing something important," the parent suggested.

"More?"

"Unintentionally, you might not help me, my child or his teacher," the parent said looking toward the young woman to her left. In fact, you might make matters worse."

"What should be done?"

"We need to 'operationalize' our terms," the parent indicated.

"Right!"

"How'd I do?" Mom asked.

"You did great."

OPERATIONAL DEFINITIONS

While we will revisit this issue when looking at ways to establish academic and nonacademic programs, we need to touch on it now. To be effective, behavior-pairs must be clearly stated. Clarity is not solely for the benefit of a consultant as he talks with a teacher or parent. Students or adults being asked to consider alternative ways of behaving will understandably benefit from knowing which behaviors are not only preferred by others but likely to bring them more of what they value. Clear definitions are best accomplished through a process known as "operationalizing."[2]

WHAT THE INDIVIDUAL IS DOING

This essential (and simple) procedure requires only that you describe carefully what the subject is *doing* rather than using a common, but often misleading, term to represent the behaviors. You will know if the operationalizing process has been effective if everyone knows precisely what the individual is doing that has been called into question. Look once again at the previously listed behavior-pairs:

Desired Behaviors	Undesired Behaviors
1. Being cooperative	1. Being defiant
2. Not being aggressive	2. Being aggressive toward peers
3. Completing school work	3. Refusing to attend to school work
4. Not being irresponsible	4. Being irresponsible
5. Eating solid foods	5. Not eating any solids

While the flavor of each pair is somewhat evident, only one clearly describes what the individual is and is not doing. Did you guess that number 5 is probably the clearest? Although we might wish to know more about which solids are desired, it is likely that we could see what was and was not eaten if we observed the individual during mealtime. Would we be able to observe the other pairs with equal ease? While the temptation maybe to say "yes," the answer is probably "no." Even number 3 (completing school work; refusing to attend to school work) is not as clear as it could be. I'm going to inquire, "What does the individual do when *refusing* to work? Does he argue, sleep, throw things?" There is a two-fold reason for such intense clarification. As a consultant, of course, I must know what the individual is doing. Less obvious, perhaps, is that I will want to help the individual understand *precisely* what he or she is doing and not doing that has created the difficulty. Clear, observable behaviors will assist me with both endeavors. To help you with this requirement, consider asking yourself the following two questions when faced with a behavior that is in need of clarification.

1. What was the individual doing that lead me to state he or she was defying requests, being aggressive toward peers, refusing to work, and being irresponsible?

2. What does the individual need to do in order for me to know that he or she is complying, not being aggressive, working at his or her tasks, and not being irresponsible?

CLEARER COMMUNICATION

The above two questions need to be asked every time a potentially confusing term has been used. You simply answer the questions according to your own specifications. There are *no* absolute definitions, and operationalizing does not require that everyone define the terms in the same manner. All the process requires is that everyone knows what everyone else is talking about! Let's try the first pair and see what happens.

Desired Behaviors   **Undesired Behaviors**

1. Being cooperative   1. Being defiant

"Looking at the undesired behavior first, I would say that 'being defiant' isn't very clear so we'll need to change that to 'being oppositional,'" the teacher offered.

"Can you see a person being 'oppositional'?" I asked.

"Well, when someone is being oppositional he's . . . maybe . . . not following requests, arguing, you know, being defiant," she continued smiling as she searched for words.

"This is not easy, I know, but you've given us a clue. You suggested the individual was not following requests and was arguing. Those behaviors are reasonably observable."

"You would change the behaviors under the undesired column to 'not following requests' and 'arguing'?"

Undesired Behaviors

1. Not following requests
2. Arguing

"Yes, if that's what the individual in question was doing. You simply write down what he is doing, *what you see him doing* that you believe is not desirable."

"Then being cooperative isn't correct either," the parent suggested.

OPERATIONAL DEFINITIONS

Desired Behaviors

1. Being cooperative

"It's probably what we want in the long run, but you're right, it does need to be refined. The student may not know what 'cooperative' behavior represents—he may not know what he's supposed to do. Let's help him."

"How about follows requests when first asked," the teacher said.

"That's a good start."

"And never argue?" the mother asked shaking her head slightly. "I'm not sure I'd agree to that. Sometimes arguing is very desirable," she pointed out.

"That is a tough one. Maybe we're lucky and the student in question doesn't argue too much," I suggest smiling.

"No, that's the easy way out," she challenged. "Let's say we would like the person to think about what is being said and justify why he disagrees. Perhaps learn to accept some points of view even if they're distasteful to him."

"You can define the term any way you wish so long as all of us know what is preferred."

"I think you just snuck out of that one," Mom said, staring at me.

"You're right!" I answered.

The task often is not easy. But the issue behind it is important, particularly for the individual being discussed. Mystery is great in books and movies. But when it comes to helping people avoid all sorts of negative things that may happen as a result of their undesired behavior, mystery has no place. I never end a conversation with someone who is seeking help until I know, without question, which behaviors are being viewed as undesired, and which ones are being considered to take their place. Without that information, it's difficult for me to move on. Without that information, it may be impossible for students to correct their own behavior. When a teacher admonishes a youngster to "stop misbehaving," or tells her to "behave herself," or "be responsible," or "be more considerate," or makes any number of other requests that may be difficult to interpret, the youngster will have to be very lucky to figure out precisely what she *is to do.*

_____ "I WANT HIM *NOT* TO DO THOSE THINGS" _____

"Then there's another problem," the parent said looking toward the teacher. "Do you see it?" she asked.

"I don't think I do," the teacher replied.

"Let's see if *he* does," she teased, now looking at me. "Bring back all the pairs."

Desired Behaviors	Undesired Behaviors
1. Being cooperative	1. Being defiant
2. *Not* being aggressive	2. Being aggressive toward peers
3. Completing school work	3. Refusing to attend to school work
4. *Not* being irresponsible	4. Being irresponsible
5. Eating solid foods	5. Not eating any solids

"Thank you. Look at numbers 2 and 4. Well?"

"You're having a problem with the word 'not' under the desired side?" I asked.

"I knew I was right," she responded enthusiastically. "You can't use the word 'not' when talking about desired behaviors. *Not* being aggressive, *not* being irresponsible doesn't tell the individual what to do. It tells him what *not* to do which is all the undesired side tells him! That won't help him much."

Technically, Mom was right. No doubt she also realized that teachers and parents, in fact, do not want the individual to continue with the undesired behaviors. It was, after all, the undesired behavior that got all this started in the first place. But the word "not," usually positioned in front of the undesired behavior, often won't help the individual understand the desired alternative behavior. While the issue may seem small, it can be significant.

_____ WHAT DO YOU WANT HIM *TO DO*? _____

When possible, you need to communicate some active behavior that is preferred: Instead of "not scream" you might consider "talk calmly;" in place of "not running through the hall," the suggestion "walk" might improve things quickly. Instead of "not fighting," practicing with "share your feelings," "keep your hands by your side," "talk to me," might help the individual understand a desired alternative. The list, of course, could be endless. The key to this issue is to develop some clearly stated, *active* behavior that is incompatible to whatever was determined to be undesired.

MODELING THE DESIRED BEHAVIOR

Once the desired behavior has been determined there remains one last component to this issue of developing behavior-pairs. **You may need to show the individual what it is that you desire, and you may need to show how to do it.** How extensive your modeling of the desired behavior must be depends, in large measure, on the ability of the individual to understand what you prefer. Some individuals will "pick up" the desired alternative quickly. Others may need many practice sessions. There are, obviously, no rules of thumb with this issue. I've spent weeks, rather than minutes, working on desired alternatives. The time has been well-spent. Be patient. If the desired behavior is important, your time will be worth the effort—both to you and to the one you're caring for.

| 2.4 |

NOTES

1. Macht, J. (1975). *Teaching our children.* New York: Wiley.
2. Macht, J. (1980). *The slaying of the dragon within: A question of educational/psychological diseases of school children.* Littleton, CO: Jem.

SUMMARY

KEEP IN MIND

1. Although "undesired" behaviors most often draw our early attention, it is essential to remember that behaviors occur in pairs: An undesired behavior will have a desired counterpart.
2. For students to behave more acceptably in your presence, they must know that desired counterpart: what you prefer them to do.
3. By establishing clear behavior-pairs, you will be:
   a. Increasing communication between you and the student;
   b. Improving the chances that you and other adults will respond more consistently to the student;
   c. Decreasing the chances of responding only to a student's "undesired" behavior.
4. As you list or discuss the behaviors that will compose your "pairs," keep the behaviors directly observable. Make sure you (and the student) can actually see them occur. If you list behaviors that are not observable, neither you nor the student may know specifically the nature of the offending or desired behavior.

5. To help you develop observable behavior-pairs, think about what the individual is doing that is warranting (or should be warranting) your attention. The "doing" component will be the observable component.

6. When establishing the desired side of the behavior-pair, try to avoid placing the word "not" in front of the undesired behavior. Instead, develop an active behavior; some action you can see the student doing.

7. If you need some additional structure regarding the developing of the behavior-pairs for a particular student, consider the following:

    a. Take a piece of paper. Divide it in half with a pencil mark. On the top of the left half, write the word "Desired." On the top of the right half, write the word "Undesired." Since you probably will have noticed the student's undesired behavior first, write down all the individual's behaviors that you believe are not acceptable. Initially, don't worry about the language that you use to describe the behavior. (You will save yourself some time if you write down what you see the individual doing, but initially, you can use any words you wish.) On the opposite side of the listed "undesired" behaviors, think about what you would like the student *to do*. Go through each listed behavior and reword them so each will be observable: Each will indicate something the student is doing, or something you would prefer he or she would do. Once completed, you will have several behavior-pairs.

What Do You See?

| 2.1 | The next time you have the opportunity of watching (or working with) a group of students as they are behaving, working, or studying, check yourself to see how often you notice the "desired" things they're doing. See if you have fallen into the habit of "seeing" only that which is disturbing to you.

What May Happen If You Don't See the Desired?

| 2.2 | Any guesses as to what may happen to the frequency of a desired, potentially productive behavior if it is never noticed by a teacher? Besides the effects on the behavior, any guesses as to how students might feel if their efforts are rarely noticed? One more question: How old do you have to be before you no longer need any recognition from people who are important to you?

Observable Behaviors

| 2.3 | Read the following scenario. Develop the behavior-pairs. You should be able to develop at least three pairs. Make sure both

sides of the pairs (the desired and undesired) are observable.

John's behavior was beginning to interfere with his teacher's ability to run her classroom. When he would first enter the classroom, he would often be boisterous to a point of bothering the other students. He would rarely raise his hand when a question was asked to the entire classroom; instead he would call out his answer even while another student was speaking. Most disconcerting, however, was his lack of respect for either the teacher or fellow classmates. It was as though he was the only one in the room.

John's teacher decided to develop a program to help the youngster learn to control his own actions. Before discussing the situation with John, she kept a careful record of the behaviors that appeared to be the most difficult. Once her behaviors-pairs were established, she met with the young man.

Helping the Student Know What to Do

| 2.4 | Imagine the frustration experienced by a student who is requested to behave in a particular way, who wishes to comply with the request, but does not understand what it is that he or she is supposed to do. "Be a responsible citizen," a youngster is told. "Beg your pardon?" the child might respond, before adding, "What do you mean by that?" Chances are slim that you will walk up to one of your students and make such a request. On the other hand, you might nonchalantly say to the student, "Behave yourself, okay?" Well, not much difference between the two requests if the youngster is uncertain about what each entails. Given the "flagged" sentence: "You may need to show the individual what it is that you desire, and you may need to show how to do it," what steps might you have to go through to help the student understand what it means to "behave yourself?" Hints:

1. You may not have fully decided what it means to "behave yourself."
2. The child has no idea what it means to "behave yourself."
3. "Behave yourself" implies that it is possible *not* to behave yourself—a potential behavior-pair?
4. Modeling? Practicing?

Try listing the steps involved. Remember, your goal is for the student to understand (and thus be able to comply with) your request.

CONSIDER AS WE LOOK AHEAD

1. Behaviors (desired and undesired) do not occur in isolation; they occur within the natural environment.
2. This natural environment is an ever-active force that constantly changes; that constantly requires that we adapt.
3. If we believe people's behavior to be unrelated to their natural environment, we will not see their uniqueness. To understand individuals, we must go beyond what they do. We must see them and their behavior as existing within their natural environment; their own natural setting.
4. A classroom, a workshop, a special facility, all represent a portion of the natural environment. You, as the teacher, are part of that environment. You, as the parent, are part of the environment. You as friend or adversary are part of the environment. You and your surroundings will influence not only what individuals do, but who they are, both to themselves and others. You will influence individuals whether you intend to or not.

3

THE NATURAL ENVIRONMENT, THE UNIQUE INDIVIDUAL

The teacher turned toward me. "You seem predominately concerned with what the individual is doing," she said. "You've only spoken of behavior. Are you not equally concerned with what may be responsible for the behavior? For as long as I can remember, psychologists have written and lectured on the importance, moreover the necessity, of viewing unacceptable behaviors as representing the tip of an 'iceberg'; that the behavior itself maybe less significant than what lies at its base. I'm certain that many of your readers will be somewhat familiar with the concept of 'symptom substitution'[1]—the notion that dealing only with the observable, 'surface' behavior and not with the 'cause' of the actions will subtly set the stage for further difficulties. In fact, you alluded to that concept when you warned against 'fixing' the behaviors in isolation without considering the relationship the behavior holds with other variables. Is that not the basic thrust of 'symptom substitution'?"

"I am most assuredly concerned with what variables may be influencing the observed behavior," I answered, "and I am strongly opposed to viewing behaviors in isolation. The concept of 'symptom substitution' is a viable concern in the field of physical medicine. If a physician treats the symptoms of a severe infection and does not

— 23 —

resolve the underlying factors that have produced the symptoms little more than momentary relief may be accomplished. That would not be the physician's goal. I recall a kindergartner who was described by his teacher as a wild hare both at school and home. The child was first 'treated' by spending time in a special facility for 'emotionally, behaviorally disturbed' children. His behaviors were thought to be 'symptomatic' of 'emotional disturbance' and 'hyperactivity.' That approach and the assumptions that produced it didn't help his behavior. He was then evaluated by a physician who specialized in allergies. It was discovered that the child was allergic to cats, three of whom slept with him in his bedroom at home. Once the animals were removed, his behaviors improved dramatically both at home and school. His behaviors were, in a medical sense, symptoms of his particular physical system.''

INTERNAL "CAUSES": A GLANCE

"When educators and psychologists use the term 'symptom,' " I continued, "they likewise often think that everyday disturbing behaviors of students are related primarily to underlying, *internal* problems that exist *within* the individual. That attitude and logic, I believe, moves us toward treating in isolation. **The scenario involving the medicated first-grader mentioned in the previous chapter is a perfect example of what can happen when our thinking is limited to 'diseases' and 'symptoms'. There were many variables operating that influenced how that child behaved. The professionals who advised and prescribed the medication paid little attention to those other variables.** To ignore them is not the same as saying they do not exist. Indeed, they *do* exist, and there's an excellent chance despite the chemically altered behavior, the child will find another way to gain what he values and needs."

"You mean other undesired or disturbing behaviors may surface in the classroom because additional variables within his aggregate environment were not considered?"

OUTSIDE "CAUSES": A GLANCE

"Yes. Once you see how the natural environment influences behavior, you'll understand how that can happen. We are adaptive beings, and the process of adaptation occurs in relationship to what exists and is occurring, as you suggested, in his aggregate or *total* environment. Part of that environment exists *outside* the individual, and an individual's problem may be related to some

3.1

'underlying' variables that are presently operating outside of his body. Historically, the outside forces have been misunderstood and often neglected. The metaphor of an 'iceberg' where only the tip is seen, where significant material lies underneath the 'water's' surface thus defying easy observation, is assuredly a valuable theoretical concept. But that which many professionals posit as lying underneath the surface almost always refers to some inner conflict that existed *within* the individual. Difficulties that exist *outside* the individual often are not thought worthy of investigation."

"In the case of the first-grader, you're referring to his teachers," the young professional suggested.

"And his assignments, and what values exist with those assignments and any number of other factors—his interests, preparedness, and his support systems."

"By support systems you mean his parents?"

"Parents, too. Without looking at all those factors, thinking the child is the one with the problem, an internal problem, producing the disposition to fix in isolation, the child, adaptively, will discover other ways, and be taught other ways, to satisfy his needs. What is learned and eventually manifested may be no more desirable than what precipitated the medication in the first place."

"The child would be no better off?" the teacher pondered.

"That possibility exists."

"Then it is critical that we be aware of the power these outside variables that exist in what you're calling the natural environment exercise over behavior."

"Without that information, it is not likely that our efforts toward remediation will be successful. The *only* reason for beginning our discussion by focusing on behavior is that behavior is the focal point of our initial concerns. But behavior does not occur in isolation."

"It occurs within the natural environment."

"Definitely," I answered.

"Then to understand a student's classroom behavior, its place and purpose, and to develop successful methods to deal with it, whether we are referring to academic or nonacademic activities, we have to look at the relationship between behavior and the environment," the teacher suggested.

"We must look at what the student is doing, what he is being asked to do, our expectations for him, his preparedness to complete the work, our preparedness to assist him, his previous experiences and present attitudes, as well as our own experiences with him and attitudes toward him."

FOUNDATIONS OF BEHAVIOR: A COMMON
—————————————— THEORETICAL THREAD ——————————————

Common to nearly every theory of personality is the belief that behavior does not occur in isolation. Almost without exception, and regardless of specific theoretical biases, humankind as seen through the window, is depicted as an active, motivated, "energy system"[2] behaving within the structure, forces, and influential aspects that are unique to both ourselves and that which surrounds us. It would be nearly impossible to find a personality theorist who was not concerned with the effects motivation had on human actions;[3] who did not believe that "an adequate understanding of human behavior will evolve only from the study of the whole person;"[4] who did not believe that "the subject should be viewed from the vantage of the entire functioning person in his natural habitat."[5] While the theorists often differ sharply on what constitutes influential forces, they collectively hold that an individual's behavior should not be viewed as occurring in a vacuum, isolated from his or her physical and environmental systems. Although they do not use the term 'natural environment' to represent the systems they speak of, a mere cursory view of their thoughts and writings clearly shows their deep concern for viewing each person within the totality of his or her *own* world, no matter its complexity or simplicity.

"You're suggesting that Freud's 'psychoanalysis' and Skinner's 'operant conditioning' have something in common?" the skeptical school psychologist asked.

"Yes, as do the tenets of Piaget, Jung, Kurt Lewin, Tolman, Carl Rogers, and most any other major contributor to the field of psychology you wish to name," I responded.

"Aren't you pushing things a little?"

"How so?"

"I don't recall that Skinner was enamored by the concept of the unconscious. And I doubt Freud had much use for token systems and M & M candies. Who besides Jung believed in the power of 'inherited ancestral experiences'?" the psychologist asked. "And find me someone today who aligns himself with Sheldon's 'Constitutional' psychology—you know, that fat people are jolly, skinny people are shy, and red-haired folks all have swift and violent tempers."

"You're missing the point. Each and every theorist, even those who characterized themselves as atheoretical, disavowed the notion that Man is an independently, capriciously functioning being, without ties to some base or foundation. Yes, some theorists were more concerned with the biological basis for behavior; others more interested in the environmental basis for behavior. Some placed more emphasis on unconscious variables; others seem determined to view only that which was readily observable. But all saw Man's behavior as a *function* of something; that it did not occur whimsically. All strove, in their own ways, to identify lawful relations between behavior and whatever was believed to be most influential. Identified lawful relations would, they believed, allow them to predict with some degree of confidence how an *individual* would behave given identified factors."

"Is that such a critical point?" the psychologist asked.

The Individual: A Glance

"It's no small issue," I answered. "Many of us today have lost sight of the individual and his ability to adapt to his unique environment. We view the *individual* without seeing either his biology or his surroundings. We see him as an 'average' child, growing and developing in an 'average' social arrangement, possessing an 'average' biological system. In schools, particularly, we evaluate the student with instruments that are based on norms or averages; speak of the student as though he were merely a representation of the average. Few, if any, of the theorists who provided us with the ground work upon which to understand the individual spoke of 'average' people. Most, because they were concerned with the well-being of the individual, intended for us to speak of the individual, evaluate the individual, develop remediation for the individual."

"From a consultant's position, the individual, his uniqueness, is paramount," the psychologist reflected as he thought about his own responsibilities.

"The professional consultant's view, assuredly. But the same can be said for parents, teachers, therapists, and anyone else who is asked to help an individual in jeopardy: Each are consultants in their own right. Recognize that once you bypass the individual in favor of the expediency of groups, you lose the flavor of the individual who is placed within the group; the very flavor that is needed to intervene successfully. As soon as you fail to see the individual with respect to his natural environment as it exists within his school and home, fail to see clearly his unique self and the uniqueness of that which surrounds him, as soon as you become more concerned with how an individual compares with someone else, rather than how he compares today with how he was yesterday, you have forfeited the very information that will help you help him."

THE NATURAL ENVIRONMENT'S COMPOSITION AND ROLE

The natural environment consists of two major divisions: one that exists outside our bodies, and one that endures within. The outside component is composed of all of the people who make contact with us; all the places within which we work, play, visit, and study; all our material possessions; everything that provides us with information; and anything that we can see, hear, taste, touch, or smell. The inside component includes our present thoughts; recent and distant memories of all we've experienced involving successes, failures, joys, and disappointments; feelings both emotional and health-related; our physical strengths and weaknesses; whatever genetic predispositions we might have; and anything unique that we carry within the privacy of ourselves. **The natural environment encompasses everything about us that produces our individuality, and no two natural environments can ever be exactly the same.**

| 3.2 |

AN ACTIVE, ONGOING FORCE

The natural environment is not a passive entity that sits in life's balcony oblivious to what's going on. To the contrary, it is an ever-active force that continuously impinges on every sense organ and sometimes, perhaps always, leaves a trace or replica of the impingement within the physiology of the brain. Further, the "stamped" memory may not be simply a black and white, two-dimensional, dull reflection. It may be anything but: a remembrance embellished with emotions ranging from joy to pain; an incident that seeks repetition or begs for future avoidance. The impingement may be remembered forever, may be remembered in parts or whole, or may be forgotten as quickly as a baby drops a boring toy. To the degree that it is remembered consciously or otherwise, it can affect present and future emotional, cognitive, and motor behaviors. Regardless of what happens with the momentary incident, the natural environment continues its actions for as long as we continue breathing. It presents situations that set the stage for our behaviors: to analyze, think, react, decide, then behave, and perhaps learn something that could enhance future growth. It is an enigmatic system that was neither invented nor developed by humankind; a system that has garnered the attention of thousands of scientists, poets, and philosophers; a system capable of producing an Albert Einstein, a Helen Keller, and a Jonas Salk. It has also produced a Hitler.

The Influence Begins Early
_____ and Continues through Life _____

If we accept the transmission of genetic strengths, errors, and predispositions as being part of the natural environment, then it is accurate to state that the natural environment begins its influence at conception. In all likelihood, the "day-old infant" has already experienced much more than her age might otherwise suggest: She is certainly not a "blank page." If we accept the data showing that newborns are capable of learning from their first breath, then the pages on which their stories are written begin filling up as soon as an infant is held in loving arms.

While some of the above may be debatable in certain professional quarters, the following is not: The natural environment influences the everyday behavior of a maturing 8-day-old as well as the behavior of a maturing octogenarian. The _process_ producing the environment's influence remains relatively constant regardless of age: both of these individuals will constantly find themselves in the midst of their external and internal systems; both will be affected by environmental reactions to their behaviors; both individuals will learn to adapt to what they experience. The 80-year-old and his or her younger counterpart will tuck away, in the privacy of their thoughts, any number of three-dimensional images, laden with colorful emotions, that will help them behave in a manner that will bring them what they value.

_____ Idiosyncratic Influence _____

Regardless of a child's age, he or she will have had direct experience with the natural environment since the moment of birth and, perhaps, earlier. How the child perceives, remembers, and acts upon the experiences is often difficult to determine. Rest assured, however, that he or she is perceiving, remembering, and behaving in accordance with what has happened.

> The young couple and I were seated on the floor of their family room; their 14-month-old daughter remained nestled next to her mother's side, appearing suspicious of my presence. I had met with the family twice before, and had learned quickly to avoid imposing upon the child's "territory." If our eyes met, she would instantly begin to cry and stretch her small arms toward her mother as though begging to be rescued from a frightening situation. If her mother stood, even for a moment, the child's soft face would grimace; her arms would extend and the desperate screaming would begin. The initial call for assistance had occurred a week earlier. Mother's voice was filled with fatigue and apprehension. "I can't answer the phone, sit alone in a chair, drink a quick cup of coffee without her in my arms. If I leave her for a second, she wails until I pick her up. I

can't even go to the bathroom alone," she said, her words and tone without humor.

By the end of the first visit, I had been informed that the child had been born with a moderate condition of low muscle tone, most noticeably in her lower limbs. Her crawling skills were extremely limited; she could move herself a few feet from where she sat, but the exercise was difficult and laborious. For most of her young life, she had been carried in her mother's arms. If she desired something, she would cry, raise her arms, and be carried to what she wanted at the moment. Since she had yet to develop functional words, her crying was her means of communication; since she had yet to develop adequate ambulatory skills, her mother was her vehicle. Without the presence of her mother, the child's present world narrowed significantly.

"Why can't she be like other children her age?" Mom asked me as we sat in the family room. Referring to some of the children in the neighborhood, Mother added, "They're content whether their mothers are with them or in the kitchen. They don't raise their arms and expect to be carried every place. And they certainly don't scream when their mothers walk away."

"The others haven't had the same history," I suggested after briefly reminding the mother and father of their child's developmental uniqueness. "I doubt they've been held as much or carried as much. Their verbal skills are probably a little better, and they can get around a little easier. Your youngster is doing what she has discovered to be successful—for her, asking, by crying, to be with you in your arms is, presently, what she knows. She's comfortable, and probably doesn't know that you're annoyed and desirous of things to change. We can teach her alternative ways of behaving, but she'll always be her unique self. **Try not to compare her with the other youngsters—their natural environments and the accompanying effects have been different from the very beginning of life.**"

| 3.3 |

_____ INFLUENCING THE WHOLE PERSON _____

"Are children truly influenced by the natural environment from their first breath?" the parent asked.

"Earlier," I answered quickly. "While we have much to learn about the factors that impact upon the developing organism, several things are readily apparent. With human beings, the term 'zygote' is used to represent the cell that is the union of an egg and sperm. The zygote is formed at conception. The more familiar terms 'embyro' and 'fetus' refer to the organism as development within the womb continues. If, at conception, the produced cell contains a third 21st chromosome (a condition known as 'Down's Syndrome'), the produced child will travel a different road through life than he would have, had the extra chromosome not been present. Since the natural environment includes genetic determinants, this individual will be influenced by his natural environment from the *moment of fertilization.*"

"He will be 'retarded,'" the parent said.

"That's a poor term to use. It carries such excess baggage, and it produces attitudes that can unnecessarily affect the child's future in a negative way. Further, it doesn't tell us anything of practical use about the individual. The child is simply different than he would have been had he received the expected allotment of two 21st chromosomes. More to our point, the genesis of those differences occurred at the moment of conception."

"I never thought of it at that way," the parent said. "I guess personalities, intelligence, maybe even certain behaviors also get their start at the moment of conception."

"The ice may be a little thinner with those areas," I answered, "but to the degree that there are genetic predispositions toward personality or behavioral traits, those traits would have their beginning the moment the egg and sperm combine."

"And intelligence?"

"That depends on the *type* of intelligence we're discussing. Are we referring to 'functional' intelligence—the type involved with our daily activities; 'artistic' intelligence—that which is shown by consummate professionals of the arts; 'organic' intelligence—the electrochemical composition of the brain, as well as any number of other types?"

"I wasn't aware that there were different kinds of intelligence," the parent stated.

"Let's just say there are different views of what the term 'intelligence' represents."

"If I think about it, I would guess that the functional type is something that has to be acquired, like learning to come in from the rain or at least figure out how to open an umbrella. **But the organic type or the artistic type might be tied more to what a person is born with,"** the parent reflected.

	3.4

"There's little doubt that organic intelligence is a real entity, and that it has its inception very early. Many things, gender, eye-color, body-type, reflexes such as sucking and eye-blinking have a transmitted genetic base. The configuration of brain nerves and chemicals probably has a similar base. As of now, precisely what represents organic intelligence, and how to measure it, remains a mystery. While purely speculative, its hard to believe that a Mozart, Einstein, or Van Gogh could have manifested their accomplishments without a running start from an atypical combination of genetic materials. It's something we may never know for sure."

"But it is possible that the physiological part of the natural environment might have given those people their start."

"Possibly. At the same time, remember that the same natural environment has the capability of *impeding* what it may have started or *enhancing* what originally was a deficiency. It's a question of reversibility versus irreversibility."

"That's too complicated for my brain," she admitted.

"At times, mine too, but let's take a shot at it. What do you suppose might happen if a developing fetus is deprived of nourishment? What might happen if the birth of the child was dangerously premature? What could be the outcome if during pregancy a woman took medication that affected the developing organism?"

"I remember the 'thalidomide babies,' " the parent answered quietly. "That was horrible."

"What was thought to be a harmless tranquilizer turned out to be far from harmless. That drug, because it existed, was part of the natural environment. It influenced development just as would a dearth of nourishment or a noted prematurity of birth. Endowments provided at conception are not uneqivocally irreversible. On the other hand, what effects might an enriched environment or a fortunate circumstance have on a youngster whose genetic makeup speculatively was not quite as extraordinary as a Madame Curie or a Count Basie?"

"Like being taught by a master teacher?"

"Or being adopted by a special family or raised by exceptionally devoted parents," I added.

"The youngster might do considerably better because of the fortune that had come his way," the parent answered. "The given genetic, physiological part of the natural environment might be changeable, reversible."

"Very changeable, very early."

" 'Your' natural environment is a potent force," the parent offered.

"It does have the ability to influence."

"That, I believe, is an understatement," the parent smiled.

A PERSONAL ADMISSION OF IGNORANCE: TUNNEL VISION

When I first began my graduate studies, my field of vision of the children I worked with resembled a narrow, tunnel: I stood at one end; the child was visible at the other. I saw only the youngster, and often only a small part—usually the behavior that had created some concern. Two superlative teachers (no doubt presently enjoying the Arizona sun), a wide range of experiences, and countless, unique children, parents, and professionals provided me with a wide-angle lens that now enables me to see much more than the small figure that appeared suspended in space, unattached to anything else. Today, many of the people who seek my assistance often mirror my once limited perspective, seeing "the problem" isolated from its position in the natural environment. Such "narrowness" is understandable for their training is frequently "field-specific": They concentrate on their respective fields of expertise, be it language, motor movements, curriculum, physical health, etc. When I enter their domains, my knowledge is often equally narrow. (Thank goodness most of us adhere to a team approach!) Teachers and parents, on the other hand, rarely enjoy the luxury of being experts in only *one* field. Their skills are required in all of the above areas, multiplied on occasion by ten. Because of all they are expected to do, their seeing only "the problem" is quite understandable.

To help you visualize the individual, the natural environment, and "the problem," I have borrowed, loosely, a pictorial aid developed by Kurt Lewin, a noted psychologist born in 1890. Lewin viewed humanity as we live and interact with our environment, and it was not by accident that he chose the term "life space" as the theme of his figures.

THE TOTAL LIFE SPACE

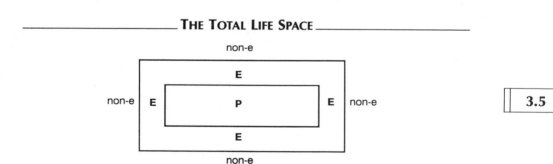

3.5

In its *simplest* form, the life space is composed of three variables: P, E, and the non-e. The letter P stands for person; the E stands for the actively engaging environment; and the "non-e" represents the part of the environment that is momentarily or forever unknown to the individual person. As the figure indicates, the person is pictured surrounded by his or her active environment; outside that environment rests the part of life that has yet to enter into the person's perceptions. The P could be you or me or anyone we work with; the E would be the environment within which each and all of us live; and the "non-e" could be any object, experience, or piece of information that lies outside of our present knowledge. Probably, "P" and "E" are easy to understand—simply look at yourself and where you are at the moment and, again in the simplest of terms, you have your "P" (you) and your "E" (where you are and all that exists around you).

The "non-e" might be a little more difficult to identify with. Let me offer a quick example. Early this morning, I was at a special care nursery, at a local hospital, working with a 10-month-old boy. The infant had been within the confines of the hospital's walls *since birth:* he had not been home, not gone outside, not met any adults other than his mother, father, and hospital staff. While 10-month-olds differ markedly from one another, it should be easy, given that his entire young life had been spent in the hospital, to imagine much of what exists within the youngster's "E" and "non-e." Before entering the hospital unit, I was *not* part of the youngster's world. (I was in his "non-e".) However, as a direct consequence of my presence and interventions, and the child's ability to know both, the youngster's "P" and "E" became slightly more complex as a result of my being. His natural environment, its internal and external components, were affected by a stranger who rather quickly became associated with the "pleasantries" of a full stomach brought about for the first time by eating food from a spoon. Like the 10-month-old, our "person," "environment," and "nonenvironment" are continuously being altered by that which has been familiar for a long time, and that which has just come into existence. As the personality theorists suggested, we are active energy systems living within an energizing environment. The complexities of both begin at conception and do not end until we've taken our last breath. All that lies in between is nothing short of mind-boggling.

_____ THE "PERSON": ALL THAT WE ARE_____

```
┌─────────────────────────────────┐
│                                 │
│                P                │
│                                 │
└─────────────────────────────────┘
```

The P represents the summation of everything we are: the ways our heads work, our ability to think and problem solve; our memories of familial and cultural experiences—those pleasant, those not; our acquired feelings, values, and preferences; and our unique physical and genetic structure. It is a representation of mind, body, and infinitely more than just their combination, a representation of everything that makes us unique. It is a complicated, marvelous puzzle that has pieces in place before birth. As we develop and grow, we continue to store the chromatic slides that document our experiences, along with our emotional associations with the experiences. While many of us will share comparable experiences, our individual perceptions, interpretations, and reactions to those experiences may be quite dissimilar. It is where we keep the many faces and facets of our unique internal and external systems. **Its uniquenesses are responsible for two children of the same age being vastly different; two adults, having lived the same three decades, being at opposite ends of a continuum on any number of variables; and two Heads of State acting as though they were not from the same planet.**

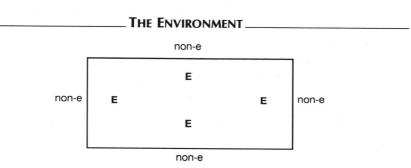

| 3.6 |

THE ENVIRONMENT

While infants, as they first enter the world, already possess many attributes, their external world, as it personally relates to them, is often seen as having little impact on their cognitive and emotional behavior. This appears to be a limited view, based more on professional prejudice than knowledge. Various studies have shown that neonates discern unpleasant odors,[6] that at one week of age they prefer looking at checkered-pattern discs rather than plain discs,[7] that newborns can learn to turn their head in a particular direction when reinforced for doing so,[8] that the presence of strangers can alter the response patterns of infants,[9] that when infants begin to crawl they can discriminate between shallow and deep cliffs,[10] avoiding the latter while approaching the former. These and other studies suggest that the newborn's environment is not an empty space. Rather, the "new" environment possesses *cues* (known as stimuli) that the newborn's "person" appears to have the ability to recognize, respond to, and discern.

THE ENVIRONMENT'S CUES

As infants mature, more cues, capable of influencing what they do, how they think, what they explore or avoid, enter their environment, whether the environment represents home, school, or any other place they may find themselves:

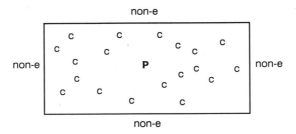

| 3.7 |

And before long, the P is surrounded by these cues (c) that can come in many shapes, sizes, and colors.

"What do cues actually do?" the parent asked.

"They *help* us learn, help us process information, help us become more aware of and sensitive to our surroundings, and help us figure out how we should behave. They guide our actions and eventually allow us to predict how our environment is likely to react to our behavior. A growling dog, for example, can warn us to do something besides approach the animal. A quiet dog, with wagging tail, can increase the chances we'll touch the canine. The animal's growling, tail wagging and/or quiet behavior are observations that are the cues. In a school setting, when solving the math problem 3__2 =, a pupil will need one of several 'cues' ('+', '−', '×')', before he will know what to do. When learning to read words and write sentences, a student will need to be exposed to, and eventually understand, many informational cues before becoming successful at those tasks.

"Cues can be anything that impinge upon one of our sense organs; they are around us continually," I continued. "A traffic light is a visual cue, as is the time displayed on our alarm clock. A mother's stern voice is an auditory cue, as is the whining of a fire engine's siren. Sour milk can provide an olfactory cue. If tasted, it will provide an additional, easily discernible cue. The sharp edge of a chipped cup is a tactual (and visual) cue. A thought, pleasant or otherwise, 'popping into our head,' a feeling bursting from our stomach, can alert, remind, or move us. A letter, positioned in a word, a word located in a sentence, a sentence mentioned in a paragraph, all provide certain cuing information. A child's cry, a stabbing chest pain, a dark swirling sky, steam rising from a coffee cup, or smoke billowing from a distant house are all cues that, depending upon our experience and maturation, can provide us with important information that will help us choose appropriate responses. It would be nearly impossible for us to function, read: survive, without cues."

MOST INFORMATION CUES NEED TO BE LEARNED

"What do you mean 'experience and maturation'?" inquired the parent.

"Most of the cues that influence us are neutral at first. Someone, or the natural environment, must teach their meaning. A traffic signal, for example, will not have the ability to guide our walking or driving behavior until we understand the meaning of the light's different colors. That ability comes from experience and the development of our cognitive systems."

"Could the teacher's or classroom's cues have had an effect on that first grader who was medicated for his attention and work difficulties?" the parent asked.

"Not only could, but did! Remember, behavior does not occur in isolation: That child, I assure you, was influenced by many of his environment's cues. He learned what to do and what not to do in the presence of those cues in order to obtain what he valued at the moment."

"He learned?"

"He was *taught* the meaning of the cues, perhaps not intentionally, but taught nevertheless."

"By his teacher?"

"Teacher, peers, parents, time of the day, subject matter; any or all could have been involved in the teaching/learning process," I explained.

"And what he learned could have played a part in his inattentiveness?"

"A very big part," I answered.

CUES: A CLOSER LOOK

My first assignment as a consultant is to ascertain the nature of the presenting problem. Once the undesired behaviors have been carefully described and the desired alternative behaviors have been determined, I begin looking for any environmental cues that appear to be associated with what the individual is doing and failing to do, both academically and nonacademically. For a brief period of time, my concerns are less with how the individual's immediate environment is responding to his or her actions—what the teachers and care-givers do when the individual acts, and more with the identification of what circumstances seem to be present when the behaviors occur. Specifically, I try to determine whether any observable cues may be "setting the stage" for both the troubling behaviors as well as the more desired alternative actions. The identification can help me understand what changes within the individual's environment may be needed to assist the individual in finding more beneficial ways of behaving.

The following example will demonstrate how cues exercise their influence. The situation described is not at all unusual: Similar scenarios occur in many classrooms and special facilities.

Mark's parents received a letter from school requesting their presence at a meeting to discuss their son's behavior. The letter, signed by the school's psychologist and principal, indicated concern that Mark might have a problem that was interfering with his willingness to work and ability to comply with his teachers' assignments. The letter did not come as a complete surprise: Mark's homeroom teacher had also expressed her concern through various notes sent home. The parents and teacher had discussed the problem twice before. On both occasions the teacher had indicated that Mark was a very active child, that it was possible that his activity level was interfering with his ability to concentrate. The family physician had been contacted. A thorough examination provided no explanation for the "hyperactive" behavior. The nine-year-old's parents and I were friends, and they asked me to attend the meeting.

The tone of the meeting was supportive and friendly. The psychologist, three teachers, and the assistant principal represented the school. The homeroom teacher, who was Mark's math teacher, and the psychologist accepted the responsibility for describing what the young boy was doing while in school. The psychologist admitted that he had been minimally involved, that he had watched Mark on two occasions during math class, and that he had observed the child's "hyperactive" behavior during class time.

The homeroom teacher explained, "He's an intelligent boy, yet his work is below par. I'm concerned he may be having great difficulty concentrating. I believe we should consider a test battery to see if some attention problems can be identified," she suggested, looking toward the psychologist.

"I think we're being premature," spoke Mrs. Fox, one of the other teachers.

"How so?" the assistant principal asked.

"Mark has no problems in my class."

"Could you be more specific?" the assistant requested.

"He's attentive, calm, interested, polite. His work is fine. He's certainly not hyper," she answered, "at least not with me."

The young assistant principal faced the psychologist. "Have you had a chance to see him in Mrs. Fox's class?"

"I'm sorry, I haven't," the psychologist replied.

Mark's mother looked at me. **"I don't understand. Why is he calm and doing well in one class and having difficulty in another?"**

"Many possibilities," I responded. **"It may be related to the curriculum, the size of the classroom, his own feelings and perceptions about his performance, the composition and style of the class, the feedback he's receiving, and any number of other possibilities.** What's important," I stated, "is that his behavior appears specific to a set of circumstances: He's behaving differently in the presence of different cues. We'll need some additional information before knowing what to do." I turned toward the assistant principal. "Can you free your psychologist for a few hours so he can take some data?"

"Yes," the man replied. "Tomorrow," he added, nodding as he wrote himself a note.

The psychologist confirmed the teacher's observations. Most of the differences between the two classes were subtle, were easy to overlook, but were measurably related to the curriculum and the teachers' styles. The two teachers discussed their classroom approaches, worked together, and made a few alterations in the math curriculum.

3.8

_____ CUES AND BEHAVIOR-PAIRS WITHIN THE LIFE SPACE _____

What may be apparent from the above example is that students do *not* always manifest the same behaviors under all conditions. Thus, once the behavior-pairs have been determined, I seek to identify the conditions under which both the desired and undesired behaviors do and do not occur.

When we can identify the cuing differences that appear to influence both sides of the pair, we know that something within the individual's environment, frequently relating to either the environment's feedback or the type of work being required, also differs. In the case of the student, the youngster was experiencing more success in one particular class, and apparently found it easier to concentrate on what was asked of him there. From a diagnostic standpoint, this information is critical, for it can tell us that given the right circumstances, the individual behaves quite desirably. From the standpoint of remediation, we learn what needs to be done to help the individual increase his or her desired responding.

THE CRITICAL CUE

3.9

One of the most important observations you can make is the fact that there are conditions under which the *undesired* behavior *does not* occur. Whether it be at school, home, or special remediation locations, the confirmation that undesired behaviors are tied to specific cues can provide us with a wealth of information, not the least of which is what we must do to help the individual with those behaviors.

Why is the aforementioned observation so valuable? When we observe the cues that are guiding the behaviors, we gain knowledge of how the environment is reacting to the behaviors, and we learn something very important about the individual: When conditions are right, the individual behaves desirably. When conditions are right, the client is *not* as "disabled" as we may have thought. That observation has enormous ramifications for our remediation and our attitude.

SCHOOL-RELATED CUES

Behaviors observed in regular school settings are almost always tied to specific cuing situations; they do not occur continuously. It is important, therefore, to recognize the conditions that appear to "set the stage" for the undesired actions, as well as noting the conditions under which the undesired behaviors do not occur. Again, these notations should be documented prior to any intervention efforts that focus exclusively on an individual's behavior. It is often easier and more productive to provide students with alternative ways of behaving by first working with the cuing or antecedent conditions that appear tied to the students' actions, *then* supporting the more alternatively desirable behaviors the changes bring about. An example should help clarify this important suggestion.

I was asked to look at a kindergarten youngster who was described, by her teacher, as one of the most explosive children she had ever seen. The child, as a result of her behavior, had already experienced the near-gamut of "negative" sanctions the teacher had at her disposal: being confined to her chair during activities she seemed to enjoy; missing recess periods; mandatory visits to the principal's office; several letters sent to her parents, and, no doubt, a few periods of yelling and threatening on the part of the teacher. When I arrived at the class, I was informed that the child was being considered for review by the special education resource people for assistance. When I spoke with the teacher, there was little question she was quite disturbed by the child's actions. Fortunately for all concerned, the teacher had a few patient threads left within her system and was willing to help me gather some data before involving the special education team.

DATA COLLECTION: A GLANCE

Observing the child for a relatively short period over two days revealed the following: By and large, she was a well-behaved, most pleasant child. Most of her school-day went smoothly, cooperatively. Indeed, the child had the most beautiful of deep-brown eyes that would sparkle radiantly, accompanied by an equally bright smile, when she was engaged in activities that appeared to be to her liking. What was most apparent, was the fact that during those periods when the child behaved acceptably, even admirably, little attention was provided for her efforts. All the attention, it seemed, turned to her (on her!) during the brief period where she was asked, along with her classmates, to practice printing her name, a milestone most of the other children had successfully accomplished.

By the time I arrived, the child no longer "struggled" with the letters of her first name. Instead, she would throw her pencil or crayon across the room, rip her paper into small pieces, and exclaim the moment the practice sessions began, with a pitch that might have broken fine crystal, that she had no intention of even trying, what in her judgment was, an impossible task. (She later confided in me that she also thought it was a "dumb" task; "I already know my name," she informed me proudly.) What remediation was required entailed little regarding her protestations—her behaviors were viewed as a distant second to the academic task that appeared associated with them. Three interventions were undertaken: first, to show her the value of being able to print her own name; second, make the task easier and more successful for her with the use of *informational cues*—dots and dashes and arrows and colors; third, spacing very brief practice sessions throughout the day rather than having them occur en masse during one designated period of time. After some twenty two-minute name-writing practice sessions, accompanied by encouragement and support provided by the teacher, the problem was resolved. Most critically, her willingness to try the exercise made it easy for the teacher to show appreciation for effort.

The issue of cues, as they relate to student behavior, certainly is familiar to you, although you may have forgotten how you may have relied on them while being in grade school. As a youngster, did you ever need to pass someone a note containing the most vital information? If so, it's not likely you chanced the activity while your teacher's eyes were locked into yours. More probably, you waited, somewhat impatiently, until the teacher turned his or her back to you before the critical news was passed to your eagerly waiting friend. Just as the class bell, day of week, or announcement of an assignment, provide you with important information influencing your behaviors, so perhaps the class you were in, the material you were working on, or the presence of the dreaded or welcomed substitute teacher(!) set the stage for activities that would not have occurred had the situational cues been different. In the above respect at least, things (and students) haven't changed much: Different cues still set the stage for different behaviors; students still use them to determine when the time "is right" to behave in various ways; and teachers still need to be aware of which cues seem to be associated with which behaviors.

I sat with the school's psychologist and resource teacher while they discussed a sometimes delightful, often less-than-beguiling 4th-grader who was rapidly working himself into an enormous hole. Several of the schools' staff had experienced enough of his "acting out" to want him forever removed from their classes and their building. After meeting with the youngster and discussing the matter with his homeroom teacher (who wished to do whatever he could for the boy), I realized that placement in a special class for "behavior disordered" students was the route several teachers desired for him (and themselves). Not atypically, the youngster was pleasant and cooperative as he and I sat together. A few moments of "probing" his academics showed that he was quite proficient at the three "R's." When I asked him how things were going, he gave no indication of the impending decisions that were right around the corner.

CUES AND RESULTING BEHAVIOR

I urged the psychologist, resource, and homeroom teacher to begin searching for and documenting which cuing conditions seemed to be associated with the youngster's behaviors. The following was discovered:

1. The youngster was cooperative and productive while working one-on-one with his homeroom teacher.
2. He was equally successful while working alone with the resource teacher.
3. He was somewhat less cooperative but still productive while the homeroom teacher worked with the entire class as a group.
4. Cooperation and attention to assignments were nearly nonexistent in art, music, and physical education.
5. Most of his troubling behaviors occurred when he sat next to, or was in close approximation to, his good friend, Dustin, who was equally boisterous and nonproductive in art, music, and PE. The homeroom teacher had long since started keeping the boys a safe distance apart during class assignments, but had not communicated the arrangement to anyone else.

The obtained information clearly indicated that while the youngster was not "disordered," he was, indeed, disorderly under easily discernible conditions. After speaking with all the teachers involved, it became equally apparent there existed wide disparity between their classroom guidelines, expectations, and assignments. With some reluctance (but with some "soft" insistence on the part of the school's principal), the teachers met together to evaluate their own methods of working with the youngster. Additionally, the resource teacher and homeroom teacher sat with the two boys and applied their own "soft" insistence to help the youngsters realize what was expected of them.

Because of the importance of identifying which cues seemed to be influencing which behaviors, I would advise you to take the necessary time to note the following:

1. The conditions under which the desired side of the behavior-pair are most and least likely to occur
2. The conditions under which the undesired side of the behavior-pair are most and least likely to occur

Take your behavior-pairs, write them down, and search for the following:

Behavior-Pairs

Cues in the *Presence* of
Desired Behavior

Cues in the *Absense* of
Undesired Behavior

```
    c                          c
    c....P...B..fb             c....P...B..fb
    c  c                       c  c
```

If you can locate the above, you've accomplished the first critical step toward remediation. You can then begin speculating on a second critical issue: a behavior's purpose.

CUES AND THE BEHAVIOR'S PURPOSE

Rest assured, undesired and desired behavior serve a purpose. Unfortunately, the student or client may be the only one who knows, readily, what that purpose may be. "Purpose," initially at least, is a private event, tucked comfortably away within the client's "person." Our determination of a behavior's "purpose" is second-hand, usually accessed by way of observation. There are times, of course, when we can ask individuals why they've behaving in a certain manner. If their cognitive skills are sufficiently advanced, and they are willing to share an intimate part of their "persons" with us, they might just tell us what we need to know. Often, "purpose" is not determined so easily. You'll have to dig for it by watching the natural environment at work—specifically the interaction between behavior, cues, activities, and feedback. You'll need to watch the interactions carefully; they can escape notice when you're swamped with a hundred responsibilities. You can give yourself a head start, however, by asking a few questions: "What cues are present when the undesired behavior occurs?" "What purpose might the undesired behavior be serving—what is the 'payoff' for the individual?" "Is someone accidentally providing him with something he values when he behaves undesirably? Has the individual learned to predict how different members of his environment will react to him, and does he behave differentially in response to those reactions?"

MOTIVATION: A GLANCE

Finally, if you have developed clear cues for behavior-pairs, and the individual possesses the necessary skills and experiences to interpret what has been established, there may remain an additional variable that will need your attention: the individual's willingness to participate in the program. As the personality theorists suggested, we are beings influenced by personal motivation. If an individual can see some value in what she's being asked to do, chances are excellent she will become a willing participant in the carefully thought out exercises you have provided. If value is *not* perceived, the individual, adaptively, will, with persistence, find another means to gain what she believes is important. Such adaptability is, by all observations, an inherent part of us. We have the ability to make choices and, as has been seen, the natural environment has the ability to reinforce those choices even though the adaptive behaviors may be only momentarily beneficial to the individual who has selected (or been taught) to travel a particular road. Fortunately, the natural environment can be assisted. We have the ability and knowledge to provide different roads: We can help people, young and old, find alternative ways of behaving. Whether we decide to exercise our ability and knowledge in behalf of someone else is also governed by choice and values. We can sit on the sidelines and blithely watch the natural environment take its course, or as a function of dedication and strong commitment, we can step into the arena and take on the challenge: helping others help themselves.

"This is all very complicated isn't it?" the parent reflected.

"It will become even more so," I responded. "We're now going to look at an additional variable, 'environmental feedback,' that also influences what we do. In place of looking at all the intricate components involved with an individual's behavior, it's a lot easier to assume the child or adult is the one with the problem, then, expediently, fix what is seen as 'maladaptive.' Rarely, however, does expediency translate into efficiency. We might accomplish something for the moment, but moments have the habit of fleeing."

ENVIRONMENTAL FEEDBACK

In addition to everything else about us that makes us unique, our behavior plays a prominent role in what we are. Our "person," thus, is composed in part of our behavior (B). We are, to no insignificant degree, what we do, and what any two of us do can vary dramatically.

What is evident is that cues within our environment, alone, cannot account for the variability in human behavior. Genetic predispositions, along with intrusive, and perhaps supportive, events occurring intrauterinely no doubt play a role—babies do enter the world with measurable behavioral variability. The work of countless physicians and psychologists have made that abundantly clear.[11] But our behaviors are influenced by more than just those two important components. There is another potent force that affords behavior some of its flavor and character: Environmental feedback and the individual's ability to interpret the value and meaning of that feedback (fb) appears to account for much of what we do. **That our behavior is affected by personally meaningful consequences is no longer problematic: The evidence for this is clear and incontrovertible.**

3.10

BEHAVIOR IN THE LIFE SPACE

In any given situation, be it in the living room at home, the classroom at school, the waiting room of a doctor's office, or in the arms of a loving parent, the life space can be viewed as an environmental location, where an individual actively participates cognitively, emotionally, and motorically (B) in the presence of any number of discernible *cues* (c).

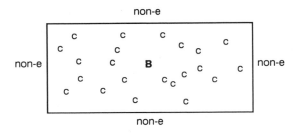

Like cues, environmental feedback can represent anything occurring within the environment that impinges on our senses. Unlike cues that occur behavior, this feedback occurs *during* or *after* our behavior and it affects what we are *now doing* and what we may do in the *future.* Environmental feedback is directly related to adaptation and learning, and it has been demonstrated many times that very young infants (along with very "old" adults) possess the ability to be influenced by the feedback their natural environments provide. Individuals' behavior, therefore, is a function of

1. Whatever predispositions they carry within their "persons"
2. Their present developmental level
3. The cues that exist immediately prior to the behavior
4. Their cognitive ability to discern the meaning and value of the cues
5. Whatever effects *prior feedback* has had on their behavior
6. Whatever effects *present feedback* is having upon their behavior
7. Any number of other variables that are unique to an individual and unknown to an onlooker

SCHOOL-RELATED CUES

The life space, considering one very simple scenario—a student sitting in her classroom, working on an assignment—can be depicted as follows:

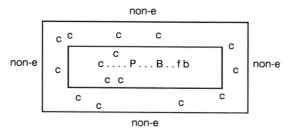

3.11

The *cues* (c) represent the classroom, the academic materials, the class-mates, the teacher (what he's doing; where he's situated), the time of day, whether it's sunny or raining outside, along with a "handful" of other variables; the student's *person* (P) represents her interest in what she's doing, her state of hunger or fatigue, her memories of similar experiences and their outcomes, her present emotional state, her ability to gain enjoyment and success from what she's doing, her perception of the materials as well as of herself, her predictions as to what will happen as a result of her efforts, her developmental, cognitive skill level, and again a "handful" of other personal components; the student's *behavior* (B) represents what she is actually doing. The natural environment's *feed-back* (fb) represents what occurs as she is working (or not working), as well as what will occur once she has completed her work.

"I understand the cues, and the importance of the child's uniquenesses as he works in the presence of the cues. But the idea of feedback is not as clear," the parent said.

"Almost anything that an individual experiences within his environment can provide him with information about what he is doing and, perhaps, influence what he will do in the near or distant future. Feedback is that information, and it helps all of us adapt to our environment. If by accident we touch a hot stove we might learn to avoid careless movements when we're cooking: we'll concentrate a little harder on what we're doing so as to avoid future burns. If we get a speeding ticket, we might learn to drive a little slower—at least for a while. If we fall on an icy sidewalk while running, we might learn to walk more cautiously the next time we notice the frozen conditions. Check-marks or x's, happy faces or stickers, placed on a student's paper are forms of feedback, as are gold watches and badges offered for exceptional service. A smile or a frown, a pat on the back or the behind could be other examples. An infinite number of environmental reactions are potentially capable of influencing behavior, even the behavior of a very young person."

"At birth?"

"Perhaps before birth," I responded, "although research on the overall effects of the environment on the yet-to-be born child is in its infancy. We do know that 2-to-4-day-old, full term babies can be influenced by their environment's feedback in the form of sugar water, smiling, touching, and much more,[12] and that age, by any standard, is quite young."

"So feedback can represent any number of things provided by people or experienced as a result of events within an individual's external environment," the parent suggested.

"Yes, but that's only one type of feedback, the type that's *outside* the individual."

"I'm not sure I understand."

INTERNAL FEEDBACK: PLEASANT

"There's long been talk of 'intrinsic' or 'internal' feedback that can equally influence the behavior of people," I said.

"Internal?"

"Yes, that which occurs within the individual's 'person.' The noted psychologist Jean Piaget believed, for example, that the infant, as early as one month of age, had the ability to receive positive feedback from his own behavior—a sort of 'primitive intrinsic reward' system.[13] Certainly early genital exploration, where the child fondles his own sexual parts, produces an internal sensation that is likely intrinsically pleasurable. I've worked with young children whose optic lenses were surgically removed due to the formation of cataracts. Many of these children will place their index fingers against their upper or lower eyelids and literally manipulate the positions of their eye balls in order to change the visual images they see. The new images, the differences of light and color, brought about by their behavior, produce intrinsic feedback that the children undoubtedly sense as positive."

"I never thought of internal feedback in that way," the parent said. "Children could behave in lots of ways simply because they feel good about doing it."

"Absolutely. You can watch 3-month-olds, while lying awake in their cribs, having a good old time cooing, kicking their legs, and raising and lowering their bodies apparently simply for the sake of the activities.[14] What feedback they receive is from themselves, from their own bodies.

"Is it always positive?" she asked.

_____ Internal Feedback: Unpleasant _____

"Not always. In fact, it can be very unpleasant. Not long ago, I was involved in a case where such a circumstance existed."

Jesse came into the world nearly six weeks earlier than was predicted. As sometimes happens, the premature birth created difficulties for him and his family. His vision and motor skills were impaired, requiring thick lenses and constant physical therapy; by the age of two, his intelligible speech was limited to a handful of words that seemed barely connected to the world around him, prompting intensive speech and language intervention. Despite the obvious deficiencies, the child had that mystical spark that brightened his ever-curious eyes, providing his parents with reason for hope. At about 30 months of age, however, Jesse's developmental journey turned downward: He stopped eating. He had never been a ravenous eater, but had consumed enough solids and liquids to keep his small, frail body going. Now, he refused any foods and reluctantly accepted only minimal amounts of liquids. The change hadn't occurred all at once. Rather, it began slowly with rippling protests when his mother placed him in his high chair and attempted feeding. Not knowing what else to do, Mom would remove him from the chair when his outcries became too much for her; she would hold him tightly within her arms. He would then quiet and relax immediately. As days passed, Jesse seemed to do whatever was necessary to be removed from the chair. It was as though he was testing hidden waters known only to himself.

Preliminary examinations by the family's physician failed to disclose any easily identifiable problem, and the parents were urged to be patient and keep trying. Jesse made their efforts difficult: Gradually, inexorably, his screaming at feeding time increased, as did his thrashing and turning away from an oncoming spoon. Soon, just placing him in a high chair set the stage for an intense tantrum that continued until he was removed from the chair and placed away from the kitchen. The physician decided to hospitalize the youngster, and ordered a series of tests to examine the child's gastrointestinal system. The tests revealed a serious problem with the youngster's gall bladder. The doctor speculated that each time Jesse swallowed food, he experienced considerable pain.

"The child knew he hurt, but no one else did," the parent reflected.

"That's right. The feedback he was receiving was private, internal. It escaped initial detection."

"But it taught him not to eat, right?"

ADAPTING TO INTERNAL FEEDBACK

"Like all of us, Jesse was an adaptive individual. If the physician's speculations were correct, Jesse hurt every time he ate. Eating, therefore, was *followed* by pain. Jesse likely discovered that not eating was *followed* by an *absence* of pain. Thus two very basic forms of internal feedback—pain and no pain—began teaching Jesse adaptive behaviors."

"And you indicated that the child began thrashing and screaming as soon as his parents placed him in his high chair. Was the high chair a cue?"

"Precisely. Jesse, besides being adaptive, was quite a sharp youngster. He knew that the high chair meant eating."

"And pain."

"That's right. The feedback from his environment taught him that as well. In fact, the painful feedback changed the 'emotional' meaning of nearly everything that was associated with eating. The sight of a spoon, his high chair, the very kitchen of his house—through their association with eating's painful feedback or consequences—"signaled" his cognitive and emotional systems that more discomfort would return if he ate. **The cues set the stage for the acquisition of a behavior that would enable Jesse to avoid the pain: The youngster did what was adaptive—he stopped eating!**"

"That is frightening."

"That's adaptation to the natural environment," I responded.

"What eventually happened to him?"

The decision was made to remove the child's gall bladder. Surgery was successful, and after the child had undergone a thorough reexamination of his swallowing mechanisms and internal tract, he was allowed to return home. His parents felt confident that the worst was over: The source of the internal, painful feedback had been removed, thereby eliminating Jesse's need for the adaptive noneating. On paper, the parents' expectations were logical. Frequently, however, the natural environment appears to function illogically. Jesse continued his refusal to eat. His screaming and thrashing did not subside; indeed, they intensified. The simple sight of a spoon became the trigger. His reaction was immediate, explosive, and persisted until spoon, food, and high chair were removed from his visual field. The child began losing a dangerous amount of weight and body fluids. Out of necessity, he was returned to the hospital where a stomach tube was surgically implanted to allow feeding and hydration throughout the ensuing days. Once home, Jesse's parents continued their efforts at oral feeding. They met with little success. The hospital staff had no suggestions. The hope was that Jesse would turn himself around at some time in the near future.

|| 3.12 ||

"That's a heartbreaking situation. I can't even imagine how difficult it would be having to struggle with something that seems so natural as eating. Didn't he ever eat anything by mouth, even after the tube was implanted?"

"He did take a few bites," I answered, in a manner requesting the parent to pursue her question.

"He took a few bites and there wasn't any physical pain?"

"That's correct. Keep going," I urged.

"If you're hungry and you eat, the eating should provide *pleasant* feedback. If the feedback is pleasant, you should continue eating. If the eating continued without discomfort, the high chair and spoon would no longer be cues that 'signaled' trouble. After all, Jesse's natural environment started the mess; it could have ended it."

"Well said. Unfortunately, Jesse and his parents were a little unlucky. The child had taken sparse amounts of food through the mouth after the gall bladder had been removed; the food had been digested without the previously experienced painful feedback. The natural environment *should* have 'told' the child—through the absence of pain—that eating was okay. Another child, no doubt, would have started eating: problem resolved. Jesse didn't. Perhaps his memories were very vivid, very frightening. Kids, from their beginning, differ in their reactions and perceptions. Sometimes, the natural environment doesn't appear to work in anyone's behalf."

FEEDBACK: NATURAL AND INTERNAL, ARTIFICIAL AND EXTERNAL

While the environment's feedback can take many forms and influence all behavior, what is sometimes overlooked is that, in its purest sense, feedback can literally affect life: not only its quality but whether it continues. Various researchers have described what can happen to infants whose environment fails to provide minimal sensory stimulation: the infants whither, some die.[15] Spitz (1945), for example, reported that throughout history, from 31.7 to 90 percent of babies in foundling homes died in the first year of life.[16] The researcher spoke of the possible devastating effects that can occur in the absence of "mother love"—a phrase representing, among other things, the importance of "mothering" an infant, a phenomenon often wanting in institutional-type settings. Papalia and Olds (1978), perhaps considering the issue of the absence of "mother love," posed the question: "What, after all, do mothers do?"

Their answer: "They give babies a wide spectrum of sensory stimulation: They pick them up, cuddle them, rock them, speak to them, play with them, love them."[17] Mothers *and* fathers and a host of other significant people provide the babies with feedback—interactions that can assist an individual to developmentally go forward, stand still, or retreat into a paucity of life, or less.

The environment's feedback begins from birth to influence both the acquisition and frequency of behavior—whether behaviors will or will not occur in the near or distant future. Further, it assists in attaching value and meaning to the surrounding cues within an individual's life space, and it influences the individual's perceptions of environment and self. To no small degree, the environment's feedback begins to impact on whatever predisposed "personality" attributes an individual may possess, as well as shape the very flavor and character that will help the individual become what he or she will be. Behavior, thus, is significantly affected both by the feedback it produces *naturally,* as well as feedback that is *contrived*— whether it is planned by someone external to the individual, or whether it occurs accidentally, at the whim of the natural environment.

NATURAL FEEDBACK: A GLANCE

When Jesse stopped eating, his adaptive behavior was being influenced by natural feedback. The adjective "natural" is used because the pain Jesse experienced was *not planned,* but was a function of the child's physiology and was a direct result of the child's eating behavior. Further, Jesse did *not* have to learn that "pain" was uncomfortable, something to be avoided. He, like nearly all children, was born with the physiological and cognitive abilities to make that discrimination. Thus, Jesse discovered that when he swallowed food, his body reacted with pain. No one manufactured the outcome; no one outside of Jesse's body contrived, or "gave" him, the pain. In the same way, light produced by manipulating the position of eyes, stimulation from rocking back and forth, from sucking fingers, from cooing, produce their own feedback within an individual's "person." Natural feedback is a potent motivating source. It can influence a wide variety of behaviors, some, as in the case of Jesse, that can lead to disastrous consequences. Those of us who work with severely involved children and adults see other examples of "self-defeating" (although still adaptive) behaviors that push our remediation attempts to their very limits. Perhaps all "self-stimulating" behaviors fall under the category of behaviors that are maintained by their own natural feedback or consequences. Those that debilitate growth and development, given treatment constraints, are often intractable.

At the same time, and on a brighter note, natural feedback can produce and maintain many desirable behaviors.

——————————————— INTRINSIC REINFORCEMENT ———————————

"I was hoping you would add that heading," the psychologist broke in. "Your 'natural feedback,' that which I term 'intrinsic reinforcement' can influence behaviors that are highly valued. Some of us read, listen to music, solve math problems, explore our environments, purely for the enjoyment inherent in those activities. There's an intrinsic value to them, producing a natural high," he said exuberantly.

"Some of us even write because we enjoy doing so," I added quickly.

"Then you would wholeheartedly support teachers concentrating on helping students discover natural, positive feedback for academic efforts? That parents should do the same when spending time with their children at home?"

"Of course. As a father, I couldn't be happier than when I watch my own children read for the sake of reading, study their algebra for the sake of personal, mental enlightenment, work in school purely for a sense of intrinsic success. I never enjoy visiting with a school-aged child whose academic endeavors have nearly ceased for want of any reason to continue. If I could write the student's script, I would have him studying and developing for purposes of bettering himself, of feeling better about himself. But what I want, what many of us want, doesn't always happen. It must be understood," I continued, "that the natural environment doesn't always write the scripts or develop the life space that produces what we might all wish for."

"That sometimes it produces behaviors that are detrimental to the individual," the psychologist stated.

"Very much so," I responded. "When it does, our immediate concern moves from how we might wish for things to be, and shifts to what can be done to help the individual. If a student is not working, we need to provide him with a reason to do so."

"You would give the natural environment a helping hand through the use of *artificial* feedback," the psychologist suggested.

"Either that, or we can sit on the sidelines and watch the downward spiral continue," I said. "I haven't worked with or known too many professionals who are comfortable with that option. Most, like myself, prefer to jump into the arena and do something beneficial."

_____ Artificial Feedback: A Glance _____

The term "artificial" is used when feedback is not a direct, logical result of a behavior; the feedback may be planned by someone outside the child or it may follow behavior accidentally. The relative value of artificial feedback, unlike natural feedback, is *learned* through repeated experiences. Whether a particular form of artificial feedback is or isn't valued by an individual depends on the *perceptions* of the individual; whether it will or will not alter or maintain behavior also depends on the *perceptions* of the individual.

Like natural feedback, artificial feedback can be a strong motivator. Indeed, a large percentage of our everyday behavior is influenced by artificial consequences—consequences that are not a natural outcome of what we do, but are provided by people and events. Intentionally or otherwise, artificial feedback can increase, decrease, or maintain existing behavior. It is frequently a major tool used by consultants when their assistance is requested. The planned use of artificial feedback is employed when natural feedback has *failed* to increase or maintain the occurrence of desired behavior.

_____ When the Natural System Fails _____

"You had to use artificial feedback with Jesse, didn't you?" the parent said, "because the natural environment had not shown him that eating was safe and intrinsically pleasurable."

"Short of ignoring the situation, hoping Jesse would have found his own solution to the eating problem, artificial feedback was the only option," I responded. "Most children eat successfully because the behavior reduces gnawing hunger pangs, as well as providing the opportunity for experiencing pleasant tastes. Under such conditions, artificial feedback is rarely needed. Eating has come under the influence of the natural system. Jesse's history, however, had interfered with the natural system's progressions."

"What did you do?"

"I helped him understand that nice things would happen when he swallowed food; that he would be able to experience what he valued when he would eat. I used toys, mirrors, and anything that he liked, then I showed him how he could gain access to those valued objects."

"Did the program work?"

"Not immediately. It took several meals for Jesse to understand the process involved. After a couple of days, however, his protesting nearly ceased and he began to eat willingly. Soon, the cues that had signaled trouble began to tell him that pleasurable things would happen when he ate."

"So you manufactured the relationship between his behavior and the feedback you provided. That's why it is called 'artificial.'"

"That's right," I responded.

"What happened after he began eating consistently?"

"What would you guess happened?" I pressed.

FROM ARTIFICIAL TO NATURAL FEEDBACK

The parent thought for a moment. "Well, you indicated that you use artificial feedback only when natural feedback fails to maintain the desired behavior. **I would assume that you would continue with the artificial approach until the more natural feedback takes over.** In the instance of eating, natural feedback would be pleasant taste and the removal of the sensation of hunger. So as soon as Jesse learned that eating brought him those natural outcomes, the artificial feedback that you used was no longer needed."

3.13

"Exactly. Once Jesse began to eat without pain, a different set of natural and artificial consequences began to exercise their influence. He started enjoying the tastes of various foods and drinks when they touched his tongue, and his physical system quickly taught him that the discomfort from hunger could be temporarily eliminated by eating. Such "natural" contingencies reduced the need for the mirrors and toys that had been provided when he swallowed and withheld when he failed to swallow. When eating occurred without incident, "strange" things began to happen—strange, of course, only to Jesse. His parents were able to take him to restaurants, the sights, sounds, and aromas of which must have been tremendously exciting, and he was able to experience his first birthday party with friends, all of whom sat around a table and savored the hot dogs and ice cream and cake that many children devour with the most pleasant of thoughts and feelings. That sight had to be tremendously exciting for Jesse's parents. Artificial feedback helped all of this to occur."

NOTES

1. Ullmann, L.P., & Krasner, L. (1965). *Case studies in behavior modification* (p. 2–15). New York: Holt, Rinehart and Winston.
2. Hall, C. S., & Lindzey, C. (1957). *Theories of personality* (p. 224). New York: Wiley.

3. Ibid., p. 5.
4. Ibid., p. 6.
5. Ibid., p. 6.
6. Lipsitt, L. P. (1971). Learning processes of human newborns. In Ira J. Gordon (Ed.), *Readings in research in developmental psychology.* Glenview, IL: Scott, Foresman.
7. Fantz, R. L., & Nevis, S. (1967). Pattern preferences and perceptual-cognitive development in early infancy. *Merrill-Palmer Quarterly, 13,* 77–108.
8. Siqueland, E., & Lipsitt, L.P. (1966). Conditioned head-turning in human newborns. *Journal of Experimental Child Psychology, 3,* 356–376.
9. Fouts, G., & Atlas, P. (1979). Stranger distress: Mother and stranger as reinforcers. *Infant Behavior and Development, 2,* 309–318.
10. Gibson, E. (1970). The development of perception as an adaptive process. *American Scientist, 58,* 98–107.
11. Brazelton, T. B. (1973). *Neonatal behavioral assessment.* Philadelphia: Lippincott.
12. Lipsitt, L.P., Kaye, H., & Bosack, T.N. (1966). Enhancement of neonatal sucking through reinforcement. *Journal of Experimental Child Psychology, 4,* 163–168.
13. Piaget, J. (1952). *The origins of intelligence.* New York: Norton.
14. Lamb, M. E., & Campos, J.J. (1982). *Development in infancy* (p. 137). New York: Random House.
15. Spitz, R.A. (1946). Hospitalism: A follow-up report. In D. Fenschel et al. (Eds.), *Psychoanalytic studies of the child,* Vol. 2, (pp. 113–117). New York: International Universities Press.
16. ———(1945). Hospitalism: An inquiry into the genesis of psychiatric conditioning in early childhood. In D. Fenschel et. al. (Eds.), *Psychoanalytic studies of the child,* Vol. 1 (pp. 53–74). New York: International Universities Press.
17. Papalia, D. E., & Olds, S. W. (1978). *Human development.* New York: McGraw-Hill.

SUMMARY

KEEP IN MIND

1. It is the individual with whom we work; it is the individual, rather than the mythical "average" child, who must garner our attention. If you are teacher of a group of 30 students, you are, in effect, a teacher of 30 individuals.

2. These 30 individuals will have been (and will continue to be) influenced by their unique natural environments.

3. The natural environment does not solely influence observable behavior. It affects all that encompasses individuals: what they do, yes, but also how they feel and think.

4. The natural environment's influential processes remain relatively stable regardless of an individual's age:
    a. Each individual will find him- or herself in the midst of his or her internal and external systems;
    b. Each will be affected by environmental reactions to his or her behavior; and
    c. Each individual will adapt to whatever he or she has experienced.

5. Evidence clearly indicates that an individual is capable of learning from at least the earliest moments after birth. This means that an individual is capable of being influenced by his or her environment from that beginning. The environment, then, can begin to have an impact on an individual's behavior, thoughts, and emotions very early in life. This means that two individuals, from an environmental perspective, can begin to acquire differences within days of being born.

6. Evidence also indicates that children, from birth, appear to have different strengths, weaknesses, predispositions, and personalities. Thus two individuals, from a genetic perspective, will show inherent differences as soon as the opportunity to do so arises—perhaps with the first soft smack to their bottoms, or their first drink of Mother's milk.

7. Given environmental and genetic forces, much of which still remains a mystery, it is little wonder why we, as people, differ so; it is little wonder why many professionals urge all of us to see a youngster for what he or she is—a unique individual, not merely a member of a group.

8. All of us function within our unique life space. We are influenced by how we feel and think (our "person"); by what we see and hear (the "cues" that surround us); and by the reactions our environment provides to our behavior (the "feedback" that occurs when we act).

9. Most of the information we derive from the surrounding cues must be learned. A red traffic light will only guide our behavior after we have experienced the meaning of the light. Similarly, a + sign, next to a list of numbers, will only guide a student's behavior after she has experienced the meaning of the "addition" sign. Without our ability to discern the meaning of cues, we would experience great difficulty surviving.

10. All of us use cues to help us determine how we should behave. We do

not respond in the same fashion in the presence of everyone. While the way we act is dependent on many factors, some of those factors include who we are with and where we are: environmental cues.

11. With experience, students can predict how different teachers (and other adults) will respond to their behaviors. Students can then use the presence or absence of the adults (cues) to determine not only what to do and what not to do, but how the environment is likely to respond (feedback) to their actions. Cues, then, do more than simply "set the stage" for behavior: They can alert us to the possible consequences of our behaviors.

12. Cuing differences that may be influencing a student's behavior can be very subtle. Class size, curriculum, teacher mannerisms and employed feedback, specific classmates, assignments are a few examples of school-related cues.

13. While it is important to identify which cues are influencing the desired and undesired actions within a behavior-pair, it is especially critical to identify the conditions, the cues, under which the undesired behavior does not occur. Once you can determine that there are times when a student does not "misbehave," or does not manifest the undesired behavior, you know the individual can manifest the desired behavior if the conditions are right. It is essential to identify those conditions: the conditions that set the stage for the *presence* of the desired behavior: the conditions that set the stage for the *absence* of the undesired behavior.

14. When you experience a student who is having academic and/or social difficulty in your presence, remember to make a note of the following:
    a. The conditions under which the desired and undesired behaviors are most likely to occur
    b. The conditions under which the desired and undesired behaviors are least likely to occur
    The accumulated information will tell you about the student's adaptability, values, and perceptions of the present circumstances. The information will also provide you with ideas for remediation.

15. That our behavior is affected by the consequences it produces is no longer problematic. All of us constantly experience feedback from our environment; all of us learn what to do and what to avoid as a result, in part, of the environment's feedback.

16. Feedback can be divided into two basic groups:
    a. natural, internal, intrinsic
    b. artificial, external, extrinsic

17. While various definitions and descriptions have been assigned to the different types of feedback, the crucial differences appear to be as follows:
    a. Natural feedback occurs as a direct result of a behavior. Its

"positive" or "negative" value requires no learning or experience: The feedback or "sensation" is provided by the individual's physiological system. Natural feedback is often said to be internal, or intrinsic to the individual.

b. Artificial feedback is not a direct result of a behavior; it is something provided by someone; its "positive" or "negative" quality must be learned. Artificial feedback emanates from outside the body: Someone provides the feedback. It is said to be external or extrinsic to the individual.

c. Both natural and artificial feedback are integral parts of all remedial programs.

18. All feedback (natural and artificial) influences the future probability of a behavior: the likelihood that a behavior will occur again.

19. All feedback (natural and artificial) is a necessary component of growth and development.

20. All of us provide feedback; all of us receive feedback; all of us adapt to feedback. The environment's feedback (natural and artificial) again, helps us learn what to do.

The Breadth of Your Thinking

| 3.1 |

You are a teacher of 28 children in first grade. All of the children are about 6 years of age. Most of the youngsters are quiet, attentive, dutiful, seemingly willing to do anything to please you. A few of the boys, however, are somewhat rambunctious, somewhat unruly. You raise your voice, they quiet down, but when your back is turned, their playfulness begins anew. One of the boys, a bit more than playful, seems forever on the move. He seems to have no interest whatsoever in your first grade curriculum. His attention, what there is of it, is off someplace not confined by any brick walls. He is a problem. You've talked with him; he seems to listen; but then he doesn't seem to listen. He can't tell you *why* he doesn't like what you're doing in class, but he can tell you that he doesn't like it. When you ask him what he'd rather be doing, he shakes his head with uncertainty. He smiles when you tell him that you'd like to be his friend, but as soon as you're finished talking with him, he dashes off at lightning speed. The child's mother and father can do little more than sigh when you share your concerns. They, too, have observed similar behaviors. (You haven't panicked yet; you're just concerned. You like the child!) The parents ask you if they should consider talking with the family physician about medicating their child. You indicate comfortably, "Not at this time." You add, "There are many variables and components that can contribute to a child's inattentiveness and unruliness that do not warrant medication." You state, "I'd like to check some things out before I advise you to speak to your family physician." Try the following exercise.

List all the variables and components you can think of (that have *nothing to do* with the child's physiology) that might contribute to a 6-year-old's "excessive" activity level and accompanying inattentiveness to classroom academics. Imagine yourself and the child being in your classroom. Compare your answers with your colleagues. The more answers the better.

What Makes Us What We Are?

| 3.2 |

a. List as many factors as you can think of that play a role in producing an individual's uniqueness, i.e., the individual's "person." (Hint: Think of a youngster from the point of conception to the present day. There will be many general factors, and an incalculable number of specific factors.)

b. As the child's teacher, do you believe you will be able to learn how much influence (and what kinds of influences) the above stated factors have had on a student's present daily activities? (When considering this answer, be realistic. Indicate how you will obtain the information. Remember, you will have many students to concern yourself with.)

Be Cautious When Comparing

| 3.3 |

Please reread the scenario on page 29. Note that I suggested to the child's parents that they not compare their daughter's behavior with the behavior of similarly aged children. In actuality, many of us constantly compare the behavior of one child with the behavior of others with the hope of gaining some insight into whether the child in question is progressing and developing "normally."

Question: What is there about the natural environment that requires extreme caution when making comparisons between children of similar age? (Hint: Remember, the natural environment exists within and from without an individual.)

Question: Why do you think parents are so prone to believe that children close in age should be expected to behave similarly? Have the fields of education and psychology had some influence on such parental beliefs? Can you specify the nature of the influence? (Hint: Some theorists believe that children have built-in clocks: Their development is almost exclusively determined by physiological maturation. Other theorists point out that no evidence exists for such an assertion.)

Innate Intelligence

| 3.4 | Although we are somewhat ahead of ourselves, take a moment to speculate on what you believe the term "innate" or "organic" intelligence might mean. (Remember: The term "innate" and "organic" precludes any "post-conception," environmental influence.) Question: Have you ever heard anyone describe a person as being a "born" teacher? What would have to happen, or what would have to be involved, in order for someone to be a "born" teacher?

Your Personal Life Space

| 3.5 |
    a. Wherever you are at the moment, list some of the general components of your own life space. (Find a youngster, age 8 to 12 years. Ask him or her to do the same. You can help the youngster as much as you wish, but be attentive not only to his or her answers, but the cognitive methods the child uses to produce the answers.)

    b. Generally speaking, what is the relationship between the life space and the natural environment? Are they the same? Different?

Cautions, Once Again

| 3.6 | Have you ever found yourself wondering how someone else could be "so stupid" or be "so weird" because they believed something (or acted in a way) that you could not fathom? A Review: What is there about an individual's "person" that requires you to be very careful when comparing one child with another? One adult with another? The following request may not be easy, but try it if you'd like: Identify, in *your* judgment, the most hideous, the most fiendish individual you have knowledge of—someone, perhaps, who lived within the last century. See if you can "justify" his or her actions/beliefs/behaviors by placing the individual, historically, within his or her natural environment. In other words, was there something about the individual's natural environment that somehow explained,

perhaps again, justified, the horrible actions? To deal with this issue, you will have to be completely objective in your view; you will have to keep your personal biases isolated. It will not be an easy task. That, in itself, will tell you something of your natural environment and the influence it has had on you.

Surrounding Cues: Yours, Your Students'

| 3.7 |

a. Describe the many cues that are around you at the moment; that are influencing what you are presently doing.

b. Think about a child in your classroom (or one who you imagine will be in your classroom). What cues might be present that will influence his behavior?

Different Cues, Different Behaviors

| 3.8 |

Identify a youngster who is having difficulty in one class, but who is doing well in another (or a youngster who is behaving differently in the presence of two separate teachers). Observe the student under both conditions. List what you believe represents the important differences between the two conditions that may be influencing the student's behaviors.

When an Undesired Behavior Does Not Occur

| 3.9 |

Discuss with your colleagues why it is so important to know that there are conditions under which an undesired behavior does not occur.

Influential Feedback: That Which Influences You; That Which Influences Your Students

| 3.10 |

a. Over the next several days, list examples of how your natural environment's feedback has influenced your behavior.

b. With each listed example, try to categorize the type of feedback into:
(1) natural, internal, intrinsic
(2) artificial, external, extrinsic

c. List a few examples of environmental feedback that will be found in your classroom, feedback that will influence your students' behaviors.

The Classroom Life Space

| 3.11 | Note all the components in the diagram opposite box 3.11. If you have access to a school classroom, try to identify one simple scenario, and identify and describe the components that would relate to the "cues," the "person," the "behavior," and the "environment's feedback." If a classroom is not available, use your own present surroundings to identify and describe the components.

When a Student Decides School Work "Ain't Worth It"

| 3.12 | Jesse stopped eating because he experienced persistent pain when his body attempted to digest food. Come up with a school-related scenario where a student, adaptively, might decide that it is best to stop working; that school is something best avoided. (Work on this question. It has enormous ramifications for all of us who teach.)

A Personal Experience

| 3.13 | Can you recall any personal experience where artificial reinforcement was used to help you become involved in an activity (that you weren't initially thrilled by) that later became something that you really enjoyed; something that was "reinforced" by its own natural feedback?

CONSIDER: AS WE LOOK AHEAD

1. While we know that cues play an important role in guiding our behavior, it is now necessary to look at an additional variable that also influences what we do: motivation. The desire and willingness to participate and cooperate in academic and social programs is, as you know, very important.
2. From our own experiences, we've learned that if students see value in the task at hand, they're more likely to become involved in what is being asked of them. We've also learned that in the absence of any perceived value, it is often very difficult for any of us to become interested and involved in an activity.
3. You will now see that there are ways for you to influence your students' "state" of motivation. You can help youngsters see the value that exists in all academic tasks.

4

THE NATURAL ENVIRONMENT'S POSITIVE FEEDBACK

USING FEEDBACK

Once the behavior-pairs have been established, and the influential cues have been identified, our attention must turn to how the natural environment, through its positive feedback, influences behaviors. Please note I did not preface the word "behaviors" with the word "desired." The omission was not an error. We must not lose sight of the fact that the natural environment's feedback can increase the occurrence of *any* behavior, desired or otherwise. The natural environment teaches us *what to do* in order to gain access to what we value. For desired behaviors to occur more frequently, we must make sure the procedures to be discussed influence the *desired sides* of the behavior-pairs.

The professor's expression resembled the satisfied smile of the cat who had swallowed the canary. "Finally, we arrive at your stock and trade," he declared pointedly.

"How's that?" I asked.

"A rose by any other name is still a rose," he offered as though intoxicated by some ethereal gas.

"I've heard that expression before, but not in the present context," I responded.

4.1

"You've talked about 'feedback' and consequences, natural and otherwise. **But the truth is you're talking about conditioning, stimulus-response, salivating dogs, and the rest.**"

"You've got your theories a little mixed up," I suggested.

"That's no big deal," he reacted, swallowing his own air.

"No?" I softly challenged.

"Not at all. It all means the same—training animals to jump through hoops. Exercising your power over someone else. Leading us all to water and *making* us drink."

"I beg your pardon?"

With a face now red from his own flatus, he stated, "Despite the camouflage, despite your efforts to make the truth sound different, more appealing, here's where you bring out your chocolate bribes, your cherished M & M's."

"I do have some in my desk, if you'd like one," I said, hoping to bring sanity into the conversation.

"You have them in your desk!"

"Yes. Would you like *one*?" I repeated patiently.

"Is it free?" he asked sarcastically.

"Free? I had to pay about 50 cents for them!"

"No, I mean do I have to *earn* it?" he sparred.

"For you, it's a freebie."

"I'm grateful for your generosity. You probably use them with your students . . . shape their behavior," he muttered as he slipped several candies into his mouth.

"With my students?" I chuckled, hearing his muffled suggestion. "Let me think for a minute . . . M & M's with my students, to shape behavior?" I asked rhetorically, smiling at my colleague's confident face. "Yes, come to think of it, I did use them once. . . ."

I had been lecturing to one of my undergraduate classes on the importance of understanding the complexities of the natural environment's ability to influence our behavior. Believing that an active demonstration, rather than further lecturing, would better serve that purpose, I decided to run an "experiment." At the conclusion of a Friday class, I solicited the help of two students and asked them to bring a couple bags of M & M's to class on Monday. I requested that they not say anything to their classmates, and to meet me in my office a few minutes before class was scheduled to begin. When Monday arrived, I told the helpers we were going to try to influence the "writing" behavior of the students in the class. I gave them the following directions: "When we enter the room, don't say a word to anyone. As soon as you see any student writing or scribbling or doodling, walk to the student, place an M & M on his or her desk, and then look for another student who is moving the pencil point on a piece of paper."

(Writing was selected as the target behavior because it occurs frequently —at least at the beginning of class! My intent was to review several theoretical points; the chosen behavior was not too important.) The three of us went to class. As predicted, several students were writing as we entered the room. Without hesitation, one helper went to a writer and presented her with an M & M. The student looked up, laughed, ate the candy, and continued writing. Her neighbor saw what had happened. He, too, began writing and promptly received his candy. Within two minutes, 95 percent of the students were scratching away at their papers. Most everyone was laughing, talking, *but* still writing. The helpers and I were running back and forth dropping candies everywhere.

REINFORCEMENT IS NOT MAGICAL

There were, however, four "anarchists" sitting in the back of the room. Not only were they not writing; they had yet to touch their pencils. Their faces were covered thinly with smug, indifferent expressions; behind the puffed lips, however, rested smiles. I walked to the back, positioned myself in front of the "ring leader." The rest of the class turned to watch the "confrontation." (It was all very friendly!) I stared at the leader; she stared back. It was the moment of truth. She stood her ground. The class had been witness to the lesson I wanted them never to forget: there's nothing magical about the environment's payoffs, no matter if they're M & M's or anything else. I was about to return to the front of the room to review what had happened, but the ring leader's voice stopped me.

"This is the dumbest thing I've ever seen!" she exclaimed. "I know what you want me to do . . . you want me to write. I'm not going to do it," she proclaimed proudly. I nodded approvingly: her choice was fine. "Besides," she stated quickly, "I don't like M & M's." Her classmates laughed heartily. "Now . . . ." She paused as though to gather her thoughts and to gain my undivided attention. *"If by chance you have some chocolate covered peanuts!"* Ah, yes, the natural environment. As it happened, on my way to school that morning I had stopped at a convenience store. I had purchased two bags of M & M's for the students . . . *and* one bag of M & M chocolate covered peanuts for *me!* The bag of peanuts was hidden in my back pocket. A full smile covered my face. Calmly, my hand went to my pocket, and I produced the yellow bag with the large, printed letters. The class roared, once recognizing what I held in my fingers. The chief "anarchist" fumbled through her purse, found a pencil, and began to scribble enthusiastically. Her comrades followed suit. Each received a chocolate peanut. I ate three of them as we all enjoyed the moment.

"I think what you did was abominable," the professor remarked. "Really? What was so terrible?"

"Now that you used candy to get them to write, they'll only write, from now on, for more candy. They'll probably grow up expecting candy everytime they do anything."

"College students?" I asked, dumbfounded.

"Well, maybe not candy, but other *things.*"

"College students?"

"Yes! I remember reading a noted psychologist's view that . . .

Often a child who has been constantly rewarded with objects . . . learns to negotiate in material terms. He demands rewards for achievement and may show little motivation at school unless a parent promises to give some *thing* as a trophy for acceptable performance. **Over and over I have been consulted by parents of young college students who lacked motivation and refused to study unless they are promised a new sports car if they achieve a B average.** These children never seem to get any inherent pleasure out of what they do, since they tend to evaluate their accomplishments in terms of the material things that can be acquired by their efforts. . . .[1]

| 4.2 |

"College students! A sports car when they achieve a B average?! You had to search far and wide for that one," I responded, shaking my head."

"It took some effort," he conceded.

"Do you think such a foolish thing is frequent?" I asked incredulously.

The man sat quietly for a moment, reflecting on his words. "Come to think of it," he said, his head listing slightly to the left, "my son, a sophomore in college, isn't the most productive student. He does okay, but . . . You know, he'd never come to me and say, 'Hey, Pop, how about an MG if I make a B average?'"

"I'm happy for both of you. By the sound of things you'd have to purchase a house with a 30-car garage," I remarked. "Now let's see, you did indicate that there are times when he does work hard at his studies?"

An Issue of *What* Is Valued

"For sure," the proud professor/father responded. "Particularly when he finds a class to *his liking,* you know, one that *he's interested in,* one that *he values,* one that *provides him with success.*"

"Hmmm. Doesn't that tell you something?" I asked, with no hope that he'd figure it out.

"Huh?"

"Never mind. What's his college major?"

"He's studying the existence of vestigial relics."

"Like his father," I suggested.

"Huh?"

POSITIVE FEEDBACK/VALUES: A DEFINITION

4.3

A positive reinforcer is anything an individual will put out effort to obtain. It is anything he values, anything he will work hard to procure. ("Working hard" means behave.) Note that the definition includes the term "anything" but does *not* include the terms "pleasant" or "enjoyable." Positive reinforcers represent one of the natural environment's reactions. When they follow a particular behavior, they affect it. Further, they affect that behavior in the presence of the environment's cues. When an individual comes to understand that his behavior has produced what he values and has noted which cues were present at the time the payoff occurred, he will be able to predict which of his behaviors may produce the payoff the next time the cues present themselves.

Years ago, the sometimes disparaging nickname of "M & M psychologists" was pinned on a group of professionals who attempted to help youngsters with their behaviors by providing the children with positive feedback. The "positive" payoffs often were the "melt-in-your-mouth" candies, and the professionals could be seen carrying bags of the sweets almost everywhere they went. I remember, as a graduate student, eating as many as I gave away. I also remember I'd frequently forget I had them in my pants pocket; and remember vividly the mess when I removed the pants from the washing machine.

AN ADMISSION OF IGNORANCE: NAIVETE

Many of the children involved in the early experiments were fond of those little candies; they *worked hard* to receive them. Others, frankly, could have cared less! More than once, a child I was working with looked into my eyes and asked, "Don't you have anything else?" I suspect my initial reaction was: "You mean there *is* something else?!" As a fledgling, my knowledge of values and reinforcement was not very thorough; it was tied more to magical thinking than to an understanding of the power and complexities of the natural environment's motivators. Fortunately, a very special child taught me a priceless lesson.

I had been working on my PhD for a short time when one of my major (and most admired) profs requested I help a little girl learn to wear her glasses. With a minuscule layer of confidence, I accepted the challenge. Upon meeting the child, the layer became thinner. She was 7, nonverbal, knew neither her name nor her whereabouts, was nonambulatory (she didn't walk), not toilet-trained, and she ate only puréed food. She was born with cataracts that were removed shortly after birth. She had undergone exploratory heart surgery for an aortic pulmonary "window" before she had passed her second birthday. She was the thinnest "string bean" I had ever seen. The thickest of glasses had been prescribed to facilitate her vision, but she refused to wear them for more than a few seconds. She would allow them to be placed over her eyes, but her small hands would pull them down almost immediately. I was told she would be permanently blind if she persisted in not wearing her glasses. She had enough problems; she didn't need that burden as well.

My initial efforts were based on magic: My knowledge of valued payoffs had grown beyond M & M's, but not much beyond. Banana pudding had been added. I had just successfully taught another child to discriminate her name from the names of the other girls in her residential cottage. Once accomplished, the active youngster was able to locate and use her own toothbrush and not everyone else's. The child had a passion for the tasty pudding and worked diligently for the stuff. My head told me that if banana pudding worked for one child, it would work for another. That's *all* it told me. With that limited knowledge, I began working with the glasses-wearing problem.

I brought the frail child and her thick glasses into a small room within the laboratory of the state facility, gently placing her in a sitting position on the floor. I raised the glasses to her eyes, fixing the frames on her nose and ears. Instantly, I gave her a spoonful of the "magic potion." Reluctantly, she swallowed the pudding—the expression on her face said she'd never do it again. Not so reluctantly, she removed her glasses. I persisted; she did the same. After some fifteen minutes I removed her from the small room and placed her on the floor of the laboratory's main room. It had been a humbling experience, one that always has value for graduate students. At that moment, the main room was relatively dark. There were only two sources of light: a soft, orange glow from a special fixture on the ceiling and a thin stream of intense sunlight that poured through a thread-like crack between the double doors of the laboratory's main entrance. The latter illumination was some thirty feet from where I was standing. While the child laid quietly by my feet, I talked with my professor seeking whatever help he would provide. After a minute or two, I looked down toward where I had left the child. She was gone. Frightened, I glanced everywhere but was unable to locate her. A fellow student yelled: "She's over there!" pointing toward the building's double doors: she was bathing in the stream of sunlight. I walked quickly to her and raised her into my arms. As I brought her back to the center of the room, I told her that she had scared me.

BEING TAUGHT BY THE CHILD

4.4

Had she understood my words and had the ability to speak, she would have questioned *my* ability to graduate from grade school. Once again I placed her on the floor. She remained stationary for one tick of a clock. **My mouth hung open as I watched her drag her slender body back to the sunlight, to where the sun shone directly into her eyes. She breathed heavily from the expended energy, smiled satisfyingly at what she had attained.** As clearly as with the most articulately spoken words, her behavior showed me what *she* valued. Moments later we were back in the small room. This time, no pudding. A lantern, capable of producing a strong beam of light, rested in my lap. After some four hours of hard work, she accepted the glasses as part of herself.

As fate would have it, I saw her fifteen years later. Glasses-wearing had become a comfortable, daily part of her behavior, maintained by the natural reinforcing feedback of better vision. As I sat with her, I recalled the lesson she had taught me: Watch what individuals do; they will let you know what they value.

FROM ARTIFICIAL TO NATURAL FEEDBACK, ONCE AGAIN

4.5

"You used a contrived program with the young child to help the natural feedback take over the responsibility of maintaining glasses-wearing?" the parent asked.

"Yes."

"And once the child found value from her glasses, the contrived program was no longer necessary, right?"

"Right."

"So it is possible that a parent might use a sports car as a part of a contrived plan, hoping that eventually the college student would learn to continue his studies for their inherent enjoyment," the parent speculated.

"A parent has that option, although it's likely not to bring about the desired end of inherent enjoyment in studies. For that matter, a parent has the option of offering a sports car to a 5-year-old for brushing his teeth!"

"That would be crazy . . . and wrong."

"Crazy, no doubt. But wrong? That's a different story. The word represents a value judgment. When considering contrived payoffs for remedial programs, the term, initially at least, is best avoided. Depending on the situation, we need to place all options on the table, then eliminate those that either do not fit within our preferences, or are not wise given our long-range goals. While I would suggest a parent would be foolish to use a sports car as an incentive for anything, the word 'foolish' is also a judgment, based upon *my* value system. Today, for example, several school districts are paying high school students money to attend classes, hoping to decrease truancy. A controversial approach, to be certain. Personally, I do not approve of it. I judge it to be a poor 'band-aid' solution, one that overlooks some very important issues that we will discuss later. Again, however, that's a judgment on my part. I suspect there exists a vestigial relic who would judge that banana pudding, as well as light from a lantern might be also be wrong and foolish, despite the possibility that one or both might help an individual acquire an important skill.

FEEDBACK IS ALWAYS AN ISSUE

The department where I was a graduate student sponsored various speakers who would stand before us and share their thoughts, biases and theories. The purpose was to broaden our outlooks, give us something to think about. One such invited speaker presented his views on positive reinforcement. He was *against* its use in any form. He believed the only true, valuable reinforcement had to come from *within* the person; that reinforcement *given by someone else* was next to worthless, perhaps harmful. He chided those of us who, *by plan*, gave children hugs when they behaved desirably, who provided the youngsters with extra privileges when they worked especially hard, who "plopped candies into a child's mouth" (his phrase) when part of a goal finally had been attained. He stated that a child would be better off *not* doing something than doing it because someone provided him with a reward (his word) for an activity the child found worthless (like wearing glasses or using one's own toothbrush, I remember thinking). He added that children will learn what to do when they discover the value inherent in the activity. "Do not walk in with your 'bag of tricks,'" he insisted. "The child will find his own way." When he finished his lecture, the room full of students remained quiet. The authority received little more than a sprinkling of applause, mostly from the professors who felt some empathy for his position. The speaker's face, earlier full of smiling confidence, turned flat, pale. It appeared as though he wished to retract some of his views, or, at the very least, soften them. With polite formality, the professor who had sponsored the lecture nodded toward the speaker, indicating the session was over. By all appearances, the guest seemed hurt by the near total absence of recognition for his efforts. A few of us went to him and offered thanks for his willingness to speak to us. He remarked: "I guess I stepped on a few toes." We answered: "Heads, would be more accurate."

"Do you believe his views were wrong?" the parent asked.

"They couldn't have been more wrong. Feedback is part of the natural environment—nobody invented it. Everybody needs it; everybody works for it, everybody offers it; and most importantly, everybody will eventually find it."

"What do you mean 'everybody offers it'?"

"Watch the natural environment at work. Watch it in schools, homes, lecture halls, business offices, anyplace. You will see people interacting with people: parents with children; teachers with students; bosses with workers. There will be words of thanks, words of admonishment; there will be grades offered, bonuses given (or retracted), promotions promised or made possible, all depending on effort or being at the right place at the right time. Gold watches, colorful flowers, words of appreciation are available, all depending on effort or caprice. Environmental feedback is everywhere: Everyone has access to it; everyone, if they feel the least bit of interest toward someone, offers it. I assure you the speaker compliments his students and shows them his disapproval. His grades are feedback, as are his words of encouragement and support."

"He receives the same from his academic superiors," the parent commented.

"We could ask him about his raises, his promotions, his received and desired professional recognition."

"All contrived?"

"Well-earned, perhaps, but contrived nevertheless."

"And if he doesn't like that type of system, he could escape from it by living in a cave."

"He didn't impress me as someone who could survive in a cave," I answered, "but if he did, it would be because of his ability to adapt to the cave's natural environmental feedback."

"So no one can escape *it.*"

"Not while we're alive."

DEBATE TYPES, NOT THEIR IMPORTANCE

"If that is true, then the type of feedback is the central issue," the parent suggested.

"Yes. Those authorities who find fault with rewards and reinforcement are really expressing their disapproval over *types* of rewards and reinforcement, and not the issue of feedback. Sports cars are out; '(sincere) feelings and (personal) reactions to . . . behavior' are viewed favorably.[2] They all recognize that feedback is an essential part of growth and development. They just disagree on what type of feedback is most beneficial to the individual.''

"That does present a problem, though," the parent said. "How's that?"

GO BEYOND YOUR PERSONAL PREFERENCES

"Look at your definition of a positive reinforcer: it is *anything* that an individual values; *anything* he will put out effort to obtain. It is the individual, then, who decides what is and what is not a positive payoff for *him*."

"That's correct."

"So the authorities who are talking about what should and should not be used as reinforcers are imposing their own values and judgments on everyone else. They are saying what 'should' be, without consideration for an individual's 'person'—his history, experiences, perceptions, predisposition. It's easy to say what 'should' be, but what 'should' be may not represent what 'is.' ''

"Is that a problem?" I asked as though I didn't know.''

THE STUDENT'S PERCEPTIONS ARE ESSENTIAL

"Of course," the parent stated. "Suppose 'sincere' feelings and 'personal' reactions aren't valued by an individual. **If there is nothing magical about banana pudding, why would anyone assume there's something magical about adult attention, no matter how sincere and personal the person was who offered it.** If I don't trust a person, don't like the person, or don't know the person, I doubt I'm going to be 'hot' about his attention. If I'm a student, and I haven't experienced a great deal of success with my studies, I doubt I'm going to be 'turned on' by 'inherent enjoyment' of academic progress. There's nothing magical about that, either. My gracious, I never realized how simple and nonproductive it is for someone to tell someone else what they *should* value."

"It is easy. At the same time, I'm sure those people who sit in soft, cushioned chairs and suggest the 'shoulds' are all speaking with good intentions. Many of their 'shoulds' are easy to embrace. It would be nice if all our behaviors were motivated by intrinsic, personally satisfying, values that produced long-term, beneficial, self-fulfilling, behaviors. Unfortunately, it just doesn't always happen that way."

4.6

"The arena, again," the parent remarked.

"Again and again. So long as the natural environment doesn't give us what we would hope for . . ."

"We step in," the parent said, nodding.

"We step in, yes."

TEMPORARY CONTRIVED PROGRAMS:
INTO THE ARENA

We step into the arena only when the natural environment has not produced behaviors viewed as desirable. When consultants do intercede, our goal is to help the desired behavior occur frequently without the need for feedback that is unrelated to the behavior itself. All of us would much prefer that students read for the enjoyment that comes from the activity rather than having the behavior maintained by "gold stars"; that youngsters communicate for the "inherent" value of interaction rather than for being hugged and told "good talking"; that children eat their food, study their math, brush their teeth, wear their glasses, and be respectful and thoughtful of others for what "inherently" exists within those activities rather than for the "bells" and "banjos" that often are necessary. All of us, teachers, psychologists, therapists, want desirable behavior to occur frequently, comfortably, naturally, purely for the sake of the activities' *worth*. I've never met anyone who was thrilled with the use of "bells" and "banjos," and most of the folks I've met would prefer to eat M & M's rather than doling them out as "rewards."

But the consultant knows that the potential or real worth associated with an activity is often not experienced. For an individual to "taste" the worth of an endeavor he must first know that worth exists. Frequently, individuals seen in consultation do not realize that certain behaviors have the ability to produce specific payoffs: They have yet to learn, for example, that wearing of glasses can help them see their world more clearly, that communication can enhance interaction, or that the reading of a book can introduce them to both outcomes. Obviously, before glasses-wearing, communicating, reading, or any other behavior can produce valued payoffs, these must be experienced. Before those "desired" behaviors will occur frequently, seemingly naturally in the future, they must produce an effect perceived as positive by the one who is participating in the activity. That's a fancy way of saying that the behavior must produce a positive "payoff." If glasses-wearing painfully distorts the world, if communicating proves ineffectual and embarrassing, if reading is too difficult or frustrating, the activities will possess no "inherent" value: They will not occur on their own. Jesse showed us that something as simple as eating does not always produce anything close to positive feedback.

_____ HELP THE STUDENT DISCOVER INHERENT WORTH _____

Our task, therefore, is to give inherent worth a chance to influence. We can make every effort to associate a desired behavior with a positive, naturally occurring, effect. Long before a problem exists, we can show our children the value "inherent" in the activities we desire. If the natural environment doesn't throw us an unwanted curve, if the child continues to experience worth from his or her efforts, "bells" and "banjos" un-related to the activity will occur so infrequently we won't be aware of them. If, however, the natural environment turns its back on us, we take the following procedures and help the natural environment work for us.

FEEDBACK POSSESSES NEITHER _____ WISDOM NOR MORALITY _____

There is a second reason why we step into the arena to lend the natural environment a helping hand. Look once again at the opening paragraph to this chapter:

> Once the behavior-pairs have been established, and the influential cues have been identified, our attention must turn to how the natural environment, through its positive feedback, influences behaviors. Please note I did not preface the word "behaviors" with the word "desired." The omission was not an error. We must not lose sight of the fact that the natural environment's feedback can increase the occurrence of *any* behavior, desired or otherwise. The natural environment teaches us *what to do* in order to gain access to what we value. For desired behaviors to occur more frequently, we must make sure the procedures to be discussed influence the *desired sides* of the behavior-pairs.

By accident, by circumstance, by errors of omission or commission, the natural environment can teach an individual to behave undesirably: "The natural environment teaches us *what to do* in order to gain access to what we value." If we discover that one of our behaviors produces an outcome to our liking, chances are good we will manifest that behavior again in the presence of particular cues.

Feedback is an effect. It simply occurs. It, in itself, is not guided by knowledge or intent. It has neither morals nor wisdom. It is incapable of caring about right or wrong, good or bad, desirable or undesirable. As with a bolt of lightning, a stream of warm sun, a smile, a light touch or harsh spank, it just happens. It occurs at a point in time. It has the ability to influence behavior.

If feedback possessed morals, wisdom, and caring, I would never have met Jesse or any of the other youngsters and adults I've seen over the past

4.7

twenty years. I wouldn't, today, be visiting the 3-year-old whose tantrums have reached intolerable proportions, or the 24-year-old whose aggressive actions have sent an aide to the hospital. But morals, wisdom, and caring are not a part of feedback. It operates, often without detection, always without concern. It teaches without foresight or knowledge of its own effects:

Erin has discovered that when her mother says "bedtime," screaming, for reasons unknown to the child, gets Mom to change her mind.

c........P.............B................**f b**
"bedtime"   Erin   screaming   delay bedtime

Mike has learned that when he throws food on the floor, he must leave the table and go to his room.

c........P.............B................**f b**
table   Mike   throw food   leave table, go to room

Jeremy knows that if he clowns around in class, he will have to sit by himself in the back of the classroom.

c........P.............B................**f b**
class   Jeremy   clowning   sit by himself

Jesse discovered that when he ate food, he experienced pain.

c........P.............B................**f b**
food   Jesse   eating   pain

Feedback happens. It doesn't know what behavior is being influenced.

Although not always, feedback is most often provided by someone: parent, teacher, etc. Occasionally, stomachs and heads that are in disarray, stove elements left on, walls that are in the "wrong" place, and cabinet doors left open provide us with feedback. Generally, however, the feedback consultants are most interested is that which occurs at the hands of the significant people within an individual's life space. We know that through *no fault,* and without intent, feedback can begin to produce an increase in behaviors eventually deemed undesired. When the behaviors reach proportions that raise concern, resulting in a call for assistance, the consultant takes his caring and knowledge and offers help to those involved. This, as you may have guessed, is the arena.

SPECULATING ON BEHAVIOR'S PURPOSE

The issue of a behavior's purpose has been mentioned several times. Because this issue is so important, we will be returning to it now, as well as throughout the remainder of the text. Among other things, the determination of purpose can tell us something of an individual's perceived value of the feedback he or she is experiencing. That information will provide us with ideas for remediation. Let's run through a typical sequence that a consultant might face.

First: A phone call or message is received requesting assistance.

Second: Clearly stated, observable behavior-pairs are determined.

Third: Data are collected to ascertain what conditions may be setting the stage for both the desired and undesired behaviors.

Fourth: We return our attention to the undesired behavior.

The above inquiries will provide us with the following:

```
        c........P.............B
        cues                 undesired
                             behavior
```

Next, we need to determine how the natural environment is reacting to the undesired behavior.

Fifth: Data are collected to determine what feedback is following the behavior.

```
        c........P.............B............?
        cues               undesired
                           behavior
```

—————————— INITIALLY, AVOID CHARACTERIZING FEEDBACK ——————————

4.8

As in the four examples of feedback we just saw, it is essential that we simply document how the environment is responding to the behavior. At this stage, **we do not describe or speak of the feedback in terms of "positive" or "negative" or any such words.** *All we do is to write down what is happening after the undesired behavior has occurred.*

c........P.............B................**f b**
table   Mike   throw food   *made to leave table,*
go to room

It may be difficult to maintain "neutrality" during this phase. We often draw premature conclusions about the positive or negative "flavor" of feedback. Most often, quick conclusions, prior to collecting more information, will tell us only about *our* values, rather than the values of the individual in question. We will return to this issue shortly.

Now we turn our attention to "purpose."

Sixth: What purpose might the undesired behavior be serving? What might the individual be gaining from the behavior? What is the possible "payoff" for the behavior? *Why* is the individual manifesting the behavior?

"I believe you've just opened Pandora's box," the psychologist suggested.

"Excuse me?"

"Pandora. Hephaestus' mythical woman. The box that contained all the evils that could plague Man. The question Why?, and the speculation of purpose behind behavior will open the floodgate. Everybody and his brother is going to have ideas *why* a behavior occurs."

"Is that bad?" I asked.

"Come on, now," he chided. "Suppose someone suggests that Mike throws his food because he's been taken over by evil spirits."

"I suspect that possibility exists."

"It wouldn't ruffle your feathers?"

"My feathers? No."

"How about if Mike's behavior is said to be a result of his 'insecurity' or feelings of 'hostility' toward his parents?"

"If such were offered, I wouldn't roll over and expire."

"All right, try this one: Mike throws food because it is his way of unconsciously demonstrating his sexual prowess."

"We could place that one into the hopper as well," I answered.

"Okay, what hidden agenda do you have this time," the psychologist asked smiling.

I returned his smile. *"Any* idea about why a behavior occurs is legitimate so long as it can be *tested."*

"How in the world could you possibly test for evil spirits, insecurity, or unconscious displays of sexual prowess?"

"Fortunately, that's not my problem. I would never suggest those ideas were related to food-throwing or anything else," I stated. "I don't see those issues existing through the window that governs my thinking."

"But other consultants might offer those ideas as causatory variables," the psychologist suggested.

"Then it would be their responsibility to offer evidence substantiating their views."

"You know that some parents and other professionals will buy into those ideas even without substantiating evidence," the psychologist said. "They'll accept them because an 'authority' says they are true."

"That does happen, I know. Personally, I would hope that all people who seek assistance would think carefully, logically, about what might be responsible for behavior; that they wouldn't be too quick to accept an idea simply because it sounds good or novel. By accepting an idea without consideration for other possibilities, they might overlook something important."

"Like 'payoffs' "?

"Yes. Regardless of one's view through the window, we would be making a serious mistake if the question of payoff and purpose for behavior does not enter the discussion. Psychologists have long since been aware that payoffs for undesired behavior can lead to an increase in the behavior. It's hardly a new view."

In the 1960s, when reviewing a case involving a serious behavior, one psychologist stated:

> If you want an explanation for this behavior . . . I believe we can account for all of it with one general principle: *it pays off.* It pays off for the individual who can't seem to find other . . . behaviors to get him what he wants.[3]

When reviewing a series of research articles describing such behaviors as "social isolation," "regressed crawling," and "crying," two further psychologists stated:

> These three studies of nursery school behavior indicate clearly how a behavior "paying off" may lead to its increase."[4]

"Determining the value of a payoff requires that we consider the individual's perception of how the environment is responding to his behavior, isn't that so?" the psychologist asked.

"Without question," I responded. "Do you recall the discussion the parent and I had a while back regarding reinforcers and values?"

> "It is the individual, then, who decides what is and what is not a [reinforcer] for him," [the parent said].
>
> "That's correct," [I responded].
>
> "So the authorities who are talking about what should and should not be used as reinforcers are imposing their own values and judgments on everyone else. They are saying what 'should' be, without consideration for an individual's 'person'—his history, experiences, perceptions, predisposition. It's easy to say what 'should' be, but what 'should' be may not represent what 'is.'"

——————— DETERMINING THE PAYOFF/PURPOSE OF BEHAVIOR ———————

Whether one is "hot" or not about his environment's reactions rests within the domain of an individual's "person." Perceived value is a private event. Receiving banana pudding could be something valued. Then, so could any number of things: a spanking, or adult attention, studying hard, being by oneself, listening to music, embroiling oneself in an argument, being sent to one's room, or most anything else. Our task is to enter an individual's private world to determine how he or she values the occurring feedback. The task is not as difficult as it may appear. We have at least two means to ascertain that information.

LET THE STUDENT'S WORDS HELP
——————— YOU UNDERSTAND PURPOSE ———————

We should try, when possible, to ask individuals to share their thoughts and perceptions:

```
   c........P.............B................f b
  table     Mike        throw food     made to leave table,
                                          go to room
```

"Hey, Mike, how come you persist in throwing food on the floor?"

"Am I goin' to be punished for telling the truth?" the youngster asks hesitantly.

"Absolutely not. For the sake of science, you're home free. We want you to share your 'person' with us."

"You guys are strange. But if you promise . . ."

"We promise."

"My mom is a great lady. But she cooks the worst chicken fried steak imaginable. I can't cut it, much less chew it. If I dump it on the floor, she sends me to my room. You promise . . .?"

"We promise!"

"I've got a bag of Pepperidge Farm Goldfish, the lightly salted kind, under my pillow. I go to my room, turn on the tube, and eat fish. Not bad!"

"No insecurity?"

"Nope."

"No evil spirits?"

"Nope."

"No sexual prowess—the kind that's unconscious?"

"Say what?"

"If we can determine the payoff's value from the individual's perception, we can begin developing ideas that will show the person what alternative behaviors are available that could lead him to what he values," the psychologist said.

"I'm not sure there's much we can do with wooden chicken fried steak, but in most other instances, determining payoffs can help us develop programs," I responded. "In Jeremy's case . . .

```
c . . . . . . . P . . . . . . . . . . . . . B . . . . . . . . . . . . . . . fb
class      Jeremy           clowning            sit by himself
```

4.9

. . . it would be helpful to figure out how he feels about sitting by himself. Is it something that he values? Is he 'working hard' to be removed from the classroom's activities? Does he clown around in all his classes or in a particular one?"

"That last question refers to the business of cues, doesn't it?"

"Yes. If he 'misbehaves' in only one class, that tells us something about his perceptions of both the class and the immediate environment's feedback."

"So he may be working hard to be removed from one class's activities rather than those in all of his classes."

"Yes."

"But why would a youngster work hard to be removed from a class?"

"I don't know. Let's ask him."

"We're doing fractions and I don't understand them," Jeremy admitted, apparently embarrassed. "The teacher calls on us to answer questions; I can't answer them. When he puts me in the back of the room, he doesn't ask me anything," the youngster pointed out.

"Do you like sitting by yourself?" we ask.

"Not really, but it's better than looking stupid."

"So he clowns to avoid looking bad in front of his teacher and classmates," the psychologist said.

"It looks that way," I responded.

"He's not working hard to get something; he's working hard to *avoid* something."

"That's right. 'Avoiding something perceived as unpleasant' is another type of payoff."

"Sitting in the back of his class won't help him learn his fractions, though. It's only going to make things more difficult for him later."

"I'm afraid you're correct."

"His teacher should do something about teaching Jeremy fractions rather than isolating him from the class. I mean, the kid's behavior is his way of telling us that the math is over his head."

"Very possibly."

"So in this instance, the payoff—sitting in the back of the room, avoiding looking foolish when questions are asked—tells us how to help the child. If he were successful with fractions, he could remain with his friends. His friends would be happy; his teacher would be happy; and Jeremy would be happier. And we found all this out because we asked the youngster to share his private views."

"Sometimes it is that simple. We now know Jeremy's math curriculum needs revamping."

IF WORDS ARE NOT AVAILABLE, WATCH BEHAVIORS

Determining the value of payoffs is somewhat more difficult when an individual's cognitive and language skills are deficient, either due to development or trauma. Under those conditions, we must watch carefully the individual's behavior and note the types of feedback that are occurring. If individuals repeat the behavior that appears to produce the feedback, it is safe to speculate that the feedback holds some value for them. A child, for example, who consistently plays with a certain toy is likely receiving something of value from that toy. Her words aren't necessary; her behavior tells us of her perceptions. If an individual's frequently occurring undesired behavior is repeatedly reacted to in an identifiable manner, and the individual continues manifesting the undesired behavior, the environment's reaction may be something the individual wishes repeated—it may hold value *for him or her.*

When attempting to determine payoffs for the nonverbal individual, three essential issues must be considered. First, we must maintain "neutrality" regarding *our* perceptions of the feedback. A common error, for example, is our assumption that a particular environmental reaction is, *ipso facto,* "negative," something an individual will wish not to experience. We expell a student from school; we send another to his room; we remove a third from an activity; or invoke any number of other reactions that, from our view, are intended to help students "mend" their ways. To our chagrin, we may discover that the individual wishes to be expelled, or finds it advantageous to be in his room rather than participate in an activity that he would prefer to avoid. By maintaining "neutrality," simply noting exactly how the environment is responding, we'll be in a better position to access the individual's perception of the reaction.

Second, we may lose sight of the purpose for a behavior when we indicate that the environment does not respond to the behavior the same way every time it occurs. Feedback does *not* have to occur consistently to be influential. The statement: "When the child behaves in a certain way, sometimes I do one thing, sometimes another," indicates the behavior is being attended to variably or occasionally. If the occasional feedback is valued, the behavior that produces it will grow more persistent, thus occur more often. Again, it is necessary to describe the behavior along with *what* feedback is occurring, and *when* it is occurring.

Third, it is often necessary to figuratively look at individuals' life space through a microscope in order to determine the purpose behind their behavior. While the "whole" picture will provide a sense of what is happening, a "microscopic" view will often show us the unique relation between behavior and the environment's reactions. A colleague of mine shared the following story:

She was working on a toileting program with a nonverbal, nonambulatory, 5-year-old cerebral palsied youngster. The child had begun to use eye-pointing as a means of communication. Various pictures would be shown to the child when he seemed to want to express a need. After noting which picture drew the child's visual attention, the therapist would have a better idea of what the child desired.

Once the child had learned the purpose for the toilet, the therapist wanted him to understand how communication could functionally manipulate his environment. Rather than placing him on the toilet for many minutes, waiting for an "event" to occur, the therapist wanted the child to learn that looking at the picture of the toilet would result in him being taken to the bathroom. Gradually, the procedure was working: When the child "needed" to go to the bathroom, he would look at the toilet picture, the therapist would take him to the potty, and he would urinate or defecate. The process was laborious. The child would have to be wheeled into the bathroom, removed from his wheelchair, placed on a mat in order to remove his pants, then picked up and placed on the toilet seat. The child's motor involvement precluded his assistance: The more he tried to help, the tighter his muscles became. Getting the child from his classroom and onto the toilet would often take twenty minutes. After several days of success, a problem presented itself: The child would look at the picture, be placed on the toilet's seat, and engage the therapist in smiling, gestural play rather than doing his business. By all observations, the youngster was enjoying himself immensely. The therapist, however, wasn't. She had three other children to care for, and she couldn't afford the time the child was suddenly requiring.

A not too "microscopic" analysis suggested that the child was using the picture cue as a means to gain considerable one-on-one attention from the therapist, whom he liked very much: He learned that by focusing on the picture he could be removed from the classroom and have the therapist, and their play, all to himself. For the sake of the other children, the situation could not continue. The therapist quickly showed the child that he could have his desired one-on-one, in class, *after* he urinated or defecated. This slight change in *when* the valued feedback was provided got the program back on track.

By taking a closer look at the relationship between behavior and the environment's feedback, we can often determine what purpose the behavior may be serving. Doing so will help us devise a program that will be beneficial to all parties involved. Remember, if an individual continually repeats a behavior that produces the feedback, there's a good chance the individual is working hard to receive the environment's reaction. The reaction, then, whether it appears "positive" or otherwise, whether it occurs consistently *or* occasionally, is valued.

DETERMINING PAYOFFS FOR DESIRED BEHAVIOR

Not every environmental reaction is valued the same way by every child, and what is valued by a youngster today may not be valued tomorrow. Like adults, children's interests and values change as growth and development continue, and an environmental reaction that once was something to work hard to obtain may become something less important or something to work to avoid. While this variability can play havoc with our programs and plans, it is, nevertheless, a part of a natural growth process. For a reason that may not be initially obvious, it is essential that we stay in constant touch with an individual's changing preferences. Let me bring back the earlier mentioned six points that are involved in a consultant's queries. There's a seventh that must be added.

First: A phone call or message is received requesting assistance.

Second: Clearly stated, observable behavior-pairs are determined.

Third: Data are collected to ascertain what conditions may be setting the stage for both the desired and undesired behaviors.

Fourth: We return our attention to the undesired behavior.

Fifth: Data are collected to determine what feedback is following the behavior.

Sixth: What purpose might the undesired behavior be serving? What might the individual be gaining from the behavior? What is the possible "payoff" for the behavior? *Why* is the individual manifesting the behavior?

Turning our attention to the desired side of the behavior-pair, we ask:

Seventh: Does the desired behavior serve a purpose—Is there a payoff for the desired behavior? Does the individual see a reason to behavior desirably? What does the desired behavior bring him or her?

"If an individual learns that from all his available behaviors, his desired behavior is what brings him something of value, he'll be inclined to behave desirably. If he discovers that his desired behavior does not bring him something of value, he'll be less inclined to behave desirably. Is that view too narrow?" the parent asked.

"From my perspective it's not too narrow," I responded.

DESIRED BEHAVIOR MUST PRODUCE A VALUED
PAYOFF, INTRINSIC OR CONTRIVED

4.10

"Then, for a desired behavior to occur, it must produce some valued payoff for the individual."

"Yes."

"And you indicated that what is valued doesn't have to be something material?" the parent asked as she reviewed her notes. "And it doesn't have to be something given by another person."

"No, not material, and not necessarily provided by an outside source."

"The payoff could be a sense of accomplishment, discovering something that satisfies curiosity, a desire to help another person, or just feeling good about participating in an activity," the parent continued.

"A desired behavior's payoff could be those or any number of other 'internal,' self-pleasing, feelings."

"The bottom line is that the desired behavior must produce something valued by the individual. If not . . ."

"The behavior will not occur," I responded.

"When you set up your remediation programs, how do you tell whether you need to provide an external, artificial payoff?"

"The individual's behavior will let me know," I answered. "Once the desired behavior has been determined, I look to see what, if any, feedback is occurring when the desired behavior is manifested. An individual who is working hard at a task, or behaving in a desired fashion, *is* receiving something of value."

"Something positive."

"Maybe," I responded.

"Oh, I remember. The desired behavior may enable the individual to avoid something seen as unpleasant."

"That's right."

"And if the desired behavior is not occurring?"

AWARENESS, ABILITY, COMFORT

"Then one of several possibilities are evident. First, the individual *may not know what behavior is desired.* Second, he may know what is preferred, *but he can't do it.* Third, the individual *may be frightened by the behavior.* Fourth, he may know what is expected, may have the ability to do it, may not be frightened by it, but *may see no reason to do it.*"

"So you would provide him with a reason to put out the effort," the parent said.

"It's not always that simple. Do you recall Jeremy's problems with fractions? You could provide him with every incentive in the world, but if he doesn't understand the arithmetic, the offered incentives will do little but frustrate him."

"In that case, you would teach him what he needs to know, then provide him with a positive payoff."

_____ ARTIFICIAL TO NATURAL, ONCE AGAIN _____

"At that point, an artificial payoff may *not* be necessary. Jeremy might continue working on his fractions because he finds them to be fun and challenging. *We only provide contrived payoffs when natural or intrinsic feedback fails to maintain the desired behavior. We do so with the long-range goal of helping the more natural payoffs take over.* Let me share an example with you."

I've been involved with a little boy for several months. The child has a metabolic disorder that has seriously affected his cognitive skills. Nevertheless, the youngster has a lot going for him. He's very personable, he's got a great smile, he loves to explore his environment, he enjoys listening to records, and he's a wizard with ten-piece puzzles. But he doesn't speak, and he's never successfully been able to tell his parents or teachers many of the things he wants to do. When I first met him, I noticed that he would charge up to an adult, grab an arm or sleeve, and first grunt and then scream as though he wished to share something important. The adults would lead him around the room, desperately trying to determine what the little boy wanted. Frequently, the scene would produce frustration for all involved, and, on occasion, the youngster would become so worked up over the adults' inability to understand his desires that his screaming would evolve into a full-blown tantrum.

My sense was that if I could help the child with his communication difficulties, many of his adaptive, "undesired" behaviors would disappear. I could have, of course, provided him with any number of positive payoffs for being quiet rather than screaming or tantruming, but that course of action would not have resolved the "underlying" problem. Teaching a nonverbal child *to be quiet* would be as absurd as it sounds.

One morning I sat with him at a table in a relatively nondistracting corner of the classroom. I knew, from observation and discussion, that the child enjoyed puzzles, music, and cereal-treats. I had brought four large picture cards with me: One card displayed a picture of a record player; one showed a puzzle; one showed a box of cereal; and the last one was blank. I placed the card that pictured the cereal box on the table. Directly behind the card, I had placed a bowl of dried cereal. His initial reaction was to grab for the cereal. It was evident that was what he wanted, but it was not what I wanted. I wanted him to learn that despite his inability to speak intelligibly, there was another effective way to communicate his desires. I stopped his hand before it reached the cereal and redirected it to the picture of the cereal box. As soon as he touched the card, I gave him a few pieces of cereal. Predictably, he gave no indication that he understood the process behind what we were doing. He again lurched for more cereal. Again I redirected his hand toward the picture card. When he touched it, I gave him a few more pieces. As he ate the treats, he stared into my eyes. "If you want something, point to the picture," I said to him. He hesitated for a moment, then went for the bowl. I stopped him, and this time *he* layed his hand on top of the card that pictured the cereal box. After giving him some additional treats, I gently touched his wavy hair and told him how proud I was of his efforts. Before he had completely chewed the cereal, and while he looked into my eyes, he touched the card. He was given more treats. After several more successful trials, I brought the picture of the record player and placed it next to the cereal box picture. I knew that if he were going to use the picture cards as a means of communication, he would have to look at the cards (rather than me!), and discriminate between them. He noticed the additional card on the table, but was more intent at looking at me. As chance would have it, his hand went to the record player card. I shook my head "No," and placed his hand on the cereal card. With each subsequent trial, he began to look for the cereal card before placing his hand on it. Despite my changing the position of the two cards, he looked for the pictured box of cereal before making his choice. The minute I brought the classroom's record player to the table and placed it behind the picture of the record player, he slammed his hand on the record player card.

Within a few days, all four cards were on the table. He seemed to enjoy taking turns at which card he would touch: He learned that the cereal card brought him something to eat; the record player card brought him a few minutes of music; and the puzzle card brought him his favorite ten-piece puzzle. He touched the blank card only once, almost as though he wanted to see if there was any magic attached to it. His picture communication book now has twelve reduced-size pictures. He carries it with him wherever he goes. His teacher is helping him discriminate the letters of the alphabet. The hope is that soon he will be able to spell, as well as point out his desires. The child's natural environment has taken over.

"You had to teach the youngster the desired pointing and looking behavior, teach him how to do both, and then teach him what payoff the behaviors might offer him," the parent said.

"That's right, and as soon as he put it all together, he took off. In a sense, he learned how to learn. On one occasion, he found a picture of a bicycle in a magazine and brought the picture to his teacher. There was no small bike available at school, but after the teacher called the child's parents, a shiny red and white tricycle was waiting for the youngster when he arrived home from school. And a new picture was added to the child's book."

"That's really exciting," the parent exclaimed.

"I know the child would agree."

"Would you have been as successful had you not used those artificial reinforcers?" the psychologist asked.

"Certainly the cereal, puzzles, and record player made the process easier," I responded, "but given the child's innate skills, it's possible that, eventually, success might have been achieved without them. The child, however, might have experienced a lot of pain in the process. I chose to use them because I wanted the learning experience to be pleasant and fruitful, quickly."

"Were you concerned that he would learn to use communication solely for the purpose of accessing material objects?" the psychologist asked.

"Not at all. Once his skills improve, his natural environment—his parents and teachers and friends—will introduce him to the beauty of sharing ideas and feelings," I answered.

"That will be difficult for him, won't it," the parent suggested.

"Difficult, but possible. He's now learning the value of interaction, and so long as that interaction provides him with purpose, he'll continue to explore ways of using his acquired skills."

"To think it got started with puzzles and a record player," the parent said.

"Let's say those items assisted. He came into the class knowing much about communication. The objects just helped him learn more."

"Do you use the same approach with problems other than communication?" the parent asked me.

"I'm not sure I understand."

"I mean, do you identify activities that your other patients enjoy and use them in your developed programs?"

"Whenever I am asked to help someone, I always spend time finding out what the individual values. If I am going to assist someone's acquisition of desired behaviors, I will need to determine what he's willing to work for."

"Then you will help him learn how to access the valued objects," the parent added.

"That is one of my intended goals. But remember, what is valued is not always an object."

"It could be the approval or appreciation of an important adult," the psychologist said.

"Yes."

_____ WATCH WHICH BEHAVIORS RECEIVE FEEDBACK _____

The first time I saw the 9-month-old he was securely buckled into a car seat placed atop the mattress of his hospital crib. The young physician who stood by my side filled me in on the child's difficult history. The child had been abandoned at birth; left at the doorstep of a fire station located in a city not far from Denver. When the child was taken to a hospital, it was discovered that his lower intestines had not developed properly, and surgery to correct the problem had been performed immediately. Further, it was found that he had a condition known as hydrocephalus (an accumulation of fluid within the cranium), and a shunt (a channel through which the excess fluid could drain into the stomach) was implanted in the infant's skull to prevent further damage from swelling. For reasons unfathomable, (presumably to allow the child to die quietly) the infant had been placed, and basically left unattended, in a crib in the far corner of one of the hospital's units. He was discovered by a resident physician while on routine rounds, and was immediately flown to his present location. The initial surgery to correct the intestinal problem had been far from adequate, and the child, once again, had to 'go under' the knife. Those problems aside, another had surfaced: The child had never eaten any solid food, and the present methods used to maintain him, intravenous feedings, were becoming more difficult due to the collapsing of his veins. As I gazed upon the child, I wondered how he had made it this far. He was a most engaging child: He had bright blue eyes and a full head of blonde hair. If death was around the corner, the child didn't know or accept it. His smile was captivating and his energy was boundless. He waved his small hands gleefully at the mobile that was attached to his crib and his eyes never missed a passing nurse or attendant physician. A strong bond had grown between the adults and the youngster and the mutual affection that was offered no doubt sustained his life, as well as the efforts of those dedicated to him. But he was not eating, and the physicians believed that the possible gains from further surgery to correct his nutritional problems might be outweighed by the intrusive procedures. The child was the first 'failure to thrive' youngster I had seen and I felt completely overwhelmed. The young physician quietly sat by my side. For the moment, the child was in better shape than we were.

Through all the movement and controlled chaos that often is germane to a busy special care unit, a crystal clear picture stood out: A minute rarely passed without a nurse stopping by the child, touching him, talking to him. He would stop whatever he was doing and drink in the warm affection that poured forth. Part of my head asked, 'Could he learn to initially swallow food in order to obtain that endearing attention?' It was worth a try. I took the physician's arm and together we gathered the nurses into a group. To say the least, they were not pleased with my idea. But the child was important enough for them to put aside their displeasure.

I positioned several of the nurses at the far end of the child's crib. They were asked to smile, clap, and wave their hands at the child; his eyes never left them. The remaining nurses were asked to stay outside the child's visual field. I located a large piece of cardboard and brought it next to the crib. The physician mixed a small container of baby cereal and apple sauce, and joined me at the child's side. I placed a small quantity of the mixture on the tip end of a tongue depressor. After taking a deep breath, I placed the card board directly in front of the child. The nurses, the mobile, all that the child valued, disappeared. Surprised, his eyes and mouth opened wide. I immediately, carefully, placed the cereal and apple sauce on the middle of his tongue, and without hesitation, removed the cardboard 'blind' exposing the excited nurses. In truth, the child had several options: He could have held the food on his tongue or he could have spit it out. He didn't do either: He swallowed. The nurses clapped and shouted wildly. The child was allowed five seconds to enjoy their displayed affection before the cardboard once again removed them from his sight. A second, small amount of food was placed on his tongue. This time he held it in his mouth for a brief moment, then swallowed. The cardboard was removed. On the fifth 'trial,' the physician took over the job of manipulating the blind and the food. Within one hour, the child had consumed all the mixed cereal and apple sauce—about two ounces. More important, he learned that swallowing brought him what he most valued. (The nurses and physicians learned the same.) During the afternoon session, the blind was no longer needed. The nurses simply remained quiet until the child swallowed. Six months later, the child was adopted by a loving family.

_____ TAPPING THE INNER WORLD _____

Occasionally, I am asked to describe the most difficult case I've been associated with over the years. While several come to mind, one case stands out as being my most trying and frustrating experience. It involved twin boys, born prematurely. Both were congenitally blind, both hydrocephalic, neither were verbal, and both were self-abusive. I first met the boys when they were about 2 years old. Today, they're 14. While they did learn to walk and become toilet trained, I'm sorry to say that neither have progressed much beyond that over the years. Despite the efforts of many professionals, teachers, therapists, psychologists, and physicians, the boys have no adequate communication system, they are both tucked away in their isolated worlds, and their self-destructive behaviors have only worsened. Both are living in group homes, and while new programs are constantly being tried, the best that can be said is that, with the exception of the self-abusive hitting and biting, they are not regressing. Seeing the boys always reminds me that we all have much to learn about helping individuals who are heavily burdened.

Recognizing that I'm about to affix myself to wall, suitable for pins or darts, one issue beyond all others stands out in my mind as being a contributing, if not predominate, factor in our collective inability to help these boys over the years. None of us, independently or acting as a team, have ever been able to tap into the youngsters' value systems. We've never been able to find anything the boys were willing to work for, even sparingly. We've never been able to compete with whatever motivation they carry in their private worlds. The search for natural or contrived leverage has been ongoing, literally, for years. It will, of course, continue.

A VARIETY OF VALUES

There is an eighth step in the sequence previously mentioned. Let's review the seventh.

Seventh: Does the desired behavior serve a purpose—Is there a payoff for the desired behavior? Does the individual see a reason to behavior desirably? What does the desired behavior bring him or her?

The eighth speaks of an idea best described by the phrase "menu of values." A menu of values is a "reinforcement menu." It lists the many activities, objects, and reactions individuals find of worth. It tells what they are willing to work to obtain. It tells something of their perceptions and preferences. It can contain anything from enjoying math to enjoying sitting under a tree; from enjoying a kind word to enjoying a warm hug. Anything! (Even a sports car.) We do *not* determine the list; the individual does.

Eighth: What does the individual value? What is he or she willing to work hard to obtain? What are his or her reinforcers?

Miss Locke had a unique approach that she used at the beginning of each school year. She would spend several days talking with her students so she could get to know them and they, in turn, could learn something about her. She would tell them what she hoped to accomplish, while asking them what they would like to accomplish during the school year. Usually, by the middle of the first week of school, she made the following statement to her students.

"I am going to do the best I can to make this class interesting and fun. Yes, I did say fun. I will ask you to do some things for me and, in turn, I will try to do some things for you.

The very first item on our agenda is for me to find out some of the things that interest you. I do not necessarily mean classroom subjects, but things or activities that you would like to do beyond classwork. Games, activities, hobbies that you enjoy—that's what I would like to know about. I am going to pass out a piece of paper to each of you. On the paper you will see ten lines. I would like you to fill in as many of the ten lines as you wish with things you would like to do. You are in fourth grade now, so I know that there are many fun things you enjoy. If you will share them with me, maybe we will be able to do some of them in class."

Miss Locke passed the papers to the entire class. The excitement was evident. One of the boys raised his hand. "Is it okay if we put down something like going on a picnic?" he asked.

"Yes," she answered, "that's just fine."

That evening Miss Locke took the papers home. As expected, there were approximately 200 suggestions. Fortunately, as was also expected, there were over 100 duplications. Of the remaining choices, a few were not practical. One child wanted to visit the moon. Another wanted to go to Disneyland. Another suggested that he be allowed to stay home and forget school for a couple of years. However, for the most part, the suggestions were practical and administratively feasible. She tallied the remaining list and decided on the 25 most popular.

Among them were the following:

1. Going on a picnic
2. Playing with paint
3. Going to the library to see film strips
4. Playing games in class
5. Reading various magazines
6. Learning to sew
7. Talking with a neighbor
8. Talking about hobbies

In addition to a few more, there were three that were the most popular. One, Miss Locke expected—a visit to the Busch Gardens Zoo. There was another that was a little surprising—a field trip to a 7-11 store. But of all the ones that were submitted, going outside and looking for bugs was the one that floored her. In all the years that she had used the reinforcement menu idea, this one had never been mentioned. However, if some of the kids wanted to do it, it was fine with her—"as long as the bugs are kept in jars," she was to tell them at a later date.[5]

When the natural environment falters, and fails to teach and maintain desired behaviors, our ability to intervene successfully depends in large measure on our acquiring ideas of what an individual values. Several of the programs to be described, those that increase as well as decrease behaviors, use identified "reinforcers" to help the natural environment right itself. We were never able to establish a menu for the twins. In our ignorance, we were unable to tap into the natural environment in a way that would have benefited the two boys.

Fortunately, most individuals seen by consultants do not guard their values so secretively. Most, indeed, wear them on their sleeves. The eighth step asks us to identify and note them. The task is not difficult. A piece of paper, a pencil, eyes that are willing to see, and ears that are willing to listen, are the only tools needed. What can be obtained will help us influence the desired side of the behavior-pairs. That's what we're all about: Helping individuals find alternatively desirable ways of accessing what they value.

"FREEBIES" VERSUS CONTINGENCIES

We have but one more topic to discuss before looking at various ideas to help influence desired behaviors. This particular issue carries considerable importance, and I would ask that you give it very serious thought. If you are comfortable with my biased view, I believe your chances for successful redirection of undesired behaviors will be markedly increased.

A most cursory look at the natural environment indicates that the vast majority of positive payoffs enjoyed by adults must be *earned:* The food on our table generally arrives only after some effort has been put forth; the clothes on our back requires the same. Tropical vacations taken in the dead of winter are rarely handed to us on a silver platter. We usually have to motor our derrière in high gear before such a luxury can be enjoyed. Even meaningful relationships, marriage, friendships, and the like, require commitment, consideration, and occasionally taking out the garbage before they can be lasting and totally fulfilling.

In technical language, valued payoffs are said to be *contingent* on (*dependent* on) many, often specific, often identifiable, behaviors and actions—generically called work! Less technically, we have to put out effort for what we want, for what we value. We do have access to a *few* "freebies"—payoffs that are dependent on just being alive: love and caring from devoted parents who (despite the "terrible twos" and mercurial adolescent years) never seem to tire of "unconditionally" providing their affection; warmth from a log fire, a cooling breeze in summer; the musical and painted notes from favorite artists; the beauty of a star-filled night are but a few.

HEAVENLY FREEBIES

Conversely, many children discover early (and come to expect) that the vast majority of their payoffs at home are of the "freebie" type. There's an unending supply of ice cream sandwiches in the fridge, a music box that always plays, a bike that can be ridden any time, a quantity of toys in the closet outnumbered only by the entire inventory at Sears. At school (during the early years) it's snacks at 9:00, recess at 11:00, movies at 1:00, and free time at 2:45. (I'm exaggerating a little!) The "freebies" are always there; they'll always be there! For what seems an infinite number of glorious years, the stuff just keeps pouring in. It can be termed "unconditional giving!" No requirements, no contingencies.

DREADED CONTINGENCIES

Then one day, the natural environment mentions something about a work ethic, usually after a moderate explosion due to frustration—"*Forget this unconditional business. No television until you finish your homework!*" (That's what happens at home.) "*No recess because you horsed around in language arts!*" (That's what happens at school.) One lovely, serene, innocent, moment in time, the life space changes. A new expectation is imposed—or at least mentioned: "Before you get what you want," the environment states, "you must do what I want." The individual's reaction (said with words or actions): "I like the way things were. I didn't have to do nothin' to get those things! You mean I gotta work?" If the parent, teacher, therapist answers, "Yep," then enter: the *contingency* system!

EXPLICIT CONTINGENCIES ARE OFTEN NECESSARY

Certainly not excluding "freebies," the methods we are about to explore lean heavily toward the contingency system: The child is *expected* to behave desirably in order to gain access to what he or she values.

Personally, I have yet to encounter a teacher (or family) who has operated exclusively on an either/or basis; all have had some balance between the "freebie" vs "contingency" approach. Yet, quite a few of us have gotten ourselves into a position where "freebies" far outnumber their counterparts.

In the *short run,* the "freebie" system is easier. It requires less time and effort on our part: We do not have to set up guidelines that specify what must be done; we do not have to watch the child's behavior closely; we do not have to go out of our way to provide artificial, meaningful payoffs when necessary—when the natural environment has ceased to work for us; we do not have to withhold payoffs when the desired behavior fails to occur. We allow the natural environment to "float," (in other words, we "float") hoping the child will learn what we desire. It is easier in terms of effort. It may not, however, teach the behaviors *we* desire.

While universal goals are always debatable, one possibility seems to stand out: We want the individuals we care for to be "self-directed." We want them to have a say in their own destiny—not be a Ping-Pong ball that is paddled around by forces difficult to see, name, or control. We want them to incorporate the lessons Life teaches so they can use the lessons to further their own cause. We want them to learn to regulate their own actions, making it less necessary that an outside source will be needed to regulate what they do. We want them to know how to access both the valued natural and artificial payoffs their environment provides. We can call the process of becoming a self-regulated individual by any manner of name, but the goal will be the same: We want individuals to be able to care for, and be able to take care of, themselves.

SELF-DIRECTED BEHAVIOR:
KNOWING THE COMPONENTS

People who are self-directed know not only how their environment influences their behavior, but know also how they can influence their environment. They are better able to understand and predict the contingencies that exist within their life space. **They have learned to say to themselves, "when I do 'A,' 'B' happens; when I do 'C,' 'D' happens," and they can describe, with a high level of accuracy, the "A's" and "C's" (behaviors), and the "B's" and "D's" (the payoffs).** They can more easily determine what will happen as a result of what they do. They can weigh the pros and cons of their actions and choose more accurately how to obtain what they value, and what will best serve them in the future.

| 3.12 |

_____ DEBATE: INTERNAL DRIVE, EXTERNAL INFLUENCE _____

The practical question, of course, asks how self-directed behavior comes about. Perhaps the renowned psychologist Carl Rogers was correct when he said:

> Gradually my experience has forced me to conclude that the individual has within himself the capacity and the tendency, latent if not evident, to move forward toward maturity. In a suitable psychological climate this tendency is released, and becomes actual rather than potential. It is evident in the capacity of the individual to understand those aspects of his life and of himself which are causing him pain and dissatisfaction, an understanding which probes beneath his conscious knowledge of himself into those experiences which he has hidden from himself because of their threatening nature. It shows itself in the tendency to reorganize his personality and his relationship to life in ways which are regarded as more mature. Whether one calls it growth tendency, a drive toward self-actualization, or a forward-moving directional tendency, it is the mainspring of life. . . . It is the urge which is evident in all organic and human life—to expand, extend, become autonomous, develop, mature—the tendency to express and activate all the capacities of the organism to the extent that such activation enhances the organism or the self . . . it is my belief that it exists in every individual, and awaits only the proper conditions to be released and expressed.[6]

Dr. Rogers' view suggests the capacity for self-direction, for self-realization, is an innate component of the human being. This would mean that the capacity is present at birth (actually at conception if it is genetically transmitted). While not attempting to read more into his statement than intended, it appears that he holds with the belief that we are blessed with a "forward-moving directional tendency" that will lead us to find and secure that which will "enhance the organism or the self." To the degree that my interpretation is correct, the natural environment (parents, teachers, experiences) found in every individual's life space, rather than _influencing_ the directional choices that we make, basically provides "the proper conditions (for the innate tendency) to be released and expressed."

Dr. Rogers' belief is easy to embrace. But like so many expressed tenets in our field, it would be difficult to either verify or refute. Therefore it remains a belief; one that can be adhered to or denied. A part of me would like to believe it is true: It is optimistic, uplifting, spiritually satisfying. But the part of me that has worked with children and adults for many years makes its acceptance impossible. I've seen both the natural and artificial environment at work. It does more than set the "proper conditions for . . . expression." It influences what will be expressed. It shapes, molds, and sets the stage for future behavior. It is not "a passive entity that sits in life's balcony, oblivious to what is going on." It is an active system that teaches! It can raise individuals to the heights of personal achievement or lead them to the brink of their personal demise. It can teach them to manifest self-improvement or self-effacement. It can move them to explore that which is new, or tell them to be satisfied with what is. It can take endowments and embellish them, or it can take endowments and lessen their potential. It can teach what to love and what to hold in prejudice. It can teach consideration, respect, responsibility, or their opposites. While our children may have an innate capacity to creatively adapt, it is the natural environment that shows them what requires adaptation, along with what actions will best serve that end.

LEARNING TO BE SELF-DIRECTED

Everything I have seen tells me that self-directed behavior must be taught and must be learned. Left to its own means, the natural environment will do the teaching for us. What may be learned, however, may run counter to what we desire; what may be learned may run counter to what the children, in their future, may desire. True, as days pass, the natural environment, of its own impetus, will teach the "A's" and "C's" and "B's" and "D's" for us, but the contingencies learned may be far from those that produce personal good or personal enhancement. For the desired to happen, either the brightest fortune must shine, or we must become involved.

The contingency system promotes the acquisition of self-directed behavior by teaching what can be loosely called a "cause" and "effect" relationship between behavior and payoffs. When the desired behavior has been determined and communicated, either through words, modelling, or practice, and the valued payoffs have been identified, either by asking or observing, the contingency system, carefully employed, can help individuals acquire the behaviors that, in the *long run,* will serve them best. But remember this: Carefully planned or not, the contingency system is always in operation; our intentions aside, it may, with equal ease, teach individuals to behave in many ways that will *not* serve them best.

SOMETIMES TOUGH LESSONS MUST BE LEARNED

I had been called by a local school district requesting assistance with a severely involved, nonverbal 11-year-old boy. When I arrived at the child's school and greeted his parents, I was handed his three-inch thick confidential file. Typically, the youngster had been "painted" with a wide vary of confusing professional colors: He was described by some as "autistic," by others as "retarded," by yet others as "learning disabled." What I saw, as I looked at him, was a strapping 5-foot, 6-inch, 150-pound individual who, at times, would work diligently at the tasks his teacher had established, and who, at times, would refuse to work, preferring instead to sit back in his chair and roll his head and eyes in circles. I also noticed the "pain" written on his parents' faces as they watched their child vacillate between being productive, attentive, and interested, and drifting away into a space that only he could touch.

"If he would only pay more attention to what he's being asked to do," the mother said to me as she, her husband, and I stood in a far corner observing the child, "I believe he would make more progress. But he's so inconsistent; it's like he needs to go away for a few minutes, go off into his private world."

"Has that been occurring more often of late?" I inquired.

"At school, yes. At home, we spend so much time with him that we don't give him that chance. He's our only child," Father explained, his eyes fixed on his son.

"Do you both visit school often?"

"We try to come at least two or three times a week. His teacher said we could come everyday if we wished, but we can't," the mother indicated.

"He does work harder when they are here," the teacher said after joining us. "He particularly works hard for his father," she added, touching the mother's shoulder.

"He does do better with his father," Mother agreed. "They have a marvelous relationship. Look at him now," the woman said, pointing toward her son, who was swaying back and forth, not touching the materials on the table. "He knows we're here, and he wants his father by his side. All Father has to do is to stand next to him and he'll start working." I turned toward the teacher and silently asked if Mother's appraisal was accurate. The teacher nodded "yes."

"Go to him," I requested of the man. "Do whatever you ordinarily do. Be yourself."

The youngster continued his swaying until the moment Father touched his arm and whispered something in his ear. Instantly, as Mother had suggested, the child's demeanor changed: Without looking at his dad, the child returned his attention to the tasks and began working diligently. Equally interesting, the moment Father walked back toward us, leaving his son's side, the head and eye rolling began. Father stopped his movement, returned to his son, and the child once again began to work. "Do you see how he *manipulates* us," Mother said, her words reflecting confusion, not anger. "He will do that at home, too."

Manipulating: A Glance

I caught her eyes and said softly but with intent, "He's *supposed* to manipulate you. That's adaptive behavior. Be thankful that he knows how to manipulate. Without that skill, his plight would be much more difficult.

Understand that *we* have accidentally taught him what needs to be manipulated. He wants his father by his side. He has learned—been taught—what he must *do* to accomplish that. Again, it's a good sign."

"But how do we stop the manipulation?" the woman asked.

"You don't ever want to stop it. Manipulation, growth, even survival are all interrelated. We need to change some of the particulars but not his ability to do what is necessary to gain access to what he values. Do you mind if I try something?" I asked. "I would like you to stay here. I'll ask your husband to stand with you, away from your son." I motioned for Father to join his wife, then I took the teacher's arm and she and I walked to within five feet of the now swaying child. After explaining the plan to the teacher, I walked back to the parents. "Mr. Smith," when I give you the signal, I'd like you to walk directly, quickly to your son's side. Do what you always do when you're with him, but watch me as well. When I motion to you, I'd like you to take one step away from your son. Watch me again, and I'll let you know when to return to his side."

The teacher, as requested, stood about arms length behind the child: His swaying was rhythmical and persistent. I nodded toward her. She immediately walked to his side and placed her hand on his shoulder. The swaying ceased, and the child, as though feeling comfortable, began working. I turned to the father: "Go quickly to him, and stand where the teacher is now." The child looked up briefly, saw his father approaching, then returned his gaze and attention to the task before him. Father, again, whispered something to the boy as the teacher moved slightly away. After a few seconds, I motioned Father to take one step from the child's side. The child's work continued. Father returned to his son and touched his shoulder. As directed, Father then moved several steps from his son. The youngster hesitated for a moment, then removed his hands from the task and began swaying. Reflexively, Father took a step toward his son. I immediately shook my head "no," and motioned Dad to walk further away from his son. The boy's mother grabbed my arm tightly. "He wants his father," she said painfully.

"I know," I answered quickly. "But he must learn that attention to task will result in his father's return, not the swaying and head rolling." She grew quiet, uneasy. "Hang in there," I asked, smiling toward her. "Let's try this a few more times." I motioned to the teacher to once again redirect the child toward his work. With her by his side, the child complied. Father seemed to know exactly what to do. Once he saw his son attending to the task, he stood next to him. Gradually, he moved ever so slightly away, then returned quickly. After several more practice periods, the father moved a few feet from his son, then returned so long as the child continued his work. Shortly, the father positioned himself some five feet from the youngster. Not unexpectedly, the child stopped working and began swaying. Patiently, nervously, Dad stood his ground. Three very "long" minutes passed before the child, without prompting, went back to work. I heard (and felt) Mother sigh as Father quickly went to his son, hugged him and whispered into his ear. Within an hour, the child continued his work even though his father was standing by his wife, some twenty feet from the child. Father, Mother, and teacher alternately, briefly, returned to the child's side touching him as he worked. Twice within the hour, the child "tested" the new contingency. Without prompting, he redirected himself toward his assigned task.

"There's so much in that example, I'm not sure where to start," 4.13
the parent said taking a deep breath. "The behavior-pairs: attending to work versus swaying and drifting away. The cues: The child used the adults' proximity to know when to and when not to work. Purpose. It's so obvious. He learned that when he stopped working, he could get someone to come to his side. The natural environment, what you're calling the contingency system, taught him the rules that were operating: Stop working and someone will come to you. He learned the 'A's' and 'B's' with no problem. He learned what to do to get what he valued. Then, when his environment changed, he learned the new rules, the new contingencies. That's amazing."

"Not so amazing. He's an adaptive youngster."

"But it had to be very difficult for him."

"Frankly, it was much more difficult for his parents, particularly his mom. You could sense how desperately she wanted to run to his side when he stopped working."

"But that would have only reinforced him for not working, correct?" the parent said.

"As painful as it was for the parent, and believe me I could feel her anguish, her child had to learn the lesson that work produced what was valued. Without that lesson, it is unlikely the youngster would have learned to attend more consistently to his important tasks."

"Not an easy lesson for us to learn," the mother thought outloud, invested in her own private thoughts.

——————— An Exercise in the Adult Use of Power? ———————

"No, it's not. To the casual observer, it might appear mean or inconsiderate of an individual's feelings to require that the targeted behavior, the desired behavior, occur first before the valued payoff is provided. To some, it no doubt seems uncomfortably like one person exercising power over another, and that issue has always stirred strong feelings and reactions. The popular author Dr. Thomas Gordon, in his *Parent Effectiveness Training* book suggested

> The stubborn persistence of the idea that parents must and should use
> authority in dealing with children has, in my opinion, prevented for

centuries any significant change or improvement in the way children are raised by parents and treated by adults. . . . My own conviction is that as more people begin to understand power and authority more completely and accept its use as unethical, more parents will apply those understandings to adult-child relationships; will begin to feel that it is just as immoral in those relationships; and then will be forced to search for creative nonpower methods that all adults can use with children and youth. . . . It is paradoxical but true that parents lose influence by using power and will have more influence on their children by giving up their power or refusing to use it.[7]

"I didn't interpret what you did as exercising power over the youngster, rather more as responsibility for his welfare," the parent said.   .

"I'm afraid that's the problem with words, attitudes, and an interpretation of someone's personal motivation," I responded. "I suspect Dr. Gordon would have interpreted my actions as a display of power."

"Do you think you were using your power?"

I hesitated for a moment before answering. The words "power," "control," "influence," carry so much excess baggage that it is easy to view them negatively. "I did exercise power," I stated, "the same power I exercise when I prevent my own youngster from running across the street without looking for oncoming cars, or refusing to allow him to eat a dozen donuts before sitting down to dinner. Professionally, if there is something I can do to assist a child in finding a better way to adapt to his environment, I will not turn my back on the child, regardless of emotional judgments made about my personal motivation. I will not allow him to beat himself or consistently fail in school or behave in a way that is breaking up his family. I'm certainly not going to sit back aimlessly while he spends hours drifting off into space; not if I can find a method that will teach him the importance of attending to task so he can learn something that will help him become more independent, more fully functioning. If my interventions are perceived as a 'big' person exercising power over a 'little' person, then that is a issue the perceiver will have to deal with. I don't have a problem with the term 'power' as it may be used in the above context. When any of us step into the arena, taking on the awesome responsibility for assisting another human being, what 'power' is exercised is certainly not for the sake of the exercise. It is to explain with words or show with actions what the natural environment has done, and what it may be able to do to further growth. It is to take the contingency system that operates continuously whether we like it or not, whether we know it or not, and change it! We have the power to influence what the environment is doing. But even without plan or intervention, the natural environment's contingency system will teach an individual the "A's" and "B's" that are operating within his life space regardless of the views or intentions held by folks outside the space. The individual *will learn* to manipulate the environment according to the lessons the environment has taught him."

"I see what you're saying: Being a part of the environment affords me the opportunity to become actively involved. Personally, I'm prepared to watch what I am doing, to see what part I'm playing. But before we go on, I must share that I am having a problem with something you've said a couple of times."

"What's that?" I asked.

MANIPULATING THE ENVIRONMENT: A NEEDED SKILL

"The term 'manipulate.' You seem to be suggesting that to manipulate is an asset. To me, it seems so negative, so devious. I have this vision of someone, sitting off in some cobwebbed corner, plotting something evil."

"I thought that might get you. Your characterization 'negative' is kind. Deplorable, despicable, would be more accurate. It's almost as though the word itself cannot be spoken without a reflexive facial contortion that reflects disgust. The word doesn't warrant such a reaction. In every scenario that I have presented to this point, the child or adult in question has learned how to obtain what was valued, in part, through his or her ability to manipulate the environment. Would you begrudge Jesse's attempts to be removed from his high chair when he knew that eating would bring him pain? Of course not. Yet he was manipulating his environment—his parents! How about Mr. Smith's son. He learned how to bring his father to his side. He was taught how to bring his father to his side! The youngster was doing the best he could to obtain what he wanted, and his father accidentally reinforced the manipulating, adaptive behavior. If we can discover what or who the individual is manipulating we can learn something of his perceptions, his values, and our feedback. A word that can lead us to all that can't be half bad."

"So if I believe my child is manipulating me, I should look to see what I am providing him when he manifests his behavior," the parent said.

"Exactly. Don't disgustedly turn away from the word. Use it to gain some insight into the life space. In fact, embrace the word. It will tell you what 'A's' and 'B's' are operating. It will tell you what needs to be done to alter an undesirable situation."

"Embrace? I'm too old to change my reaction to it. Learn something from it? That I can do."

_____ NOTES _____

1. Salk, L. (1972). *What every child would like his parents to know* (p. 76). New York: Warner

2. Ibid, p. 75.

3. Mees, H. (1964). *How to create a monster.* Unpublished manuscript.

4. Ullman, L. P., & Krasner, L. (1965). *Case studies in behavior modification,* (p. 25). New York: Holt, Rinehart, and Winston.

5. Macht, J. (1975). *Teacher/teachim: The toughest game in town,* (p. 79). New York: Wiley.

6. Rogers, C. (1961). *On becoming a person,* (p. 35.) Boston: Houghton Mifflin.

7. Gordon, T. (1970). *Parent effectiveness training* (pp. 164–193). New York: Plume.

_____ SUMMARY _____

KEEP IN MIND

1. The feedback from positive reinforcement can just as easily increase undesired behavior as desired actions. You must watch which of the individual's behaviors are receiving your valued attention and recognition.

2. A positive reinforcer is *anything* an individual values; it is *anything* the individual will work hard to obtain. There are no universal positive reinforcers; there are no blanket reinforcers. When working with a classroom full of students, you will encounter many different values and interests: Said differently, you will encounter many different examples of positive feedback. Never hesitate to sit with individual students and ask them to share with you what is important to them. Knowing their values will help you relate better, as well as help you develop effective programs for them.

3. Feedback not only affects the frequency of behavior, it affects the frequency of behavior in the presence of specific cues. Note: A student behaves in a particular manner in your presence. You provide positive feedback immediately after he manifests his behavior. Chances are increased that given your presence, he will manifest the same or similar behavior again because he expects his behavior will once again result in the previously experienced feedback. Assuming his behavior is perceived *by you to be desirable,* all is well: It will occur again in your presence. If, however, the behavior is perceived by you to be undesired. . . .

4. Your students will show you what they value; they will show you what they are willing to work hard to obtain. If you, inadvertently, offer a payoff that is not perceived as positive, your students will let you know. The critical question remains: Will you change what you have offered? Will you accommodate your students?

5. Everyone uses feedback; everyone is influenced by it. What differs among us is what each of us values; what each of us will work hard to obtain. The debatable issue is not that positive feedback is important and necessary; the debatable issue is what type of positive feedback is important and necessary to each of us as individuals.

6. If you aren't certain what individuals value, consider: (a) asking, or (b) observing closely their actions. Anything individuals do frequently, talk about frequently, or think about frequently is, for them, something of value.

7. Never underestimate the importance for having something of value for an individual student: "If an individual learns that from all his available behaviors, his desired behavior is what brings him something of value, he'll be inclined to behave desirably. If he discovers that his desired behavior does not bring him something of value, he'll be less inclined to behave desirably. . . ."

8. When possible, develop a reinforcement menu for the students in your classroom. You want to have at your disposal a nice variety of values the students can choose from.

9. Your goal is to bring desired behavior under the influence of its own worth: You want desired behavior to be maintained by natural, inherent reinforcement. To bring that outcome about, it is often necessary to get the desired behavior started! Frequently, a contrived, artificial program will accomplish that end: It will get the behavior started, thus increasing the chances the student will see the value within the activity. Once that occurs, the artificial program may no longer be necessary.

10. When discussing the types of feedback students receive from their environment, initially avoid categorizing the feedback as "positive"

or "negative." Instead, clearly write down how the environment is responding to the individuals' behavior. Example: In place of saying, "I praised the student for her effort," describe precisely what you did: "I said to the student: "I'm pleased with what you accomplished." Although disappointing, it may turn out that the student did not value the fact that you were pleased. Given such a circumstance, two outcomes are likely: (a) you *didn't* "praise" the student, and (b) whatever she did that produced your reaction will not be affected in a positive manner. Stay neutral: Simply describe what you did and what effect it seemed to have.

11. Behavior always has purpose: It produces something of value to the individual. Whenever you evaluate an individual's behavior, consider what purpose it may be serving. Ask yourself: "What is the payoff for the behavior? What is the student deriving from his behavior?"

12. Contingencies, the relationship between behavior and the environment's feedback, are a part of life: Nearly everything we do is associated with some sort of feedback, be the feedback natural or artificial. Contingencies, therefore, need to be a part of (only a part of!) what you do within your classroom: You have expectations for your students; they have expectations for you. Discuss how you intend to respond to what they do; request how you wish for them to respond to what you do.

13. All of us need to know the relationship between our behavior and how our environment will respond to what we do. Security, in large measure, comes from our ability to know that when we do "A," "B" will happen. Help your students understand that a "lawful," predictable relationship, within your classroom, exists between what they do and how you will respond. Help them to become more self-directed; help them predict that when they do "A," "B" will occur. You want your students to know (to be able to predict) what will happen as a result of their actions. They must be able to run a private dialogue: "Here's the situation; here's what may happen; here's what I will do." Knowing that "B" occurs in conjunction with "A," often helps the individual evaluate what to do.

14. Do not be "turned off" by the term "manipulate." Manipulating the environment is an essential activity. It can, indeed, enhance an individual's very survival. If you believe that a student is purposely manipulating you, (a) find out what the student is doing; (b) find out what purpose this behavior serves; and (c) decide whether you are pleased with those actions. When an individual manipulates, he or she is attempting to obtain something he or she values. If you aren't pleased with the choice of behaviors, help the person acquire alternative ways of achieving the goals.

Clarifying Theoretical Models

| 4.1 | There's a sizeable difference between the theories that speak to "salivating dogs," and "stimulus-response." Take a moment to differentiate between the theoretical views of Ivan Pavlov, a Russian physiologist, and B.F. Skinner, an American psychologist.

Motivation for School Achievement?

| 4.2 | What motivates you to work hard at your academic studies? (Do you think someone in your family is going to fork over a new BMW if you make a "B" average?)

Individual Preferences

| 4.3 | What is the importance of the term "anything" that is included within the definition of a positive reinforcer?

Learning from a Child's Actions

| 4.4 | Reread the story opposite the ICON box 4.4. What did the child show me through her behavior? Would I have been successful with the child had I persisted with banana pudding? What might happen if you tell all your students that they can have extra recess upon completion of their reading assignments? What will you do if they aren't all equally excited?

From Artificial to Natural

| 4.5 | Describe the case similarities, regarding the positive feedback procedures that were used, between Jesse and the child who was taught to wear her glasses. Why wasn't artificial reinforcement needed once eating and glasses-wearing reliably began to occur? Suppose the problems, instead of being eating and glasses-wearing, were reading and writing. Can you fashion a scenario where artificial reinforcement would initially be used to start those behaviors; where eventually natural reinforcement would eventually maintain them?

When It Comes to Values, Look beyond Yours

| 4.6 | Why is it necessary to go beyond your personal preferences when considering what types of positive feedback you intend to use in your classroom?

Your Feedback

| 4.7 | Watch yourself over the next few days. Note the types of feedback you provide your friends and colleagues. Do you think they were influenced by what you did?

Stay Neutral at First

| 4.8 | Why is it important to avoid characterizing feedback as "positive" or "negative" when you are initially investigating how the environment is responding to behavior?

Behavior's Purpose

| 4.9 | Review Jeremy's case, page 81. Questions:
a. Why is it so important to first speculate upon, then test out, the purpose for a behavior?
b. Suppose you had two professionals discussing Jeremy's case, each one holding different views through the window regarding the case's "dynamics." One professional might suggest the child's "clowning" was a sign of insecurity, perhaps emotional disturbance. The second might suggest the "clowning" was a means for the child to avoid doing his work. One might suggest the behavior was "inappropriate" and "maladaptive." The second professional's judgment might be the opposite. Would determining the behavior's purpose shed light on which view was more accurate?

A Behavior's Payoff

| 4.10 | Visit an elementary school or day care center. Take a piece of paper and, with a pencil line, divide it in half. At the top of the left-hand column write the letter "R" for behavior; on the right side, write the letters "fb" for feedback. Watch the interaction between the students and their teachers. Write down some of what the children do, along with the types of environmental responses the behaviors produce. Identify some behaviors that appear to be undesirable—either to you or to one of the teachers. See if you can speculate on the behaviors' purposes. If possible, bring your materials back to class and discuss your findings with your colleagues.

Looking for Bugs?

| 4.11 | If you want to have a most enjoyable experience, try this: Visit a highly heterogeneous third or fourth grade class. Ask the teacher if you can have 10 minutes to compile a reinforcement menu. I believe you will be floored by what the kids value; what they want to do.

Your Self-Directed Behavior

| 4.12 | Think about your own life space and all the significant contingencies presently operating. List several examples of the "A's, B's, C's, and D's" that are currently involved both in your studies and personal life. (Remember, the "A's" and "C's" represent behavior; the "B's" and "D's" represent how your environment likely responds to those behaviors, i.e., "When I do 'A,' 'B' happens.") If feasible, find a school-aged student (preferably middle or high school). Ask the individual to share some of his or her presently operating "A's and B's."

Putting It Together

| 4.13 | This is a difficult but very important exercise. Visit a classroom, K–6. Identify a child who is having difficulties. Watch the child as he or she interacts with the teacher and classmates.
  a. Note the behavior-pairs that appear to be operating.
  b. Determine the cues in the presence of which the behaviors are occurring.
  c. Speculate on the purpose for the undesired behaviors.
  d. Determine the "A" and "B" contingencies that seemed to be influencing both the desired and undesired behaviors.

CONSIDER AS WE LOOK AHEAD

1. As we look at the procedures available to increase behaviors, you will notice how they mirror the contingencies and operations found in everyone's life space.
2. Notice that the procedures have no inherent magic or worth. Their value and effectiveness are directly related to your skills when using them.
3. You will now see how artificial feedback systems can help a student find natural value in many activities.

5

Using Positive Payoffs to Further Growth and Development

The consultant has at his or her disposal only a few ways, incorporating positive payoffs, to assist the natural environment in bringing about and maintaining desired behavior. The few methods use either "attention/recognition," "material payoffs," logical outcomes, or their combination. None of them are magical; all of them are familiar; none will be effective without effort and planning; and all require that the individual values the payoffs that are being used. All are intended to teach individuals which of their behaviors will produce what they value, and all are intended to help the desired behavior get started so, when possible, the behavior can eventually come under the influence of more natural payoffs. The planned use of any of the following ideas must *not* begin until the following information has been compiled.

1. The behavior-pairs must be established. Decide carefully what you wish for the individual *to do*—the desired behavior, and what you eventually want him or her *not to do*—the undesired behavior. You must assume responsibility for this determination. You may, of course, consult with the individual to seek out his or her preferences, but the final decision ultimately rests within your hands. If you feel that you are too involved to make the decision, seek outside opinions. Above all, the decided pairs must be directly observable. Both you and the individual must eventually learn what behaviors

constitute the pairs. You will not be able to "catch" the desired behavior until you know what actions represent that behavior.

2. Once the pairs have been established, carefully observe and note the occurrence of the undesired behavior, as well as the payoff the undesired behavior is producing. If the individual has learned that the undesired behavior enables him or her to avoid what he or she perceives as frightening or dangerous or too difficult, positive payoffs for an alternatively more desired behavior (from your perspective) will not prove beneficial to either you or the individual. As you will see in the following chapter, *undesired behaviors always serve some purpose*—they are producing something of value to the individual. Programs that incorporate positive payoffs must be placed on hold until that purpose has been identified and resolved. If you need some "structure" regarding this last point, keep in mind young Jesse: No amount of positive payoff would have influenced him to eat so long as he continued to experience pain from his natural system. The adaptive noneating, the "undesired" behavior, enabled him to avoid that pain. Resolution of the problem required that the circumstances that produced the pain be dealt with *before* employing methods to influence the desired alternative behavior.

3. You have determined what the individual will work hard to obtain. Establish your "reinforcement/value" menu. Remember, there are no universal "reinforcers." Concentrate, therefore, on what the individual finds of value. If you know the individual well, you will have ideas as to what he or she values. If you are not pleased with the individual's choices for what he or she is willing to work for, introduce the individual to other options, allowing him or her to experience the potentially valued components. If you are not certain what may serve as a positive payoff, watch the individual carefully. His or her behaviors will help you gain access to what he or she values. Most any behavior or activity the individual participates in frequently may be incorporated within the "menu."

ATTENTION/RECOGNITION

Far and away, providing attention and recognition for the initial acquisition and ultimate maintenance of desired behaviors is the easiest method for us to use. We don't have to visit the store or open a cabinet to get them. We carry them with us no matter where we are. Attention and recognition are provided through speaking, touching, glancing, hugging, and the like.

USING POSITIVE PAYOFFS TO FURTHER GROWTH AND DEVELOPMENT

PROCEDURES

For attention and recognition to effectively influence behavior, keep the following four issues in mind:

1. Immediacy
2. Potency
3. Description
4. And one I will leave unmentioned for the moment.

IMMEDIACY

Attention and recognition needs to be offered as close to the desired behavior as possible. Offering words of thanks or affectionate strokes when the desired behavior has occurred will tell the individual that you appreciate what has occurred. It will also increase the chances the behavior will occur again in the future.

Attending immediately to desired behaviors is essential for individuals whose verbal skills have yet to develop sufficiently to benefit from what are called "verbal mediating responses." "Mediating responses" help "bridge" the gap between when the behavior occurred and when the attention is used. Indicating that you are appreciative of something that has occurred hours (or minutes) earlier, requires complex cognitive skills if it is to be effective. If the individual possesses the verbal and cognitive skills to "process" the delayed feedback, the offered attention may still be effective. The general rule of thumb regardless of the individual's verbal skills, however, is to provide the attention immediately after the desired behavior has occurred.

POTENCY

The issue of "potency" is important in the following respect: Words of appreciation and thanks are positive payoffs only if the *person* offering them is valued by the child. There is nothing automatically special about being told one is a "good boy" or "good girl." The emotional quality of words is neutral at first. They develop value as they become associated with caring people. Physically abused, neglected, deprived, or consistently reprimanded individuals may adaptively mistrust anyone who comes close to them. In order for your words and affection to maintain their positive attributes, the positive relationship between you and the individual must also be maintained. Quality time together, attentive conversation, respect, an appreciation of perceptions, helping individuals feel good about their efforts, are only a few of the variables that build and maintain the relationship.

DESCRIPTION

You need to tell individuals, in the clearest words, what they did that warranted your sign of appreciation. The response, "Thanks for closing the door," as an example, can accomplish many things. It tells the individual you appreciate something he or she did; it says what that something is; it increases desired behavior—helps the person understand what you would like done in the future under similar cues; it promotes self-directed behavior; it gives the individual practice with words and how they are used; it provides him or her with a sense of accomplishment (albeit a small one); it shows the individual you are aware of his or her efforts; that you care about these efforts; it can make you both feel good about each other. Not a bad return for just a few words. I'm not suggesting that you must add the description of the behavior every time you observe something desirable. Such might become stilted and tiresome. A warm wink from a caring eye after the behavior has occurred can be just as powerful. Just remember, the individual must know what he or she did that warranted the wink. It's not likely that closing doors, giving someone else a chance to answer a question, or placing a chair under a desk provides any sort of "natural" payoff. For these "desired" behaviors to occur, artificial payoffs in the form of appreciation will be needed, at least occasionally.

"BEHAVING FOR ATTENTION"

You must watch carefully which of the individual's behaviors are gaining your attention. Recognition and attention can increase *any* behavior, not just the ones you want increased. We all need recognition in some form. The people you care for are adaptive individuals who also need recognition. They *will* find a way to gain access to what is valued. If no one pays attention when they are behaving desirably, they will find other means to gain what is valued. I'd settle for a dollar everytime I've heard someone say, "He's just doing that for attention" when describing an undesired behavior. If I received another dollar everytime the person speaking passed the observation off as a casual, insignificant comment, I'd be on my way to a sandy beach—at someone else's expense. Take a second to think about the phrase: "He just behaves that way *for attention.*" Shouldn't something else be said after the observation and speculation has occurred? Any ideas? How about behavior-pairs for a starter? If he's doing the "undesired" for attention, what's happening with the *desired* side of the pair? What's its payoff? Why not show the individual how to do *that for attention!*

"That's it? That's all there is to recognition and attention?" the young student asked. "Come on, there's got to be more."

"That's about it," I answered. "You observe a behavior that you're pleased about, you share that information, and you show your appreciation. It's not very complicated."

"How about sincerity. The kid's going to know whether you're being a hypocrite."

"If your tone of voice is as flat as a pancake; if your face is grimaced from anger; if you cover your mouth, turn away, and talk as though you were conversing with a caterpillar, the individual will pick it up."

"I don't know," the student said. "I've heard kids can see through smiles."

"If so, its because they can see something else written on your face or communicated with your body. Be sincere. Problem resolved."

"But I'm sure sometimes I'm not going to feel sincere," the young student stated.

"Then don't say anything."

"If I don't say anything, and he's done something really special, he might not realize how much I appreciate it . . . or how much I would appreciate it if I were sincere," he said flinching from his own confusion.

"My guess is that if you observe an individual doing something special, you feel good about it."

"Yeah, I suppose you're right."

"But there is more, isn't there?" the parent suggested.

NEGATIVE ATTENTION

"What are you thinking of?" I asked.

"Negative attention, for one thing. I've seen some kids work for it, and that's difficult to understand." she said.

"Yeah, now that's confusing," the student echoed.

"The reason why we become perplexed over such a situation is due to the word 'negative,'" I answered. "Take out the term 'negative' and you're left with the observation that the individual is working for attention.''

"But the individual seems intent on being told, often in a loud voice, often spoken with anger, that he should stop doing something. Instead of stopping, he continues his antics. It's as though he enjoys being yelled at,'' the parent indicated.

THE INDIVIDUAL'S VALUES

"Remember the construct that I've called the child's 'person'? It is that 'person,' the private part of the individual, that decides the value of an environmental reaction. When we use the term 'negative,' we're describing our perception of the reaction, not necessarily the individual's perception.''

"Are you suggesting that an individual might perceive being yelled at as a positive payoff?'' the parent asked.

"Technically, yes. In the same sense that a spanking could be a reaction worth putting out effort to obtain,'' I said.

"No,'' the student muttered. "Who in their right mind would do a dumb thing like that?''

"An individual, most certainly in their right mind, who has discovered that the only way to gain attention is to do something that results in being yelled at or spanked or placed in a corner chair,'' I said. "Strange from our view, sad frankly, but not impossible.'' Dr. Lee Salk has pointed out:

> No child wants negative attention if positive recognition is forthcoming. There is no inherent desire to behave badly. This is a learned phenomenon, based upon your reactions to your child. If you offer no positive satisfaction or positive attention and only attend to your child's needs when he is misbehaving, you are, in a sense, encouraging this rather unpleasant means for getting your attention.[1]

"Any kid who wants to be spanked must be mentally disturbed,'' the student reacted as though he had forgotten his general psychology classes.

"No, sir. You didn't listen to what Dr. Salk suggested. The youngster is doing the best he can to gain what he values. If there is something 'disturbing' about such a scenario, it is the inability or the unwillingness of the child's environment to find something desirable that warrants a different form of attention.''

"Again, behavior-pairs,'' the parent said.

"Always behavior-pairs," I answered.

"So we must always be attentive to something good the individual has *done*," the parent stated, "then when we see it we should recognize it."

ATTENTION FOR BEING, NOT ONLY FOR DOING

"I think we should always be on our toes so we have the opportunity, if we wish to exercise it, to 'catch' the child doing something good, recognizing it with our appreciation. But not always because the child has done something good. Sometimes it's real nice just recognizing the child. Dr. William E. Homan, a pediatrician and author has suggested:

> *Praise the child more for being, more than you praise him for doing.* . . . We quite properly praise and reward our children when they make a good effort and when they achieve a measure of success. . . . Parents generally react favorably to a good report card or to a kind and thoughtful act on the child's part. This is all well and good, and profitable and proper. However, it is too easy to let these accomplishments become the child's major or sole source of praise, reward, acceptance, and love.
>
> It is important that the child receive the greater measure of praise and love *unrelated to his achievements and successes.* The child should have the opportunity to see that a good report card and a thoughtful act merit a pat on the head, a slap on the shoulder, a smile, a warm word of encouragement, even perhaps a silver quarter; but he should see more often that he receives the greater reward of five minutes of cuddling, ten words of praise, a friendly tousling of the hair, and perhaps even a one-dollar bill when he is producing nothing.[2]

"Recognizing him for simply being. That's love and caring. That's the name of the game."

"And the individual won't think he's receiving the affection because he's done something at the moment?" the parent asked.

"If you tousle his hair every time he bops his sister and never tousle it any other time, you'll likely produce a problem," I answered. "But that's pushing things to an extreme, and if you're on your toes, noting and recognizing desirable behaviors, it won't happen."

"You're talking about 'unconditional positive self-regard,'" the student blurted. "That's Carl Rogers' stuff. Appreciation for being and becoming."

"It has its place," I responded.

"Right on!" the young man hollered.

THE "WHEN . . . THEN QUICKIE"

If you have feelings for people, if you care about them, care about their welfare, acknowledging who they are and what they do is as natural as spring rain. It becomes something that you like to do, something you want to do. So long as you recognize that attention is often a highly valued payoff, recognize that it can influence both sides of the behavior-pair, and realize the importance of attending to the desired side, you will increase the opportunities for the desired behavior to be acquired and maintained through the use of a wide variety of "social" payoffs. Occasionally, however, attention and recognition are not, in themselves, sufficient to help a desired behavior get its start. They, along with the natural environment, need assistance.

The "When . . . then quickie" earns its name because its components provide a quick way to resolve spur-of-the-moment, minor difficulties that could become major ones. It can be an easy way to nudge a desired behavior forward, giving it a chance to be influenced by attention, recognition, and perhaps natural payoffs. It is capable of maintaining order in the midst of near-chaos, soothing frazzled nerves, satisfying two peoples' needs nearly at the same time, and accomplishing this and more without one yell, one threat of solitary confinement, or worse. According to questionable sources, it was discovered . . .

by a Grandma thousands of years ago. Her laboratory consisted of four walls, a mud floor complemented with sparse furnishings, and a thatched roof that leaked when it rained. As so often happens, the discovery occurred accidentally. She was babysitting her grandson; the child's parents were out hunting venison. She had made the boy a luscious apple pie; it was sitting atop the stone stove, cooling. He wanted a piece of the pie. Understandable. Grandma wanted him to finish his peas. Also understandable. She sensed a conflict was imminent. Stormy lines were forming on the child's small face—he was used to freebies. Grandma was determined to introduce the concept of limits. She thought for a minute: "He wants pie. I want him to have peas. I should be able to figure something out." Suddenly, from the deep recesses of her mind, it came to her. She turned and faced her cherished grandson. Her words were soft, clear, confident. "Tell you what, Buster, *when* you eat your peas *then* you can have a piece of pie!"

Instantly, the grandson's brewing anger faded. Finally, someone had given him some help in figuring out what he was expected to do.

"You mean all I have to do is to eat these green things, and then I can have a taste of that epicurean delight?"

"You got it, Buster."

"Not a bad deal," the youngster muttered, munching away at the little green things.

STUDENTS LEARN TO MAKE CHOICES

The "When . . . then quickie" teaches individuals something about contingencies, teaches them something about making choices. It says their environment has requirements and that completion of those requirements is necessary before they have access to what they desire. When used correctly, it gives individuals a taste of control—they decide if they wish to put out the effort to obtain what they want. As they consider the choice, they learn something about limits.

The beauty of the procedure is its simplicity. Generally, you don't have to guess what represents the desired payoff: The individual makes that known clearly. Most often it is something immediately at hand. If you believe no requirement is necessary for the individual to have what is desired, he or she receives it. The payoff becomes a "freebie." If, however, you believe that before the person can have what he or she wishes a specific behavior is required, indicate that you need the person to complete some activity before the reinforcer will be available: "When you do what I want, you may have what you want." (To my knowledge, no child has ever totally fallen apart on hearing the converse "if you *don't* do . . . you *can't* have. . . ." Like others in my field, I prefer the positive, active approach. It provides the individual with more information.)

PROCEDURES

For the procedure to be used correctly, there are only a few items that need remembering:

1. You need to watch and listen carefully to what individuals do or say. They will either show you or tell you what is valued at the moment.
2. You need to make a very clear statement as to what must be done in order to receive what is desired. Watch your words! Don't say "be responsible," or "be nice" or "mature." Spell out exactly what you expect.
3. You must make certain individuals have the skills to do what you are requesting.

4. Occasionally, you may need to refresh an individual's memory about the "contract's" particulars. Remind the person of what he or she is working to obtain and what must be done to fulfill the condition. I have found it helpful to mention the "reinforcer" first: "Remember, you can have a piece of pie after you finish your vegetables."

5. You must be fair! Once the task is completed, and assuming nothing unusual has happened that presents another problem, (see later) you should follow through with what you have stipulated.

One of the responsibilities I had as a graduate student was to build switch-and-lever boxes that were used with children to help them communicate with their environment. Most of the devices (the ones I built, at least) were crude but reasonably effective. The graduate students had a small shop within the laboratory where the creations were developed. Because of limited space within the entire building, the shop often served as a "classroom" where various objectives were taught to the children being served. In addition, the room was used by volunteers from the community who worked with the children on letters, words, and numbers. On one particularly beautiful summer day. . . .

I had been working alone in the shop trying to build a switch box. After some fifteen minutes, I heard a knock on the closed door. When I opened it, I was greeted by an elderly woman who was holding the hand of one of the children who resided at the state institution. She asked if she and the child could use the room to work on a number exercise. I invited them in and pointed to some available chairs. Then I went about my business trying, unsuccessfully, to be invisible.

It quickly became evident that the woman's chosen goal was for the child to count from 1 to 10, a feat I knew he could do from my experiences with him. Although my back was turned to both, I could tell the child was not interested in complying with the volunteer's requests. He'd say a few numbers, then stop. I could almost feel his eyes peering at me, wanting to know what I was doing. Not wishing to interfere, I tried not to listen to either the lady's pleas or the child's refusals. Finally, the frustration was too much. I turned just a little. As I suspected, the youngster was aware only of my presence, interested only in my efforts at trying to find the right nut for the right bolt. I turned fully, holding several nuts and bolts in my hand. "Would you mind if I offer a little help?" I asked the woman politely.

"Please do," she answered, her voice reflecting a little disappointment in her own efforts.

"You want to watch me play with these things?" I said to the child, showing him the shiny metal objects. He nodded rapidly, smiling from ear to ear. "Okay, you can watch in just a second. This nice person would like you to do something. She wants you to count from 1 to 10. As soon as you do that, you can stand by me and watch. Is that okay?" His head shook so fast I thought he was going to hurt himself.

I did not get a chance to turn around. He immediately turned to the woman: "One, two, three, four, five, six, seven, eight, nine, ten," poured fourth. Then, like a jack-in-the-box, he bounced to where I stood.

I had performed no great feat. Rather, I recognized what the child wanted and what the environment (the volunteer) wanted. Assured that the child could handle the task, I said, "When you count your numbers from 1 to 10, then you can watch me." Notice I did not say, "Come watch me, *then* count." I could have done so, but that would not have been the "When . . . then quickie." The desired behavior comes *first,* the payoff *follows.* The child might have told me, in no uncertain terms: "I changed my mind. I don't want to watch you play with those dumb nuts and bolts!" My answer would have been calm, straightforward: "If that is your choice, fine."

—————————————— **LESSONS TO BE LEARNED** ——————————————

While I might have wanted to waiver, to try to convince the child how much fun watching would be, I would have lost the opportunity for teaching several lessons:

1. There are contingencies in life.
2. The natural environment often sets limits on behavior.
3. Children have some control over their environment.
4. As a result of choice, children can influence their environment.

It is possible that after the child digests all the lessons, he develops a change of heart: "I changed my mind again. I'd like to watch." Again calmly, a restatement of the contingency: "Fine. As soon as you count, then come watch."

—————————————— **VARIATIONS** ——————————————

As with all procedures, there are variations and exceptions. A situation might present itself where it would seem appropriate for the payoff to come first: "I promise to do my homework as soon as I come back from the movie," a student states. Suppose you accept the conditions. If the child follows through on returning from the show, no problem. If the child fails to carry through with her part of the "contract," then in the future, for a while at least, the correct order of behavior *then* payoff should be enforced. Another child might have had a very difficult day. You want him to have something of value to lift his spirits. He knows you have bought ice cream for dessert. Your prefered rule has always been "finish all your dinner, then dessert." There's nothing wrong with an occasional compromise: "Eat two pieces of meat and one spoonful of potatoes, and that will be enough."

CLARITY

The language you use when stating the contingency must communicate both sides of the "contract." See if you can determine what difficulty may exist in the following: "As soon as you clean your work area, you may go to the library." First, there may be no difficulty. The student may be sufficiently familiar with the statement to know exactly what she must do. If not, confusion might arise. "Do I have to sweep the floor?" the student might ask. The culprit is the word "clean." It would be better to replace the word with the precise chores expected: "As soon as you place your books in the desk, and chair under the desk, you may go to the library." Such precision takes a little longer, but if it decreases any misunderstanding, the time spent is worth while. It is also helpful if some parameters are attached to the payoff side. "When you put the books away, etc., you may go to the library for fifteen minutes." How about a problem with the following: "As soon as you finish your assignment, you may go to recess." Again, no problem may surface. Notice, however, that the "contract" says nothing about the work being correct, or even approximately correct. "Speed" may be the end product, not accuracy or effort.

THE "WHEN . . . THEN" ATTITUDE

The principle behind the "When . . . then quickie" is the expectation that the individual will behave in a designated manner prior to receiving the sought-after payoff. If one of your goals is for the individual to understand and to come under the influence of such contingent payoffs, then initially the *concept* on which the "when-then" attitude is built is *more important* than either the behavior required or the reinforcer offered. Practicing the concept helps individuals acquire the attitude, helps them understand how it works, and lets them know that in your presence, at least, that's the way their environment operates. If you have the aforementioned goal, then look for ways to practice the concept. Each time the individual requests, either by words or actions, something he or she values, the opportunity for fostering an understanding of the process presents itself. A few practice sessions during the day or week will show the individual how the process works.

> "Dad, I'm going to ride my bike?"
> "Sure, dear, but take a minute first to hang your coat in the closet."

> "Mr. Jones, may I go to recess?"
> "Yes, Billy, but bring me your math paper first."

There is an implied contract, an expectation, in the above examples. One thing has to happen before another will happen. Compliance with the agreed-on specifics, by both parties, helps teach the "When . . . then" attitude. The attitude sets the stage for the individual to say "When I do . . . then. . . ." As you recall, that is the beginning of self-directed behavior.

I am not suggesting that the above "minicontracts" are necessary all the time. "Freebies" have their place, and as mentioned, the spontaneous tousling of hair and affectionate squeeze dependent on nothing but being, cannot compete with any planned, artificial system. My experience, however, has shown that continual "freebies" void of any "When . . . then" mind-set, produces an expectation that things come without effort. Payoffs become expected more as a function of the passing of time rather than quality of performance. If life worked that way, the word "disappointment" would not exist. Life within the natural environment is rarely that way, and the sooner individuals are introduced to the reality of limits, the less likely disappointment will come as an overwhelming shock. Conversely, as they come to understand reasonable limits, it is more likely individuals will learn how to control access to their values.

> "You mean all I have to do is to eat these little green things; then I can have some of that scrumptious apple pie? Thanks, Grandma, that's not a bad deal. You sure make my world easier to understand."

FUNNY MONEY AND OTHER
COMMUNICATING DEVICES

When the environment fails to communicate clearly, the absence of desired behavior is more likely. If our language is sufficiently muddled, our provided messages about expectations and outcomes may fly stories above an individual's head. The result may be that the individual neither understands what is desired nor what payoffs are being made available. Given the confusion, the adaptive individual will find a means of acquiring what he or she needs. The choice may be less than what we desire. When such a situation exists, the consultant occasionally finds it necessary to employ an often complex artificial system to teach *the people* responsible for the individual how to communicate precisely what is desired and what payoff maybe forthcoming.

This final procedure is being mentioned for three reasons. First, it has historical significance. Second, it can be very effective for certain individuals, who, because of their developmental levels, have difficulty tolerating delayed feedback and who need more than attention and recognition to maintain their desired behavior. Third, it can be the most difficult to administer. Ideally, we do not wish to use it. If we have done our job adequately, we should rarely need to use it.

THE SYSTEM AS IT EXISTS
IN THE NATURAL ENVIRONMENT

To a large degree, the procedure approximates the circumstances that govern the working life of nearly all adults. We labor at an activity, we receive payment for our efforts from an outside source, and we use the payments to purchase both our necessities and luxuries. While our labors, payments, and purchases differ, the basic system remains constant, and while we may, on numerous occasions, fret over what we must do to gain payments for our labors, most of us, nevertheless, work and behave acceptably within the system.

We've seen, however, that the natural environment is capable of producing and maintaining behaviors that would never be a conscious part of a care-giver's plan. It can happen in homes and schools. It can also occur, dramatically, in institutions for the developmentally delayed and behaviorally disturbed. The system seems to go haywire, producing disheartening behaviors that seem more at home in a Faustian play than in a hoped-for caring world. Sometimes the manifested behaviors appear so entrenched as to be unchangeable, relegating the living to a life unenvied by anyone. The fictional movie *The Snake Pit* shockingly becomes a nonfictional work. There are many factors that go into producing these results, and it is easy to throw stones at those in responsible positions, or explain away the bizzarre with psychological jargon. It is often difficult for the concerned to make meaningful changes. Many years ago, a young psychologist took his skills into such an arena. With some license, this is the gist of what happened.

5.1

THE ARENA

On entering the institutional facility, and with little more than a glance, the psychologist noticed the effects the institution's natural environment was having on those incarcerated. Many adult patients, old beyond their years, were mute by choice rather than by physical anomaly, combative at the slightest cue, resistive to interventions intended to alter what had become habituated, and seemingly satisfied to be utterly and completely isolated from what little freedom was available. Some had not talked, had not emerged from their adaptive shells, in years. The staff's explanation for the behaviors? "The patients were *ill*"—a simple, terribly naive explanation. " 'Ill' as they may be," the psychologists thought, "the patients had no reason to be otherwise." Their individual environments had, without intending, set up contingencies to keep them as they were. His recorded observations confirmed his suspicions. Those who were combative and resistive received inordinate attention when being so. When they quieted, they were left alone. Those patients who piled heavy sweaters on their perspiring bodies were constantly engaged in conversation about such an "abnormality." Little fuss occurred when a desired alternative was observed. Those who remained silent were continuously told how important it was to speak, but their occasional utterings brought considerably less than did the quiescence.

With permission, the psychologist chose to change the natural environment. He decided to *pay* the patients to be less "ill." It was an arduous task. Habits had been etched, and behaviors were resistant to change. He took a barren wall on the ward and placed machines against it that dispensed coffee, candy, and smokes. He devised tokens the machines would accept. The patients were shown the machines, shown the tokens, shown how to use the tokens. The patients were told through words and modeling how to earn the tokens; they were told which of their behaviors could bring them what was in the machines. Some did not understand the explanation. The psychologist knew that understanding of his words was *not* absolutely essential. He stood close to those whose language skills had deteriorated. Their slightest utterances immediately produced a token. The slightest sign of compliance produced a token. The slightest effort toward emergence from obscurity produced a token. Soon, although not instantly, utterances, movement out from the dark, and exploration began to occur more frequently. Soon, behaviors that hadn't been used in years began to produce payoffs to the liking of the patients. The "new" natural environment, through tokens that were exchanged for valued artificial reinforcers, showed the benefits of speaking, walking, cooperation. The staff began to use attention and recognition, first at the request of the psychologist, later by their own choice, to faciliate the acquisition and maintenance of the "new" behaviors. The staff's natural environment, too, had been changed. They were exhausted by the combativeness; they welcomed the patients' cooperation. Their therapeutic efforts brought them payoffs. The "token economy" had helped to produce change. At that point, behaviors that were functional and capable of enhancing life began to come under the influence of the environment's natural contingencies—artificial consequences became less essential. The benefits were calculable. The precedent was set. Other facilities adopted the psychologist's methods; other "lost" people were helped to find themselves.

YOU DETERMINE COMPLEXITY

You have control over the complexity of the system by limiting or expanding the number of behaviors you wish to influence. A system that targets a single behavior is considerably easier than one that involves five. The rule of thumb is to start small and build gradually, if the latter becomes necessary. Frequently, once the process involved with the system is learned by all parties, it can be discarded in favor of more "natural" or "logical" approaches. This process, then, is what I would ask you to attend to. You will see immediately that the system, while it holds promise for short-term concerns, is not one that is intended to replace the natural environment. Whether it is used by teachers or parents to help with the behavior of one child or a group of students, its purpose is to help the adults develop a more effective way of communicating and providing feedback. With that in mind, let's see what this approach is all about.

Many years ago, fresh from graduate school, I supervised a system that attempted to influence *six* behaviors simultaneously. Never again! I practically had to live with the parents and their son, Eddie. (In retrospect, had the scenario occurred today, Eddie would have been seen as "having an attention-deficit-disorder" and probably would have been placed on medication. "Attention/behavior"-altering drugs weren't in vogue when Eddie was a child, thus "treatment" focused on the child's family environment rather than his physical system.) The parents needed constant assistance: They had a very difficult time communicating their behavioral preferences to their son. Once realizing they were the ones who needed to look closely at what they were doing, the process to help them began.

_____ PROCEDURES _____

Let me run through some of the practical components you'll need to consider if you decide to use this procedure.

1. Behavior-Pairs
2. Type of Tokens
3. Back-up Reinforcers/Reinforcement Menu
4. Delivery System
5. Penalties
6. Exchange System

BEHAVIOR-PAIRS

You need to identify the specific behavior creating difficulty and determine its alternatively more acceptable counterpart. Make sure both behaviors are observable. I would strongly suggest that you select only one behavior-pair to work with. Both you and the individual need to succeed and learn the processes involved within the system. If too many behaviors are worked with simultaneously, success and learning may be difficult to come by. In Eddie's case, the desired side of the behavior-pairs were as follows:

1. Going to bed on time
2. Doing homework
3. Following requests
4. Getting dressed (in the morning)
5. Chores
6. Putting clothes in the hamper

Typically, school-related behavior-pairs will focus on class assignments, coming to class on time, following directions, answering questions, and the like. In special facilities, the behaviors might include work assignments, outbursts, lucid conversations, indicating needs, and similar activities. As may be evident, you would determine the undesired behavior, develop its alternative, and proceed.

TYPE OF TOKENS

The token can be almost anything. Tallied points were used by Eddie's parents. Professionals have used poker chips, pieces of paper, and funny money ("Monopoly" bills). The individual can have some say in the choice. The token just needs to be something you can easily store, something you can keep track of, something that won't be misplaced or guided into wrong hands. You wouldn't want to use watermelons, although their seeds would be fine.

BACK-UP REINFORCERS/REINFORCEMENT MENU

With rare exceptions, a dollar bill, itself, is meaningless. It has value only if it can be exchanged for something else. No doubt there exists someone somewhere who keeps thousands of dollar bills hidden in a mattress. For that individual, having the pieces of paper nearby is enough. Most of us, however, have a different use for them. With equally rare exceptions, the poker chip, the funny money, and the colored sticks have value only if they, too, can be exchanged. I have seen a few people who enjoy accumulating points for the sake of accumulation. They had no interest in exchanging even one point.

The back-up reinforcer is precisely what its name implies. It is something of value; something the points and tokens are exchanged for. There are several ways to determine the back-ups. Individuals will tell you; you can watch and note what they like to do; you can sit with them and develop a reinforcement menu that lists items of value, or you can provide them with many "enticing" objects and activities and see which ones they like. The obtained reinforcement menu is an integral part of the system. Since present-day values change, often rapidly, it is advisable to have many alternatives available.

Not long ago, I was asked to help a youngster who had been hospitalized due to a serious infection within his liver. One of the staff's major concerns with the child was his unwillingness to eat enough food to maintain his caloric needs. The 4-year-old seemed quite content to sit and nibble for over an hour on the smallest portions of food, and once meal-time was over, he invariably had failed to consume enough nourishment to satisfy a baby pigeon! (Out of necessity, a tube had been placed into the child's stomach, via his nostril, that enabled the medical personnel to provide the child with sustenance sufficient to fight weight loss.)

The staff had attempted to develop a motivational system for the youngster to improve his eating, but their efforts had proved unsuccessful. "We can't find anything reinforcing for him," one of the nurses complained in a voice reflecting the staff's overall frustration and concern. "He doesn't seem to like anything," the nurse pointed out. In reality, the child liked a lot of things. The problem was that the medical personnel hadn't looked in the right places.

5.2

They forgot that any activity a child frequently enjoys can serve as a reinforcer. They had made the error of thinking that reinforcement was limited to TV, sweets, and social attention. They forgot that many other items also could be reinforcing to a child. The head nurse and I positioned ourselves at a far end of the unit, and we watched the child as he played with other patients, looked at pictures in a book, carried stuffed animals in his arms, shot a small pop-gun into the air, took sips of root beer from a can that he informed me was *his,* and generally enjoyed his freedom to walk and skip around the premises. In less than 15 minutes, the nurse and I compiled a *reinforcement menu* that listed at least 10 available items. On the following day, a motivational system was put into effect. Once the child experienced several trials of the "when-then" contingencies and realized, for the time being, that there would be few "freebies," he began to eat. Stable weight gain eventually allowed the nasal tube to be removed, and the child's eating soon came under the control of the natural reinforcers of pleasant tastes and reduction of hunger. The artificial motivation system was no longer necessary.

You have the final say as to what is included on the reinforcement menu. If you believe candy is out, orange slices are in, fine. Remember, however, that orange slices may *not* be valued, and thus not be reinforcers. You might like them; you might like for the individual child to like them. But. . . . Many more times than not, a token system is only as good as its back-up reinforcers. Eddie's self-determined back-ups were:

1. Treats	9. Movie
2. TV time	10. Eating out
3. Fishing equipment	11. Record album
4. Money (max $1.50/week)	12. Having a friend over
5. Staying up late	13. Staying at friend's
6. Chess game	14. Picnicking with family
7. Dessert	15. Fishing with Dad
8. Small toy	16. Baseball glove/bat

Every item on the list was something Eddie had received in some quantity *prior* to the initiation of the system. For the most part, however, they had been "freebies." The exceptions: Dessert had always been contingent on Eddie's completion of dinner; money—"allowance"—had been given only after Eddie did a few chores. The remainder were available to the child pretty much on a noncontingent basis. The system changed that approach. Eddie seemed undisturbed by the proposal of the contingent system. (I sensed he welcomed the structure.)

DELIVERY SYSTEM

Chips can be placed in jars; points listed on a piece of paper; pegs placed in a pegboard. The governing principle should be that the individual can see how well he or she is doing. The visible accumulation of chips, points, or pegs can be reinforcing in itself. The delivery of the token should be accompanied by a sprinkling of hair-tousling and warm words, along with a *clear explanation* of what the individual did that warranted the payoff. By keeping in mind, again, that the system's overall purpose is to teach the care-giver how to communicate more clearly what behaviors are desired and what payoffs will be provided, it should be evident why explanations and demonstrated recognition are so important. Eddie's parents, for years, had fallen into the trap of basically responding to their son when he had misbehaved. They had forgotten how important it was to let their son know that they appreciated the desired things he did. Eventually, the entire system used with Eddie was replaced by words that conveyed guidelines and appreciation, along with occasional "when . . . then" quickies that helped the youngster know what he was expected to do. That more natural way of relating to Eddie did not occur immediately; his parents needed the structure of the system to help them monitor their own actions.

Determining how tokens or points should be delivered can be either simple or complex. An individual might receive one token each time a desired behavior is manifested. This was the approach used with a 5-year-old who had a swallowing problem and by necessity had to be fed by a stomach tube for most of his life. After the problem was corrected, he had to learn to eat food by mouth. For this youngster, each swallow of solid food brought him a poker chip that he later exchanged for something he valued. (The tokens were only needed for a few weeks.) Another individual might receive a token for participating in an activity for a determined period of time. This approach was used with a young student who needed to wear a patch over one eye in order to use and strengthen the vision of his other eye. He received a dried lima bean (his choice!) for each 15-minute period that the patch was worn. The beans were exchanged for time for playing Scrabble with his parents when he returned home from school. (Again, the tokens were only needed briefly.)

As the above examples indicate, tokens can be earned for a certain *number* of behaviors, as well as a certain amount of *time* engaged in an activity. The target behavior determines whether "frequency" or "duration" is the critical feature.

Eddie's circumstances, as you might have guessed, were more complicated. Look once more at his targeted desired behaviors. The undesired "pairs" are likely apparent.

1. Going to bed on time
2. Doing homework
3. Following requests
4. Getting dressed (in the morning)
5. Chores
6. Putting clothes in the hamper

As can be seen, the behaviors included some that were more "frequency" oriented: numbers 1, 3, 5, and 6; and some that involved "time": numbers 2 and 4. (The reason number 4 was viewed as involving "time" was because he often took many minutes before completing the activity. It should be noted that Eddie had no difficulty dressing himself; he simply procrastinated. If Eddie had a motor problem, the dressing behavior would not have been included within the system.) The youngster received 1 token when he went to bed at the time requested, 1 token for each request that was followed, 1 token for each chore completed, and 1 token when his soiled clothes were placed in the hamper. He received 1 token for each 15 minutes of homework, and 2 tokens if he dressed within 10 minutes after being requested to get ready for breakfast.

"You'd need to be an accountant to keep track of the tokens," the parent stated.

"Close, but not quite," I responded quickly. "Remember, it's a lot easier working with one or two behaviors. Six, all at once, is nearly impossible."

The accumulation of tokens is one thing. What to do with them is another: one can only fondle them for so long. In schools and special facilities, there's often a "store" where an individual can exchange the earned tokens for special experiences (such as going outside to collect bugs) or material objects (treats, pencils, books, etc.)—again, very similar to what we do with our dollar bills. For all purposes, the reinforcement/value menu becomes the "store." The individual knows that a certain number of tokens will be required before the experiences or objects can be obtained. Our responsibility is to determine the exchange "value": In other words, how many tokens will be required before an individual can go get the jar and search for bugs. Fortunately we have control of the "value" system: We don't have to read the newspaper to see how the dollar has fluctuated against the yen or ruble.

To keep this explanation "brief," I'll make suggestions as though we were dealing only with two behaviors. (I'd need a full chapter to explain what was done with Eddie.)

1. The first step is to look at the reinforcement menu and determine how often you wish the individual to have access to the store's items. How many minutes of free time will you allow the individual to have? How many snacks? How much allowance can be earned? How many games of Scrabble are you willing to play? You must set some limits on the quantity of payoffs; otherwise you'll spend your entire day as a sales clerk behind a counter of goodies. That will do more than frazzle your nerves. Check each item on your payoff menu and decide how often it can be earned. You can't allow an individual to visit Disney World every day! The "big" items will require more tokens. The smaller items will be easy to obtain. Above all, remember that you want the individual to experience success and therefore access to what is valued, as well as learning the process behind the system—that payoffs come from effort. Don't set your exchange value yet. There are other things that need consideration first.

2. The second step requires that you determine, or estimate, how many tokens the individual can earn during a given period of time. Let's assume that the two target behaviors are following requests and completing math (or work) assignments. Now, ask yourself the following: "How many math problems can be completed during an assignment period (or how many work-related tasks can be completed in an hour or so)? The answer is dependent upon several factors but knowing how many "completions" have occurred in the past will provide you with some approximation. If the individual is given one token for each correct response, you'll have an idea as to how many she can earn in a given period of time. (You can, of course, provide one token for every two correct responses.) How about following requests. Technically, the individual will be able to earn tokens commensurate with the number of requests you make. If you make 10 requests, she can earn 10 tokens. You must determine how many requests you generally make each day. If you have no idea, you'll have to watch yourself over a few days in order to sample your own behavior. If you generally make 3, then 3 tokens would be the maximum. So, if everything works out perfectly, you'll know the total number of possible tokens the individual can earn per day. In the case of the child who wore the patch over his eye, the exercise was only required for one hour per day. One token could have been given for every 15 minutes, thus 4 could have been earned. The "swallowing" child had more control over the situa-

tion. The parents, rather than watching their behavior, kept track of the number of swallows the youngster usually took per meal. It, of course, varied depending on what was served, but they were able to determine an approximate number of swallows.

3. The third step requires that you attach a number value to each token. For example, 1 token can be worth 5 minutes of Scrabble time; 1 token will equal 15 minutes of bug-finding; 5 tokens can be worth a dime; 10 tokens can be exchanged for a bag of peanuts or can of juice; 60 *million* tokens will result in a trip to Paris. This part of the system is in your hands. Review your menu, figure out how often the items are to be made available, determine how many tokens (under the most ideal situation) can be earned, then place a value on each token. At this point, assuming you've explained all of the above to the individual, she will know what she must do to earn the "store's" items.

PENALTIES

What do we do if the individual fails to manifest the desired behaviors? What in the world do we do if the individual manifests both the desired and undesired behaviors at different times? Imagine this: An individual is asked to follow 6 requests. He complies with 3 and chooses not to follow the remaining one. He's earned, let's say, 15 minutes of free time (each earned token worth 5 minutes of free time) and he's quite satisfied. He could have earned a total of 30 minutes of free time but he decided not to. Now we turn to a controversial issue: Should the individual be penalized for failing to behave as desired? Put slightly differently, should the individual be penalized for behaving undesirably? If you are using clear behavior-pairs—two opposite behaviors, incompatible to one another—the two questions are basically the same. The individual either complies or he doesn't; the two can't occur simultaneously. Here's where you will have to make an important choice: Do I attach a penalty to the undesired behavior, or do I allow the absence of total possible earned time to be the penalty? I'll share my biases.

While penalties may be controversial, they are, nonetheless, inherent in both the natural environment and any use of a token system.

Mom and Dad were having difficulty teaching their child to keep her room relatively clean. Their major concerned centered around empty soft drink cans and candy wrappers that were often buried under piles of dirty clothes. After many requests failed to help the youngster remember what she was to do, namely throw the refuse into the garbage can, the parents, not so calmly, told the child that if *one* can or wrapper was discovered, she would not be allowed to spend time with her friends for 24 hours. After missing several valued hours with her companions, the child began to regulate her own behavior.

While there was no token involved in the above example, the child understood that she would have to *pay* a penalty (loss of time with friends) for failing to comply with her parents' guidelines. As described, the parents' rules produced an "all or none" scenario. Suppose the parents had selected a second option, slightly more complicated, to help their child understand the family's requirements.

During an evening meal, the parents explained the following to their daughter. "We want you to learn to throw your food trash into the kitchen garbage bag. The exterminator is making a fortune off your lack of memory, and we'd prefer that you not sleep with creepy crawlers. We know you'd like to spend time with your friends, and we want you to do so. We will check your room daily. You will start each day with six tokens, each worth 30 minutes of time that you can spend with your friends. If we find no trash, you may exchange the tokens for time spent with your friends. The piled, soiled clothes are not a big problem. When you run out of things to wear, you can do the wash. The spilt crumbs and liquid are a big problem. If you throw the wrappers and cans away, you can be with your friends for up to three hours. However, each found wrapper or can will cost you two hours of free time, including telephone time."

When the parents finished their explanation, they asked their child to review the requirements. Once certain that she understood the behavior-pairs and the consequences for each, the guidelines were put into effect.

In the second example, the daughter could have earned all, none, or part of what she valued. It was her choice. In both examples, behavior-pairs were influenced and penalties occurred. The daughter had a choice of what to do, but she learned that there were consequences attached to her behavior. Suppose, in the second example, explicit penalties for the undesired behavior were not included. Instead, the parents indicated that each wrapper and can disposed of in the garbage can would result in 30 minutes of earned free time (up to a maximum of 3 hours.) The youngster could have thrown 6 items in the trash, earned her 3 hours with friends, or thrown 4 items away, earned time, and still have enough refuse in her room to fill a garbage truck. This scenario would be very similar to that of the individual who complied 3 times, failed to comply 3 times, and still earned 15 minutes to do as he wished.

So long as you believe in establishing limits for an individual's behavior, some form of a penalty format will exist. Persistent behavior beyond limits guarantees penalties. Penalties should be sufficient enough to bring the individual's attention to the undesired behavior, but not so severe as to make it impossible for him to gain access to what he values. Beyond the above, there aren't any hard, fixed guidelines to be followed. The verbal individual can be consulted for ideas, or you can experiment with varying degrees of the loss of valued payoffs. If you aren't certain whether you wish to incorporate explicitly stated penalties within the system, try doing without them and watch what effects occur. They can be included at any time. Just be certain to discuss the change with the individual.

EXCHANGE SYSTEM

The exchange component is essential for several reasons. First, it shows the individual that her effort and accumulated tokens are of value. Second, it shows her how the system works: Desired behavior allows access to what is valued. Third, it can show her that the more she works, the more she can earn—up to a point. Often, I will spend time during the beginning of a program showing the individual how the exchange process works. This is particularly the case with an individual who has problems benefiting from verbal explanations. I'll actually model the exchange: provide her with a token, accept it from her, then immediately offer her something of value. Once I believe she understands the exchange process, I will devise a task for her, have her complete it (guaranteeing success), provide her with the type of token to be used, then exchange it. The critical issue is for the individual to understand that her behavior yields something of value. Practice is often essential in order to understand the process.

DATA COLLECTION: MONITOR
THE SYSTEM'S PROGRESS

If you intend to try some variation of the above, by all means, keep it simple. If you try it and you fail to observe your intended outcomes, do not be dismayed. There's nothing magical about the approach. Ask yourself some questions:

1. Have you, accidentally, begun to provide attention to the undesired behavior?

2. Have you altered the way the system was designed? Are you allowing the individual to have the back-up reinforcer *without* requiring him or her to complete his or her part of the bargain?
3. Are the requirements too stringent? Does the individual believe that it has become next to impossible to gain access to the payoffs?
4. Has there been a breakdown in consistency?
5. Has the reinforcer lost its value? Do you need to reevaluate the back-up reinforcers?
6. Has the system become too "mechanical"? Are you remembering to complement it with attention and appreciation?
7. Has the individual grown tired of the system?
8. Have *you* grown tired? Do *you* want out from under the funny money?

Token systems are needed only when there has been a breakdown in communication and consistency, or when you're dealing with large numbers of individuals and can't divide yourself into 28 pieces. What does the system really do? It teaches us to watch what *we* are doing! It teaches us to talk, to listen, and to bring things into focus. It teaches us to watch more carefully what the individual is doing. It teaches us to "catch him doing something good." It teaches us to provide him with positive payoffs, affection, recognition, and an occasional surprise when he does something good or when he's just his marvelous self. It teaches us to *communicate more clearly*—the individual knows what is expected, knows that things happen as a result of his behavior. It helps us help the individual. If we learn to do the above, we can get off the system. If we are doing all of the above, we don't need the system!

POSITIVE PAYOFFS: PROVIDING A
REASON TO BEHAVE DESIRABLY

Frequently, all of us throw around a word that suggests we've forgotten how difficult it can be to figure out our natural environments. The word: "Should." The sentence: "The individual *should* behave desirably." Frankly, when discussing desirable and undesirable behaviors, the word would be best left out of any discussion. It's a dumb word, a word most often used by parents and professionals when they have become frustrated. (Later, we will discuss the "value" of the term when looking at behaviors that are associated with physiological maturation.)

From a practical standpoint, what the individual *is* doing is infinitely more important than what you, or anyone else, states the individual should be doing. No doubt, there will be times when you believe someone has had enough experience within his or her natural environment to meet your expectations. The fact remains he or she is not doing what you would prefer. While there are several reasons why an individual may not be behaving as you wish, one explanation for the absence of the behavior is that the person *sees no reason to do it!* There's no payoff. The requested behavior has no value; it makes no sense; it ain't no fun. Take a walk in this person's shoes. Think what it would be like to have to watch an ant traverse a hundred yards of burnt grass. The bottom line: The individual is not doing what you want. Give him or her a reason to do it. Step into the arena. Help the natural environment bring the behavior under the influence of natural, logical payoffs. Artificial systems are often the necessary first step toward that end. We can debate this issue of payoffs and spout platitudes until we have no breath. That's not going to help much. What will help is our willingness to show the individual that something of value, natural, logical, or contrived, something other than a sports car, can come from his or her efforts.

SPECIAL CASES

More frequently, consultants are called upon to assist individuals whose skill levels, in many areas, are significantly limited. With the growing movement across the country to "deinstitutionalize" severely handicapped individuals, bringing them within the mainstream of life, along with the greater frequency with which severely involved children are being served at young ages within public schools, many professionals are facing a population whose needs and problems often surpass the professional's educational and practical training. More times than not, the skilled professional becomes so only after many years of working with the population. Even then, these difficult individuals, with all their uniquenesses, can cause us to return to the "basics" before a transdisciplinary team can determine the best means to provide the needed assistance. Along with cognitive and motoric developmental assessments, determinations of physical strengths and weaknesses, evaluations of learning style, communication style, and emotional reactions to the natural environment, there remains an additional concern that I believe warrants our consideration. I'd like to bring that variable to your attention at this time.

LEARNED HELPLESSNESS

As you recall, individuals' behavior begins to come under the influence of their environment shortly after (if not before) birth. What is indeed learned, what is perceived as meaningful, what ultimately will have an effect on future development is, for the most part, unknown. This is especially so for the "special" child whose visual, auditory, speech, motor, neurological, or cognitive domains may be significantly impaired. When the child is eventually seen for professional services, the developmental specialist will spend many hours evaluating how far the child's development has progressed. Apart from the developmental delays that will be identified, the specialist is keenly aware that the special child is highly susceptible to something often referred to as "learned helplessness." Such a situation is nearly impossible to avoid: Due to children's unique attributes and difficulties, the early relationship between children, parents, and care-givers inevitably teaches youngsters that most, if not all, of their needs will be met regardless of what behaviors they manifest. During the earliest developmental period, this situation is not a cause for concern or alarm: Children must be cared for when they are not capable of caring for themselves. The "normal" routines involving systematic bedtime, eating, playing, communicating and the like often must be interrupted in order to help children through the trials that they are experiencing. The establishing of behavioral rules and limits, common to normally developing children, are bypassed in favor of a receptive environment that accepts (on occasion, endures) whatever children do.

Unfortunately, the natural environment does not sit by idly during this early developmental period. Lessons are being taught and being learned. "When . . . then" scenarios are presented and acquired, and children, more accurately than may be estimated, learn the patterns their natural environment provides. Frequently, what children learn is that payoffs come with little effort on their part. Frequently, and unknown to the children, their "handicapping" conditions have set the stage for their care-givers to respond differently than if they were not handicapped: they are pampered, rather than pushed to do more; their environment is one of protection, rather than one that promotes advancement. During the earliest developmental period, this situation is understandable. Still, it has its effects, and when they reach the age where the educational system has been mandated to provide services, they often carry what they have learned into the classroom. Without meaning to sound unduly harsh, they expect "freebies." Frequently, they receive them: cookies and crackers and cheese are just there. They are required to do little to receive them.

LESSONS MUST BE LEARNED . . .

The child blessed with an intact body will likely suffer few setbacks from this "freebie" regime. Eventually, parents, teachers, and those other significant people within the natural environment will, at some point, begin to impose limits. They will teach the child that something, perhaps asking or pointing or naming, must occur before the cookies and crackers are forthcoming. The "intact" child will learn the new lessons with relative ease: He or she will learn what must be done in order to gain what is valued at the moment. Conversely, the "special" child, the one who needs the most assistance, may not know precisely what must be done to receive what has been made available. Instead, he or she may sit and wait for something to happen, or may reach or vocalize or meander *until* something does happen! Something, of course, will happen, for it always does.

. . . LESSONS MUST BE TAUGHT

But the "special" child may neither know what that something is nor, more importantly, what must be done to have some control over what happens. This child, rather than learning how to manipulate the environment with behaviors that help him or her develop, becomes a more passive recipient, often without direction. And all of this happens with the most humane intentions: protecting the child so as to make him or her feel loved and comforted. While the child may be protected and loved, nonetheless he or she acquires "learned helplessness." Without intentional exaggeration, the child becomes, or appears, more handicapped than he or she is, and pointedly, is the one who suffers the most.

Our task is to provide children (or adults) with a means to demonstrate whatever abilities they possesses, as well as learning the process that valued payoffs come from their self-initiated, easily identifiable, developmentally enhancing actions. Once these lessons are acquired, the developmental specialist will be in a stronger position to assess individuals' cognitive level, and thus be able to provide therapists and teachers with ideas as to the types of curricular activities that will best serve individuals' growth.

We can use any number and kind of vehicles to help the individual with the lessons: working "cause" and "effect" switch toys, pointing to pictures, vocalizations, touching someone's hand or a part of one's own body, placing small, colored blocks in a cup, or almost any other activity that is observable, specific, and commensurate with the individual's physical abilities. The means are not as important as the ends.

I had been asked to look at a young girl who was a preschooler at a local Cerebral Palsy Center. When I first saw the child, she was wrapped in her teacher's arms as they both sat on the floor of the classroom. Although the teacher was reading a story to the seven other youngsters, she seemed more intent on keeping the young girl nestled close to her chest. Upon closer inspection of the child, I noticed a heavily scarred, callused area of tissue on her left wrist. The area was inflammed, and appeared to have been bleeding recently. The teacher's assistant soon joined me and we began to quietly discuss the child. "The child has been with us for two months," the assistant whispered, "and we have no idea what she knows or what she can do. The Palsy has limited her use of her right side, although she can walk with little difficulty. She doesn't speak, doesn't make her needs known, rarely attends to any activities other than eating. We've never seen her smile or give any indication of joy. She won't play with any toys, and she seems oblivious to the other children. If she is placed in a chair or allowed to roam freely, she bites her left wrist with incredible force. The only time she doesn't bite herself is when one of us holds her tightly," she explained as she looked toward the teacher and the child. "She has no father, and her mother works all day. After school, the child stays with her grandparents until the mother picks her up. Mother reports that her daughter's biting is very frequent when they are together, but it rarely occurs when she's alone with her grandparents."

"Have you verified that?" I asked.

"Yes. We did a 'home' visit at the grandparents' and we saw no biting for nearly an hour."

"How do you account for that?"

The aide hesitated briefly before answering. "The grandmother used to hit the child with a stick when the biting started. Now, the woman simply keeps the stick in plain view of the child and that appears to be a sufficient deterrent."

"I assume you've told the grandmother that she needs to stop using the stick," I said.

"We've told her, yes," the aide responded.

"What's your best estimate of the child's visual and auditory acuity?"

"Everything we've seen tells us that her vision and hearing are normal. Beyond that, we're in the dark."

As the class shifted activities, the teacher, holding the child tightly, walked toward us. As though they had done so many times before, the assistant took the child into her grasp and led her out of the room. "Physical therapy," the teacher explained, as we watched the child leave. "If you'd like to see her in action, go with her." I observed her briefly. The moment the physical therapist attempted any work, allowing the child's left hand to be free, the biting began. Therapy ended. The child's bleeding wound was cleaned and dressed, and she was returned to the teacher's waiting arms. "We've got to stop the biting," the teacher said, her voice reflecting her fatigue and frustration.

NEITHER THE LEARNING NOR THE TEACHING MAY BE EASY

"We've got to do that and more," I answered supportively. "Let me just sit for a few moments and observe." The only time the child was not held by one of the adults was during snack. With her small right arm draped against her side, the youngster ate as many of the peanut and jelly crackers as were offered, and she had no problem holding and drinking the cup of milk that was refilled three times. As soon as the table was completely cleared, her teeth and left wrist met, and she bit herself through the gauze dressing. I stayed a few more minutes, then left the school, assuring the teachers I would return the following morning.

The teacher, the child, and I sat together in a small therapy room located a short distance from the classroom. "She has no way of telling us what she wants, other than to bite to be held. At the same time, I'm not even certain that she realizes that biting results in her being in your arms," I began as I softly touched the child's cheek. "I hope I'm wrong: I hope she tells herself that when she bites, you will hold her. That, at least, would indicate an accomplished cognitive skill level. Beyond that, if it's there, I doubt she has any idea how to access what she wants, what is expected of her, and what might happen if she would refrain from biting. She apparently knows there's a harsh stick around someplace; that some people use it but most don't. Her environment has provided the most limited of information: Bite and you get held or struck; don't bite under certain cuing situations, and you don't get struck. That's not much to build a life on. I'm going to try to teach her that nice things can happen if she'll do something besides biting." I brought the small lever box that I had picked up from my university office and placed it on the table. "I will teach her that if she will press this lever she can have a small snack. Maybe she'll learn to press the lever to get into your lap, or have you read her a story, or anything that she might value. The lever will be her way of communicating. It will be the first step toward teaching her that biting is not the only way of communicating."

"If she learns that, maybe we can teach her to point or gesture or vocalize so she can tell us something about herself," the teacher suggested. "Then, maybe, we can determine some of her developmental skills."

"That's what we're shooting for," I answered. It didn't happen immediately: even young children do not relinquish their acquired habits easily. Understandably, she had no idea why I held her left hand tightly, why I lifted it from the table and placed it on the lever, why I praised her excitedly when the combined force of our hands depressed the lever creating an audible click and the lighting of a small, red bulb, why she received a small bite of cookie immediately after the appearance of the clicking sound and illuminating light, why I had to use my strength to keep her wrist from her snapping teeth. It required ten struggling trials before I was able to gradually weaken my grip on her hand, before she began to listen for the click, look for the lighted bulb, and open her mouth so as to receive the cookie. It required three additional sets of ten trials before I could allow her to work the lever on her own, feeling reasonably confident she would not tear at her skin. It required twenty further trials for her to learn that she was to wait until I showed her a large card with a cookie glued to its surface before pressing the lever. It required only three trials for her to learn to wait for the presented card, press the lever, and feed herself the small piece of cookie that I had placed by the lever box. It required only one trial for the learning to transfer to the classroom. The box accompanied her to the physical therapy sessions. The therapist worked with her for a few moments, then provided her with the box and the piece of cookie after she pressed the lever. The speech therapist used it as she evaluated a more complex augmentative communication system. She taped a plastic cup to a separate card and showed the child that the same lever could bring her a drink if she desired. The frequency of biting, in school, under specific cuing conditions, decreased rapidly. Plans were drawn to show the child's mother how to use the lever and the cards. It was only a beginning, but a hopeful one. The long range goal was to lessen the child's reliance on the lever box, to show her that the lever was not the only means to access what she valued. None of us were able to predict how long that would take, but we remained optimistic. In a relatively short period of time, she had learned a way, other than biting, to control a small portion of her environment's reactions. It would be nice to believe that the child felt better about herself as a result of her newly acquired skills. Time and her future remained her allies.

HELPING INDIVIDUALS HELP THEMSELVES

When you work with an individual, among the many other things you must think about, ask yourself whether the person *knows how to access his or her environment's payoffs.* Difficult as it may be, look beyond an individual's "undesired" behavior. Look instead at the individual's motoric and communicative strengths. Identify a desired, productive, volitional response the individual can manifest with comfort and reliability. Determine what the individual values, and slowly, patiently demonstrate through modelling and practice how that identified response can allow the individual to have something to say about how his or her environment works. Initially, the individual may resist the change you are requiring. As we said, many of us do not like to give up old habits. But if you've done your homework well, you might be able to teach alternative ways of responding that will open new doors to an individual's world allowing him or her to experience much that presently he or she does not know exists. Ironically, if we fail to provide reasons for the needed exploration to occur, individuals may see little reason to try new things: People will stay with what they know, what is comfortable, and the subsequent absence of growth will make them appear more "disabled" than they really are.

I recognize fully that interventions as described with the biting child take considerable time and effort. In special schools and similar facilities, we have to determine how to free professionals from their other duties so as to provide the initially required one-on-one assistance. However, our initial investment, if we are successful, will ultimately reduce the need for such intensive remediation. The biting child's teacher and aide no longer had to spend many hours of the school day protecting the child from herself. The child's progress enabled them to devote more time to the other children (and themselves).

SUPPORT AND ENCOURAGEMENT

A second "special" circumstance that is associated with positive feedback is one more familiar and less complicated. It involves the use of attention as a means of support and encouragement. I previously mentioned that when employing attention/recognition as a means to help a behavior get started and be maintained, the attention should follow closely the occurrence of the desired behavior. There will be occasions, however, where the same attention serves a more important purpose than felt recognition and appreciation. It provides individuals with a sign that you are with them, supporting them, while they experience or acquire a new or difficult behavior. It can be seen when the caring teacher, through warm words and soft touching, helps a student through a task that may be new and frightening. It can also be seen when a loving parent assists the child with his first step on a carpeted floor or his first nibble of a strange-tasting food. While the benefits for the above may seem obvious, it is sometimes overlooked. I bring this issue to your attention for I do not wish for you to believe that expressed attention, recognition, and appreciation must always follow a desired effort. It can be just as beneficial before and during an individual's exposure to an untried or frightening circumstance. I want you to realize that although there exists well-established guidelines as to how to use much of what we have discussed, there also exists variations that must be considered when viewing the uniqueness of individuals and the situations within which they find themselves. I'd like you to remember that there is no magic inherent within the procedures we have discussed to this point, that artificial, positive payoffs have their place, but they are not end-alls or cure-alls, that "when . . . then" agreements, funny money, contingent attention, and the like, are to be parts of programs and not programs in themselves.

SUBTLETIES

It shouldn't come as any surprise that sometimes individuals fail to manifest a desired behavior for the sole reason that they don't know what to do or are not certain how to do it. Other times, individuals may know what to do but are not certain where to do it. And occasionally, a desired behavior may not be manifested because they don't know anyone wants them to do it. Under such conditions, "bells" and "banjos" take a distant back seat to the ingenuity of the care-giver's guiding hand intended to teach individuals desired responses.

"I DIDN'T KNOW YOU WANTED ME TO DO THAT!"

Edmund Halley's comet visits our planet roughly every 75 years. If a person is truly fortunate, he or she might have the opportunity of observing the phenomenon twice in a life time. The same person, as teacher, parent or other professional, might observe another equally rare occurrence once or twice during his or her working years: an individual failing to manifest a desired behavior because she didn't know anyone wanted her to do it. Whenever I am called in to assist an individual, I always assume that such a discovery is at hand. "Do you know what your parents want you to do?" I ask the youngster, whether she speaks or not. "How does your teacher want you to behave?" I ask every student I sit with. "Do you have any idea what anyone wants you to do?" I always inquire. When the rare "I didn't know they wanted me to do that," occurs,

I turn to the individual and say, "Do us both a favor. Try doing the following. . . ." It never hurts to ask; nothing is lost in the process; everything can be gained. No "quickies," no trumpets, no contingencies. Just words that ask the individual to bring his or her behavior under his or her own control. It doesn't happen often, but every once in a while, the individual, gloriously, answers, "Okay," and proceeds to do what everyone wants. What a pleasure!

SOMETIMES PLANNED FEEDBACK
IS BEST AVOIDED . . .

"You're saying that there are times when artificial payoffs of any manner do not enter the situation," the parent suggested.

"Absolutely," I answered. "There are times when an individual truly does not know what to do or how to do it. Payoffs are not the issue. Our teaching, guidance, and support take precedence."

"Sometimes we have to make ourselves available, like just being there with no planned purpose in mind," she said.

"There are times when we must sit quietly and listen to words, understand and accept expressed feelings, provide unconditional support and love, show appreciation for someone's being rather than his doing. An individual who is momentarily experiencing pain from disappointment, rejection, or perceived failure, needs acceptance, perhaps guidance, certainly support, and certainly not a contrived contract. I have seen change and growth occur more from the establishment of a trusting friendship, more from an offered, helping, caring, outstretched hand, than from an offered, manufactured item."

With a smile, she replied, "Helping an individual understand that he is appreciated for what he is. Helping him build a strong sense of self by letting him know that he is important, special, and valued."

"To be honest, I've never fully understood the total meaning of such terms as 'self-worth,' 'self-esteem,' or 'self-concept.' The terms are often bandied around by professionals like swirling snowflakes in a blizzard. Regardless of definition, what seems apparent is that feelings of positive worth, the power that comes from perceived self-value, the sense of personal importance, the knowledge that one can succeed at what is held as significant, are, in part, the cornerstones that can help an individual take a chance at moving forward. Sometimes, through no fault or plan, those 'states of mind' are no closer to the touch than our world's nearest star. Artificial payoffs, at best, are intended to bring them within reach. They were never developed to become the sole of what one reached for."

──────────── . . . SOMETIMES IT IS ESSENTIAL ────────────

"The natural environment can work in strange ways," I continued. "It can fool an individual into thinking that adaptive, purposive, functional behaviors, like biting, not eating, not caring, not working at a task, are the only ways to achieve what is valued. Our goal is to alter that thinking; to show the individual that the natural environment can support alternative ways of behaving. For that to occur, we must show the individual that an alternative exists, and we often have to provide him with a reason to give it a chance. A carefully planned, provided 'bell" or 'banjo" just might be what the individual needs to feel comfortable taking the first step skyward. Once accomplished, he might be willing to take the second step on his own."

──────────────── NOTES ────────────────

1. Salk, L. (1972). *What every child would like his parents to know* (p. 162). New York: Warner.
2. Homan, W. E. (1969). *Child sense* (p. 15). New York: Bantam.

──────────────── SUMMARY ────────────────

KEEP IN MIND

1. Before using any positive reinforcement feedback, consider the following:
   a. Make certain clear behavior-pairs have been established.
   b. Make certain the undesired behavior is not receiving any positive feedback.
   c. Make certain you have an active, potent reinforcer available.
2. When initiating a reinforcement program, try to provide your positive

feedback immediately after the occurrence of the desired behavior. The phrase, "Catch the child doing something good," should read: "Catch the child immediately!"

3. When employing an artificial reinforcement program, make certain individuals know which of their behaviors produced your positive feedback. Describe as clearly as possible which desired response was appreciated. "That was a great answer!" tells the student what you appreciated. "I liked the way you listen to what I had to say," indicates what you would like the student to do again in the future. Most of us, it seems, do like to know what we did that pleased the important people in our lives. Happily, many of your students will see you as being very important.

4. Experiment with various "When . . . then" quickies when faced with sudden, yet clear, problems. Watch or listen carefully to students: they will let you know what they value. Determine what you want them to do. When applicable, put the two components together: "When you do __, then you can do __." A very simple "When . . . then" quickie can often prevent a minor difficulty from becoming a major problem.

5. Contrived, artificial reinforcement programs are used only when the natural environment has failed to teach and/or maintain desired behavior. When you are faced with a student who is failing to manifest a desired behavior, you have two choices: (a) you can ignore the situation, hoping somehow it will right itself, or (b) you can jump into the arena: You can provide the student with a reason to put out the effort; you can try to help the desired behavior get started, hoping that the natural environment will soon exert its influence. Those of us committed to the welfare of children rarely choose option (a).

6. Concentrate more on what *is* happening rather than what you believe (or hope) *should* happen. Your remedial programs will need to be based on what is occurring now!

7. When working with the "special" populations, be particularly alerted to the concept of "learned helplessness." Try to help parents see the importance for developing active, forward-moving programs; programs based on the expectations that children can succeed, that they can grow. Don't allow a "handicapping" condition to weaken parental efforts. "Feeling sorry" for a child rarely helps the child grow.

8. When working with your chosen population, make certain you demonstrate to your subjects how they can access that which is of value to them. If individuals do not know how to access their reinforcers through desired means, they will learn how to access their reinforcers through what *you* may perceive to be undesired means. If that is not to your liking, take the time to model and practice alternatively more desired ways that will lead to the acquisition of what is valued.

Life's Funny Money

| 5.1 | Write a brief paper showing how the components and purposes for a "token system" operate in real life. Make sure you cover the following:

      a. behavior-pairs
      b. types of tokens
      c. back-up reinforcers
      d. delivery systems
      e. penalties
      f. exchange system

High-Probability Behaviors

| 5.2 | Psychologist David Premack is noted for an important principle. Find out the specifics of the principle and how they are used in classrooms. Question: How are the "When . . . then" quickie and Premack's Principle related?

CONSIDER AS WE LOOK AHEAD

1. If you fail to provide students with a reason to behave desirably, and they see little reason to do the same, you will have opened the door for them to obtain what they value by behaving undesirably.
2. Undesirable behavior often interferes with growth and development; it is this interference that warrants our efforts to redirect the undesired actions.
3. We now turn our attention to undesired behaviors. You will see:
    a. Undesired behaviors serve a purpose.
    b. You will need to determine the nature of that purpose.
    c. You must help students find a reason to behave desirably.
4. Fortunately, there are several ways to influence undesired behaviors by concentrating on their desired counterparts.
5. Often, however, the undesired behaviors must be dealt with directly. We will now look at several procedures designed to influence the undesired side of the behavior-pairs.

6

THE NATURAL ENVIRONMENT'S INFLUENCE ON UNDESIRED BEHAVIOR

SEEING UNDESIRED BEHAVIORS

Occasions will arise where students will place themselves in jeopardy as a direct result of their own actions. Without intervention, the behaviors can begin to affect detrimentally the students' academic and social progress. Unattended, the behaviors can begin to acquire a place and purpose within the students' life space, perhaps narrowing their very future. Often students do not realize that alternative, more productive ways of behaving can provide them with the values they seek. One of our roles is to help them see those alternatives.

"Can we go back to the young girl who was biting her wrist?" the psychologist asked. "I've been thinking of her situation as it compared to Jesse's not eating. If I have been following you correctly, then I believe the two cases have much in common. Both behaviors, for example, were undesirable, at least as viewed by the adults in the children's life space. Both behaviors, from the children's perspective, served a purpose: Both produced a change in their environments' feedback."

"The biting child most definitely exercised control over her environment's feedback. She learned how to remove herself from selected activities, and her behavior produced measurable adult attention. Jesse, of course, did what he could to avoid pain. His noneating also controlled some of his environment's feedback," I responded.

"But the behaviors were quite extreme," he interjected.

UNDESIRED BEHAVIORS DEVELOP
SLOWLY, UNINTENTIONALLY

"Yes, but it took time for them to become so severe. More than likely, both behaviors insidiously reached their extremes due to accidental circumstances."

"How so?"

"Neither family intended for their respective child to acquire the behaviors that required assistance. Whatever produced the behaviors started slowly, unnoticeably. A child doesn't learn to bite herself overnight, and the likelihood is strong that Jesse's internal and external environments gradually taught him how to avoid the painful feedback."

"In other words, you and the other professionals entered the picture long after the behaviors had started," the psychologist said.

"That's right, and it is an important point. By the time any of us see the manifestation of a specific undesired behavior, that behavior already has been influenced by many environmental factors, most often unremembered and unidentifiable; any *present undesired behavior*, no matter its severity, has been built upon less severe behaviors."

"Could you describe how the above could happen with the two children?"

"I can try to piece the puzzles together, but remember, I'm only speculating from my perspective. Another consultant's view through the window will be different. The specifics involving family dynamics are almost always lost over time; few, if any, parents document each and every problem observed with their youngsters, much less their reactions to the difficulties. In the beginning, the behaviors may seem inconsequential, thus not worthy of special notation. The biting child, when very young, perhaps objected to something her mother requested of her, let's say going to bed one evening or eating something different for breakfast or just taking a bath. The child may have cried enough to have the mother rescind her request."

"The child was able to avoid an unwanted situation by crying."

"Perhaps. Then, at a later point in time, Mother may have become impatient with the crying and insisted that her child comply with whatever was requested. Another child might have complied. This child didn't. Rather than acquiesing, the child's crying escalated to a boisterous tantrum . . .''

"And the mother gave into the child's demands. If so, the child learned that crying would no longer work. To get what she wanted, she would have to try another approach—tantrum," the psychologist suggested.

"Very possibly. Then, still later in time, Mother may have refused to give into the tantrum. The child, angry, frustrated, consciously exploring an alternative or trying hard to tell her mother what she wanted, I don't think anyone can be certain, bit her own wrist and either produced a mark or blood."

"Which Mother could not handle," the psychologist said. "Scared for the child, she gave in again. Accidentally, the child learned that biting, and not the previously successful tantruming, would result in what she wanted."

"Accidentally, the natural environment taught the child that lesson."

"Do you believe Jesse learned his noneating behavior in a similar fashion?"

INTERACTIONS BETWEEN BEHAVIOR AND THE NATURAL ENVIRONMENT

"I can't be certain, but based on his parents' reports, Jesse first tried to avoid the pain from eating by turning his head away from spoons. Then he tried to close his mouth tightly. That didn't work either. Then he tried, unsuccessfully, to push the spoon away from his mouth. Eventually, he learned that screaming and thrashing resulted in a *brief* respite from food. His parents, out of necessity, and not realizing what their son was experiencing, still fed him despite the 'tantrums.' For a long time, Jesse was not able to discover a way to avoid his experienced pain. That, of course, did not occur until the physiological problem was resolved. In both cases, the behaviors started on a small scale, seemingly benign. By the time I observed them, they were no longer benign."

"The acquisition process was the same, but Jesse didn't choose biting. Instead, he closed his mouth, thrashed, or screamed when trying to avoid what he didn't wish to experience," the psychologist stated.

"Those behaviors worked for him," I indicated.

"Any ideas why one child chooses one behavior and another chooses something totally different?" the psychologist asked.

"I'd only be able to speculate again, and I doubt I could support

my guesses," I responded.
"Regardless, the behaviors had to be changed."

DIFFERENT INTERVENTIONS: A GLANCE

"For the sake of the children, yes."
"Which presents a couple of interesting observations. The noneating and biting were decreased using different methods. The noneating was stopped by providing positive payoffs for eating, and the biting was reduced by teaching the child to initially communicate through pressing a lever. Once the undesired behaviors were stopped, the desired alternatives came under the influence of natural, positive payoffs, different payoffs than what had earlier been experienced: Jesse began to gain weight, presumably felt better, and presumably found eating to be inherently pleasurable; the biting child began to discover a way to make her needs known, a way to positively manipulate her environment. The children discovered other reasons to behave desirably, other means to successfully influence their environments."
"I would see it that way," I responded.
The psychologist paused for a moment. "Can we change directions for a minute? There's something I wish to ask you."
"Certainly."

THE EFFECTS OF "PUNISHING"
UNDESIRED BEHAVIOR: A GLANCE

6.1

"What would have happened had you chosen to simply punish the undesired side of the behavior-pairs: Jesse's *not* eating and the preschooler's *biting*. The behaviors were 'life-threatening' in Jesse's case, and assuredly debilitating for the young girl. They had to be stopped."
"That is an important question," I responded. "I'll share with you that the preschooler's mother was upset with me because I *didn't* 'punish' the child, specifically, didn't slap her child's wrist when she first bit herself in my presence. The mother resisted my explanations when I told her that I needed to see if there were any *conditions* under which the child would *not* bite, that I had to begin speculating on what purpose the behavior held for the child, and that I had to observe how her environment responded to her when the biting and any acceptable, alternative behavior occurred.

Unable to convince the woman that a smack might be counterproductive, that it was something I was not comfortable with, that it would be totally unacceptable to the school administrators and teachers, I asked her if she had ever slapped her daughter when observing the biting.''

''Many times,'' she answered impatiently.

''Without meaning to be disrespectful to her, I just pointed to the woman's child when she once again bit herself. Then I looked at the mother: 'It hasn't been very effective, has it?' I asked. She reluctantly allowed me to watch what was happening.''

THE INDIVIDUAL'S PERCEPTION

''I'm surprised the mother's many slaps did not stop the biting,'' the psychologist stated.

''Why surprised?''

''Being slapped *must be aversive,* something the child wouldn't want repeated,'' he said, more as a question than a statement.

''You haven't done your homework,'' I chided.

''I've missed something?''

''Probably forgot something,'' I answered. ''Let me ask you this: is an M & M candy a positive payoff for a child?''

''Maybe, maybe not,'' he said after thinking quietly.

''How about a spoken word of appreciation?''

''It might be, but then it might not be.''

''How about going outside and looking for bugs?''

He laughed. ''You're right, I forget. Well, I didn't really forget,'' he said, quickly correcting himself. ''I just didn't transfer what I had learned from positive payoffs to negative payoffs. The *individual* is the one who makes the determination as to what is positive *or* negative. A slap might be a 'punisher' for one child, but not for another. Having to forgo a particular activity might be very unpleasant for one person, but acceptable, even positive for another. I understand.''

''We need to keep in mind that just as there are no universal positive forms of feedback, there do not appear to be any universal 'punishers,' feedback perceived by everyone to be aversive.''

''Not even something as radical as electric shock?'' the psychologist questioned.

''Not even that.''

Even when electric shock [is] used . . . differences in personal histories make the definition of 'aversive' much more complex . . . Some people report that shock has a pleasant 'tingling' effect and they act accordingly.[1]

"One of the *least* important reasons why I didn't choose to punish the young child's biting is that I had no notion of what she would perceive to be aversive. 'Pain' applied by an outside source might not have been viewed by her as 'painful.' There's nothing magical about the term 'punishment,' " I continued. "Many professionals approach the issue of decreasing behavior rather haphazardly. They assume that various environmental reactions *will be* 'punishing' without considering the individual's perception of the reaction or the individual's history that produces that perception. More important, had I simply punished the behavior without looking at numerous other factors, I wouldn't have known what the environment was doing that maintained the undesired behavior. If I had successfully reduced the biting, without dealing with the total environment, there's an excellent chance the child would have discovered another means, perhaps equally undesirable, to manipulate her surroundings."

"You might not have discovered the purpose for the behavior," the psychologist responded, now suddenly subdued.

Undesired Behaviors Have
a Desired Counterpart

"Precisely. Further, **reducing an undesired behavior without determining what should take its place is having the cart before the horse. With the biting-child, it would have been easy to conclude that 'not-biting' would be the desired alternative, but 'not-biting' as you may recall, is not an active behavior; it's a passive nonbehavior.** The youngster would have gained little help in learning what to do—what to do that would have been in her best interests. Not much progress occurs with that approach."

"Had you simply applied punishment, you would have been guilty of fixing the behavior in isolation," the professional said, more to himself.

"Very possibly. Sometimes that has to be the approach of choice. When an undesired behavior is life-threatening, there's often little time to gather data reflecting what is happening within the life space. Under such a condition, you might have to stop the behavior first, then figure out both its purpose and what responsibilities the environment holds for the behavior. But imagine the consequences for Jesse had I 'punished' his not eating

| 6.2 |

while he still had a problem with his gall bladder. That would have been disastrous for him.

"Attempting to reduce and redirect undesired behaviors," I continued, "always requires careful thinking and planning. We have several procedures available to bring about a reduction of an undesired behavior. Their availability, however, doesn't give us license to use them casually, without thought to what we are doing, and why we're doing it. For sure, a sharp reprimand might stop a behavior in its tracks, momentarily. Requiring that an individual sit in a chair, removed from others, when he screams or has tantrums might bring about a brief cessation to the screaming. Withholding a privilege when a youngster 'acts out' might temporarily redirect an aggressive reaction . . ."

"Medicating a youngster for failing to attend or follow directions might make a child more compliant, less a disruptive force," the psychologist interjected.

"Yes. But if the disruptive, disturbing, undesired behaviors are seen only in isolation, unattached to work assignments and studies, 'owned' by, and occurring only as a function of, the 'transgressor,' the procedures may provide little more than transient relief *for the adults* who are most bothered by the behaviors. The benefits for the child will likely be problematic."

THE DYNAMICS OF UNDESIRED BEHAVIOR

6.3

Undesired behavior is always reflective of something, always connected to something. It always tells us something about individuals and the world in which they live. It never occurs in isolation. It always has purpose. If it is *not* a *direct* result of a physiological condition, a condition that stems from a physical problem or a supposed genetic predisposition, then regardless of its severity, it is learned and brings the individual feedback that is valued.

UNDESIRED BEHAVIORS WITHIN THE LIFE SPACE

It is imperative that we observe the undesired behavior as it occurs within the individual's life space. We should note the cuing conditions under which it occurs and those under which it doesn't.

<u>c</u>

<u>c</u>...P...B..fb

Our observations need to be both microscopic and holistic. If we can identify which cues seem to set the stage for the behavior, we might be able to resolve the problem by rearranging the cues, by informing the individual the cues are about to present themselves, or by having the individual practice alternative ways of behaving in the presence of the cues.

"An example?" the parent asked.

"Certainly. I had known a 6 foot, 1 inch, 19-year-old, developmentally disabled young man for several years. Ordinarily, this strong, nonverbal individual posed no behavioral difficulty, in terms of aggressing, for those responsible for his welfare. He seemed to sense when he was losing self-control and would walk to a corner of his classroom or his bedroom in the group home and sit for roughly 30 minutes before returning to the activity he was involved with. The staff rarely had to guide him to a quiet corner, and he required physical restraint only twice in a four-year period. Recently, he had changed living quarters from the group home to a supervised apartment that he shared with a similarly aged young man. The new living arrangement had necessitated a move to a new high school that served significantly more students than his previous educational facility. His classroom was located on the bottom floor of the building where the environment was quieter and more easily supervised. I had received a call from his new teacher after he had become violent on two separate occasions, collectively assaulting his teacher, several regular students, the school principal and one of the high school's security guards. No one was hurt; they seemed to understand that the young man had not intentionally desired to cause injury.

"After I spoke with the teacher and her staff, it became apparent that a common thread tied the two incidents together. The first outburst had occurred by a drinking fountain. The regular students, during break, hurriedly converged on the fountain without noticing that the young man, guided by his teacher, was about to take a drink. Suddenly surrounded by the noisy throng, the young man attempted to flee from the commotion but was unable to do so because of the many bodies around him. When several of the regular students tried to calm him, their efforts only frightened him more. Eventually, with help, he was led to a quiet room off the principal's office. Two hours were required before he gained control of himself. The second incident occurred several days later as he entered an assembly. Again, unexpectedly, he was thrust into a large, noisy crowd of students who were waiting for the assembly meeting to begin. His agitation was shorter, but as intense. Several men were required to remove him from the auditorium and guide him to his classroom. He calmed within a half-an-hour and engaged himself in an activity his teacher had provided.

"After the young man's teacher recognized the commonalities of the two situations, she avoided placing him unexpectedly in the midst of the laughter and commotion common in the school's hallways. Together, we developed a plan to gradually introduce him to such cuing situations for it was believed that he had to learn to tolerate, to the best of his ability, a modicum of noise and movement that would be present both at school and an eventual work setting."

Sometimes cues that set the stage for undesired behavior are not as obvious as those that influenced the 19-year-old. A new, unpredictable person who enters an individual's life space might be sufficient to produce a change in behavior. An altered routine of predictable daily activities or the behavior of a classmate or sibling might be all that's necessary to bring about a dramatic change in behavior. Most assuredly, a change in how an individual feels, such as an ear ache, can also produce the same end. An essential *first* step in remediating an undesired action, therefore, requires determining what antecedent circumstances seem to hold influence over the behavior. Often, a few days of careful observation will help us identify important cues.

UNDESIRED BEHAVIORS HAVE PURPOSE

In addition to considering what cues might be influencing an undesired behavior, it is also necessary to consider a second issue: As difficult as it may be to reconcile, learned undesired behavior is always adaptive and purposive.

"The behavior provides the individual with some feedback that is valued," the parent suggested.

"That's right."

"No matter how disruptive or severe?"

"In my judgment, the behavior is still reflective of the individual's attempt at adapting to his present environment."

"Would you go as far as saying that the behavior is a *function of* the present environmental events?" the psychologist asked.

"Help me with the phrase 'function of,'" I asked him.

"I think by saying 'function of' I mean 'caused by,'" he explained.

DIFFERENCES BETWEEN CAUSING
AND MAINTAINING BEHAVIOR

"Before addressing your question, **it is necessary to distinguish the difference between behavior being 'caused by' and 'maintained by' certain circumstances,**" I answered. "The term 'cause' generally refers to conditions or events that were responsible for producing, initially, some 'effect.' The 'cause,' then, could be viewed as the precipitating event, the circumstance that *started* whatever effect we are now observing."

6.4

"Like a fire being started by, or caused by, a burning match," the parent offered.

"Or vomiting being initially caused by ingesting tainted food," the psychologist said.

"Both correct. But the burning fire and persistent vomiting, although caused by identified events, *will not be maintained* by those same events. A fire is maintained by combustible materials, and vomiting that has no physical cause can be maintained by environmental feedback."

"So while undesired behavior might be historically *caused* by some circumstance it might, today, be *maintained* by any number of environmental variables," the psychologist summarized.

"Exactly."

"When you suggest that an undesired behavior, no matter how disruptive, is adaptive, you're speaking of the behavior's relation to the person's present day environment," the man continued.

"Present-day, as well as the individual's recollections of how his environment previously responded to, and influenced, his behavior in the near or distant past," I added. "Keep in mind that the individual has the ability to predict how his *present* environment is likely to respond to his actions. This ability to predict is related to his remembered *past* experiences with cues and feedback."

"I understand the distinction you are drawing between behavior being 'caused by' and 'maintained by' events," the parent said, "but I'm intrigued by this whole business of causes. Like so many terms, we seem to use the word 'cause' almost as though we always know what they are. Are we that certain of the causes for undesired behavior?"

CAUSES ARE ELUSIVE

"I'm afraid the identification of true causes for undesired behavior is more difficult than most of us realize," I indicated.

The causes of erratic, disturbing, debilitating human behavior have always been a puzzle, which now seems insoluble. All that is clear is that such behavior stems from a complex interaction of many factors. These factors have long been known, but the exact role of each has never been fully understood.[2]

Most educators and researchers would agree that it is impossible, even erroneous, to assign a single cause to effects as complex as . . . academic achievement . . . [and other important behaviors].[3]

"Despite the difficulty, if we can identify a cause for a behavior, wouldn't we obtain important information?" the parent asked.

"Absolutely. As I mentioned earlier, it was critical that we discovered the effects thalidomide had on the developing embryo. Determining the presence of a significant hearing loss is invaluable. Recognizing the influence an additional 21st chromosome can have on physical development was important. But the clarity of those 'causes' are exceptions. Most causes, if indeed they exist, are nearly impossible to identify. We can, and have, invented a whole slew of them, but identifying and inventing are not one in the same."

"The real issue is whether the 'causes' can be reversed," the psychologist said. "Identifying them is one thing; changing them is another."

SEE BEHAVIOR AS IT PRESENTLY EXISTS

"Which brings us back to the issue of what may be maintaining the undesired behavior today," the parent stated.

"If our hypothesized 'causes' can neither be verified nor reversed, the practitioner must concentrate on the present effects the natural environment appears to be having on the target behavior," I suggested. "To do otherwise is a waste of valuable time. Rest assured, we will always continue our search for causes, but while the scientific search goes on, we have people who are in need of assistance now."

UNDESIRED BEHAVIOR PRODUCES FEEDBACK

The *second step* when remediating an undesired behavior is to observe the behavior and carefully note how the environment is responding to it. If we keep in mind that behavior is adaptive and purposive, we will be more inclined to see the present relationship between the behavior and its surrounding environment.

```
        c
    c....P...B..↑B
```

Again, the issue is not what is "causing" the behavior, rather what may be maintaining it today.

When noting the environmental feedback it is necessary to describe our observations in neutral terms—simply write down what reactions are occurring. The individual will tell or show us what value exists within the feedback. The *third step* involved with remediating undesired behaviors requires, therefore, that we determine the individual's perception of the value of the feedback. We can sit with individuals and ask them if they like what's happening . . .

```
        c
    c....P...B..f b
```

. . . or we can watch individuals' behavior . . .

```
        c
    c....P...B..f b
```

. . . and observe, given the feedback that is occurring,

```
        c
    c....P...B..↑B
```

whether the behavior continues or whether its frequency decreases. As stated several times, *individuals* decide the value of the feedback. Their words and/or behavior will tell us what is valued and what meaning, if any, the feedback holds for them.

IS THERE A DESIRED ALTERNATIVE AVAILABLE? A GLANCE

The *fourth step* in our remediation program is to determine if the individual knows of, and has the ability to manifest, a desired alternative behavior. If he or she doesn't know of one, don't expect it to occur. If

| 6.5 |

he or she does know, but the environment fails to provide positive feedback when it does occur, it would be foolish to expect it to continue. If the person knows what is expected, but *doesn't* have the necessary skills or experiences to demonstrate the desired alternative, then *our* expectation that the behavior "should" occur is a major error.

UNDESIRED BEHAVIOR IN PERSPECTIVE

The most clear-thinking, patient, logical person, professionally trained or otherwise, often loses perspective when faced with an annoying, disruptive, or dangerous undesired behavior. All that seems to matter is that the behavior must be stopped, *now!* The behavior achieves its center-stage position, illuminated by glaring lights—it's all that's seen. The felt frustration, anger, fear, and exhaustion experienced in the face of the behavior can blind us to the position the behavior occupies within the life space. Indeed, the life space, the natural environment vanishes. The felt emotions can blind us to the whole individual; the good things he or she does also vanish. All that is seen is the undesired behavior, in isolation. Often it is treated as though it exists by itself, owned by the individual, unaffected by surroundings, unaffected by past experiences, unaffected by present circumstances. The concepts of adaptability, of purpose, of functionality, give way to judgments of "maladaptive, inappropriate, or dysfunctional." Individuals manifesting the behavior are not viewed as doing what they can, perhaps all they know, perhaps all they've been taught, to acquire what is valued; they are seen as diseased or disturbed, labeled, categorized, and boxed. All done with the best of intentions. All done with expediency.

Undesired behavior is only behavior. It does not warrant being elevated beyond that. It is something the individual is doing. It is not all the individual is doing. It is connected and associated with a much larger picture than itself.

In the six years the 12-year-old boy had been in the school district, he had been placed in, and eventually removed from, nearly every special education program the district had at its disposal. Because of his age, the district was now compelled to transfer him to a middle-school, and into another program. The administrators knew they were merely passing the proverbial buck. The youngster, in fact, had always been a puzzle. On the negative side of the ledger, he did not speak; he had a documented history of being abusive toward his teachers and himself, and frequently he ran from a classroom and had to be chased down a hallway to prevent him from running into a busy street. He ignored most directions, refused to sit with his classmates during a group exercise, choosing instead to sit by himself in a corner. If pressure was applied to have him join the group, he would attempt to bite the teacher or himself. If circumstances required the slightest adjustment to a classroom routine, he, again, would manifest his aggressive behaviors.

Conversely, there were times when he would grab a pencil and legibly write his name, address, and phone number on a piece of paper. He could solve complex addition problems; he could read, and by pointing to words or nodding his head, he could answer questions about the reading material. For a brief period of time, during the mid-point of his educational experiences, he had been assigned to a special program and classroom that contained a personal computer. If given the opportunity, he would sit at the computer and successfully, enjoyably, run education programs designed to facilitate reading, comprehension, vocabulary building, and mathematical problem solving. Records indicated that when he was asked to allow another student to use the computer, he would bite himself or the adult who had made the request. His father had left the family when the student was very young. The boy lived with his mother and grandmother, both of whom expressed deep love and concern for him. Neither, however, were able to handle his aggressive acting-out; they learned not to make any requests; they allowed him to do whatever he desired. As a result, when he arrived at home from school, he would change into his pajamas and sit in front of the television set until dinner. Afterwards, he would return to the television until he went to bed. It had become an accepted routine.

THE COMPLETE CHILD FORGOTTEN

There had been many formal psychological evaluations performed over the years. Invariably, because of scores obtained on "intelligence" tests, he was diagnosed as "retarded." One examiner said he was "autistic." Others indicated that he was "neurologically impaired." Many opinions were offered as to which of the district's programs would best fit the youngster's needs, but with the exception of the phrase "provide structure and reinforcement," little direct help was offered to his teachers. As the years passed, the natural environment pushed him further into the abyss that I was to see.

Occasionally, a special education administrator from the district would call my office and ask if I had a graduate student who would be willing to work with some of the district's pupils. I always attempted to accommodate the requests, for the work provided excellent experience for my students, as well as providing a service to the district's children. Most often, I would have a PhD student go to the school and help the particular child, but it happened that when the phone call came, all my students were busy with various activities and could not free themselves. However, a young undergraduate who had taken one of my classes came to me expressing interest in gaining experience with special children. Since the district's administrator had provided only the briefest picture of the child she had in mind, neither my student nor I knew of the severity of the problem. We both would learn quickly.

My undergraduate student called me after observing the child for 12 hours over a three-day period. "I think I need to see you," she said, her voice colored with urgency. "I'm lost." She came to my office that afternoon. She walked in as though numb from head to toe; sat with the same demeanor; handed me her data sheets with eyes threatening to pop from their sockets. "He's under a table almost all day long!" she said, abruptly breaking her silence. "He goes to music for 30 minutes; has lunch for 30 minutes; then he goes under a table, lies down with his hands covering his face. The teacher goes to him every once in a while; asks him if he wants to join the group or work on a project. He doesn't say anything. He hides his face. If she takes his hand, he bites his arm. The teacher walks away. He's under the table for hours!"

"Under a table?" I asked incredulously. "Hours?"

"Hours, under the table," she replied as though the phrase was on a tape recorder.

"Did the teacher tell you what she wants you to do?"

"Yeah, get him out from under the table!" she stated, shaking her head in disbelief. "I'm supposed to get him to do work; get him out from under the table, have him sit down next to the table, and get him to do something. How am I supposed to do that?" she asked, her hands trembling. "Did I tell you he bites?"

"Yes, you did," I answered calmly. "What does the teacher do when he bites?"

"She either walks away or she and her aid make him sit in an empty clothes closet that has no doors. He *likes* to sit in the clothes closet! It's like *he* leads them to it. He stays there for a few minutes; then he takes himself back under the table!"

"Okay, now relax, you're doing fine. Let's look at your data."
After reviewing the incredible information, I looked at her. "What
do you think you should do first?"

SIMPLE SOLUTIONS ARE RARELY EFFECTIVE

Somewhat composed, she answered, "If I want him to sit, I've got
to give him a reason to get out from the table. Should I try M & M's
or something like that?"

"Can't hurt. Try it."

"He doesn't like M & M's," she said returning the following day.
"He doesn't like Fruit Loops, orange slices, raisins, or pretzels. I
don't think he likes me!"

"Do you have any idea of something he values, something he
might be willing to work for?"

"Nothing, other than he likes to stay under the table."

"I want you to go back to the classroom, talk with the teacher to
see if she has any ideas of what he might be willing to work for.
Watch him carefully, then come see me this afternoon."

"The teacher has no ideas," she told me after sitting down in
my office. "She removed the table, however. Now he lies down in
the coat closet all day!"

"I'll meet you in the classroom tomorrow morning," I said.

THE ARENA

The youngster was lying on his stomach in the alcove that had
once been a open closet for young students' jackets. Had it not
been chosen as a self-imposed haven by a troubling child, it would
have been without purpose. But the child was there, as far
removed from his teacher and classmates as possible. I sat in a
chair in the middle of the room and watched him carefully. As my
student had described, his hands were covering his face, but upon
close inspection, only partially covering his eyes. He could see
what he wanted, when he wanted. I, now, was the target of his
gaze. When our eyes met for the briefest of moments I waved a
greeting. He immediately turned his head toward the wall, able to
see nothing but the shadows of his palms. Slowly, I walked to him
and sat on the floor by his side. I gently rubbed his back and said a
few words, watching carefully for his reaction. He quickly turned,
almost jumping into my face. His eyes ran quickly but thoroughly
over my face, then he collapsed to the floor once again closing

himself behind his hands. I stayed by his side for a few more minutes, talking and rubbing his back. He did not look at me again until I stood and walked back to my chair. He, indeed, watched my every move.

FIND AN ACTIVITY THAT PRODUCES
SUCCESS FOR THE STUDENT

The teacher's aid came over to me. "I've been with him for two years. The teacher is new; she's the second teacher this year," the aide said quietly. "None of us are sure what to do with him."

"I'm certain he can be difficult," I said sincerely.

"Not always," she quickly responded. "Sometimes he's an angel. He reads, you know. And writes. I've seen him do math problems," she said as though wishing he would do them all again.

"He does what!" I exclaimed.

"Yes, and I've seen him work a computer."

"Give me a break," I uttered with exasperation. "He reads, writes, and works a computer," I repeated as I looked at the young boy who was now watching us through opened fingers. "Thanks," I said to the aide as she returned to several of the other children. Then to myself: "He reads, writes, works a computer, but he spends most of his time either under a table or lying in a closet." I turned to find the aide. "Where is his computer?" I asked, the question suddenly burning in my brain.

"The team didn't feel it was helpful," she explained in a tone that showed her disagreement.

"Actually," the teacher said, "the team took it with them to another school."

I faced the teacher and asked, "Do you mind if I try a few things. This is a crazy situation."

I stood and walked rapidly toward the child. There was no way I was going to allow him to atrophy in a closet. Power! I had it and I was going to use it. He saw me coming, his hands now down by his sides. I took one of his hands. "You are coming with me to the table!" I said firmly. He stood but fought my efforts. His hand went to his mouth and he bit down hard. I saw it but did not acknowledge its occurrence. I placed him in a chair and turned it to where he was sitting directly across from me, looking into my eyes. "I know you realize what is going on. I won't let you stay there," I said pointing to the closet, "not now." His hand darted to his mouth. Again he bit himself. "You've been doing that for many years. I saw you do it. Do it again, if you wish. Maybe one day you'll learn that biting isn't necessary." He took the wet, reddened hand from his mouth and thrust it before my eyes so I could not help but see it. "It's not a pretty hand; I'm sorry," I reacted with distance as I showed him mine. "Mine looks better. I don't bite."

EXPERIMENT WITH A WHEN . . . THEN CONTINGENCY

He began to stand but I stopped him quickly. "Do you want to get up?" He nodded "yes." "If you want to get up, then touch my hand," I commanded, holding out my palm, needing to see if he would be willing to accept the imposed limit. Without hesitation, he took my words into his brain, processed them, understood the "When . . . then" contingency, and gently touched my opened palm. "Thank you," I replied. "Now you may get up." He stood and walked back to the closet. He sat down, hands by his side. "You think it's better over there," I said to him clearly from my chair. "It's not! It's better here!" I brought him back to the table. "If you want to get up, touch my hand." He hesitated for a moment, then reached for my fingers. "Fine, you may get up if you'd like." He did, but he stood by my side. I quickly asked the teacher for paper and pencil. "Sit down," I stated to him. I had to guide him into the chair. "This is a pencil and this is paper," I remarked, pointing to the objects. "Write your name." It was not a request. It was a command. He took the pencil and carefully, beautifully, printed his name. "Write your address." He complied with ease. "The city where you live." "The state." The letters flowed without effort. "Write what school you go to." He looked into my eyes. "What school do you go to?" I repeated. He continued looking toward me. I took the pencil, wrote the word "school" on the paper, then handed him the pencil. *He* wrote the name of the school clearly, as though he had been doing it for years!

I had visited the school on numerous occasions and knew the teacher in the next room. I also knew she had a computer. (A computer in the next room!) She welcomed the youngster into her room. The teacher turned on the computer and inserted the discs. He waited patiently for the red, loading light to go off. Unassisted, unattended, he sat in front of the computer for an hour, reading instructions, filling in blanks, answering questions. He did not bite himself once. He did not seek the solace of table cover or closet walls. Before leaving the school, I went to him. He took my hand and squeezed it warmly. I returned his expressed emotion, touching his cheek.

My student went back to his class the following day. Within

hours, she had him working problems at a desk in order to earn time at the computer. Before three days passed, he worked at his desk in order to have access to the computer for ten minutes! While my student stayed with him, there was no biting, no need for escaping.

"But what's going to happen to him when I leave," she asked me as we sat together sipping coffee. Her voice was uncertain, as though she feared the answer to her own question.

"That will depend on the school. They know what must be done. If the personnel will learn to concern themselves less with his undesired behaviors and more with his strengths, he'll be all right."

"If not?" she asked pointedly.

THE BLINDING EFFECTS OF UNDESIRED BEHAVIOR

Undesired behavior that is persistent, disruptive, dangerous, or just annoying can diminish our perspectives to where the total picture in which the behavior occurs gives way to single snapshot that plays and replays endlessly. We see only the behavior, we are bothered by it, and we want to get out from under it. As difficult as it may be, it is essential that we step back from the narrow view and place the behavior where it belongs: squarely within the total life space. With a deep breath, we must force ourselves to return to the basics: Undesired behavior is adaptive, purposive, functional, and, *from the child's perspective,* appropriate.

REDIRECTING BEHAVIORS

The decision to reduce undesired behavior is based on more than the behavior's annoyance or disruptiveness. By far the most important justification for reducing undesired behavior is that it impedes an individual's personal growth. Lying under a table, or within the confines of an unused closet, does not promote progress. Tearing viable tissue, either by hand or teeth or any similar manner, accomplishes little other than personal destruction. Not communicating, not complying, not attending when alternative actions will help someone learn important educational and life-supporting lessons, results in little other than the waste of precious time. Individuals who continue to move further from outstretched arms intending to provide a brighter future, whether of their own volition or not, rarely understand the ticking clock that is working against them. *Undesired behavior can become a comfortable part of a routine.* It can become an ingrained part of an individual's personality or behavior repertoire. It can become like a lace veil, concealing a part of the individual that is better. Without purposive intervention, it can spread, covering the individual like a blanket.

Reducing undesired behavior, however, is often easier to talk or write about than accomplish in fact. The available procedures, again, are not possessed of magic. There is no exotic "wand" or singular method that will work across the board for all individuals under all conditions. Frequently, the consultant must "experiment" with various procedures before discovering a plan that will accomplish the intended goal of reducing undesired actions.

DISCIPLINE PROGRAMS: MORE
THAN REDUCING BEHAVIOR

"And almost without exception, any effective plan will have a positive feedback component," the young teacher pointed out. "Some of my colleagues seem to forget that. They 'punish' children when they run down the school hallway, but they fail to notice them when they're walking. They show their displeasure when a student has not completed an assignment, but they make no issue when the opposite has occurred. They're quick to withhold a privilege or isolate a youngster from a group when observing an unacceptable behavior, but their efforts stop there as though they believe they have taught an invaluable lesson."

"But they are *disciplining* the students," the parent suggested.

"Not by a long shot," the teacher reacted. "All they're doing is requiring that some penalty be paid for a misdeed. That's not discipline."

"I'm a little confused," the parent admitted. "I always thought punishment and discipline were nearly one and the same."

6.6

"I didn't mean to sound curt," the teacher apologized. "It's just that I'm adamant about this issue."

"Please continue," I requested.

"I've heard what seems a hundred inservices on what to do to decrease disruptive behaviors: pink slips, names on board, visits to the principal, loss of privileges, isolation, expulsion. The only thing I don't remember the speakers suggesting is paddling a kid's behind. Those reactions do not constitute discipline. They're just an easy, often ineffective, means to deal with a complex situation."

"You never use any of those approaches?" the parent asked.

"I'm sure I've used them all, excluding expulsion, at one time or another. But they are only a minuscule part of what I do."

"You use them when disciplining a student," the parent said.

"This may smack of a semantic argument, but I do not see myself disciplining a student, not like applying discipline as if it were a procedure. Instead, I develop a discipline *program* for a student that contains many components. I develop rules, regulations and expectations for desired behavior, as well as undesired behaviors. I consider procedures to deal with both the undesired behaviors and the desired alternatives, and the student and I practice the relationships between my expressed expectations for behavior and what consequences will occur when both the desired and undesired actions occur. I make every effort to help the student understand the relationship so he can begin governing his own behavior. I don't wish to spend the time standing over him with a big stick. He needs to learn how to monitor his own actions. He'll only be able to do that if he recognizes there are expectations, limits, rules, regulations, and consequences."

"Self-directed behavior," the parent stated.

A Reminder: Undesired Behavior as It Relates to Assigned Tasks

"Yes. But that's only a start. My discipline program considers the tasks I've assigned to the student, and how well he succeeds at those tasks. I never develop a program without considering the student's academic and social history, his perceptions of school, me, and himself. I never begin a disciplinary program without speculating on what purpose the undesired behavior may be serving, and I do nothing until I have a clear picture of how the individual's environment, which includes myself, is responding to the undesired and desired behavior. Perhaps most important, I carefully compile a list of the student's *strengths* before I even consider decreasing an undesired behavior. Frankly, had the latter been done with the student who spent so much time under the table, he would have spent more time at a computer, learning."

"You do all of the above before you initiate any punitive actions to decrease and redirect undesired behavior?" the parent asked.

"Yes, ma'am. It is easier to simply isolate, withhold, or slam away, but they're stop-gap methods at best. They could also be ruinous."

"How so?" the parent inquired.

_____ FROM ARTIFICIAL TO NATURAL FEEDBACK _____

"One of our ultimate goals is to help desired behavior come under the influence of natural feedback. We want our students, or any individual, for that matter, to experience whatever inherent joy there is in the academic or life-supporting activity he's involved with. The artificial systems we use, positive or negative, are intended to help that goal be realized. Positive systems help the desired behavior get started. Negative systems redirect undesired behaviors so the desired alternatives can be influenced through positive means. Imagine the plight of an individual, however, if most, or all, of his academic experiences are negative; if everytime he turns around he's isolated or something is taken from him. Remember that young student, Jeremy I think was his name, who was placed in the back of the room because he clowned around during math class? Not much chance to find that math can be enjoyable when you're isolated from the work. There was an example where 'punishment' (which turned out not to be punishment!) was used without any planning, or thinking for that matter. It was an ignorant 'slam-bang, get to the back of the room' approach. Indeed, the approach was for the benefit of the teacher, not the youngster. I don't believe that's part of our job description. His teacher should have made math palatable, if not enjoyable, successful, if nothing else."

"And the student's undesired behavior would have stopped without any punishment," the parent concluded.

"In that case, perhaps," I remarked, "but it doesn't always turn out that way. Sometimes, a negative sanction is needed in conjunction with all the teacher just indicated. Do you agree?" I asked the young professional.

"For sure. I'd prefer never to use any negative procedure, but sometimes students force me into the position where I must teach limits and rules. Students, and individuals in general, sometimes forget that they aren't the only ones who occupy the planet . . ."

Discipline is absolutely necessary. . . . Discipline is essential to healthy growth and development and is an integral part of learning. . . . Teaching [an individual] to follow the rules and regulations helps him adjust to the world and engage in socially acceptable behavior. In this way, [he] learns to be aware of the rights of others and to respect those rights. Moreover, discipline directs [the individual's] interests outside of himself so that he does not function solely in terms of his own impulses without regard for other people's feelings.[4]

"But at the same time, negative procedures can never be used alone. Without being combined with positive feedback for alternative behaviors, the procedures will scarcely be effective," the teacher added.

> Whenever possible, reinforcement should be part of all programs of behavior change. Continually scanning for good behaviors and reinforcing them, especially with people whose histories have been problematic, should become second nature to you.[5]

NEGATIVE SANCTIONS TEACH ONLY WHAT NOT TO DO

"This will no doubt sound naive, but why is it so important to combine procedures," the parent inquired. "I've never given that any thought."

"Primarily because *negative procedures only teach an individual what not to do.* While knowing what not to do is helpful, knowing what to do is more valuable," the teacher answered.

"Positive procedures teach individuals what to do. I remember," the parent indicated.

"Because of that," I stated, "this discussion should emphasize to you the need for using positive feedback. That need holds true regardless of the uniqueness of the individual you're working with: child, student, adult; regardless of the setting in which you find yourself: home, school, or special facility.

"Perhaps one of the most important lessons I've learned over the years," I continued, "is that negative procedures implemented to decrease the occurrence of undesired behaviors are the weakest, the overall least effective methods in any discipline program. I've also discovered that using aversive procedures can become an easy habit, a habit often requiring little thought. All we see is the undesired behavior and we want it stopped immediately, if not sooner. That disposition becomes our central focus. We sometimes forget there's a tomorrow. We sometimes neglect to plan for tomorrow."

THOUGHTS ON CONTRIVED *AVERSIVE* INTERVENTION

Every procedure designed to decrease the occurrence of an undesired behavior contains an element of *aversive* or *punishing* feedback.

Aversive feedback includes *anything* an individual will work hard to *avoid;* any feedback that occurs after a behavior that results in a decrease of that behavior; anything an individual perceives as aversive. There are some qualifications, however. There are no universal forms of aversive feedback. *The individual decides what and what is not aversive.* What may be perceived as punishment by one individual may be viewed quite differently by another. What may be perceived as punishment one day, may be seen by the same individual as meaningless the next day. What a consultant sees as punishment may be looked upon by the individual as just the opposite.

Punishing consequences are defined solely in terms of the effects they have upon behaviors. Whether a consequence is or is not punishing, can be known *only* after you look carefully at the effects the consequence has had on the individual's behavior.

If you use feedback you believe is aversive, when in fact, according to the individual's perception, it is not, he or she will *not* work to avoid it.

AVERSIVE FEEDBACK: A SEMANTIC ISSUE

"You've just stuck your professional neck on the chopping block, and I imagine there will be many people who will be more than pleased to remove it from your shoulders," the psychologist stated with a hint of disbelief.

"What did I do wrong?"

"The term 'aversive.' You used it. Do you realize the outrage you've just elicited?"

"It's just a word," I suggested with complete innocence.

"You think so? Not in certain circles. I'm surprised you didn't come up with another term."

"What purpose would that have served?" I asked.

"You don't wave a red flag in front of a charging bull."

"Not intentionally."

"Well, you just did it," he replied.

"I didn't mean to."

"Somehow I doubt that."

"Give me a few minutes. Maybe I can make restitution."

"Good luck," he said, walking rapidly away from my side.

THE INTENT BEHIND THE WORD

The procedures to be presented next *are intended to be aversive.* They are intended to tell individuals that their behavior cannot be accepted given its intensity, frequency, location, or its effects on themselves or others. Whether we softly turn away from the "misbehavior," refusing to acknowledge its occurrence, whether momentarily we remove an object or privilege valued by individuals, whether we remove them briefly from a setting, or whether we require that they perform some task or be prevented from engaging in an activity, we are using an aversive means to *communicate* an important message: The behavior cannot be accepted. While we experience no pleasure when using aversive methods, we nevertheless recognize the need for their occasional use. Individuals do behave in ways that are neither in their own or others' best interests. Some of the behaviors seem guided by curiosity and exploration, some are learned through modeling others' actions, some are taught unwittingly by members or circumstances within the natural environment, and some appear related to an emerging independent self. Whichever it is, if the behavior is seen as impeding growth, creating disturbance, or endangering the individual or others close by, the behavior must be redirected to allow an alternative desired behavior to come under the influence of the natural environment.

WHAT IS PUNISHMENT?

| 6.7 |

If we take a moment to see the overall purpose for punishment, we will be in a better position to use it correctly. **The first item to remember is that punishment—its benefits and liabilities—has always been, and always will be, with us. It can occur naturally and/or unintended—an individual's behavior inadvertently produces it, or it can occur as part of a carefully designed program.** Examples of its *unintended* occurrences are numerous.

> A child is told not to "play" with matches. The warning may not be heeded or understood. Curiosity will bring a tender finger and a lit match in close proximity. Often, one exposure to "natural punishment" is sufficient to teach the child to stay away from matches.

> Three winters ago, some friends and I went to Mexico to escape an unrelenting cold spell. Having been raised in Florida, I was familiar with the sun's effect on unprepared skin. One of my friends chose to ignore the warnings and the sun tan lotion: He never left the beach or the blazing sun the entire first day. He did *not* go near the beach the remaining four days! His feet were so swollen he could not wear shoes; his skin so burnt, he could wear

no clothes. He did not have a good time. We went back to Mexico the following winter. My friend's behavior was markedly different—the experienced aversive feedback had taught him the value of protection and moderation.

Naturally occurring punishment, the kind that taught my friend to be more cautious about exposing himself to the sun's rays, has been an effective teacher for all of us. It has helped us to *walk slowly on an icy sidewalk; to be careful about the first bite of a hot pizza; to protect our eyes with glasses when we ski; to avoid three sets of tennis when our exercise for months has been little more than adjusting dials on a TV set.*
In the preceding paragraph, I mentioned four activities:

1. Walking slowly on ice
2. Being careful about the first bite of pizza
3. Protecting our eyes when skiing
4. Avoiding three sets of tennis when our muscles are without preparation

Punishment did *not* directly influence those four behaviors. Rather, the environment's punishment *affected* their "undesired" behavior-pair counterparts:

1. *Running* (rather than walking carefully on ice)
2. *Biting the hot pizza immediately* (rather than waiting for it to cool a bit)
3. *Not wearing sunglasses* (rather than wearing the glasses in the presence of the sun's glare)
4. *Playing three sets of tennis* (rather than playing one "soft" set)

Let me explain. Notice that the following behaviors result in the following feedback:

Behavior	Feedback
A. Running on an icy sidewalk	A. Falling hard, hurting oneself
B. Not wearing sunglasses	B. Painful burn, swollen tissue
C. Biting hot pizza immediately	C. Burnt tongue and mouth
D. Playing three sets of tennis	D. Sore muscles, blisters

While not affecting everyone in the same manner (some of us may be "two-trial" learners—we may have to be beaten up twice by a piece of hot pizza before learning our lesson), there's an excellent chance that the above feedback will *decrease* the occurrence of the behaviors that produced them. Therein lies the *first* purpose for punishment: to decrease the frequency of a behavior. There is, however, a *second* purpose for punishment, one that is very important. When punishment is effective, it not only decreases the occurrence of a behavior, it also sets the stage for an *alternative* behavior to be learned. This alternative behavior is one that helps the individual *avoid* the same punishment. If the previously described feedback was perceived as punishment, a person experiencing it might learn the following behaviors in order to avoid a repetition of the same aversiveness:

Behaviors Learned		Feedback
A. Walking carefully on an icy sidewalk	to	Avoid falling, being hurt
B. Wearing sunglasses	to	Avoid painful burn
C. Waiting for pizza to cool	to	Avoid burnt tongue
D. Playing one set of tennis	to	Avoid sore muscles

_____ ANY BEHAVIOR MAY BE LEARNED _____

There is no guarantee that the above alternative behaviors will take the place of the previous ones that produced the punishing feedback. *Any behavior* that enables us to avoid punishment might be learned and adopted, some of which might be "extreme," like avoiding pizza restaurants for months, or giving up tennis completely. Regardless of which behaviors are chosen (or taught), the individual will acquire a response that enables him or her to avoid further aversive feedback. As I hope is apparent, whether the acquired behavior will be seen as desirable depends on both the behavioral options available and our teaching program.

Predictably, the consultant's purpose for employing any contrived punishing or aversive procedure is two-fold:

First: To decrease the occurrence of an undesired behavior
Second: To set the stage for an individual to acquire and manifest a desired alternative behavior

The consultant's efforts are always guided by two critical thoughts. Please note them carefully.

First: Since an undesired behavior is viewed as adaptive, purposive, functional, and appropriate given the natural environment that supports individuals, you cannot decrease or remove that behavior without providing individuals with alternative means to gain access to what is valued. Pulling a behavior from an individual without replacing it may accomplish little. Individuals, on their own, will have to discover an alternative action. It may happen to be equally undesirable.

Second: Successfully redirecting individuals requires that you show them how to move toward positive feedback rather than showing them only how to move away from aversive feedback. One of the most difficult, frustrating, and dangerous scenarios in which individuals can find themselves is to be "caught" in the midst of what psychologists refer to as an "avoidance-avoidance" paradigm. Under such a circumstance, individuals' options will be severely limited.

_____ IS A PUNISHMENT SANCTION NECESSARY? _____

Punishment used sparingly and correctly, used in combination with positive feedback, used with individuals who have the skills to avoid it, will be less likely to produce the aforementioned unwanted side-effects. Before it is used, many variables must be considered, including evaluating the seriousness of the undesired behavior:

1. What is there about the behavior, if anything, that makes it serious? Is it dangerous to the individual? To another child or adult? Is it annoying or irritating?

You need to reserve punishment for behaviors that place an individual in jeopardy, create significant turmoil within the family or classroom structure, impede growth and development, or when an important lesson regarding limits must be learned. You do not want to use punishment with an undesired behavior:

1. That left alone will decrease for want of any attention
2. That is presently being maintained by accidental positive feedback
3. That may be related to a verified physical condition over which the individual has no control
4. That is tied to an absence of experience and requisite skills
5. That is occurring because the individual does not know of an alternatively desired behavior

Whenever I am asked to intercede with an undesired behavior, I always sit on the "side-lines" and view the behavior within the total picture of the presented life space.

$$\underline{c} \atop \underline{c} \ldots \underline{P} \ldots \underline{B} \ldots \underline{fb}$$

Each factor must be carefully considered before any decision is made to target on the undesired actions. Let me quickly review the issues.

REVIEW SPECIFICS BEFORE INTERVENING

First, identify the conditions under which the undesired behavior occurs. Try to identify conditions under which the undesired behavior *does not* occur. Second, note how the natural environment is responding to both the desired and undesired behaviors. It is especially helpful to know how the environment responds to the undesired behavior in the presence of the environment's cues. The cues will indicate whether the behavior is specific to a set of circumstances or specific in the presence of a particular person. Third, speculate on what purpose the behavior maybe serving. Noting how the environment responds to the undesired behavior will provide many clues regarding purpose. Noting *who* is responding as well as the precise nature of the response can provide valuable information. If a staff member has found an effective way of dealing with the undesired behavior, we need to know what that person is doing so we can *model* his or her approach. Fourth, when possible, sit with individuals and ask them to share their perceptions of the situation. The purpose or reason for the behavior may become evidently clear once individuals have an opportunity to describe their view of the picture. If we are willing to listen (and look), *individuals can teach us* a great deal about their behavior and their environment. Most critically, the question needs to be raised whether positively reinforcing an alternative, desired behavior would be sufficient to resolve the difficulty. Any time we can avoid using punishment, we, and the individual, are better off.

NOTES

1. Kanfer, F.H., & Phillips, J.S. (1970). *Learning foundations of behavior therapy* (p. 329). New York: Wiley.
2. Patton, J.R., Payne, J.S., Kauffman, J.M., Brown, G.B., & Payne, R.A. (1987). *Exceptional children in focus* (p. 35). Columbus: Merrill.

3. Dyer, J.R. (1979). *Understanding and evaluating educational research.* Reading, MA: Addison-Wesley.

4. Salk, L. (1972). *What every child would like his parents to know* (pp. 63–64). New York: Warner.

5. Sulzer-Azaroff, B., & Mayer, G.R. (1986). *Achieving educational excellence: Using behavioral strategies* (p. 184). New York: Holt, Rinehart and Winston.

_____ SUMMARY _____

KEEP IN MIND

1. A student's undesired behavior represents the smallest part of his or her total "person." Undesired behavior should never occupy "center-stage"; it must not be seen to the exclusion of everything else.

2. Undesired behavior never occurs in isolation. Always view undesired behavior within the context in which it occurs.

3. Undesired behavior always serves some purpose.

4. Undesired behavior is neither maladaptive or inappropriate. Although it may be highly undesirable, it is, nevertheless, adaptive, purposive, functional, and appropriate, given the environment in which it occurs.

5. Undesired behavior always has a desired counterpart. By supporting the desired alternative, the undesired may become less of a problem.

6. Always identify the cuing conditions under which the undesired behavior occurs and does not occur. Remember how vital it is to determine the conditions under which the undesired behavior does *not* occur.

7. When considering undesired school-related behaviors, concern yourself with what is presently maintaining the behavior rather than spending time speculating on historical causes. You can do something about what is happening *now!*

8. After you have identified the cuing conditions associated with the undesired behavior begin noting carefully (and in *neutral* terms) how the environment is responding to the behavior. Determine as accurately and concretely as possible the feedback the undesired behavior is receiving.

9. Never lose sight of the fact that undesired behavior doesn't occur whimsically. Again, it has purpose. Often the purpose is related to the type of feedback the behavior receives. Once the feedback has been identified, it is necessary to determine the student's perception of what is occurring. Does the student value the feedback? Does *he* or

she see it as positive or negative? There are two ways to identify students' perceptions: (a) ask them—often that is sufficient; (b) watch their behaviors. If the undesired behavior decreases after it has received the environment's feedback, the feedback is likely being perceived as negative. If, however, the undesired behavior increases after it has received the environment's feedback, the feedback is likely being perceived as positive. More than a few children over the years have found it quite enjoyable to be sent to the principal's office; to be made to stay after school so they could privately fall in love with the teacher; to be suspended from school for three days and "catch some rays."

10. The decision to reduce the occurrences of undesired behavior is almost always based on the belief that the behavior is interfering with the student's growth and development.

11. Discipline programs, designed to reduce the occurrences of undesired behavior requires, however, much more than the "simple" reduction of a behavior. "Punishment" and other "negative" techniques do not, in themselves, constitute discipline programs. Such programs include at the very least the following:
    a. Clear classroom rules, regulations, and expectations.
    b. Clear explanations of the contingencies that will be operating. The student will be able to say, "When I do 'A,' 'B' will happen."
    c. Clear description of behavior-pairs, as they relate to each student.
    d. A discussion, when possible, among the students reviewing the rules, and looking at why the rules are necessary.
    e. Consideration and review of the academic requirements being made of the students. The students need to be able to succeed with what is being asked of them.
    f. Consideration of the uniqueness of each student: his or her academic, social, and emotional history as they may influence present-day classroom behavior.
    g. Careful analysis of the purpose for each observed undesired behavior. "Discipline" is not directed toward the student without careful mutual discussion (when possible) of the nature and purpose for the undesired actions.
    h. A compilation of the students' strengths, what they are successful at, what is valued, what they move toward, what is important to them.

12. While negative programs can help redirect students' undesired behavior, these programs must never be used by themselves. An absolute rule governing all negative sanctions is that they be accompanied by positive programs. Negative programs teach students what not to do. Knowing only what *not* to do isn't very helpful.

13. As with positive reinforcers, there is no universal "aversive" feedback. Not everyone sees the same feedback as negative. It is the individual, therefore, who will determine whether the feedback is negative, positive, or neutral.

14. You must never attempt to decrease an undesired behavior without first deciding which desired behavior will take its place. If you simply pull away a familiar behavior (undesired as it may be), and you provide no alternative, the student will provide his or her own alternative. It may be equally undesirable.

15. Once you have decided on the desired alternative, make certain you have an active, potent positive reinforcer available to facilitate the student's learning.

16. Before intervening with an undesired behavior:
    a. Identify the conditions under which the undesired behavior is occurring.
    b. Identify the conditions under which the undesired behavior is not occurring.
    c. Note how the natural environment is responding to the behavior.
    d. Speculate on the purpose of the behavior.
    e. Determine a desired alternative.
    f. Practice the alternative.
    g. Reinforce the alternative.

Punishment Only

| 6.1 | What is likely to be the outcome if we only punish or reduce undesired behaviors? What would an individual learn from such an experience?

Passive Behaviors

| 6.2 | Review: What is wrong with "not-biting,' not-hitting," "not-screaming" as examples of desired behaviors?

Undesired Behavior and Academics

| 6.3 | Can you think of how undesired behavior may be related to a student's difficulty with his or her school work? How might school work influence a student's social/emotional behavior?

Caused By/Maintained By

| 6.4 | This is a somewhat difficult issue. Discuss in class the conceptual differences between the terms "caused by" and "main-

tained by" as both relate to present-day, undesired behavior. What do you suppose are the ramifications for "treatment" if a behavior is looked upon as being "caused by" something as opposed to being "maintained by" something?

"I Didn't Know I Was Suppose to Do That"

6.5 A simple, but potentially illuminating exercise. Locate a student who is misbehaving. Ask her to specify the desired alternative: what her teacher wants her to do. (Don't be surprised if she can't tell you.)

Discipline? What Is It?

6.6 Discuss with your classmates what is required to have a complete, effective discipline program. Is putting a student's name on the chalkboard, in front of his classmates, enough? Is sending the student to the principal enough? Is withholding recess sufficient? How about letters home to parents? Pink slips? Is staying after school, writing on the chalkboard 7000 times, "I will be a good kid!" enough?

Natural/Artificial Punishment

6.7 Watch yourself over the next few days. List examples of how your environment has provided you with natural or artificial punishment for some of your actions. If necessary, recheck the definition of an "aversive" stimulus—it is anything you'd like to avoid.

CONSIDER AS WE LOOK AHEAD

1. Limits, rules and regulations are constant companions of school behavior.
2. The setting of limits provides many benefits to both teacher and student. As will be suggested it is the student who gains the most from clearly established and enforced limits.
3. Operating within limits decreases the need for and use of negative sanctions.

7

SETTING LIMITS

In retrospect, I would be hard-pressed to identify one case I've worked 7.1 with over the years that did not, in some fashion, involve the issue of clearly stated limits and behavioral expectations. I would go so far as to suggest that the vast majority of undesired behaviors I've been asked to view have occurred, and are presently occurring, because of individuals' inability to know what their environment expects from them and what they, in turn, can expect from their environment. Rare, if ever, is the occasion where I will suggest the use of a positive or aversive procedure to influence behavior without first discussing the issue of limits and expectancies. My position is straightforward: Before any procedure is considered or employed, someone must share with the individual what behaviors are acceptable and unacceptable; someone must explain what he or she is to do and not do. Before that can happen, of course, everyone involved with the individual must decide what those behaviors specifically represent: behavior-pairs again.

THE PURPOSE OF LIMITS

When individuals are taught what not to do, they learn that there are limits within which they must behave. They learn that certain behaviors are not desired and will not be accepted, and that their environment intends to provide feedback for their actions. Once the relationship between behaviors and the environment's feedback have been incorporated, individuals better understand what they must avoid doing. They also understand how their environment intends to respond to their actions. They thus are in a stronger position to predict part of the components that exist within their life space.

It is my judgment that without clearly stated, established limits provided to help an individual understand his or her environment's expectations, it is the individual who will ultimately suffer. Many people hold to the belief that limit-setting is designed primarily for the benefit of teachers, parents, and other professionals. Most assuredly, adults benefit from the setting of limits and the ultimate compliance of those limits by individuals they're responsible for. Life is easier for adults when misbehavior is minimal. But it is the individual who stands to gain the most when explicitly stated limits are incorporated, required and practiced by his or her immediate environment. When the individual knows both what and what not to do, and compliance occurs, he or she can:

1. Avoid unnecessary punishment
2. Have greater access to valued activities
3. Experience less confusion in his or her developing world.

Let me share two recent situations:

My clan and I had gone out to dinner to our favorite Mexican restaurant; it was a Wednesday evening—a good time to avoid the ear-piercing commotion so common to "family" restaurants on weekends. We had been seated for no more than a minute when the first high-pitched shrill noise reverberated off the stucco walls. The only people who didn't turn toward the source were those patrons who were already eating and were now "used to" the crowd at the large, round table to our immediate right. Seated at that table were three adults—a man and two women. *Intended* to be seated at that table were five young children—ages roughly three to six. None of the little ones were sitting; they obviously thought the restaurant was a playground, and they behaved accordingly. After a few minutes, one of the adults screamed "Stop it!" I could tell neither who the message was for nor what actions were to be halted. Neither could the children: They continued their play. Frankly, the children's antics were dangerous. Waiters, carrying trays of hot food, had to dodge the happily hopping brood. The hostess had to do the same as she led customers to tables. One of the children discovered a door, probably to a storage room, opened it, and was pushed inside by another child. Minutes later, the child emerged, unscathed. The three adults saw what was happening but chose for the moment to ignore everything but themselves. Then it happened. It was random and governed by the lightest of thoughts. The man, a parent of one of the children, lurched from his seat, grabbed one youngster by her small arm, and dragged her forcibly to her chair. She began crying in pain. Her face clearly showed she had no idea what had happened or why it had happened. Almost immediately afterwards, the two women stood and attempted to gather the other children to have them put on their jackets. The harsh yanking and wrenching gave the appearance of a tag-team wrestling match. It would have been humorous had there been no screaming, no threats of bodily harm. But the screaming and threats were heard by everyone; there was nothing humorous about it. Shortly after they all left the premises and reasonable quiet had returned to the small establishment, my 12-year-old-daughter looked toward me: "Dumb parents!" she stated angrily. I was thinking of the little girl whose arm was nearly separated from its socket.

James and his wife had become friendly with a married couple who had two children, ages about 8 and 10. The four adults had much in common and spent many days together enjoying each other's company. After a skiing outing, James and his wife invited the couple and their two children to their house for a quiet dinner. The family was requested to bring swimming suits so they could use the heated pool.

By the time the family arrived, the air, brought in by a massive weather front, had turned frigid. It was decided to forego the pleasures of the pool. The four children were requested to enjoy the TV and stereo in the living room while the adults sat in the family room and chatted. Since the evening was to be shortened due to the weather, James's wife did what she could to hurry the dinner preparation. Everything remained pleasantly uneventful for some fifteen minutes. Then, loud noises and laughter from where the children were playing came streaming into the family room. James knew the voices were from the guests, not his own youngsters. Curiousity got the best of him after several more minutes. He walked into the living room to find the visiting two children having a make-shift pillow fight with the heavy off-white cushions from the couch. Smiling, he asked the children not to throw the pillows, telling them someone might get hurt. When things quieted down, he returned to the family room. The respite was brief. This time, the visiting children's father went into the living room. He returned almost immediately, smiling. The noise had not abated.

"They're just playing," the father pointed out as he returned to his chair. James knew of the play. Without further delay, he rounded up all the children and seated them at the table in the dining room. Despite the fact the meal could have benefited from a little more time, it was served. After the family left, James summed up his feelings: "Wild kids," he said to his wife. Two weeks passed before the family was once again invited to the house. This time the pool was used. The two children rough-housed without concern for the others. It was as though no one else existed. Thankfully, neither of them hurt themselves as they ran and jumped carelessly both in and out of the pool. Soon the children were dried, dressed, and back in the house. They charged unrestrained through the hallways, once again throwing pillows, banging into walls, sliding across the carpet. James and his wife (and their children) waited patiently for the parents to intervene. They didn't, nor had they ever! And they were quite proud of that fact—"Do you know," Mother told the host and hostess, "we've never once had to discipline the children. They have never been spanked or punished."

"We don't believe in punishment," the children's father added, standing next to his wife. "We'd rather the children learn limits from their own experiences."

Before the last words had passed the father's lips, the crash occurred—a lamp in the living room had been hit by a pillow. Glue would serve no purpose.

James picked the pieces off the floor and made little fuss over the incident. He had already decided his course of action. When dinner was finished and the evening ended, he walked with the parents and their children to their car. Before the father had entered the vehicle, James guided him a few feet away from his family. His words were unequivocal: "You and your wife are welcome any time, but leave your children at home."

It is most unlikely that the children in either of those situations believed they had done anything wrong. Indeed, they were behaving as their environments allowed and even fostered. Still there were consequences: The natural environment does not forever tolerate behavior that it judges unruly. All of us eventually learn that limits exist, that teachers, parents and significant others will step in and place boundaries upon behavior. I have to believe that the children in the scenarios would have preferred that their environments had intervened earlier—had taught them the probable consequences to their actions, as well as knowing how to *avoid* the consequences.

THE NATURAL ENVIRONMENT
ALWAYS ESTABLISHES LIMITS

There was the belief, espoused by several professionals years ago, that adults should impose only the fewest of limits on behavior; that students and children should have the opportunity of "working things out for themselves"; that through "trial and error," they would learn what was best for themselves. Structure and specific guidelines were out; planned feedback was next to nonexistent. It was a permissive attitude, not at all a "take charge" attitude. Rather, it was an attitude that assumed the natural environment, irrespective of anyone, would kindly teach what was desired. Most definitely, the children raised under those conditions *did learn limits.* It just took them longer to do so; and their parents and educators were not the primary teachers. The behaviors acquired by the children often ran counter to what was desired by their parents, and many of the children found themselves facing some harsh and confusing consequences provided by other members of their environments (school personnel and relatives) who refused to tolerate what they were doing. By all appearances, the permissive approach was a poor one—its most notable proponent, years later, apologized for espousing its view.

INDIVIDUALS NEED TO KNOW

THE ACTIVELY OPERATING LIMITS

As stated, I believe that many of the social/emotional problems professionals bring to my attention are related to the absence of established limits and the absence of clear consequences that could help to guide individuals' behavior. While the parents and teachers I speak with are legitimately concerned about their charges' noncompliance, unwillingness to follow requests, and disruptive actions, they rarely understand that without well-communicated limits, there's little reason for individuals to behave otherwise. Often, the individuals do not know that their behaviors have overstepped some boundary for they have yet to learn that a boundary exists. No doubt their "overstepping" has produced, on occasion, feedback intended to stop the behavior. The problem is that the individuals might not have a clear picture of what they did that produced the "falling roof." As you recall, one of our goals is to have individuals monitor their own behaviors, to incorporate the notion of acceptability and unacceptability within themselves. Without the knowledge of established boundaries, an individual's acquisition of self-directedness will be very difficult.

Common sense and experience strongly support the idea that children do want limits in their relationship with parents. They need to know how far they can go before their behavior will be unacceptable. Only then can they choose not to engage in such behaviors.[1]

Adults who are proficient at setting limits provide the needed structure that enables small problems to be resolved before they turn into unpleasant episodes. They are keenly aware of what is happening. They make carefully thought-out decisions, share those decisions with those they're responsible for, point out what consequences are available, explain why the consequences are necessary, solicit, when possible, ideas from the involved individuals as to what limits seem to be appropriate, reach a general concensus as to their benefits, and hold to what has been decided. The individuals know the adults are serious in their effort to teach desired behavior, know that when limits governing undesired behaviors are tested, consequences will occur. The responsible adults have great compassion for their charges and consistently demonstrate their genuine affection. They are, however, firm when firmness is called for and unambiguous when anything less would leave the individuals out on a precarious limb. For students, children, and clients, their world begins to acquire the quality of stability and predictability.

"There's also less yelling, threatening, and punishing," the parent quickly added. "Both the adults and individuals have a sense of each other's roles and responsibilities. The total environment becomes less hostile, less caustic. I believe all of us feel better about ourselves, certainly feel more confident. We know how to help each other. Believe me, that's important. Personally, I wish I had established limits and expectations when my son was younger. Had I communicated those limits I think his life would have been easier; he would have experienced more success." She paused as though surprised that she had shared an intimate part of her family's life. "I just had to say that," she concluded quietly.

"Would you like to continue?" I asked.

"Maybe later," she answered, reaching into her purse for a tissue.

COMMUNICATING LIMITS

Experience suggests we set and communicate limits most often *after* behavior problems present themselves. While "better late than never" has some credence, "better before than after" would be infinitely wiser. Just as most of us who have children make an effort to simplify the world for our youngsters by removing expensive objects when they're first learning to explore and reach, by locking cabinets and drawers that contain dangerous objects when they first discover the joy of mobility, by providing them with shoes that do not require elaborate lacing when their fingers are first beginning to move deftly, many of us begin to establish behavioral boundaries before the youngsters find themselves in the midst of trouble. Such is common practice for experienced teachers. Often, teachers establish and communicate acceptable classroom guidelines during the first week of school wishing to start the school year on the right footing. The expected behaviors are described (sometimes written on the chalkboard), sometimes they are practiced to assure that the students understand the teacher's words, and usually the professionals explain how the students' environment is likely to respond to their actions. The discussion is constructive and supportive and positive. (If teachers err, it's most often related to the language that is used to explain the limits and consequences. Some kids do not understand the concepts the teacher uses, or the teacher's explanations are too long and too elaborate. If an error has occurred, the teacher usually discovers it quickly!)

While there are several ways to *communicate* limits and consequences, I will review three that appear most popular. You will no doubt have other ideas and creative twists that will facilitate the goal of having individuals understand the boundaries that you believe are important and necessary.

PLAIN TALK

When the professional has the ability to speak, and the individual has acquired the ability to understand the spoken word, our task of communicating limits becomes relatively easy. Our words and described concepts, of course, must match the receptive skills of the one who is listening otherwise little will be accomplished other than the expenditure of energy and breath. I have purposely preceded the term "talk" in the above title with the descriptive term "plain" to remind you that words are only as effective as the hearer's ability to interpret them. Many individuals we work with can express themselves adequately. However, they do not always have a full understanding of some of their own spoken words. In addition to being careful about which words we use, it is often advisable to seek the services of a speech and language pathologist who can evaluate the individual's conceptual language skills prior to spending considerable time verbally explaining limits. It is essential that individuals understand what we are saying to them.

Dr. Ellen Reese and her colleagues offer us advice that speaks to the advantage of "plain talk" as it relates to limits, consequences and behavior change.

Most people have verbal behavior. Use it. Our language is rich in [cues] that tell us what behavior is [acceptable] or [unacceptable] in a given situation and what consequences will follow. Instructions and warnings spare us a lot of floundering around, trying to identify the contingencies that govern our behavior. There are at least four ways we can take advantage of verbal behavior in implementing a program to change behavior. First, we can state the contingencies clearly. Second, we can issue a warning or reminder that the behavior is unacceptable and if initiated or continued will be followed by a specified consequence.

"How many warnings?" the teacher asked. "Sometimes I find myself offering several."

"The fewer the better," I answered. "Repeated warnings can become reinforcing. They also can teach the individual *not* to listen the first time for the individual comes to understand that several will be provided. If we want the individual to attend to what we are saying, we shouldn't belabor the reminders and warnings.

Dr. Reese suggests . . ."

a single warning may serve as a welcome reminder and avoid the need for punishment. Third, we can explain the rationale of a program. Granted, young children who have not even arrived at a conceptual understanding of area and volume are certainly not going to understand a philosophical analysis of the mutual responsibilities that govern harmony in the home. Elaborate explanations may serve only to confuse the child or the issues. Besides, parents and teachers need not justify to their charges everything they do. But we are more likely to abide by rules when we understand (and agree with) the reasons behind them than if we perceive them as utterly arbitrary. Fourth, verbal behavior allows us to negotiate. Contingencies that are fair and acceptable to all parties can be formalized in a contract that specifies each party's responsibilities and the consequences for meeting or not meeting them.[2]

—————— CLEAR, CONSISTENT RULES FACILITATE LEARNING ——————

A clear statement of what is acceptable and unacceptable can decrease the ambiguity that often occurs in new classes and new situations at home. As you might predict, teachers, parents, and providers will have varying views on which limits are necessary. The individual, of course, is the one caught in the middle of the inconsistency; therefore it would be helpful if some consensus can be reached as to what behaviors are acceptable under which cuing conditions. While it isn't essential that everyone agree to the letter, it is essential that the individual knows the rules and exceptions to the rules that are operating within his or her total life space. The statement, "In my presence, I expect the following," at least tells individuals where your preferences lie. In your presence, they'll understand the boundaries within which they are expected to behave.

Such statements, however, are only complex sets of verbal cues and therefore it is necessary to provide feedback for adherence or nonadherence to what boundaries have been established. Again, not everyone will feel the need to provide the same (or any) feedback when desired or undesired behaviors occur within the stated limits. The statement, "When you do such and such, I will do the following," at least tells individuals what they can expect from you when they behave in a particular way. They'll understand what consequences to expect in your presence, and that's a start.

CONSISTENT FEEDBACK

If individuals do not have sufficient language skills to benefit from the spoken word, limits must be taught through consistent, predictable consequences that contain value for them. Here there is little room for ambiguity and inconsistency, particularly when limits are first being taught. As in the case of the verbal individual, behavior-pairs must be established by the care-giving adults. That is the essential first step: Decide what the individual is expected to do under which cuing conditions. Needless to say, I trust, any expectation must be based on the individual's skill level. There's certainly nothing magical about adults getting together and deciding upon rules that are intended to set boundaries for individuals' actions. Individuals must either have the skills or be taught the skills before we can expect that our expectations will be abided by. Once a good match has been established between our expectations and individuals' skill levels, it is necessary that we either practice what has been matched, or we catch individuals behaving desirably or undesirably as they make their way through daily activities. The meaning of the term "catch" is extremely important. We must watch the individual's behavior as carefully as possible so we can react to it the moment it occurs either within or beyond the determined limits. The need for us to react quickly cannot be overstated. Any semblance of a behavior that fits within the limits we've established must be responded to immediately. Delaying our response by no more than a few seconds may allow time for another behavior to take the place of the desired one, and we will have lost a golden opportunity to respond to a behavior that would have taught a rule we believe important.

PRACTICING THE RELATIONSHIP
_____ BETWEEN RULES AND FEEDBACK _____

Learning rules and limits occurs more rapidly when an individual frequently experiences the relationship between limits and consequences. When we work with an individual who experiences little or no benefit from the guiding power of language, it is often very helpful to purposely place him in a situation where he can be exposed frequently to the relationship we wish him to learn. I've watched therapists help many young children understand that if they wish to have power over their environment, they must somehow make that wish known. In a sense, it was what I did when adopting the lever device to the previously described biting child who had to press the lever to obtain what she valued. These therapists use a similar approach but without employing a lever device. Several times throughout the day, the therapist places the child on his or her lap, rocks the child briefly, then waits for the youngster to initiate any easily discernible motor movement or sound. As soon as the movement or sound occurs, the youngster is rocked gently for a few seconds. Often within a short time, the youngster learns to volitionally reproduce the movement or sound in order to reproduce the consistent and immediate feedback. This simple, but marvelous exercise, teaches children a basic "cause" and "effect" relation between their behavior and the feedback from their environment. Once the relationship has been learned, the therapist attempts to transfer what has been learned to other situations. Throughout this generalization process, the issue of limits is always present: To have power over your environment you must behave in a prescribed way. Frequent exposures to the learning scenario, combined with immediate and consistent feedback, helps children learn how to acceptably access their valued environmental feedback.

The method using frequent exposures and consistent feedback can be used in a variety of settings with individuals whose language skills are limited. I have employed the process to teach the setting of limits when working with many de-institutionalized adults who have recently moved into a group home or supervised apartment. Because of their previous living quarters, many of these individuals have little knowledge of, for example, the workings of a kitchen. They must be taught the purpose for, and the dangers of, stoves, toasters, microwave ovens, and garbage disposals. Limits regarding these and other pieces of equipment are essential for obvious purposes of safety. With guided assistance, and many practice sessions, where consistent and immediate feedback is combined with well-established limits, many of the clients can learn to use and respect the devices that most of us take for granted. Rather than allowing the individuals to happen upon trouble, which may result in natural or contrived punishment, they are taught how to avoid dangers (and negative feedback) through repeated exposures to boundaries coupled with consistent positive feedback.

———— GAMES, PUPPETS, GESTURES, SIGNS, AND SIGNING ————

There is a wealth of information available that tells us how we can communicate limits without (or in combination with) the spoken word. Whether we use games that incorporate social/behavioral lessons, puppets that play various roles, gestures that point out critical cues, painted signs or drawings that depict expectations, or fingers and hands that communicate simple and complex concepts, limits and predictable consequences can be successfully communicated to individuals whose language skills are delayed. There seems no end to the means accomplished professionals can use to establish working rules intended to teach individuals how to monitor their own behavior. However, many of the methods have nuances and complexities that are not easily described on paper. Rather than mentioning the names of a book or two that mention such methods, I would urge that if you are working with an individual whose language skills are sufficiently limited to gain benefit from the spoken word, you visit and observe these professionals in an active setting. Nearly all school systems and special facilities have within their ranks professionals whose training has provided them with creative nonverbal methods designed to help individuals understand the need, and benefits, for environment limits. Modeling their actions is often much more helpful than trying to understand the "what" and "how" as they are described on a printed page.

———————————— MODELING ————————————

It is hard to overstate the benefits of modeling. One picture can be as helpful as many spoken words. Unquestionably, when we are attempting to teach an individual to behave acceptably within the limits of his environment few, if any, methods are as effective as modeling combined with guided practice. This is the case with both the verbal and nonverbal individual. As always, note carefully which of the individual's behaviors appear to be setting the stage for difficulties. Place that behavior within the diagram of the life space so you can determine how you are responding to it. If you are attending solely to the undesired behavior, you will have to alter what you are doing.

Select an alternative behavior, preferably one that is incompatible to the undesired one. Show the individual what you want her to do. Show her and show her again. Be patient, supportive, and prepared to acknowledge her attempts at modeling your demonstrations. Space your teaching session throughout the day, over many days, under all conditions where you believe the specific behaviors require boundaries. Provide her with many opportunities to practice what you'd prefer.

> Short training sessions, usually no longer than 10 minutes each, are more effective than longer sessions. . . . Two short sessions during the same day are probably more effective than one long session.[3]

Guide her fingers, hands and leg movements while showing her what yours do. Use words, always, but demonstrate to her how to imitate your skills. Use your gestures, your body position, your tone of voice, anything that will convey the messages you intend to teach. Watch her behaviors carefully. They will let you know whether your techniques are effective. Don't expect too much too soon. Teaching new ways of behaving often produces resistance, particularly when the individual doesn't understand why the new behaviors are being requested. If you run into a problem, identify the parts and pieces that are creating difficulty, then practice them separately until they fit comfortably into the whole. Check to see if your feedback is immediate, consistent, and valued. Make sure what you are presenting is sufficiently clear and concrete to allow the individual to perceive what you are doing. You need not be the only model for the desired behavior. Have the individual watch other adults and age-peers as they manifest the desired sequence of skills.

> A model that shares something in common with the learner (for example, age, sex, interests, or experiences) is more likely to be successful than one who does not share any similarity to the learner. . . . Even though a teacher may serve as a model, other students are obviously much more similar to the learner. . . . Further, telling the learner about the similarity between the model and himself is likely to increase the probabilities that imitation will occur for the similarities may not be readily apparent to the student at first.[4]

Keep in mind that you are attempting to show individuals an active, ongoing picture of what you wish them to acquire. Your overall goal is to help individuals understand the limits within which they are expected to behave. Every move they make in that direction lessens the chance they will experience punishment from their environment.

LIMIT-SETTING TO ENHANCE SELF-DIRECTION

Limits are implemented for the benefit of the individuals we work with. They are developed and enforced to help the individuals behave harmoniously within the socially acceptable boundaries their environments have come to expect. They are intended to help the individuals understand what they are to do and not do. Once established limits become a part of the individual's "person," he is better able to guide his own behavior for he can tell himself, "when I do 'A,' 'B' happens, when I do 'C,' 'D' happens."

All of us, regardless of position held or road traveled must have a sense of personal boundaries and behavioral limits. The individuals we work with are no exception. Whether they have been strapped with any one of many foolish labels, be it "retarded," "hyper," "normal," "delayed," "disturbed," or "disabled" in any manner or fashion, the individuals must learn that there are acceptable limits within which they are expected to behave. They must learn to incorporate those limits within themselves. Our task is to consider individuals, unique from all the rest, consider their physical strengths and weaknessess—whether these strengths are visual, auditory, motoric, or all three; learning style—whether they learn better from pictures, words, gestures, or their combination; history— whether what we wish for them to learn is brand-new or partially experienced; emotions, perceptions, and preferences—whether they are fearful or uncomfortable with what we are asking; then develop for them systems that will teach them to understand and predict how their environment expects them to behave.

——————————— BENEFITS FROM BEHAVING WITHIN LIMITS ———————————

The learning of limits helps individuals avoid frequent negative sanctions that will eventually be imposed by an environment that will not tolerate unruly behavior. It teaches them how to access the many positive aspects their environments hold for them. It facilitates growth, development, progress, and self-control. Learning behavioral boundaries is critical regardless of the physical, emotional, or cognitive problems individuals carry with them. Without established limits, enforced by clear, consistent, immediate, valued consequences, the individuals, as a result of what they do and fail to do, will appear, due entirely to their behavior, more acutely "retarded," "disturbed," or "disabled." They may find themselves on the tail of a spiral that takes them far from what they and others would wish. Without established limits, without knowing what to do, the behavior of the individuals will place heavy burdens on those of us who are teachers, parents, and loved ones.

——————————————— NOTES ———————————————

1. Gordon, T. (1970). *Parent effectiveness training,* (p. 186). New York: Plume.
2. Reese, E. (1978). *Human behavior analysis and application,* (p. 178). Dubuque, IA: W.C. Brown.

3. Heward, W.L. (1978). How to teach a child to imitate. *The Exceptional Parent,* 50–57.
4. As reported in Rusch, F.R., Rose, T., & Greenwood, C.R. (1988). *Introduction to behavior analysis in special education,* (pp. 298–299). Englewood Cliffs, NJ: Prentice-Hall.

SUMMARY

KEEP IN MIND

1. Limit setting is an important part of any discipline program. It is essential that your students know the nature of the limits you have established for your classroom. Once they know of the limits (and have agreed to them), you must share how you intend to respond to the students when their behaviors stay within and fall outside of the limits that have been established. Quite obviously, it pays to have thorough discussions on limits and feedback as early in the school year as possible.
2. Limits that are clear and maintained help students avoid unnecessary negative sanctions from their environments.
3. Limits are a natural part of the environment. The sooner students are introduced to limits governing their classroom behavior, the sooner they will be able to assume more responsibility for their own actions.
4. Make sure your determined limits are clearly communicated. When possible explain the need and justification for the limits you impose.

Limit Setting

| 7.1 | Discuss with your classmates your view regarding whether limits need to be established for classroom behavior. Share what type of limits, if any, you intend to establish with your students.

CONSIDER AS WE LOOK AHEAD

1. You will now see what artificial methods are available to help reduce and redirect students' undesired responses.
2. It will become apparent that the procedures are not particularly

potent. Relying on them to direct students' behavior will be of little benefit to anyone.

3. Notice the relationship between the negative procedures intended to reduce behaviors and the positive methods intended to increase behaviors.

8

PROCEDURES AND
APPLICATIONS FOR
UNDESIRED BEHAVIORS

Whenever possible, the best way to reduce the occurrences of undesired activities is to forget they even occur and teach alternatively desirable behaviors that will take their place. Very shortly, we will begin looking at more ideas that can help dissuade individuals from behaving undesirably. You will recognize that the methods are not panaceas, not particularly noteworthy or powerful. By themselves, as they are used in everyday life, they are often weak, often ineffective. At best, they are to be a part of a discipline program, never the program itself. They can never take the place of guidance, compromise, redirecting, modeling, When . . . then quickies, and demonstrated affection and approval. They are intended to be one thing, never everything.

To build an alternative response into an individual's repertoire, it is first necessary to decide what that alternative represents. As said many times, I never begin a discipline program without asking the responsible adult, "What do you want the individual to do?" The question seeks the determination of the desired alternative behavior. I hope you interpret my redundancy as reflecting the importance of this determination. I've also mentioned several times that it is essential that you place the undesired behavior within the individual's life space:

$$\underline{c}$$
$$\underline{c} \ldots \underline{P} \ldots \underline{B} \ldots \underline{fb}$$

You must determine whether the undesired behavior is receiving valued feedback. If it is, that must be changed. You must determine whether the behavior occurs more or less frequently under different circumstances. If it does, we'll have a better notion of the behavior's purpose. This is particularly essential if an academic activity appears associated with the undesired behavior (again, we will look at this issue very thoroughly when we reach Chapter 11, the education chapter). For the moment, remember that behavior never occurs in isolation: Take the needed time to place the behavior within the context in which it is occurring. Once you have reviewed these issues, and have identified what you'd prefer the individual to do, you can begin helping that behavior occur more frequently.

There are several ways to consider this issue of increasing the occurrence of alternative behaviors: You can choose a behavior that is *incompatible* to the one seen as undesired—the two, sitting and standing, for example, cannot occur at the same time; you can choose to increase an *alternative* response that may not be incompatible but is a lot better—pointing at an object rather than screaming for it; you can choose to influence *any positive behavior other* than the undesired one—anything the individual is doing other than what you don't want him or her to do; or you can use a nifty method that provides positive feedback when an undesired behavior *does not occur for a period of time*—an individual is reinforced when he or she doesn't scream or curse or get up from his or her chair for several minutes or longer.[1]

The fourth method involving positive feedback when an undesired behavior does not occur for a period of time warrants some explanation. The first step is to identify the undesired behavior! It should be a behavior that is easily observable (it usually is), one that you can actually see occurring. The individual then receives positive feedback *when he or she doesn't do it* for a prescribed time period. This procedure, sometimes called "omission training"[2]

> can be very powerful, but there are some tricky aspects to it. The time base must be adjusted to the individual; otherwise the reinforcers will not be forthcoming often enough to promote enduring change[3]

If the individual has the habit of manifesting the undesired behavior many times throughout the day, expecting it not to occur over a long period is not likely to produce much success. Best to start with small intervals of time so the individual can learn the process involved in the procedure. After success, the time period can be stretched *gradually.*

> Because the delivery of a reinforcer depends on time rather than on a particular response, whatever the individual *is* doing at the moment is in risk of being reinforced.[4]

If the targeted undesired behavior is pulling at your clothes while you're on the telephone, interrupting you when you are conversing with another student, or speaking out in class when listening has been requested, and you wish to reduce the behavior by reinforcing its *nonoccurrence,* the individual could be doing any number of other behaviors (some of which may also be undesirable such as pulling the cat's tail or horsing around in front of the class). Obviously, you may have to specify other behaviors that you would prefer not to occur. Equally obviously, it would be "nice" for the individual to know what you'd like him or her *to do* during the "omission" experience.

Since time is a key variable with "omission training," it is helpful if the individual can both tell time and understand the passage of time. These very complex skills may not be within the individual's abilities. If not, you'll need to develop a method to allow the individual to know how well he or she is doing. A timer with a ringer can be used; a clock with a moving second hand is possible; a model of a clock where you move the hands can be considered; or you can use what I have found to be very helpful: an hourglass with falling sand. Whichever creative method you choose, just keep in mind that individuals need to have some idea as to how much time is involved and how much time is left. Again, they need to know how well they're doing.

AVERSIVE INTERVENTION

Very recently I attended a meeting to review procedures that were being used with a young, developmentally delayed student whose behaviors were creating difficulty for his classroom teacher. The school's psychologist, special education teacher, assistant principal, and a representative from the school's Human Rights organization were present. The meeting was proceeding smoothly until the psychologist began to describe several procedures she had considered would help the youngster and his teacher. The psychologist and teacher had compiled a list of three undesired behaviors they wished to reduce, along with the behaviors' desired counterparts that they hoped to increase. One of the undesired behaviors, making loud noises, was primarily annoying, not overly disruptive, and not dangerous. The second was somewhat more disruptive—the student would treat equipment roughly: He would bang his hand on the class-room's computer keyboard, as well as throw toys across the room. The third, potentially dangerous, involved pushing other students to the ground during recess period. The psychologist's proposals included pro-viding the youngster with attention/recognition when he would speak, converse, or laugh within the context of the classroom's program; provide attention and recognition and allow continued use of the computer when he would depress the computer's keys with sufficient strength to produce numbers and letters on the screen; and provide words of appreciation and continued access to recess when he would play with his fellow students without pushing them to the ground. Conversely, the teacher was to ignore the loud noises, remove the child from the computer when he mistreated it, and have him stand away from his playing classmates for ten minutes when he pushed one of them.

Beyond Personal Bias and Ignorance

The Human Right's member said: "I have no problem with the nonattending to the loud noises, so long as an effort is made to provide praise when he converses and laughs. I realize that he must not mistreat the computer although I'm concerned that you're considering removing it from him. That *smacks of an aversive approach.* Assuredly, I must voice my disapproval of the "time-out" procedure you're suggesting with the playground activities. That *definitely is aversive,* and as you know the school system does not allow aversive intervention. You will have to develop another approach," she stated firmly.

It was not the first time I had heard concern expressed over the use of "aversive" methods in schools or other special settings. Earlier in the week, the program manager for a group home had told a primary caretaker that she wasn't allowed to have a 12-year-old client assist her with washing his own clothes after the youngster, despite clear requests to do otherwise, intentionally spilled food and drink on his clothing during dinner. The program manager indicated the procedure had to be changed to a "nonaversive" method. The problem, as I see it, rests with the term "nonaversive." Look again at the definition of aversive feedback (page 170); basically *anything* an individual will work hard to *avoid.*

The "Person" Determines Aversiveness

As indicated, *any* procedure intended to reduce the occurrence of a behavior contains an element of aversiveness. The procedures need not be harsh or inhuman, excessive, or prolonged in order to be classified as "aversive." The simple turning away from an individual, ignoring his undesired actions, *is aversive if the individual values attention.* The withholding of attention is planned, contrived, and aversive. It is intended to reduce the occurrence of a behavior. It is *part* of a program intended to help the individual acquire an alternative response. Requiring that an individual use a spoon or fork while eating *is aversive if the individual prefers to use his or her fingers.* Insisting that an individual relinquish a swing so another youngster can have a turn *is aversive to the first individual if he or she wants to swing.* Preventing a child from eating stones and sticks (or a dozen sugar-coated donuts!) is aversive if he wishes to eat those items; asking an individual to forgo the pleasures of her radio when she plays it too loud is aversive if hearing tunes is desired; deciding that a student will lose time at a computer when he mistreats it is aversive if he wishes to stay at the computer. Restraining an individual who is bent on self-destruction is the lesser of two aversive conditions. The list is endless. Even when we "ignore," "redirect," and "praise," we are incorporating two (perhaps three, if the individual finds "praise" *very uncomfortable,*) potentially aversive components within that sequence. Once we are willing to remove ourselves from the "emotional" side of the term "aversive," we cannot help but notice that aversiveness, contrived or natural, "soft" or otherwise, is a part of the natural environment, not invented by a "school of thought" or a "mad" scientist.

In our efforts to avoid the very word "aversive" we have tried to develop more palatable terms. In our efforts to be more humane and considerate of the rights and integrity of others, we have altered our words. But terms do not denote a procedure. What we do, along with what perceptions an individual holds, *and what effects we produce,* declare the type of procedure being employed. The semantic issues are pervasive and not easily resolved. The contrived procedures in the following sections are intended to be aversive. Of course, whether they *are* aversive will be decided by the individual whose behavior is being remediated, *not by the people who are employing the procedures or by the people asked to judge them.* The previously mentioned Human Rights representative *decided* that having the child stand and watch others play *was aversive.* Perhaps the child wished to stand and watch. In that case the procedure, which she called "time-out," would be positive reinforcement for that child. Further, she approved of the "nonattending" method to deal with the youngster's loud noises (believing *it* was *not* an "aversive" approach), but she could not know how the child felt about the proposed "nonattending." Perhaps *for him,* having a behavior ignored represented the strongest, harshest method possible—the most "aversive" of all the techniques being considered.

WITHHOLDING ATTENTION/RECOGNITION

This procedure is designed to allow an undesired behavior to *completely* run its course with neither interference nor attention from *any source.* Initially, it can be the most difficult procedure to use: When we become upset with a behavior our inclination is to "get in there and do something." The withholding of attention as a means to reduce undesired behavior does not allow for that option. Please note the following point:

> Regardless of reason, if you withhold your attention from a behavior for any period of time, then purposely or inadvertently respond to the behavior while it is still occurring, you will make the behavior more persistent, more enduring. Reducing the behavior will then become more difficult. The individual will learn that if he "sticks with it," someone will eventually attend to what he is doing. Worse, during the early moments when he is not receiving any attention, his undesired behaviors may increase in severity and intensity. Attention given to this exacerbated behavior will begin to establish that behavior within the individual's repertoire. Many of us have seen the effects of this sequence: Small crying episodes evolve into severe tantrums; exploratory tapping of hand to head evolves into destructive self-abuse. A behavior, once easily ignored, takes on properties that make it nearly impossible to turn away from.

EVALUATING BEHAVIORS

If most of us had our way, and the undesired behaviors we were asked to look at were minor in terms of frequency, intensity, and effect, we'd ignore them, and advise others to do the same, unhesitatingly. We could then put all our energies into identifying and acknowledging alternatively more desired behaviors. All of us would benefit from such a scenario. Unfortunately, by the time certain behaviors "reach" us they have often attained proportions where ignoring them would place the individual and others in jeopardy. Once we identify the undesired behavior we need to ask, "Can the behavior be allowed to run its course?" "Will the individual or others suffer if no attention is paid to the identified behavior?"

Some people have little difficulty allowing a behavior to run its course. Others have fuses that seem to ignite the moment an undesired behavior presents itself: Not seeing or hearing it approaches the impossible. For the ignoring process to be effective, everyone in the individual's immediate environment (including classmates and housemates) must allow the targeted behavior to run its course. If you ignore the behavior, but a colleague doesn't, a curious thing will happen: The individual child will notice *who* is nearby to determine if his or her behavior will be ignored or receive attention; the child will quickly identify who will and will *not* carry through with the ignoring process.

Before any attention or recognition is withheld from the undesired behavior, it is essential to speculate on the purpose for the behavior. Often the behavior occurs because it produces valued attention. Immediately check whether you have determined a desired alternative and whether you have accidentally failed to recognize its occurrences. The undesired behavior may be the only way the individual knows how to gain access to you.

ALTERNATIVE BEHAVIORS

As mentioned earlier, you must not pull an undesired behavior from individuals without providing desired alternatives. They must know what you want them to do, what they must do to reach you. The ignoring process will *not* tell them what to do. That's the job of positive feedback.

Behaviors that have been previously maintained by attention rarely decrease immediately when the above process is employed. Learning to find a more suitable way of gaining attention often takes time. Further, the behavior may decrease over a period of time and then unexpectedly return. This latter phenomenon has been termed "spontaneous recovery."

> Even after the problem behaviors have subsided, they may crop up periodically without any clearly apparent reason. Such spontaneous recovery can prove particularly risky, because at those times, people may be caught off guard and inadvertently provide the reinforcer; or they erroneously might conclude that the procedure failed and revert to their previous practices, which would make things worse than ever. The individuals with the problematic behaviors begin to learn . . . that all they have to do is to keep behaving as they have been and eventually the reinforcer again will be forthcoming.[5]

THE SPECIFICS OF WITHHOLDING ATTENTION

A quick reminder: If, while you are withholding attention/recognition, you turn to the individual and tell him that you will not attend to his behavior, you've done just what you said you wouldn't do! If you look at him, you've done it. If you grab his arm or physically move him from you, you've done it. Withholding attention in a practical setting can be very difficult. If you are one of those folks with a short fuse, think twice before engaging the procedure. At the very least, have a colleague close by so he or she can cover your eyes, ears, mouth, and hands. At the same time, don't have them closed too tightly. As soon as the desired alternative behavior occurs, get to it with gusto.

To use the ignoring process, do the following:

1. Politely ask the individual to stop his or her undesired behavior. It never hurts to try!

2. If the request fails, identify the target behavior. Make sure it can safely run its course without attention.

3. Identify the behavior that will take its place. Make certain the individual has the skills to manifest the desired alternative.

4. If possible, explain the "When . . . then" contingency. Tell the individual how you intend to respond to both his or her undesired and desired behavior. Use plain talk. Be brief but to the point. If you choose to use the procedure, you won't be able to say anything while the undesired behavior is occuring. Speak your mind before you begin. Model the desired alternative if you have any doubts as to the individual's knowledge regarding that response.

5. When you're ready to start, start! When the targeted behavior occurs, let it go. Ignore it. Don't look, touch, warn, or plead. For the process to be effective, the behavior must be allowed to continue until it stops and is replaced by the desired alternative action.

   Very important—if you're uncertain whether you want to start the process, don't start it. Wait until you are absolutely mentally set to start, and stick with it. Starting, then stopping and "giving in," will create considerable problems for you and the individual.

6. Be aware of what the individual is doing. When you observe the desired alternative you need to recognize it.

WITHHOLDING PRIVILEGES AND MATERIAL REINFORCERS

There are times when behaviors cannot be ignored. Either the behaviors are too disruptive or they are occurring under circumstances that make it difficult for us to look the other way. A recent case involving a bright, slightly "too" independent young boy, offers an example of a second option we can consider.

Scott's misbehavior at home was beginning to stretch his parents' patience. The 10-year-old's parents came to my office seeking help with a few difficulties that included an unwillingness to comply with requests and a refusal to accept responsibility for the simplest of chores. After meeting with the parents to help them gather some information about their child's life space, I met with the youngster. As frequently happens, he was nothing short of angelic: polite, attentive, thought everything was fine; couldn't see any reason for things to change. His school work was good; he had several friends; thought his parents were terrific; liked his young life. When asked about discipline, he indicated that his parents would sometimes send him to his room, sometimes raise their voices, but that he didn't mind either. I asked him to share some of the things he liked to do. He mentioned his bike, being outside with friends, eating ice cream, and watching television, which was limited, he added with dismay, to evenings and weekends after his homework had been completed.

His parents returned to my office after collecting data throughout a five-day period. Mom said: "I'll bet he was just fine with you. He's always polite, considerate with everyone but us." I smiled, told them such was not unusual, pointing out that I was a stranger, that since I had made few demands upon him, it was easy to be nice. After looking at their "data-diary," it became apparent that being cooperative at home was somewhat more difficult for him.

"Tell me some of the things he likes to do," I asked the parents, "things he does frequently and enjoys." They had no problem listing the very same activities Scott had shared earlier. I asked them about their discipline approaches. As they described what they had tried, I checked their diary. Scott was right: being sent to his room, the yelling and warnings were not particularly effective. "Scott has access to lots of fun things," I indicated, showing them the 'reinforcement menu' they had written down. "But they're freebies: He doesn't have to work for them. Whether he complies, listens, or accepts responsibility doesn't seem to be tied into the valued activities his environment offers."

After the parents agreed to alter their approach, I met with the youngster. I showed him the list of reinforcers; he smiled enthusiastically, recognizing some of what he liked to do. "Do you want to lose those things?" I asked him in a friendly manner.

"No way," he answered quickly.

"Well, let me explain how things are going to work." He listened attentively as I showed him how the "reinforcement menu" could easily become a "punishment menu." All I had to do was add the words "lose the privilege of . . ." He didn't want to give up his bike or friends or TV or ice cream, for even a short period of time. Together, we compiled a list of behavior-pairs. I explained what would happen when he behaved desirably; what would happen when he behaved undesirably. I told him he had a choice of what to do; I also told him what would happen as a result of his choices. Before week's end, he had become much more cooperative.

PUNISHMENT MENU

As is apparent, a "punishment menu" incorporates the valued activities listed on the "reinforcement menu." The "aversive" component becomes the *loss of those activities*. For this procedure to be effective, an up-to-date reinforcement menu is needed. Usually watching an individual's behaviors or listening to his or her preferences will help you determine what is valued.

This approach can help the individual learn to avoid undesired behaviors in order to avoid the loss of his or her preferred activities. The procedure requires the following:

1. Knowledge of the individual's value system
2. Determination of an alternative behavior more desirable than what he or she is doing presently
3. Clear explanation of the "When . . . then" contingencies
4. Willingness on your part to stick to the decided contingencies

ADVANTAGES OF WITHDRAWAL OF MATERIAL REINFORCERS

There are two distinct advantages of using the withdrawal of material reinforcement as a means to decrease undesired behaviors. First, the individual, at some prescribed time, has the opportunity to "earn back" what was withdrawn. Second, she can learn that she has control over the contingencies. Examples might be: If she wishes to ride her bike, she needs to park it in the garage; if she wishes to watch TV, she needs to complete homework or chores; if she wishes to continue working on the computer, she needs to use it correctly. The described desired side of the behavior-pair tells the individual what must be done in order for the reinforcer to be available. There is also a third advantage: You need not yell or threaten. Rather a clear explanation or modeling of the contingencies is generally all that's necessary. Responsibility shifts to the individual's shoulders, presenting him or her with the opportunity for increased self-directed behavior.

It is necessary, of course, to be aware of the individual's value system. Removing some activity or item that is of *no interest* to him won't produce the desired effect.

Recently, I was asked to become involved with a highly verbal, but developmentally delayed third-grade youngster who seemed quite bent on driving his special education teacher to her wit's end. The teacher's behavior-management program consisted solely of keeping the child in from recess. I met with the young boy, and after talking with him, I discovered he didn't like recess. In fact, he *liked* being alone with his teacher. All he had to do to get what *he* wanted was to misbehave in class. (I decided to find out what there was, if anything, about recess that he wished to avoid. It turned out that a fourth-grade "ruffian," not enrolled in the youngster's special class, would occasionally pick on the youngster, and other students as well, and that situation had gone unnoticed by the playground supervisors. Once that difficulty was resolved, recess once again became valued.)

Once you have determined the valued activity or object, it is necessary to identify specifically what the individual is doing that you find undesirable, and what you would prefer he or she do instead: behavior-pairs again—the individual must know what he or she does that results in the loss of the activity, and what he or she must do to have the activity reinstated. When the behavior-pairs have been determined, explain the "When . . . then" contingency and, when possible, practice it. It will be helpful to have the individual repeat and practice the "When . . . then" components. For the preverbal or nonverbal child, your explanation may be of little help. Nevertheless, the procedure can be employed.

I worked with a severely handicapped, 5-year-old nonverbal boy who liked to look at pictures from a book. He also liked to tear the pages from the book! It took some 20 trials over a four-day period to teach him to avoid the latter. We sat next to one another, and I talked with him while we both looked at the pictures. When he started to tear one of the pages I removed the book from him for one minute. As you might guess, he was not pleased with my actions. I ignored the brief period of crying, and after approximately 30 seconds of quiet behavior, I reopened the book to the pictures. The lesson: Tearing the book results in its brief loss.

When the valued object has been determined, the behavior-pairs decided, and the contingency explained, it becomes necessary to carry through with what has been planned. Just setting up the program may be sufficient to show individuals that you intend for them to learn desired, alternative behaviors.

_____ A Variation on Withholding Privileges _____

Occasionally a situation presents itself where we'd rather not (or need not) remove all of a privilege for a period of time. With a little ingenuity, we can help individuals learn to avoid an undesired behavior by teaching them that their actions will result in the *loss of a portion* of the valued privilege.

I was called to a school to have a look at a 9-year-old boy who was, unintentionally, ruining his voice. He would speak and shout in such a rasping tone that before the school day ended, he would lose the ability to produce clear vocal sounds. The "loss of voice" was frequent and had been occurring for several years. Consultation with a speech therapist and a ear-nose-throat physician suggested that if the youngster did not learn to bring his own verbal behavior under control, thereby reducing the stress placed on his vocal cords, he could permanently damage his voice. The speech therapist urged that a minimum of one hour be set aside each day where the child remained completely silent. The task could be likened to requesting that a 3-year-old sit attentively through one of my lectures at the university.

The therapist, the youngster's teacher, and I sat with him and did our best to explain why it was so important for him to remain silent during the chosen hour. While he seemed to understand our words, assuring us he would try to remain silent, his behavior was too habituated to come quickly under self-control. The decision was reached to use the "portion-loss" procedure.

The child was an active, gregarious boy who enjoyed the socializing that occurred during lunch and the recess period that followed. The selected "silent" hour immediately preceded the lunch/recess period; it was designated for inseat work in math and reading. His teacher constructed a set of 5 by 8-inch cards that were placed on rings attached to a wooden base. There were seven cards in all. The rings allowed each of the cards to be flipped, revealing the next one. The first card had the number 60 printed on its surface. The number represented how many minutes of free time the youngster had available. The second card had the following printed on its surface: "−10/50 min" meaning that he had lost 10 minutes of free time. Each card thereafter contained a "−10/ . . ." and the number of minutes remaining for his lunch/recess period. Each time the child spoke during the target hour, the "speaking response" would *cost* him 10 minutes.

If the youngster needed assistance during the hour, his raised hand would bring the teacher to his desk. All he was allowed to do was whisper any questions or concerns. It was decided, in order to generalize the quiet verbal behavior, that he would be allowed, at a later point, to speak to the teacher in a "soft" voice. The approach was effective: The child lost 30 minutes of free time the first day; 10 minutes on days two and three, but lost no more time thereafter. Generalization of the "soft" voice to nontargeted hours was slow, especially when the youngster was in the playground. After a brief penalty period during recess was initiated, he began to "catch" himself—our ultimate goal for him.

Specifics of the "Proportional" Loss Approach

As can be seen, this proportional loss program (often referred to as "response cost"—where an individual's response "costs" him or her a brief penalty), offers an alternative means to help the individual learn to avoid an undesired behavior. If you wish to try this method, keep the following in mind:

1. Identify the target behavior. Make sure it is observable so that both you and the individual know when it has occurred.
2. Specify the desired alternative behavior. It, too, needs to be observable. The desired alternative lets the individual know what you expect him or her to do. Make sure he or she is capable of doing the alternative.
3. Identify the valued reinforcer. This proportional loss will not work if the individual is required to forfeit a portion of what he or she *doesn't* want! You may change the reinforcement component when necessary to accommodate any variability in the individual's values. Just let him or her know of the change.
4. Practice the specifics of the procedure before it is initiated. When possible, have the individual repeat the "When . . . then" contingencies—both for the desired and undesired behaviors.
5. Once the specifics are understood, stick with the technique. You need not yell or warn. The procedure, when incorporating the above guidelines, will take care of itself.

Because this approach can fit comfortably into everyday scenarios, it can be altered to fit several circumstances. One such circumstance involves the constant repetition of a request before compliance is noted. Rather than allowing the repeating of requests to evolve into an angry scene (or become an accidental means for an individual to gain attention/

recognition for an undesired behavior), the use of "proportional loss" of a valued activity can often intercede in behalf of everyone. After you have identified the bothersome scenario, be it coming home when called, getting ready for class work, completing homework assignments, or the like, sit with the individual and explain the details of the "When . . . then" contingency. It probably will not be difficult to identify the privilege to be used. Point out that each time you must repeat your request, a *portion* of the privilege will be removed. In this instance, the response component is failure to comply with a request. The cost component will be the proportional loss of the privilege. Have the individual repeat or show you the "When . . . then" contingency, as well as state or practice the desired alternative behavior that will make the "proportional loss" program eventually unnecessary.

EASY SOLUTIONS ARE RARELY SUFFICIENT

One important point bears repeating before moving to an additional procedural idea. Removing privileges, all or a portion, can become a seemingly "easy" solution to a complex situation, one that we may rely on too quickly. As mentioned many times, it is essential that we place the undesired behavior in perspective. It is telling us something about individuals and their perceptions of their world. Imagine an individual whose "entire" world consists of people taking things from him or consistently holding the threat of loss over his head. Imagine our position if we do nothing more than mirror what others have done or are doing. The chances for developing a trusting, warm relationship approach zero. Before any "aversive" method is employed to reduce one behavior and set the stage for the acquisition of an alternative one, it behooves us to see "whole" individuals, their thoughts, feelings, perceptions, and predictions of the forces that influence their actions. If all we do is teach them to avoid, providing them with no options to move toward something of value, we have accomplished next to nothing other than to further their bleak views of the surrounding world. They will adapt to that view, but their methods of adaptation may be far worse than what they are presently doing. All "aversive" programs must be used in conjunction with strongly positive programs that will help the individual go forward, not backward.

SECLUSION AND EXCLUSION: "TIME-OUT"

In my experience, the most overused and misused potentially "aversive" approach is time away from reinforcement. More times than I care to count, I've watched the procedure used basically to provide professionals with the opportunity to remove themselves from a disruptive or annoying individual. Allowing a youngster to remain under a table or in a coat closet for hours is a perfect example. Placing a child behind a screen or "blind" for a large percentage of a school day, having a child go to his room for an undetermined yet extensive period of time are other examples. Frequently, there's little, if any, "educational" value in the isolating period; rather it is a way to get the individual "out of our hair." Frequently, it is used with individuals who are thrilled to get us out of *their* hair!

_____ QUESTIONABLE BENEFITS FOR THE STUDENT _____

For three days running, at roughly the same time each day, I had walked past a small, enclosed room, fitted with a one-way mirror, and noticed the 10-year-old comfortably sitting on the floor, appearing to be counting the holes on the acoustical tile that covered the room's walls. As the consultant to the special school, I became more than keenly interested in why the child was in the room and why he wasn't in his designated classroom. Rather than opening the door and speaking with the child, I visited his teacher. "He's been very disruptive these last few days," she explained.
    "At the same time period each day?" I asked.
    "Yes."
    "What is your assigned activity?"
    "Reading."
    "How are his reading skills?"
    "He seems to be having lots of problems."
    "So you send him to 'time-out' when he becomes disruptive?"
    "I won't tolerate what he's doing," she said.
    "Do you mind if I talk with him while he's in 'time-out'?"
    "That would be fine."
    I sat next to the child and asked him why he was in the room. "The teacher says I misbehave."
    "Do you?" I asked.
    "I guess so."
    "And that's why you're here?"
    "I guess so."
    "Do you mind being here?"
    "No."
    "Why?"
    "Because I don't have to do my reading," he answered.

A school principal called me and requested that I visit with her newly hired special education teacher who was having problems with a young, very difficult child who had recently come into the district. The principal indicated that the child was spending a great deal of time in "isolation" and she wished to have the procedure reviewed. When I entered the classroom, the teacher came to me and pointed out the young boy. He was sitting off in a corner curling a thin string around his fingers. "He'll do that for hours if I let him," the educator indicated. "Or he'll find a piece of cloth or speck of dirt on the floor and manipulate it continually."

"Does he speak?" I asked.

"No. He makes a few sounds, but no words."

"If you gave him an option, what would he do most of the day?"

With a look of frustration, she answered, "He'd sit by himself, content to be away from all of us."

"Does he participate in any classroom activities?"

"He doesn't seem to be interested."

"What do you do with him?"

"When he refuses to participate I have him sit in a chair over there," she answered, pointing to the far corner of the room.

"I imagine he sits there a lot," I remarked with a slight tone of disgust.

DESIGNED TO ENHANCE, NOT IMPEDE, GROWTH AND DEVELOPMENT

Seclusion, where a student is placed in a presumed nonreinforcing, separate room, and *exclusion*, where a student usually stays within the classroom but is prevented from seeing, and partaking in, what is happening that is presumed to be reinforcing,[6] are procedures intended to teach the "misbehaving" individual a lesson that will have some positive effect on growth and development. They are intended to help individuals understand that their "misbehavior" is not acceptable, and that it needs to be replaced by a desired alternative action. They were *not* designed to impede growth or provide us with a means to avoid our responsibilities. Yet again, individuals and their behaviors must be placed in perspective. In the first case presented above, the child learned a way to avoid studying reading; in the second case, the child, *isolate to begin with*, learned nothing from the experience. In both cases, the teachers failed to understand why seclusion or exclusion is used.

"TIME-OUT" CAN BECOME VALUED

If used with care and in combination with other procedures, a brief exclusion or seclusion application may help individuals learn to control their own actions. The potency of the procedure, however, is directly related to the reinforcing properties that encompass individuals' life space, as well as individuals' ability to succeed in their environment. If the life space is not reinforcing in the first place, if it does not promote academic and social success, removing individuals from it may accomplish little more than placing them in an "avoidance-avoidance" scenario. Little in the way of desired behavior can be learned from such a scene. Therefore, in order for the procedures to be successful, individuals must value *where they are, not where they're taken or placed,* and certainly not be in a position where they value neither. Additionally, individuals must prefer to be with people and receive external feedback rather than preferring to be alone. Sometimes, however, individuals who like to be with people may decide that there are times when it is "better" to be by themselves. This was the case with the first child mentioned above. The child who was sent to the small room was a gregarious youngster who enjoyed being with his classmates. Unfortunately, his experiences with reading were sufficiently unsuccessful that he was willing to give up a little time (a 45-minute class period!) in order to avoid the classwork. Obviously, his teacher needed to help him with reading instead of sending him away from it!

Further, the isolation area needs to be as free from reinforcement as possible. If by chance, and ignorance, it turns out to be more reinforcing than where the individual is being removed from, the results could be somewhat unexpected. I learned that lesson early.

I had recently completed my training and had taken a position at a university in Florida. An elementary school principal called me one morning asking for assistance with a few students in a fourth-grade class. After a few days of observing the three boys she had expressed concern over, it seemed that the "time-out" technique might effectively teach them to stop fighting while in class. Since the procedure did not allow all the boys to go to the same location (which they would have thoroughly enjoyed), three separate rooms were needed. The school nurse's station, the principal's office, and an unused conference room were selected. The classroom teacher was an exciting, lively young woman; her class was a fun place to be, yet the initial explanation to the boys that they would lose access to the class and their teacher was not sufficient to alter their moderately aggressive behavior.

DATA COLLECTION: A GLANCE

Prior to the first intervention, data were taken to ascertain the frequency of the aggressive acts and to provide a means to determine the effectiveness of the procedure. Only two "time-out" periods were required to put a halt to the fighting of the boys who were sent to the principal's and nurse's offices. To the surprise of everyone, the third youngster's aggressiveness actually began to occur *more often*. Indeed, he rarely waited more than a few moments once entering class to exhibit some action that warranted the "time-out" consequence. Realizing the strong possibility that *I* had somehow missed something, I decided to see what there was about the conference room that was so enticing. His teacher was asked to take him to the conference room as soon as he "acted out." I waited several minutes, then quietly sneaked into the room. The youngster had opened the drapes of the room and had positioned himself in a chair up against a large window. A smile crossed my face as I saw the youngster watching with interest what was occurring on the opposite side of the window. The school authorities were building an addition to the facility, and the child had a front row seat to the goings-on. My smile broadened as I noticed one of the "hard-hats" walk to the window and wave to the child. My intervention had taken him *from* reinforcement *to more* reinforcement! With feigned sternness, I walked the child to the nurse's station. The new location resolved the acting-out problem. (The teacher decided to allow all her students to spend brief periods of time in the staffing room to watch the construction, but that privilege had to be earned!)

I'm sure you realize that it is important for the individual to know what rules govern the possible isolation period: what he or she does that warrants its consideration; what he or she must do to avoid it. I'm sure you also realize that before it is used for any behavior, the undesired behavior needs to be placed within the total picture of what is happening. If the undesired behavior is receiving accidental positive feedback from the teacher, classmates, or anyone else involved, that has to be corrected first. If the behavior appears associated with a consistently identifiable set of circumstances, such as reading, or workshop assignments, those conditions, too, must be corrected first.

If the procedure is used, someone must keep track of its frequency and its effects! It was not developed to be used whimsically or frequently. If it is used, the time period should be brief. Said slightly differently, don't forget the individual is no longer with you. That can, and does, happen! (Most professionals recommend a 2- to 5-minute period, but that suggestion is approximate. If it is going to be used, the time period must be sufficient to be viewed as "aversive" by the individual.) Further, if it is used, and the results indicate that the behavior that warranted the procedure continues to occur, the entire discipline program needs to be evaluated quickly. Of course, that should be done prior to its use.

Because of the procedure's frequent misuse, many locales won't allow it to be used, or if they do allow it, they require a written program be submitted to a review board prior to its employment. That is as it should be. It is frequently misused! Often there are many options to try prior to initiating an isolation approach, the most important of which is to take the time to view the behavior within the familiar diagram:

$$\underline{c}$$
$$\underline{c} \ldots \underline{P} \ldots \underline{B} \ldots \underline{fB}$$

Check the cues under which the undesired behavior is occurring; check to see what feedback is being used for the behavior and its desired counterpart; sit with the individual (the person!) and ask him or her to share his or her views. If the individual is nonverbal, watch his or her behavior carefully. Try to determine the purpose of the unacceptable actions. Consider a strong positive intervention system in association with another "aversive" approach prior to isolation. Never rely on exclusion or seclusion for anything, including a respite for yourself.

_____ LISTENING TO THE INDIVIDUAL _____

Often times, the most productive way to deal with undesired behaviors is to sit with the "offender" (along with others involved) and listen to his or her perceptions of what happened. This appropriately named "life space interview," is "a here-and-now intervention built around a child's direct life experiences."[7] The interview approach, developed by Dr. F. Redl (1959) "is imposed to structure an incident in the child's life to enable the child to solve the problems confronting him or her. The interviewer's role is primarily facilitative . . . .The interviewer assists the child in increasing . . . awareness of distorted perceptions of existing realities."[8] While the approach serves several purposes, part of its value lies in helping to: (1) reduce the child's frustration level, (2) support the child in emotionally charged situations, (3) restore strained child–teacher and child–child communications, (4) reinforce existing behavioral and social limits and realities, or (5) assist the child in efforts to find solutions to everyday problems of living.[9] The interviewer (teacher or significant, valued adult) *listens* to those involved in an incident, facilitates the incident's reconstruction and, if necessary, offers suggestions of alternative ways of looking at what happened. Together, the interviewer and the individual(s) "develop an acceptable plan to deal with the present problem and similar problems in the future."[10]

Whenever we work with individuals who have the ability to express their perceptions of their life space, it behooves us to take advantage of those skills in order to develop acceptable ways to avoid further difficulties. As I hope is obvious, the inclusion of the "person" in my hypothetical formula

provides us with the opportunity for allowing individuals to express their own views of what is happening. Equally apparent has been my insistence that we must develop our social/behavioral remedial programs with due consideration to the perceptions and values of individuals rather than ours alone. What we see and feel, and what individuals see and feel, may be diametrically opposed. Listening to individuals' words will help us gain access into their private world. It may be that they need little more than a warm hug and a few words of assurance and comfort to get back on their feet and continue forward. If more is needed, their shared views will help us learn what will be best for them. If we look and listen, we will discover more times than not that *the individual will teach us what to do.*

LET THE INDIVIDUAL GUIDE YOU

This point cannot be overstated. Despite all my experience, I *never* know how to help individuals until I have spent time with them, time to watch what they do and, when possible, listen to what they say. Regardless of the nature of the phone call that I receive, be it to solicit my assistance with a 20-month-old who is not eating, or a 50-year-old who is not cooperating, I never develop any preconceived notions of what should be done until I see the whole individual within his or her life space. Invariably, his or her behaviors will provide me with a course of action. If I lose sight of the individual, even for a moment, perceiving him or her to be a member of an amorphous group, predicting what should work on the basis of membership in that group, I am less likely to be of help. If I did that, it would be as though the individual did not exist. I assure you, he or she would be quick to point out my error.

GAINING ACCESS TO POSITIVE VALUES

We end this section on redirecting and reducing undesired behavior by returning to the most basic of issues: helping an individual gain access to what is valued. I wish I could take you in hand and visit and revisit many of the individuals I've seen and worked with over the years. Together we'd stand close enough to an individual's life to watch as she does what she can to find meaning and value from her efforts. On occasion, you would be witness to the mutual joy that comes from one person helping another. You'd see the dedicated professional who unselfishly provides a supportive, guiding setting where an individual can tap into himself, learn from others, and move steadily, successfully forward along a path that is bright and promising. But on occasion, you would be witness to circumstances less promising: the environment's inability or unwillingness to help the individual find reasons, or build upon his or her own reasons, to go forward. You'd see an individual who does not know how to access what his environment *could* offer. You'd see required tasks that are neither relevant or related to the individual's skill level; an environment so indifferent as to preclude stability and predictability; a system more interested in expediency, less interested in efficiency. And you'd see undesired behavior—behavior that is adaptive, purposive, appropriate and functional—but behavior that will not facilitate growth and development.

While many of our professional assignments are difficult, some so trying that we marvel at our ability to continue, one task is relatively easy: demonstrating the *process* that teaches our charges how to obtain self-enhancing, positive outcomes—both natural and artificial. **Never underestimate the importance of having reasons to go forward, reasons both intrinsic and extrinsic. If an individual has neither, and we fail to set the stage for either, our means to help the individual are seriously diminished. Concentrating mainly on reducing undesired behaviors is a fruitless endeavor.** We must provide individuals with a reason to work for something, not only to avoid something.

8.1

All Individuals: Those Strong, Those in Need of Strength

Understand further that this issue of teaching the process that leads to the acquisition of valued feedback cuts across every group, every category of individuals. Regardless of age, gender, physical or cognitive or emotional strength or weakness, individuals must know there is a reason to put forth effort to obtain what is valued. No matter the "state" of individuals, no matter what we call them, no matter what we say they have or don't have, no matter where we place them or where they find themselves, they must know how to access that which they perceives to be of worth, whether the worth is internally held or externally provided. While there are many topics in our collective fields that are cause for debate, the issue of experiencing positive feedback for growth and development is not among them. Its importance is a given.

_____ NOTES _____

1. Catania, A.C. (1979). *Learning.* Englewood Cliffs, NJ: Prentice-Hall.
2. Sulzer-Azaroff, B., & Mayer, G.R. (1986). *Achieving educational excellence: Using behavioral strategies,* (p. 159). New York: Holt, Rinehart and Winston.
3. Ibid., p. 159.
4. Ibid., p. 159.
5. Ibid., p. 169.
6. Walker, J.E., & Shea, T.M. (1984). *Behavior management: A practical approach for educators,* (p. 102). St. Louis: Times Mirror/Mosby.
7. Ibid., p. 125.
8. Ibid., p. 126.
9. Ibid., p. 126.
10. Ibid., p. 127.

_____ SUMMARY _____

KEEP IN MIND

1. If you decide to ignore an undesired behavior, consider:
   a. Can the behavior be allowed to run its course? It is too dangerous or disruptive to be given such an option?
   b. Has the purpose for the undesired behavior been determined? Have you looked at the type of feedback the undesired behavior has been receiving?
   c. Will everyone involved with the behavior be able to completely withhold attention/recognition: Will the behavior be allowed to run its course with no reminders?
   d. Has an alternative to the undesired behavior been determined? Does the student (and teacher!) know of the alternative?
   e. Has a reinforcer been identified that will be used when the desired alternative behavior is manifested?
   f. Are you aware that the undesired behavior may become a little louder as you ignore it? Will you be able to stay away from it?
2. If you decide to influence an undesired behavior by withholding privileges and material reinforcers, consider:
   a. Have you identified the undesired behavior?
   b. Have you determined the purpose for the undesired behavior? Have you determined the type of feedback it has been receiving? Have you discussed the behavior with the student?

   c. Do you have knowledge of the student's value system? Have you developed a reinforcement menu?

   d. Have you determined a desired alternative behavior that will provide the student with access to what is valued?

   e. Have you clearly explained the operating "When . . . then" contingencies? Can the student repeat them accurately?

   f. Have you decided that it is necessary to employ the "aversive" procedure? Are you prepared to stick with the contingencies?

3. Be aware of how easy it is to overuse "time-out" and "seclusion." It can become a convenient way for you to avoid working on the student's problem. Equally possible, "time-out" and "seclusion" may become an easy way for the student to avoid working on his or her own problems! If students find that when they "act out" you thoughtfully send them away from assignments that are creating frustration and difficulty, they may choose to "act out" rather than work out the academic issues.

4. Beyond the "technical" procedures described throughout the chapter, one of the most effective ways of reducing the frequency of undesired behavior is to talk with students; listen to their views; ask them for suggestions. They know that your methods for reducing behavior aren't very powerful (and they certainly aren't magical). Perhaps conversation might shed some light on how best to help students stop their "misbehaving," while engaging in more desirable, more productive alternatives.

5. Above all, concentrating solely on reducing undesired behavior is a fruitless endeavor. You must provide reasons for your students to move toward valued ends rather than having them merely move away from feedback they perceive to be aversive. Without positive reasons to go forward, a student's day can be little more than bleak.

Providing Reasons to Go Forward

| 8.1 | Reread the section "Gaining Access to Positive Values." Discuss in class what is likely to happen to a student's efforts, to his or her self-esteem, if the entire school day is spent trying to avoid that which he or she sees as unpleasant, aversive, and futile. (Hint: Trust me! The student's going to quit something.)

CONSIDER AS WE LOOK AHEAD

1. We've been talking about single behavior-pairs, cues, and feedback. As you no doubt realize, behaviors, rather than surfacing in simple, uncomplicated order, often appear in bunches: One behavior-pair

leads to another, and that one leads to another, etc. These related behavior-pairs are often called "chains" of behaviors, where each behavior-pair represents one link. In a classroom, ten links can occur simultaneously. (No one ever said teaching or working with children or developmentally delayed adults was going to be easy!)

2. Each link of the chain has its own cues and feedback systems. As any teacher (parent) knows, lots of things can happen suddenly, overwhelmingly.

3. As a teacher, parent, psychologist, you will have to deal with an occasional torrent, "ready or not," as the kids say. To effectively deal with these complex links and chains, you need to be at least one step ahead of each one. A series of question can help you gain the advantage. We will look at those questions in the next chapter.

9

CHAINS OF BEHAVIORS

In any given moment, an individual is capable of experiencing, processing, and manifesting an incredible number of mental, emotional, and motor activities. The most cursory glance at the human organism in action can't help but leave the observer with a sense of breathless wonderment. We are, indeed, marvels. Up to now, however, I purposely have focused our discussion on the smallest of components: *one* set of behavior-pairs, occurring in the presence of *one* set of cues, followed by *one* set of environmental feedback. In actuality, these "sets" represent one minuscule link in an ever-present, ever-evolving chain of sets. These minuscule "sets" are important, of course, for they often represent what the individual is doing *now*, and often "now" is all that is on our minds.

THE PROBLEM OF MULTIPLE LINKS

There is a danger in too narrow a focus, for you may be lulled into believing that behavior-pairs and their accompanying cues and environmental feedback are unrelated to pairs that might follow in the near future or those that have already occurred in the recent past. Occasionally, focusing on one link is momentarily sufficient. More times than not we must recognize that a link occupies a position next to several others, and, when necessary, be prepared to deal with each one as it is manifested. Let me share a hypothetical example that might happen in a not-so-unusual home. While noting the whole picture, try determining the many particulars.

It is 4 P.M.; a mother and her two children are home. The 7-year-old asks for a cookie. Mom says, "Okay." A moment later he asks for another. Mother explains that dinner is soon, that one cookie is enough. He stomps his foot, pouts, and walks away. Almost immediately Mother hears crying. She goes to the family room and sees the 7-year-old holding the toy his younger brother was playing with. She tells him about grabbing and sharing, and asks him to return the toy. He does, throwing it to the floor exclaiming, "I never get to play with anything!" Upset by his shouting, she suggests that he go to his room to cool down. He does, crying loudly. After several minutes, she visits with him, asking him not to become so angry, and suggesting that he watch television. Quickly he calms and goes to the TV set. Reasonable quiet sets in. Mom returns to the kitchen, shaking her head as she smells the burning chicken.

This very small piece of the 7-year-old's environment produced quite a few individual scenarios. The following represents his behaviors and the environment's feedback.

Behaviors	Feedback
1. Asks for a cookie	1. Received a cookie
2. Asks for a second cookie	2. No cookie given
3. Stomps foot	3. No apparent reaction
4. Pouts	4. No apparent reaction
5. Walks away	5. No apparent reaction
6. Grabs toy	6. Explanation about grabbing, sharing
7. Throws toy	7. No apparent reaction
8. Shouts	8. Sent to room
9. Cries	9. Visit, conversation, and suggestion to watch TV
10. Watches TV	10. Enjoys the show

All of the above occurred within a matter of minutes. The described chain was composed of 10 separate links. Each link had its own cues, behavior, and environmental feedback, and each and all of what happened was part of the child's natural environment. We can't discuss the specific effects of the experienced consequences, for we'd have to know something of the child's value system and watch his future behavior to make an intelligent guess as to what influence the feedback had. It is safe to say, however, that many parts of the chain were influenced by the manner in which the environment responded.

SEPARATING THE LINKS AND THEIR COMPONENTS

Reasonably rested and in good spirits, it is likely that most of us can handle nearly any single set of behavior-pairs manifested by an individual. Conversely, the best of us, no matter how spirited we are, may desire to "throw in the towel" after being confronted with several pairs occurring rapidly within a chain. In place of capitulation, there is a process that can help. Admittedly, the process may appear time consuming, and it might strike you as being anything but spontaneous. You might react to the soon-to-follow questions by pointing out: "If I ask all those questions, make all those decisions, hours will pass before I respond to the behavior, and by that time neither the individual nor I will remember what in the world happened!" Rest assured that practice will allow you to attain the desired spontaneity, and after a short while you will be able to run through the questions and decisions and still remember (and influence!) the behavior.

CHECK EACH BEHAVIOR IN THE CHAIN

First, you need to remember that a chain is composed of links, that some links are likely more significant than others, and that you can choose which links need remediation. Upon observing *any* behavior within the chain, your first step is to ask:

> "Do I want the behavior to occur again under the same or similar cuing conditions?"

This question is important for it begins a decision-making process that increases the chances for consistency and clear communication between you and others who are working with an individual. It is an easy question to overlook, for often times the answer seems so obvious. Even so, ask it, at least while you are acquiring the habit of this process. Let's suppose you observe something an individual has done, you ask the above question, and your answer is a resounding "Yes." You have perceived the individual's actions to be desirable—something you believe will further the individual's growth and development. Your affirmative answer offers you two choices: you can provide some valued feedback (expressed appreciation, assuming it *is* valued) which will let the individual know you approve of his or her actions, or you can allow the behavior to pass without reaction. Once an individual's desired behavior becomes a comfortable part of his or her repertoire and/or receives natural, rather than contrived feedback, your planned feedback need not occur each time the desired behavior is manifested. Occasional positive feedback is more than sufficient. However, if you decide to allow the behavior to pass without a positive reaction, and it is *not* a consistent part of the individual's repertoire, and it does *not* provide the individual with any natural feedback, then remember:

> When an individual is first learning to do something that you see as desirable, it is essential that you facilitate his or her learning. If you fail to let him or her know that you'd like the behavior repeated under similar circumstances, you might not see the behavior again for some time.

> Recently I sat with a mom and dad who were concerned over their child's *absence of compliance.* In the midst of our conversation, Mom stopped for a moment to ask the child (who was the topic of discussion) to bring his younger brother a toy. The youngster did so unhesitatingly. Neither parent said a word; there was no reaction whatsoever to the child's *compliance.* After a few seconds, I interrupted the discussion and asked, "Is that what you'd like the child to do—follow your requests?" The parents answered "Yes." Before I said another word Mom looked at me: "We didn't tell him that, did we?" Smiling, I answered, "I didn't hear anything. I doubt he did either."

When you observe a behavior, particularly when it is first being acquired, ask the question, "Do I want that behavior to occur again?" If the answer is affirmative, let the individual know how you feel about his or her actions.

Suppose you ask the question ("Do I want the behavior to occur again . . ."), and your answer instead is a resounding "No!" A particular behavior within the chain has met with your disapproval; it is not something you wish to see repeated under similar (or perhaps any circumstances.) Several additional questions need asking, the order of which is not overly important.

"Is the behavior serious enough to warrant immediate action, or can it be allowed to run its course?"

Your answer will assist you in determining which, if any, of the previously described "aversive" procedures might be necessary.

"What purpose might the behavior be serving?"

The question and ultimate answer can remind you to evaluate how you have been responding to the behavior in the past, as well as providing some insight into the individual's perceptions of his or her surroundings. It is always necessary to remember that present behavior may be related to something that has occurred in the recent (or distant) past. For the verbal youngster, the life space interview mentioned earlier might provide you with additional information that will facilitate your understanding and intervention. At the same time, always keep in mind that you need to determine whether the present environment has been inadvertently maintaining the behavior by its provided feedback. If an individual discovers that disruptive behavior produces a valued reaction, then the individual's undesired actions are *appropriate,* adaptive response.

"What alternative behavior would you prefer?"

Again, a decision-making question that will establish behavior-pairs, and facilitate learning and consistent teaching.

"Does the individual know of the alternative?"

Everything we know about kids and adults tells us they do not think the same, remember the same, perceive in the same manner, or understand events with equal clarity or ease. Sometimes individuals don't know which alternative behaviors will be perceived as desirable; they may need your guidance. Sometimes, they do not have the developmental skills to know that an alternative is even possible. When necessary and applicable, present, model, and practice the alternative, preferably before the individuals get themselves into trouble.

"What feedback would be most effective?"

Here is where you decide which approach will likely be of benefit to the individual as well as producing the outcome you deem necessary. If you have spent time with the individual, chances are good you know the individual well; know his or her value system; know what he or she works hard to obtain and what he or she works hard to avoid. Ideally, you should choose feedback that has some logical or natural relationship to the undesired behavior. If that is not possible, then you should choose artificial feedback for the determined undesired behavior that communicates clearly your assessment of the individual's actions. When faced with undesired behaviors, your purpose is to resolve the difficulty quickly with minimal discomfort for everyone. Being firm and convincing in the beginning will help the individual learn to acquire the behaviors you believe are in everyone's best interests.

"How might the individual react to your feedback?"
"Are you prepared to deal with his or her reaction?"

The fact that you have chosen to intervene and are prepared to carry through with what you believe will benefit the individual, does not mean the outcome of your efforts will be what you anticipated. Several unexpected results might occur, and you need to be prepared for those possibilities:

1. Despite your preparation, individuals may not realize what they were supposed to do. This can occur when there has been a breakdown in communication, where the words you use are beyond the individual's receptive skills, where you have failed to adequately practice the alternative, or where individuals do not have the necessary skills or experiences to behave as you would prefer. This latter possibility must be avoided. Prior to the misbehavior, you have perhaps asked an individual if he understands which behavior you would prefer. His affirmative response does *not* mean that he understands. He may answer "yes" because he believes it is what you want to hear! If you feel you have erred with your preferred limits, and the behavior is not serious, pull back the feedback and discuss the situation. If the behavior is perceived to be dangerous, try to redirect and protect the individual, do what you can to calm the situation, then when things have settled, and you have noted how the behavior fits within the individual's life space, discuss and practice the alternative.

2. The individual may continue to misbehave despite your feedback. This can occur if the feedback is not perceived as aversive, or if the misbehavior is enabling the individual to avoid something you are unaware of that he or she perceives as aversive.

DOES A PARTICULAR BEHAVIOR
REQUIRE YOUR ASSISTANCE?

There is an all-important question to ask that I believe will help you as you attempt to teach desired actions to the individuals for whom you have accepted responsibility. It is a question that will focus your attention directly on what an individual is presently doing, even though it appears he or she is doing ten things simultaneously. On observing any behavior, ask:

"Is that what I want the individual to do?"

If your answer is "Yes," then all is well. If you believe the answer to be "No," then begin the process that will help the individual learn a desired, alternative way of behaving.

SUMMARY

KEEP IN MIND

1. Whenever you are faced with a behavior that doesn't quite ring a receptive chord, ask yourself: "Do I want that behavior to continue to occur? Now? Ever?" If your answer is "yes," then simply acknowledge it and all will be well.
2. If the behavior is not to your liking, you will need to consider several variables and ask several questions. First, determine whether you need to do something about the behavior at the present moment. Might it be better for all concerned if nothing is done now, or is now the time to intervene? Your decision will likely be dependent on the severity and importance of the behavior, along with the reaction others may have had to what happened.
3. If the behavior is not to your liking, and you believe you must intervene *now*, then consider the following:

    a. Have you determined an alternatively more acceptable, desirable behavior? Perhaps the individual is not aware an alternative exists.
    b. Have you thought about what purpose the undesired behavior may be serving? Perhaps the student has found that by manifesting the undesired behavior, you are providing him or her with what is valued. If so, you will need to change what you are doing.
    c. Does the student know you are upset with him or her? Upset with what he or she is doing? Does the student know what you want done?
    d. Have you determined the student's value system? Will you have some potent contingencies available to help the student acquire an alternative way of responding? Perhaps the student sees no reason to behave differently.

e. If you attempt to provide students with an alternative way of behaving, how are they likely to respond to your request for them to do so? Are you prepared for that new link?

f. Have you asked students for their opinion of the situation? If they are fond of you, if they trust you, students might be more than willing to help you out. Ask; it never hurts to try.

CONSIDER AS WE LOOK AHEAD

1. Before looking at the many major issues associated with the education of all students, we need to take a quick glance at "compliance." As you will see, compliance, and its antithesis, are important concerns for teachers and parents.

2. Compliance, like so many behaviors, can be influenced by what we do. We will look at several components that will help you improve the compliance behaviors of your charges. If you are successful, you and your students will find your classrooms and the activities within them more successful and enjoyable.

10

VERBAL GUIDANCE AND COMPLIANCE

A large percentage of the problems that are brought to my attention are related to compliance, or more specifically, its absence. They appear to involve a relatively uncomplicated set of circumstances: an individual is doing something; you need for him or her to do something else; you ask, and expect the individual to comply with a request. What is asked is rarely out of the ordinary. Rather, the requests are made because of concerns over someone's health, convenience, safety, or self-enhancement. When the requests are followed unreluctantly, agreeably, minor problems that interfere with everyday living and developing, while at school, home, or special settings, become less frequent. Willing adherence to needed rules, limits, and expectations allow time for more important issues: the teaching and learning of skills that promote personal growth and self-directed behavior.

THE ROLE OF COMPLIANCE

"Teaching compliance requires the use of power," the parent suggested.

"The concept of compliance, helping an individual understand why adherence to certain expectations is important, and has little to do with the typical meaning of the term 'power.' It involves a process that goes far beyond producing the dutiful following of a request, far beyond one person exercising strength over another.''

''But isn't it possible that requiring behavioral compliance could be misused?'' the parent asked.

COMPLIANCE MISUSED

''All of us must constantly be aware of the purpose behind our insistence that a certain request be followed. The question of *our* motivation is central. If we require something be done solely because it makes our lives easier, then we have misused it. If it serves no other purpose than to confine or smother or keep an individual in tow, then it again is being misused. If compliance is required when the individual, in fact, has neither skills nor experiences to adhere to it, then its use is grossly incorrect.''

COMPLIANCE USED CORRECTLY

''But if it is used to help an individual attend to our words, if it is used to facilitate influence through verbal guidance rather than threats and use of punishment, then it has merit. If it teaches the individual to be more aware of his own actions as they impact on others, then it has value. If it promotes an understanding that the natural environment imposes rules and regulations on all of us, that living within those boundaries, oftentimes to our displeasure, is a necessary fact, then it will have long-range benefits that will offer more control and power to the individual over his own life.''

''Achieving compliance is not easy,'' the teacher stated. ''Many of the pupils who come to my class have no sense of what it means to be guided by words. They are so used to requests being made and then retracted that attending to what is asked or required is something that evokes little thought, much less action. During the first few days of the school year, I explain that I will make few requests of them, but I expect those that are made will be listened to and acted upon as I wish. Frankly, I'd be able to spend more time with instruction if the children's parents had practiced with compliance more diligently.''

''When the children were young?'' the parent inquired.

INFLUENCE THROUGH WORDS

''Let me answer that one,'' I asked, looking toward the teacher. ''Parents need to practice the *power* of words as soon as their children have acquired the ability to be guided by them. All of us who work with individuals need to show our charges that words are guiding cues, that the words are intended to set the stage for a behavior to occur, and that the behavior is, indeed, expected to occur. Long before children enter school, they need successful experience both with following their parents' wishes, and with seeing what happens when they make their own requests. Such experiences would provide them with first-hand knowledge of what it is like to make requests along with learning to abide by them. If we were to practice with our children when they were young, necessary compliance to rules and regulations would be more understandable and palatable when they enter school."

"There would be a lot less yelling and threatening," the teacher added. "There'd be a lot less undesired manipulation that only serves to heighten unpleasant emotions. If there exists an expectation that something needs to be done, the students need to know that the expectation exists, why it exists, and that they must get to it. Requiring that something be done doesn't happen very often. But when it does, there can be little room for equivocality."

METHODS TO ENHANCE COMPLIANCE

The majority of the difficulties associated with an individual's following or failing to follow your requests can be resolved once you understand both the long-range value of compliance and the methods available to increase its occurrence. Consider the following:

1. Compliance is directly related to verbal influence. The more adequate your verbal influence, the greater the likelihood of compliance.

2. Noncompliance is more a problem for you than for the individual, for it is you who wants something changed. The individual, frequently, is quite content doing what the moment offers without being overly concerned with what you might need. More to the point, the individual may have experienced this compliance-business before and noticed, to his or her pleasure, that if he or she ignored the request, "it" went away. A sizeable number of parents and teachers have said to me: "I ask him five times to do something, then I get tired of asking, so I do it myself." Under such circumstances, the individual doesn't need an overabundance of intellectual "nuts" and "bolts" to figure out what to do (or not do!) that's in *the individual's* momentary, best interest.

3. You must establish and enforce reasons for compliance. The indi-

vidual must know that a "When . . . then" contingency is operating—what is expected and what feedback will occur.

4. You must be aware of *what* you are asking the individual to do. The individual should not be requested to do something unless he or she has the skills to do it. More so, individuals should not be asked to follow or complete a request if the activity holds fear for them. The feared component needs to be investigated and neutralized before compliance is expected. If fear appears to be a factor, requests need to be analyzed from individuals' perceptions and personal experiences. If the task is new, we need to approach it slowly assuring success as we proceed. If individuals have experienced unpleasant associations with the task, we need to determine which parts of the task elicit comfort, and which parts elicit fear. After practicing with the comfortable components, we gradually introduce the less desired parts, providing support and, again, successful experiences.

5. You must be aware of *when* you are asking individuals to do something. The fact that you want something done *now* doesn't guarantee individuals share the imposed time-line. There are necessary circumstances when *now* is correct, but there are times when it would be best to avoid making a request, given what the individual is presently doing. A five-minute delay may be just what is needed for the individual to do willingly what is being asked.

6. You and the other significant people in the individual's life must agree on, or at least talk about, the importance of various requests. If you and someone else think in opposite directions, the individual will adapt nicely to the inconsistency. Adaptation, in this instance, rarely translates into compliance.

7. You need to realize that "compliance" is a behavior—indeed a complex set of behaviors. Initially, compliance must yield some payoff for the individual. Most often the payoff is valued attention and recognition showing that you appreciate the individual's cooperation.

TYPE-ONE/TYPE-TWO REQUESTS

For purposes of clarity, requests can be labeled as being either "type-ones" or "type-twos." The invented, shorthand names are not important, but the concepts behind them are significant. Let me first define the two categories of requests; then I'll show you their purpose.

Type-one request: A request made of individuals where they have *no* choice other than to comply. They must do

	what you have asked. There are no if's, ands, or buts!
Type-two request:	A request made of individuals where they have a choice. They may do what is asked, or they may do something entirely different.

Type-one requests are made *only* when you have decided that a particular behavior *must occur*. These requests can include any number and kind of behaviors, and it is up to you to make the decision which requests will fall under the type-one category. Since individuals *must* comply with what you have asked, you need to think carefully about which requests will be type-ones. It is essential that a type-one request *not* be made unless you are prepared to make sure the request is followed.

Type-twos differ in that they are more a suggestion than a requirement. Again, there are no predesigned lists; you must devise your own. An example might be: "It's nice outside; why don't you go play." As this is type-two, the individual has the option of going outside or staying inside. Compliance is *not* required for type-twos.

It is necessary for you and those you work with to agree on the category of the request *before* it is made. By doing so, you can support each other, let individuals know it is necessary for them to do as you have asked, decreasing the chances individuals will "play" one of you off against the other in the hopes of altering the request. When possible, it is helpful for individuals to know the "status" of the request. This knowledge can be communicated in any number of ways—a "certain" look, a raised finger, a specially worded sentence with an equally special inflection to the voice, or somewhat more concretely, "John, this is a type-one!" These indicators are *cues,* and with some practice, individuals will have little difficulty recognizing their meaning.

——————— BEHAVIORS INVOLVED WITH TYPE-ONES ———————

Up to this point, there's nothing particularly difficult about setting the stage for compliance: You decide which requests are type-ones and type-twos; you agree to make certain that all type-ones are completed; and you communicate those decisions to the individual. As you might expect, there's often a catch to things that appear simple. Perhaps you have experienced something like the following.

Johnny's grandmother was very quick to discipline her 8-year-old grandson. She came from the "old school" where respect for elders was a given, where adherence to what an elder required was expected. No explanations or justifications were necessary: "Just do what I say because I said it." She would visit the boy, and her daughter and son-in-law several times a year, and it appeared that the child did not look forward to her presence. When Grandma would walk through the front door, the youngster would exit through the back. Mother would have to go to the backyard and practically "promise the moon" in order to produce a welcoming smile. Mom had resolved to make the next visit different. "I want you to *stay in the house* and *say hello* to your grandmother when she walks in." On paper, the two requests were quite simple; *both*, according to Mom, *were type-ones*. With Mother's hand firmly on the child's shoulder, Johnny met the requirements of the first request—he stood near the door when Grandma entered the house. Mother looked toward her son: it was a cue for the second request. The child remained stoically quiet. To avoid further embarrassment, Mom withdrew the second request and suggested her son go outside and play. That request was complied with willingly. Later in the evening, Mom and son talked. "I don't like her, Mom. She's mean. You *can't make* me say hello to her." Taking this example to an extreme, the child was right—short of the methods used in the Spanish Inquisition, no one could make him talk to his grandmother. The child could choose to speak or keep silent. All his parents could do was to try to influence his choice.

The example tells us something very important about the behaviors involved with type-one requests. Let me give you two lists of behaviors. See if you can discern an important difference between them.

List A	List B
Eating	Putting on shoes
Talking	Sitting in a chair
Reading a book	Brushing teeth
Listening	Placing a bike in the garage

Remember the phrase "You can lead a horse to water, but you can't make him drink"? Barring a most unusual horse, the phrase is *wrong*. Given all the things that could be done to the poor horse, there's a 99.9 percent probability that the animal could be made to drink. The same, however, cannot be said for many individuals—at least not some of the ones I've seen over the past twenty years. Despite efforts by parents, teachers, and a host of therapists, I have encountered individuals who have refused steadfastly to manifest certain behaviors, and like 8-year-old Johnny, have said either with words or actions, "You can't make me!"

The issue of compliance partially involves the subject of control. It involves the question of *who controls the specific behavior being requested.* To appreciate the difficulty and importance of control, look once again at the above lists.

List A	List B
Eating	Putting on shoes
Talking	Sitting in a chair
Reading a book	Brushing teeth
Listening	Placing a bike in the garage

Select one behavior from List A and one from List B. Imagine that you have asked an individual to comply with the two behaviors you have chosen. (Assume you are not some diabolical demon who will do whatever it takes to force the individual to comply.) Let's say your selection from List A was either eating, talking, or listening. When the individual hears the request she states, "You can't make me." Now, the critical question: Can you physically guide her through the activity? The chances of you being able to do so are very slim. The individual, technically, has control over those behaviors. She can keep her mouth and ears "shut." Can you *influence* her choice? Certainly, but let's wait on that for a second. Now, ask the individual either to put her bike in the garage, sit on a chair, or brush her teeth. Again have her say "No." Can you physically guide her? *Yes.* (Note: I'm not suggesting you would be ecstatic about doing so, but you could physically walk her to the sidewalk, take her hand, and together put the bike in the garage. You could, in the same manner, "help" her brush her teeth, sit in a chair, put on her shoes, or any number of similar activities.)

ACCEPTING RESPONSIBILITY

Why is this so important? The topic of behavioral control has always been a controversial issue. Indeed, the word "control" is somewhat of a "buzz-word" capable of eliciting all sorts of emotional reactions. Type-one requests require that the task be completed. They require that *someone take the responsibility* for having the individual do what is being asked. If you feel uncomfortable exercising control, using your physical guidance to insure the completion of the task, then you must forgo making any type-one requests. If you "demand compliance," and then, upon hearing the individual's refusal, rescind your demand, you will be setting the stage for the individual to learn undesired avoidance responses. In place of type-ones, you will, initially, need to make all your requests type-twos, allowing the individual a choice. You should then attempt to determine why the individual wishes not to comply: ask him for his ideas, observe his behaviors, see if he can offer a simple solution to the impasse, consider what purpose exists for the noncompliance, see how you are responding to his noncompliance, determine what payoffs exists for both compliance and noncompliance, try to find a way that will help him feel good about doing what you ask.

_____ Refinements with Type-Ones _____

The vast majority of requests we make while working with individuals fall into the type-_one_ category—those where compliance is expected. If you are curious about your own use of these requests, watch yourself over the next few days and keep track of the number of times you request something of an individual where it matters little whether he or she complies. My guess is that you will want the individual to do as you have requested. Additionally, you will likely discover that:

1. You do not make many requests that are unimportant or unnecessary.
2. You are making the same request several times.
3. You are allowing considerable time to pass between the request and the individual's efforts to comply.

Let's look at some subtle issues associated with compliance.

1. Type-_two_ requests are rarely made until the individual has the necessary receptive and expressive skills to comprehend and respond to your words or gestures. Once the individual begins to gather skills in communication, we generally begin to introduce the type-twos. Ironically, _many of your type-twos are disguised type-ones._

"Would you like to go to the bathroom before going outside?" a young child who has learned to use a potty chair is asked. Nine times out of ten, the child's response is "No." Nine times out of ten, your response, following his response, is "Yes!"

If the intention was to have the child go to the bathroom, the adult might consider why the question was raised. Why not say: "We are going outside; let's go to the bathroom." The statement is a type-one, and the potty is visited. The directly stated type-one can enable you to avoid arguments and wasted time. Further, it can have a positive effect on the individual's understanding of the power of his own words. With a legitimate *type-two*, the child's answer "No" *should be honored.* That option was given to him. If, however, the request was a *disguised* type-one, and the intention was to have him comply regardless of his words, then he will discover his words have no power. He might think: "Why ask me when you already know the answer you want?"

One more example:

"Would you move your chair under the desk?" a student is asked.
She answers, "It's too heavy," as she walks out of the classroom.

If your question was a type-*two* request, then say goodbye. If you *intended* it to be a type-*one,* look at the position you're in. If you reject her answer and press her to help you, you are telling her that her opinion doesn't count much. If she protests further, you might find yourself in an unpleasant debate, something neither of you will appreciate. Pushing this one more step, you might choose to acquiesce—her protests being too much to handle at the end of a tiring school day. You can bet a pretty penny you'll hear the protests again when a further request surfaces. After all, they worked!

If your request is truly a type-two, there can be no problem, for the individual is able to do as she wishes. Disguised type-ones, however can get you (and the individual) into a real mess, and they should always be avoided.

_____ MAKE YOUR DETERMINATIONS CLEAR _____

2. Most of us do not make a lot of requests of the individuals we work with. Instead, we seem to make the same ones over and over. If we can get past the frustration of the noncompliance, or the delay in compliance, we can learn something from the needed repetition: It is telling us that our methods are not very effective. First, there's a strong possibility that the individual does not realize the request was a type-one. This may happen because sometimes you require compliance and sometimes you don't. Second, you need to cue the presence of a type-one, either through words, tone of voice, or gestures. Third, when first initiating type-ones, a "When . . . then" quickie can offer assistance. Fourth, your guiding hand insuring

completion may be necessary. Fifth, when possible, an explanation for the purpose of compliance may help the individual understand why his or her cooperation is being solicited.

You must decide ahead of time whether a request is a type-one or two. That you have made that decision, however, guarantees little. You must communicate your decision, and in the case of a type-one, you must consistently require the task to be completed. Both will aid the establishing of verbal control and help decrease the occurrences of ingenious excuses that often result in everyone becoming upset.

HAVE A TYPE-ONE COMPLETED QUICKLY

3. On those occasions where you make a type-one request, it is important for compliance to occur as *quickly* as possible. This will help the individual attend to your words, get to the task at hand, and reduce your need to continuously repeat your instructions. This is what verbal influence is all about. Individuals seem truly adept at figuring out when we mean business. They can tell by tone of voice and facial expressions if the time has arrived where they must get to work. If they are used to being asked something seven times before the law is laid down, they know how much procrastination time is being made available! Truly, I've met kids who have paper and pencil handy to keep track of how many requests have been made so they know the precise second *before* Mom or Dad or teacher are going to explode.

Before you make a type-one request, consider the following:

1. Will the individual understand what you are requiring?
2. Do you want compliance *now?*
3. Does the individual understand the concept "now?" Would it be helpful to practice the meaning of "now?" Do you need to add that word to your request?
4. Does the individual understand the importance of cooperating? Has he or she had an opportunity for input? Can you show the individual why compliance will help you both?
5. Are you in a position (frame of mind) to help the individual comply?

After you have made the request, monitor individuals' actions to insure that they are doing what you have asked. If necessary, help them get started! It is best, particularly with nonverbal individuals, to avoid making type-one requests from far away. Individuals may literally or selectively not hear you. Certainly do not argue, for they may learn to do the same. Do not allow yourself to ask them seven times; they will learn to count! Ask once, then make sure the task is done.

FEEDBACK AND COMPLIANCE

Keep in mind that compliance is not always an easy job for individuals. They may not see why something needs to be done, and may be anticipating an activity far removed from what you want them to do. Remember that compliance always involves at least *two* separate behaviors: compliance and the accomplishment of a task. When you first begin to teach individuals the importance of type-one requests, both compliance *and* the task warrant your acknowledgement.

SUBTLETIES

The purpose of establishing a clear format of type-one and type-two requests is to facilitate an individual's ability to predict his or her world. Anything we can do to promote self-directed, independent behavior deserves our strong consideration. Practicing with compliance under various conditions, including different locations and different personnel, will help the individual learn the processes involving verbal guidance. It will help him or her to understand "When I do 'A,' 'B' happens." Many of the individuals I've worked with have had little experience with a consistent environment that promotes the learning of such a relationship between their behavior and how their environment works. They neither know how to access their valued reinforcers nor recognize that their environment has specific expectations for their actions. Successful compliance can help them experience both. As said earlier, adherence to verbal guidance involves a process that goes far beyond producing the dutiful following of a request. Rather, it becomes a vehicle that allows us to teach individuals to learn for themselves.

SELF-INITIATED LEARNING

It is not unusual for individuals, once experiencing type-one requests, to begin to generalize the occasional need for compliance to situations not specifically introduced. For them to do so, however, they must have had successful experiences with following through with what you have asked.

The process, then, is more important initially than the tasks involved. Multiple practicing sessions where individuals are requested to do many small things and receive appreciation (if it is valued) for effort can help with the introduction of the process of learning to attend to words and being guided by them. Frequently, I will ask teachers and parents to purposely set the stage for these practice sessions so individuals can experience several times throughout the day the sequence that starts with a simple request and concludes with demonstrated appreciation for completion. Initially, the teaching process is time consuming for it requires our undivided attention. If our teaching approach is successful, the required practice time will decrease rapidly for individuals will soon begin to do things for us and themselves.

It is, of course, important to view the process of compliance from the individuals' perception. Little is accomplished if we constantly attempt to *make* individuals comply. If that is all we have going for us, then we will indeed be in the midst of an unwanted power play. Our goal is to set the circumstances where individuals *want* to comply both for us and for themselves. For that to occur, they must value themselves and those of us who find ourselves in a responsible position. For them to value themselves, they must know they are important; they must know they can be successful; they must know that they, as well as what they do, is appreciated. By associating ourselves with their importance, success, and experienced appreciation, we, too, will have a better chance of being seen as important and of worth. Conversely, if we are seen as only carrying a big stick, seen as part and party to an absence of success and appreciation, cooperative compliance will be a distant possibility. If our methods fail to teach the process that promotes cooperative compliance, it will not occur in our presence.

IN THE ABSENCE OF COMPLIANCE . . .

Ironically, it is individuals who will lose out under the latter circumstances. Their manifested undesired behaviors will impede their personal growth and development. In schools and special settings, they will not work to improve themselves. They will not tap into their own productive resources—to whatever degree they exist. They will be seen as having a problem, when in fact, the problem is more ours. If steps are not taken to reverse the downward spiral, they will be visited by the convenient "dragons" that have proliferated so dramatically over the past years. Sometimes, without intent, the fictional "dragons" will be conveniently reified, and will take precedence over what we are capable of doing to assist the individuals. At that point, they will indeed have a problem.

SUMMARY

KEEP IN MIND

1. When your students comply with your needed requests, your task as teacher and their role as students become easier and more successful.

2. Compliance with your words promotes what is called "verbal influence" or "verbal control." You and your students relate with one another and are guided by each other through words rather than coercion. The accompanying atmosphere becomes one of mutual cooperation.

3. Helping students become appropriately compliant requires that you be aware of the following:
   a. Students must know that you expect compliance; that if you ask them to do something, you expect them to carry out your request.
   b. Students will be more inclined to be compliant if:
      1. They understand what they are to do.
      2. They are able to do what has been requested.
      3. They see some reason to do as requested.
      4. They know you will appreciate their effort.

4. Remember the two types of requests—type-ones and type-twos:
   a. Type-ones: requests that must be complied with. No exceptions. Do not make a type-one request unless you are certain you want compliance, and unless you are prepared to make sure the request is carried out.
   b. Type-twos: students have a choice as to whether to comply.

5. If you make a type-one request and then change your mind, the following is likely to occur:
   a. You will lose verbal control.
   b. Your students will know you do not mean business; they will know that on those few occasions when you require they comply with your requests, you will likely, once again, change your position.
   c. Your students will adaptively push you; they will find ways to waste precious time; neither you nor they will be as successful as you could be.

6. When you make a type-one request, make certain it is complied with as quickly as possible. When compliance occurs, show some appreciation both for what was done and for the students' cooperation.

7. Always explain to your students why compliance with type-one requests is necessary. When possible, ask them for suggestions as to which requests should be type-ones and which should be type-twos. As you will see, once you begin making requests of your students, the

vast majority of your requests will be type-ones. Still, try to solicit your students' cooperation and input.

8. Understand that the absence of compliance opens the doors for the convenient dragons.

CONSIDER AS WE LOOK AHEAD

It remains to examine the issues and circumstances, the realities and areas needing change that all impact on your work. Consider, for example:

1. Schools. School problems. Students. Student problems. Teachers. Teacher problems. Controversy.
2. "IQ" Tests. Discrepancies between ability and performance. Controversy.
3. Learning Disabilities. Attention-deficit-disorders. Emotional disturbance. Special classes. Special curriculum. Medication. Dragons. Professional Ignorance. Parental pain; parental concern. Controversy.
4. A need for things to change. Who will take the lead in making the changes? Who must take the lead? Teachers. No controversy.

11

DRAGONS OF CONVENIENCE: EDUCATION'S DISEASES

Many things are changing within the field of education, particularly the relationship between regular and special education. There is considerable dissatisfaction with the way some professionals view "exceptional" individuals and the programs designed to provide direct services to them. My conceptions of the present state of affairs, and what I will discuss, have been influenced by both authors and practitioners who, like myself, work directly with children and adults who present problems requiring assistance. I have also been greatly influenced by the special individuals I have seen whose uniquenesses have been as varied as grains of sand. The individuals have been my most important and effective teachers. They have provided the basis for much of the following.

The material to be presented is not without controversy. While it will be embraced by some who read it, it will be reacted to with disdain by others. It will create problems both for professionals who have been taught to think otherwise, and for parents of "exceptional" individuals who have been told otherwise. Those of you who will find this book a part of your educational training may also experience confusion along with any number of other reactions; for another required reading or provided lecture may suggest that the views expressed in this text (and that are shared by many other consultants) are, to put it succinctly, wrong.

─────────── THE OPPORTUNITY TO CHALLENGE ───────────

Wrong as some may see it, know that you, just as I, have a choice of positions with which to align ourselves. That that option exists tells us most of our sought-after answers have yet to be documented to the satisfaction of everyone. It also tells us that the "truths" stated or implied by authors, speakers, or practitioners may be little more than opinions without basis in fact. Thus the door is open for disagreement and challenge; authoritative edicts, even when pontificated by the Emeritus, must be held in suspicion until all the facts are in—requiring a time period that will outlast all the present-day Emerituses. If, as student, practitioner, or parent, you sense a chord of dissonance within the fields of regular and special education, and if you are of the mind to do so, you can challenge the accepted, not solely for the enjoyment that accompanies such activity, but for the purpose of proclaiming that you have yet to be satisfied with what you've heard, read, or been told to believe.

─────────── THE DRAGONS: THEIR EVENTUAL DEMISE ───────────

It was inevitable that the "dragon" would have found its way into this manuscript. We have been associates for many years, friends at times, but not all the time. My university office wall is covered with hand drawn pictures of the beast, most often smiling benignly, standing near a young child who appears to reflect my uncertainty as to whether the creature is ally or foe. One of the pictures, sketched in pencil, was given to me by my cherished son when he was six years of age. Its position on the wall is such that each time I sit at my desk, I see the dragon staring back. It holds special significance for I know how close this child came to being drowned by the ignorance that gave birth to the fire-breathers whose powers have markedly affected the lives of countless children, parents, and teachers.

The dragons will eventually be laid to rest. The process is well under way. As with most unneeded, outdated artifacts, they will be consigned to a historian's attic along side other dusty, antiquated trinkets from the fields of medicine and psychology. We will stop our time-wasting, semantic games, halt our childish propagation of fancy but useless names, recognize our responsibilities and their worth, and, as was suggested well over a decade ago, get to the serious business at hand.

─────────── THE NAMING GAME ───────────

A "Rumpelstilskin fixation" . . . [a term coined by Dr. Alan Ross] . . . characterizes the preoccupation of some psychologists with whether a given child who manifests a learning disability is or is not brain-damaged. That question and related questions of etiology and classification often dominate psychological evaluations and staff conferences as if everything depended on that one answer. In a well-known fairy tale the chance for the princess to live her life happily ever after depends on her discovering the name of an ill-tempered dwarf. As a result she goes to great lengths to learn his name, and upon doing so, earns her salvation. Many clinicians and educators seem to engage in similar fairy-tale behavior. They act as if, could they but give the condition a name, the child would be saved. It is time that psychology and education lead the way in calling a halt to this labeling so that sooner or later, parents may follow. We must rid ourselves at long last of the mistaken notion that one of our tasks is diagnosis, "identifying a disease from its signs and symptoms." We should instead get on with the job of training, teaching, and rehabilitating the children.[1]

QUALITY MANDATED

There are numerous federal and state laws mandating that all children are entitled to appropriate (and one would hope, quality) education. As we all know, mandates are little more than words on paper: The documents do not, themselves, assure that the intent of the laws are carried out. The job of application rests on the shoulders of the field professionals who are directly involved with the individuals whose rights (and integrity) have been protected by legislation and verbal commitment. Again on paper, the task would appear to be relatively straightforward: have available a strong, well-trained group of dedicated professionals; determine the specific short and long term goals the educational system is to serve; determine what skills and assets individuals bring into the system, what the individuals will need, what experiences will be necessary, and how best to deliver those experiences assuring the individuals' growth toward the established goals. The mandates are clear: services for all individuals, regardless of differences.

THE PRESENCE OF DIFFERENCES

If all the individuals who entered the educational system were basically the same, meaning they shared similar endowments and prior experiences, shared similar skills and abilities, both physical and mental, shared the same desire and motivation to learn about themselves, the knowledge of their worlds, and what they would need to advance within themselves and their worlds, education's task would be easy. Such similarity (homogeneity) would require little more than having a dedicated teacher open *the* adequately written textbook to page 27 and say to the 30 or so students, "Let's begin." (One textbook per level of instruction and assignment would be sufficient given that all the students were basically ready for, and capable of benefiting from, the same material. Educating them would be no more difficult than buying a plain-colored sock—one size fits all.)

The Dilemma Differences Present

Suppose a system was foolish enough to believe that all students (of similar age) were ready (as a result of their age) for the same materials. Imagine what might happen if such a belief was accepted. Imagine what might happen if, unbeknownst to anyone, as a result of some heretofore unheard of quirk, a student, slightly dissimilar from those already enrolled in the class, entered the school room in order to be educated. Imagine what might happen if the quirk's effect went unnoticed until the teacher stated, **"Today we're on page 28, let's all begin."** Imagine what might happen if the new student . . .

11.1

. . . eagerly flips the pages to the one designated, looks at the material, experiences a sudden sense of emptiness in his stomach, raises his hand, uncomfortably indicating the material is slightly (only slightly) over his head. The teacher, dedicated, but trained to believe that all students entering her class are the same, also experiences a sudden sense of emptiness in her stomach. She asks her pupils to put their charcoal and slates away and take ten minutes of extra recess. With legs less than stable, she makes her way to the teacher's lounge and falls into the cushions of a soft chair.

"What's wrong with him," one of her colleagues asked after hearing of the dissimilar student.

"I don't know," the teacher answered, her lower jaw nearly touching the floor.

"But there must be something wrong? Maybe something serious?"

"Do you think so?"

"Don't you think so?"

"I don't know what to think," the teacher responded. "All I know is that he is different from the others and that's not supposed to be."

"What are you going to do?"

"I'll figure something out," she said, pressing her brain cells for a expeditious answer.

As fables would have it, she fought off her light-headedness and nausea, returned to the class, told the dissimilar youngster not to fret, met with him after class for a few moments, helped him with the problems he was having so he'd be prepared for the following day's page 29, and rode the family horse home to her mud-covered husband, who couldn't understand why she was so late. Later in the evening, a bushel of onions was delivered to the teacher by the formerly dissimilar student's mother who personally thanked the teacher for her assistance.

AN EPIDEMIC OF DIFFERENCES

Word of the teacher's efforts spread quickly round about hither and yon. Before week's end a second new student entered her classroom door. A note was pinned to the back of his shirt: "Please help this one, too. He's also dissimilar . . . only slightly."

"Another one? My heavens, do we have an epidemic on our hands?" the colleague remarked on hearing the news. "Does he look funny, different, you know, unusual?"

"He seems okay to me, he's just a little behind the others," the teacher answered, slightly more confident and less shocked than when the first dissimilar student entered her class.

"But how could he have gotten that way? He must have some kind of a condition."

"What do you mean 'condition'?"

"A problem, something wrong with his head. Maybe he's got a brain dysfunction, a little one, you know, minimal."

"How would I find that out?"

"You could ask him," the colleague suggested innocently.

"I'm supposed to walk up to him and ask him if his brain is damaged!" the teacher exclaimed.

"Don't get excited, I'm just trying to help."

"I wonder if there are more like him," she asked quietly.

"More! Can't be. I mean, if there's more what will you do with them?"

The teacher thought for a moment. "Teach them, I guess," she answered as she walked back to her classroom to see the new student. That evening, she and her husband found a live pig tethered to a tree near their house. The note attached to the rope said simply, "Thanks."

After securing the animal in the barn, the husband turned to his wife: "Keep this up and I'll put away the plow and open a supermarket."

There were, of course, more. Each day new students stood in the teacher's doorway. Some walked with slight limp, others didn't walk at all. Some spoke in short, labored sentences, some did not say a word. Some were very young, appearing as though they had yet to see their first book, others were older, rapidly approaching adulthood with needs that seemed to outstrip what the classroom could offer. A few still benefited from the teacher's brief assistance after school, some required many weeks, others seemed to benefit little despite the teacher's tireless efforts.

A REQUEST FOR ASSISTANCE

"I need some help," the exhausted teacher said, slumped in the chair of the principal's office.

"I've brought in a consultant from the city to tell us what to do," the man indicated from behind his desk. "He'll be here this afternoon."

"That's nice, but I think all I need is some additional teachers who could assist me with the dissimilar students," the woman said wearily.

"Let's wait to see what the consultant has to say."

AN INEFFECTIVE SOLUTION

Later that afternoon: "The first thing I would do is take all the dissimilar students and place them in their own classroom," the well-dressed man began as he opened his briefcase.

"Why would we want to do that?" the teacher, now sitting straight in her chair, asked.

"If you would remove all the dissimilar students, you could once again have all your students work on the important page in the book. All would be ready for the same information," the man answered.

"I don't think I ever want to go back to that approach," she responded. "I've learned a lot these past weeks."

"Such as?" the principal asked.

"Differences don't frighten me anymore. I've come to see that they are real and should be expected. They are a part of our world," she answered.

"But your job would be easier if we keep the similar and dissimilar separated," the man responded.

The teacher turned to him. Indignantly, she stated, "I didn't become a teacher because it was easy."

THE ASSIGNING OF NAMES

The man abruptly faced the principal. "I would remove the dissimilar ones from the woman's classroom, then I would test each of them to find out what is wrong with them," he said as though the teacher was no longer in the room.

"The only thing wrong with them, that matters, is that they need more help, more time, than I can offer," the teacher stated with passion.

Still ignoring her, "We need to know what to call them," the consultant continued with heightened resolution. "Once we know what to call them, we'll know what to do with them."

"Call them!" the woman protested.

The well-dressed man looked her in the eye. "Yes! Knowing what to call them is important. We can then categorize them!"

"For what purpose?" the principal asked.

"Sir, there's a new federal law that guarantees money for different educational diseases. If you have the right disease, you can get funds. All you have to do is to tell the federal government what is wrong with the students, what they need, and the money is yours."

| 11.2 |

"The students need teachers," the woman pleaded to ears that didn't hear.

"What sort of categories are you referring to?" the principal asked, holding up his hand to momentarily silence the woman.

"Do you want them *all?*" the man asked. "There are quite a few."

"Not all, just a sample," the principal requested.

The consultant reached into his brief case and found a piece of paper filled with something that, in today's parlance and often declared by way of a bumper sticker, just happens. "There's academically handicapped, aphasia, autistic, behavior-disordered, below-average learner, brain-damaged, cerebral dysfunction, educational problems, failure sets, culturally deprived, delinquent, educable mentally retarded, educationally disabled, ego-development deficiency, emotionally disturbed, emotionally handicapped, emotionally maladjusted, exceptional, genotypically retarded, hyperactive, hyperkinetic, impulse ridden, latent development . . ."

The principal moved his raised hand toward the consultant, signaling enough already. The man didn't see the hand.

". . . learning disabled, low cognitive capacity, low IQ, mentally defective, mentally handicapped, minimal brain dysfunction, overstimulated, perceptually handicapped, physically handicapped, primitive, psycholinguistically disabled, psychotic, retarded development, slow learner, socially defective, socially deprived, socially disruptive, socially handicapped, socially impaired, socially maladjusted, socially rejected, symbiotic disorder, trainable, withdrawn . . ."

"Enough!" the principal declared, his ears now ringing.

"Sir, there's more."

"No doubt. Where'd you get those things from?"

"From special education journals," the man replied confidently.

"Special education?"

"Yes. It's the new thing. I predict it will become a most important repository."

"For what?" the other man asked.

"The students who are dissimilar," the consultant indicated.

"Will you both shut up for a moment!" the teacher exclaimed, standing up. **"Funds and names and diseases! Give me a brief break. They're still children, each doing the best they can with what they have.** Some are so sharp they could nearly teach the class, not to mention themselves. Others learn more slowly, differently, but they still learn. A few present uniquenesses that I know nothing about: I'm not sure what they hear or what they see. But they're still children, and what they need is as evident as the nose on your face: They need different books, more skilled teachers, and more time to practice and experience what we can offer them."

"If you had listened to me," the consultant broke in rudely, "you'd have realized that was precisely what I said. Once we know what to call them, we'd know what to do with them. The names would tell us what is wrong with them; what they're suffering from." The man placed the paper filled with the names and placed it in his briefcase. He then stood and glared at

11.3

the teacher. "I suppose you already had an idea of what to do with the children if we hadn't named the names."

AN ALTERNATIVE: A GLANCE

"You can bet the farm on that. Identify their strengths and weaknesses. Find out what they succeed at with ease and what sets them to stumble. Develop approaches that maximize their styles. *Teach them*," she answered as she walked from the room, back to the children.

ARE THE NAMES IMPORTANT? TO SOME, YES . . .

"It really doesn't matter what terms we use to describe the students, does it?" the parent asked.

"That depends on whom you ask," I told her. "Samuel Kirk, a noted authority in field of special education, for example, has suggested that certain names are relevant while others are not. He stated that while the name 'brain-injured' has little educational significance[2] the name 'learning disabilities' has considerable value.

Many people . . . hesitate to label a preschool child as "learning disabled." Others, including myself, believe that the term is appropriate . . .. I have discussed this difference in concept with some of my colleagues who feel that we should not apply the term *learning disabled* to preschool children. They state that if a child has a language disorder we should call it "a language disorder." If a child is disoriented in space we should label the problem "a disorder in orientation." If a child has a visual perceptual problem we should label it as a "visual perceptual problem." I do not see the logic in such arguments.[3]

Other professionals," I continued, "also believe the names have educational value. The name 'gifted' has gained prominence over the years, and now we have some professionals who believe it is beneficial to combine various names, such as 'gifted-learning disabled.'[4]

"As you might expect, however, other authorities share a different point of view."

An examination of the "classificatory labels" strongly suggests that there really is no classification system within special education. What might appear to be a system is, in reality, an unsystematic crazy quilt of labels. The categories and labels do not constitute a scientific classification system. First, there is no common logic, criteria, or order within the scheme. Second, the various classificatory labels come from different disciplines, reflect different perspectives, and serve no single purpose. The crucial and fundamental inadequacy of current special education classification is simply that the scheme does not serve educational purposes.[5]

The categories used in special education for mildly handicapped students are not reliable nor valid as indicators of particular forms of education. Their use is expensive and inefficient; they cause much disjointedness in school programs.[6]

It has not been possible to construct a distinct research base for the categorical programs of special education, because the categories have been ill-defined and unreliable. The boundaries of the categories have shifted so markedly in response to legal, economic, and political forces as to make diagnosis largely meaningless and inconsistent. Accountability is unclear because the categories are scientifically indefensible.[7]

In offering these comments about the classification of students, we do not deny that the students have serious problems; it is the flawed system for addressing those problems—how the children, and even the teachers and programs, are categorized—that is in doubt. And we note that to the extent that classification systems are unreliable and inconsistent, the accountability to children so fervently desired and fought for by advocacy groups simply goes awry.[8]

Reflecting on the major review of research and practice in special education which he led in the early 1970s, the late Nicholas Hobbs said that the present classification system for exceptional children is "a major barrier to the efficient and effective delivery of services to them and their families and thereby impedes efforts to help them."[9]

| 11.4 |

"This is so perplexing," the parent said. "Some professionals tell us the names and categories are important, while others tell us they're detrimental. Am I the only one confused?"

"By no means," I responded. "Many people share your bewilderment. Many of us aren't certain what the names actually mean."

THE NAMES' INCEPTION

"Then where do these indecisive names come from? They weren't just invented, were they?"

"Frequently when authors use the terms, they bracket them with quotation marks indicating that the names are only constructs; that they aren't to be interpreted as being concrete things," I explained.

"You mean they *were* invented!" the woman exclaimed.

"I'm not certain how all the terms came about, but the most popular one, 'learning disability,' came into print as a result of a parent/business meeting in 1963. Samuel Kirk proposed the term 'as a compromise because of the confusing variety of labels'[10] being used in special education."

> In 1963 members of many . . . parent organizations met . . . to discuss the national problem of brain-injured children and to establish a national organization . . . . The parents were advised that if they were interested in educational services for their children they should use a term relating to teaching or learning. Kirk stated that, for want of a better term, he had recently used the term *learning disability* in his text *Educating Exceptional Children* to describe this diverse group of handicapped children.
>
> At the business meeting the parents discussed various terms and finally decided on the name . . . . The name and category "learning disabilities" struck a receptive chord . . . . Learning disabilities, as a separate category of exceptionality, was born.[11]

"It was voted into existence?" the woman asked, astonished.

"I would imagine a consensus was reached by those attending the meeting that the term represented what they wanted to say," I suggested.

"Then in actuality, it's only a name," the parent said, "a term used to describe other things."

"That's right. It is a construct that certain leading authorities believe is valuable. Other equally qualified authorities believe it is a 'phantom' category—that there is no real 'LD'."[12]

Closing her eyes, she paused for a moment. Then with a look that reflected an earlier, painful experience, she stared at me: "If someone told a parent that his or her child *had* a 'learning disability,' the statement would be inaccurate," she said, her face now strained and pale.

"This is a highly charged, controversial area," I answered softly, "but in my view your interpretation is correct. You've happened upon a major area of professional confusion."

"Such as?" the parent asked.

"The difference between describing an observation and explaining it," I answered.

"This is not one of your professional word-games, is it?" she asked pointedly.

"No, it's not. There is a real difference; one that can have a major impact on the thinking of professionals, as well as the type of remediation an individual receives."

CONFUSION LEADING TO AN ERROR IN LOGIC

"There might not be anything wrong with the child," the parent said, her voice reduced to a whisper.

"Not wrong in the sense of an illness or disease or an anomaly that exists within the child's physical or emotional self. Rather, the child might not be doing something that meets someone's expectations."

"Not doing something! You mean the child's behavior is not acceptable or desirable?"

"Not according to someone's predictions or preferences."

BEHAVIOR, THE BAROMETER: A GLANCE

"And because the behavior is not what someone wants or believes is right, the child is said to have a problem?"

"That happens."

"How can it happen?"

"Most of us aren't very comfortable with differences. We want things to run smoothly, according to our own perceived plan of how they should run. This is especially true with students' school performance. If something goes awry, if an individual isn't doing what we want, if he does something different than what we hoped for, we want to know why the difference has surfaced and what to do about it. No doubt the parents at that business meeting Dr. Kirk addressed were not satisfied with their youngsters' performance in school. The parents were a representation of thousands of parents who also had experienced dissatisfaction with what their children were doing. They didn't like the term 'brain damaged' or 'retarded.' They wanted their children referred to in a different way. They had the courage to speak their minds, to demand help. As a result of their efforts, much has changed. No longer are children kept in closets because they are different; no longer are parents embarrassed about seeking assistance when their children aren't like all the other children who live on the block. Schools have been mandated to incorporate differences and provide assistance. The days of 'open your book to page 27 and we will begin' are gone. Schools are now required to open books to whatever page will promote success for the child. The many advocacy groups composed of parents and other professionals now guarantee the acceptance of differences and the programming for those differences. But in their zeal to protect the rights and integrity of all who are different, they've produced a system so invested in names and labels and categories, a system so satisfied with quick and erroneous answers to complex issues, that the specific needs of the children often have been overlooked."

> Unless major structural changes are made, the field of special education is destined to become more of a problem, and less of a solution, in providing education for children who have special needs.[13]

BEHAVIOR: THE BASIS FOR DECISIONS

Consultants, because of the tasks requested of them, often see things differently than professionals who spend little time working directly with individuals in need of assistance. Consultants, like teachers and therapists, are commissioned to observe, every day, what individuals do and fail to do. They have the opportunity to watch how individuals behave throughout a whole range of daily academic and social activities. Initially, beyond anything else, they focus on the behavior of the individuals. Through the behavior, the professionals are provided with a picture of the whole person.

It is no doubt apparent why an individual's behavior is so important. Behavior is the barometer we use to determine how well individuals are doing. If individuals (children or adults) are doing precisely what everyone wants, precisely what is expected and desired of them, it would be rare, if ever, that they would be seen as having any sort of problem. More concretely, if individuals' school work is successful, if they are progressing and advancing in their studies commensurate with the expectations of their teachers and parents, they would be seen, from an academic viewpoint at least, to be doing just fine. If individuals' communication skills and motoric activities are progressing equally well, again they would be seen, from those viewpoints, to be right on the developmental target. If individuals' social behaviors meet or exceed established expectations, if they feel good about themselves, pleased with their own growth, once again from those viewpoints, they would be judged as doing well. If individuals are doing or experiencing all of the above, an educational or psychological consultant would not be requested to offer any assistance. None would be needed.

THE ABSENCE OF DESIRED BEHAVIOR

What if they aren't meeting our expectations? Little will turn our heads more quickly than when we notice that one of our youngsters (or charges) is experiencing difficulty with any one of a number of developmental tasks. It is the *absence of desired behavior,* academic, social, communicative, or motoric, that causes us to look more closely at individuals who have not met our, or someone else's, expectations. Again, the important barometer is the individual's behavior. I am not called in to help a youngster with feeding if, in fact, her eating behavior is sufficient to maintain health. Likewise, I am not called to offer assistance to a school-aged youngster or delayed adult if his behavior in school or home is satisfactory to those responsible for his education and advancement. But if the individual's behavior deviates from a real or professed "normal" path, if the individual's health, well-being, or progress takes a turn toward a different, less desired road, I, and many of my colleagues, may be summoned to offer ideas as to what may be responsible for the deviation, and how best to redirect development toward what is desired.

| 11.5 |

THE PAIN FROM CONFUSION

"This is very important to me," the parent said as she nervously placed a legal size pad of paper on the table and began to write. "I may ask you to repeat a few statements for I need to be certain that I understand precisely what you are saying. I have received so much conflicting information over the past years that I no longer know what to believe. Ever since that initial conference," she said, reflecting on the past, "our lives have been placed in a swirling whirlpool. Before, everything seemed so stable. Now, I just don't know. I've always thought myself capable of handling most anything that hurt my child," she continued, her voice heavy. "But this, this something that seems not to be a something, this experience without boundaries, without clear edges or lines that would allow us to demarcate and understand, has hurt us all." She paused. Her pain and despair were evident.

"Do you feel comfortable enough to share a few specifics?" the teacher, sitting next to the mother, asked.

"The specifics are cloudy," the woman began slowly. "About half-way into first grade we received several notes indicating that our son was not living up to his capabilities. He wasn't attending to his work to the degree desired by his teacher. He was seen as a little clumsy; his handwriting was not as legible as that of some of the other children: 'too scrawly,' his teacher had said. He was considered bright: They had given him several tests that indicated he was quite capable, but he wasn't working up to his capacity, we were told. At that first conference, we were told that he might have some neurological problem that was interfering with his efforts. The school psychologist said that he was probably experiencing significant confusion; that he was trying to make sense out of the world around him, but that it was very difficult for him to do so. The psychologist kept talking about 'soft' signs of brain dysfunction. He used the term 'brain dysfunction' so casually. It was as though we were expected to sit back and, equally casually, accept the fact that our son had something wrong with his brain. The man never knew how frightening his words were. He seemed so damned aloof, almost arrogant. At one point, he turned to us and asked if *we* could explain why our son wasn't doing as well as he should. He asked us! He seemed pleased when no answer was forthcoming. He then talked about 'learning disabilities,' about 'hyperactivity,' about deficiences," she said, her eyes filling with tears.

"Besides the handwriting, did your son's teacher tell you what else was creating difficulties?" the young teacher asked.

"She brought out a few of his class papers. He was supposed to have written something on one and he hadn't; he was supposed to have answered certain questions she had asked, but he hadn't done them all correctly. Was that so terrible? He was just a little boy."

"At home?" I asked.

"He was . . . has always been fine at home. He does what we ask, he's happy, plays with his friends. He's no more clumsy than they are. They all seem to trip over their own feet," she added with a forced smile.

"Did you share your feelings and observations with the staffing group?" the teacher asked.

"I tried, but no one seemed to listen. They had their tests. They kept talking about how he was different from many of his classmates. They didn't hear what my husband and I said. They kept talking about 'normal' this and 'normal' that; about developmental ages and the fact that our son was below the average age; about how he *should* be doing better, about how he was capable of doing better. They seemed bent on a direction and they wouldn't waver."

"How is he now?"

"I don't know," she answered with a deep sigh. "He gets special help with his handwriting, which I don't mind. He reverses some of his letters and numbers, not all the time, but he does it. He says he forgets which way certain letters are supposed to go. He knows his right from his left, but sometimes he starts the wrong way and the letters get written backwards. His reading and math are okay, but again, they keep saying that it's not what it should be for someone so bright. One teacher told me he might be gifted, but he might have a perceptual problem, a processing problem, I think is the way she put it."

"Is he in a special class?" the teacher inquired.

"Several times a week he goes to a room for 'learning disabled' students," the woman answered.

"Does *he* mind?"

"Once, in the beginning, he asked me if he was different, if he was retarded. He told me one of the kids in school said he was. I must have cried the whole night," she shared. "What was I to say? I told him, yes, you are different. We are all different. But that's good," I said to him. "It's okay to be different. I told him he was great, that he was loved dearly. He doesn't ask about it anymore." She stopped talking for a moment, seemingly on the verge of exploding. She turned to me. Words that had laid close to the surface of her mind poured forth like a torrent rain. "Now, you tell me!" she demanded. "You tell me what's so wrong about being different! What's so terrible about a 6-year-old being a little clumsy, not writing perfectly, not answering all the questions asked of him, not attending to everything presented? Do you do everything perfect?" she challenged, pointing her finger toward my chest. "It's okay for an adult to screw up, but not a child? Where's the logic in that? Have you ever tripped? Spelled a word wrong? Not been able to answer someone's meaningless question? Do you hear everything asked; attend to everything said?"

"No," I responded.

"And what's this capacity business? I can tell you the capacity of a milk container, that's easy. I know how many cookies a jar can hold. But how do *they* know the capacity of my son?" she laughed angrily. "His brain? He's not some simple, plastic, or glass container with finite walls. Could they tell me of my capacity? Yours? Anyone's? Don't you realize how foolish, how naive you sound when speaking of the capacity of a human being? And this!: Where do they get off saying that being different means that he has a physical problem! I don't care what names you people use, they are just words, names, voted on at a business meeting, or decided on by mutual consent. Couldn't there be another explanation for his differences? Why does the problem have to be inside him? Are his teachers perfect? Don't they make mistakes? Couldn't there be something wrong with the school? Are schools perfect?'' she stated, knowing the answer to her own question.

All teachers, whether they teach regular or exceptional children, frequently encounter youngsters at the preschool or elementary levels who are not responsive to instruction or who are disruptive in class. These children may evidence problems in reading, arithmetic, language, or writing or in social adjustment or motivation. Most of these pupils are probably victims of poor teaching, insufficient background experience, and/or inadequate motivation. No children are immune to the debilitating effects of these three factors.[14]

"I'm not trained in your field," the parent continued, somewhat subdued, "but I don't perceive myself to be a totally ignorant woman. I'll tell you what I see. You've got a lot of kids in one classroom. That must be very difficult for the teacher, especially if the children are not all alike, if they have different interests and skills and backgrounds and support systems. Most of the kids are doing fine—which means they are doing what the teacher wants. But you have some who, *for many possible reasons,* are performing differently than what is assumed normal or desired. A discrepancy exists between what is wanted and what is observed. That makes the teacher's task doubly difficult. This discrepancy is the critical factor, isn't it? It's what you look at. It's all you see. But what you don't see is it also represents a crucial flaw in your thinking. All of us, in every walk of life, experience discrepancies. But what you have done is to assume if there is a discrepancy between a student's behavior and what is expected of him, he's the one with the problem. I can tell you this: discrepancies can occur for many reasons, and not one of them need suggest the student is suffering from an invented, voted-on, educational disease. Children aren't television sets with broken transistors, computers with worn out chips, automobiles with outdated batteries. Yet you look upon the children as if their parts are malfunctioning. You have committed the sin of reification. You have given life to inanimate artifacts. In the process of your idolizing, you've forgotten us. Your names, and your debates over them, have taken precedence over what the children are doing; what you might do to help them." She stopped speaking, and looked toward the teacher and myself.

"Sometimes I think everyone out there is wearing earmuffs." Her words were barbed, carefully considered. She seemed drained, exhausted, her energy and emotions spent. "It's like selective deaf ears; like you have the ability to hear only what you want, what fits comfortably within your own schemes. It's like you don't even listen to your own words. You just say them because you've always said them. Sometimes, I want to give up," she said, her voice now barely audible, "because I'm so tired of talking with people who don't hear. Then I look at my son and I know I'll never give up. There's something wrong with what you people are doing," she said without a hint of hesitation. "Good intentions aside, there's something wrong. And please don't tell me that you mean well. I know you mean well. But I don't need your understanding. I need to understand what is going on."

THE DISCREPANCY MODEL

As the parent indicated, discrepancies are vital components of the educational system. They are involved in many critical decisions that can dramatically affect the lives of students, their teachers and parents. If their presence is interpreted incorrectly, any number of serious errors regarding judgments made about students and what they need are likely to occur. Understanding what they are and what they mean is extremely important.

The term "discrepancy" suggests that a particular observation is inconsistent with what the observer expected or desired. A discrepancy, therefore, requires at least two variables: one that is expected and one that occurs. The discrepancy *model* is an intregal part of every profession, be it medicine, education, engineering, or homemaking.

DISCREPANCIES: THEIR PURPOSE

Discrepancies, those that involve such serious concerns as an individual's walking, talking, or progressing in school, to the less serious observations of a lightbulb that won't turn on or a microwave oven that won't turn off, serve an important purpose: *Discrepancies alert us to the possibility that a problem exists.* They become an impetus to find out *why* something is not occurring as expected, along with what needs to be done to rectify the existing difficulties. They helped Henry Ford produce safer cars, Jonas Salk develop the polio vaccine, Margaret Mead expand our views of peoples of the world, and many educators develop better services for school children. Other examples of the discrepancy model in action are plentiful.

If a person's "normal" blood pressure was 120 over 80, and suddenly it changed to 200 over 110, the person and his or her physician would want to know why. If a child had yet to take his first step by 15 months of age, had yet to speak by 24 months of age, the question "why," punctuated with great concern, would be raised. If, however, the observed blood pressure and the child's behaviors were exactly as predicted or expected, then no discrepancy would exist and the question "why," regarding those observations, would not be raised. Without the discrepancy model, the accompanying inquiry as to what may be wrong, and the developed answers and remedies, many of us would not be alive today.

ANSWERS TO THE QUESTION "WHY": ETIOLOGY

Both the discrepancy model and the questions it encourages are essential. We humans have never produced trouble for ourselves when seeking reasons and explanations for the phenomena of our world. What difficulties we have created are *not* with the question "why," but with the expedient *answers* we have chosen to accept. Historical literature is ripe with problematical answers and explanations for a wide variety of concerns: Ravaging plagues that decimated populations were said by authorities to be caused by "evil spirits"; a woman's collective "emotional instability," fatigue, and common cold, were said to be caused by her "wandering uterus" that had been lossened from its pelvic moorings; "mental illness" was explained by a patient's "congested blood"; and a person's persistent interest in stamp collecting was suggested to be a result of his poor toilet-training experiences.

One can find little fault with authorities of the past, who when faced with "diseases" that were creating havoc, searched for etiologies (causes). That was, and still is, an authority's responsibility. In retrospect, one can question the authorities' skills when they allowed themselves to suggest that plagues were caused by "evil spirits," and that the woman's difficulty was due to a uterus that had wandered aimlessly from its appointed position. It might have been helpful for the patients of the day to have secured several "second opinions" regarding the hypothesized "causes," but it is unlikely a second opinion, in those days, would have helped much. Professional ignorance abounded; authorities of the past had few, if any, *alternatives* to the dragons they invented—evil spirits, congested blood, and vagrant uteri were in vogue, and many authorities knew no better. The professionals did the best they could with the information that was available, and it is easy for an "enlightened," present-day student of history and logic to throw stones at their efforts and conclusions. No doubt authorities centuries from now will have many a stone to toss at our modern-day dragons. Indeed, the stone-throwing has already begun: More than a few present-day experts have long since begun flinging their entire scientific arsenals at the contemporary, ubiquitous, dragons that have found their way into today's schools and homes.

DRAGONS: THE METAPHOR

Dragons are the *answers* given by authorities when asked *why* an individual behaves or fails to behave in a particular manner. In schools and special settings, they are the reasons offered by authorities to explain the *absence* of *desired*, or the *presence* of *undesired*, academic, social, or developmental behavior. The answers can speak to medical problems— why a child fails to walk with a normal gait or properly digest his or her food; education problems—why a student has difficulty learning information, following instructions, or concentrating on assignments; social/ behavioral problems—why an individual has a tough time sitting still or abiding by classroom guidelines. The question "why" seeks the "etiology" of a problem, and the answer offered represents the dragon. Placement into special classes, along with proposed treatment for medical, academic, or social/behavioral problems, often are determined once the dragon has been named by an authority. Sometimes the pronounced dragon—the authority's answer to the question "why"—is correct. Sometimes the authority's answer is wrong.

MORE THAN A SEMANTIC PROBLEM

The parent looked up from her notes. "So we have this child, this individual. We observe that he is behaving in a particular fashion. We see what he is doing, and we decide that what he's doing does not represent either what we want or what, according to some measure, we believe he should do. At that point a discrepancy is said to exist. Right so far?"

"Yes," I answered.

"The discrepancy tells us something may be wrong, so we begin to investigate what might be responsible for the absence of desired or predicted behaviors. Our investigations will help us know why the individual's behavior is different than expected. Once we determine the nature of the problem and what is *causing* it, we then institute a treatment procedure." She briefly returned to her notes. When she looked up again, she appeared puzzled.

"Is there a problem?" I asked.

"That's just it, I don't see any problem. I'm almost disappointed. I thought I would discover some blatant logical error."

"With the exception of the term 'cause,'" the teacher responded, "there is no problem at this point."

The terms "cause" and "effect" are no longer widely used in science. They have been associated with so many theories of the structure and operation of the universe that they mean more than scientists want to say.[15]

"Whenever I see one of my students experiencing difficulties with his academic work or social behavior, whether he's not attending, not completing assignments, or not performing as I would wish," the teacher continued, "I always try to speculate on what variables might be related to the observed discrepancy. If I can discover what might be influencing the student's responses, I will try to discover a solution."

"You try to find out what's wrong," the parent suggested.

"Of course," the young professional answered.

"Like whether the student *has* a learning disability?" the woman asked. The teacher and I hesitated before either of us responded. The parent caught the silence and shifted uncomfortably in her chair. "Did I say something wrong?"

The teacher first looked toward me then to the parent. "I think you just found what you were looking for."

"I don't understand," the parent said to the young woman.

"The serious error in logic," I stated. **"A student *cannot have* a 'learning disability.'"**

| 11.6 |

DETERMINING THE EXISTENCE OF A PROBLEM

My consultation is sought only when an individual's behavior fails to meet an expected level of performance. Expectations are the standards used to determine if everything is right or if something is wrong. Thus, before any professional concludes that a discrepancy exists between individuals' observed performance and their expected (or predicted) performance, the professional must have a basis on which to determine his or her expectation of how individuals *should* be performing. Many professionals, as a result of their training and biases, derive their expectations of desired performance by looking at the individuals who are being "examined"; then they do any or all of the following:

1. **They compare** an individual's behavior with the behaviors of other individuals of similar age/grade level.

| 11.7 |

2. They compare an individual's behavior with developmental norms that suggest what individuals *should* do at particular ages.

3. They compare individuals' academic performance with their measured intellectual ability or capacity (most often by using "intelligence" tests) which some professionals believe indicates how well individuals *should* be performing academically.

If a professional believes that a discrepancy exists between the examined individual's *observed* performance and the *expected* performance, the professional may conclude that a problem exists. Most often, the professional, because of his or her training, will suggest that the individual *has* a physiological or emotional problem, perhaps slight, perhaps severe. When asked *why* the discrepancy exists, the professional may respond with such *explanations* (read: "dragons") as "learning disability," "emotional disturbance," "retardation," "hyperactivity," "attention-deficit-disorder," or any number of other names. Again, given the professional's training, such conclusions and responses appear logical.

PROFESSIONAL DIFFERENCES

If *all* professionals in the fields of education and psychology were taught by their mentors to make the above comparisons and draw the above conclusions, teachers and parents would have a relatively easy time understanding what was being said or suggested regarding a particular student because there would exist no disagreements among us. All professionals would assess the same way, interpret the same way, and come to the same conclusions. Such, however, is not the case. A second group of professionals, as a result of their training and biases, view an individual's behavior differently, and draw different conclusions.

1. They will not compare individual A with individual B as a means to determine what anyone should do academically or socially.
2. With a few exceptions (e.g., walking, talking) they will be very cautious predicting what an *individual should* do.
3. They will *not* use "intelligence" tests as a measure of "intellectual capacity," and thus will not use a derived score on such a test to predict how a student should be performing academically.
4. They will see an individual's behaviors as adaptive, perhaps undesirable, but certainly not pathological. When asked why the individual is behaving "undesirably," they have available several alternative explanations for the absence of desired behavior, and none of the alternatives will suggest the existence of an *educational/ psychological* disability within the individual.

5. They might conclude they don't know what is responsible for the individual's "undesired" academic or social behavior. They would rather admit ignorance than invent a convenient "dragon." They know that even in the absence of being able to answer the question "why," much can be done.

The two views are noticeably different, and their disparities must not be glossed over lightly. Those who represent both positions are equally concerned about the welfare of the individual; both, it must be assumed, wish to do the best for the individual who is experiencing difficulties. Despite their mutual concern, however, the existing discordance will produce differing views of the individual, his or her behavior, and what programs need to be designed in his or her behalf.

THE BASIS FOR PROFESSIONAL EXPECTATIONS

The value (and validity) of *any profession's* discrepancy model is dependent on the profession's ability to accurately measure the variables that are being compared. Today's medical profession, for example, knows roughly what an individual's blood pressure *should* be, given (among other things) the person's age and body weight. Medical science has gathered data from large numbers of people over the years, has developed charts and scales that provide a barometer by which to make comparisons, and has manufactured a reasonably effective instrument that allows measurement of what is termed "blood pressure."

Imagine, however, medicine's plight many years ago when it sought to learn about blood pressure, but neither knew all the variables involved, nor had yet to develop an instrument that provided accurate measurement of what they believed existed. In the absence of such information and technology, physicians would not be able to indicate the existence of a discrepancy because they wouldn't know what a patient's blood pressure *should* be—or what it was! From all their observations, they would have known that "blood pressure" or something similar to it no doubt existed; they simply wouldn't have known its specifics. Such ignorance would not have prevented the doctor from *talking* about blood pressure, but it would have prevented other physicians from knowing what he or she was talking about. In all likelihood, the doctor wouldn't have known what he or she was talking about either. The value of the discrepancy model, as it would have related to blood pressure, would have been suspect, at best. Physicians and their patients would have shared the same darkness that comes with ignorance.

EDUCATION'S VARIABLES

Education's discrepancy model, obviously, is only as good as its ability to measure its critical variables. Since the discrepancy model is the *only* means available to determine whether a student has a problem, the importance of a valid model cannot be overstated. Thus, for a teacher or parent to receive an accurate, correct answer to the question: "Is there something educationally, emotionally, or behaviorally wrong with the child," authorities must be able to accurately measure the variables that make up education's discrepancy model. If the authorities *can* do so, then accurate, valid answers are possible. If they *can't*, then they will be in the exact position of the early physician: They will be able to talk about something, but neither they nor anyone else will know precisely what is being said.

As indicated earlier, education's discrepancy model is employed to facilitate many decisions: Class placement, presence of "handicapping" conditions, curriculum to be used with students, the development of goals and objectives, what type of therapy is needed, as well as other determinations. It is based on a comparison of the following variables:

1. The student's intellectual *capacity*	COMPARED WITH	The student's academic *performance* in class
2. How the student *performs* on various tests	COMPARED WITH	How *other* students *perform* on the tests
3. How the student *should* behave in class	COMPARED WITH	How the student *is* behaving in class

Let's see what problems, if any, exist with the variables that make up the above three comparisons as they are often used in education's discrepancy model.

ACADEMIC PERFORMANCE IN CLASS

To measure the variable of academic performance in class, one needs only to determine what specific academic area will be investigated or tested and what methods of measurement will be used. If, for example, a teacher is interested in a child's performance in math and concept formation, the classroom professional has all that is necessary to adequately measure both areas: the math books and daily exercises the student uses, his or her own innovative questions and observational skills, and the child's oral and written answers. If the teacher desires to know of a student's writing skills, paper, pencil, and an idea or two generally is all that's necessary. While standardized achievement tests can be used (and usually are) to offer an estimate of a student's academic performance, individual assessment by a teacher, using classroom materials, is a far superior method of gaining access to an individual student's unique skill level and learning style. Many standardized instruments fail to offer specific information about an individual youngster, presenting instead percentages and averages that speak to many youngsters. Further, they rarely are geared toward the precise curriculum being used by the student's classroom teacher. Frequently, they sample small amounts of material that may not offer a reliable estimate of a particular student's skills. As such, they provide information about the "average" student, the "average" curriculum, not the individual in question as she makes her way through what her teachers have planned for her. If, however, a teacher uses his own instruments to assess how the student is performing in class, this variable can be easily measured.

In some instances, a child will lack the necessary physical endowments to answer a teacher's questions in the ordinary manner of speaking and writing, and academic performance may not be easy to measure regardless of the tools employed. I am referring to a youngster who has suffered a trauma associated with what is termed cerebral palsy (CP), or other neuromuscular accidents. Great strides have been made in the past decades providing such a child with augmentative communications systems that allow professionals to sample a child's cognitive and academic work. With any child who lacks or has difficulty with communication skills, care must be taken when drawing conclusions about the child's academic abilities. The absence of behavior is *not* synonymous with an inability to behave. The child may know considerably more than his body will allow him to share.

_____ COMPARING STUDENTS' TEST RESULTS _____

Students are requested (or required) to take any number of tests that will show where each stands in relation to the others regarding a host of topics including academic subject matter and learning styles used to interpret and solve problems, questions, puzzles, and the like. For those interested, a Montana individual's performance can be compared with a purported counterpart living in Maine. Thus, for what it's worth, data can be provided indicating how students compare with other students on a wide variety of tasks.

CLASSROOM BEHAVIOR

This variable is measured by simply watching and noting what the student does. A teacher's keen eyes and ears, along with a reasonably accurate record-keeping system, are all that are necessary to know how the student *is* behaving. (For the teacher to understand what purpose the student's behavior serves, the teacher must know how the behavior fits within the natural environment.)

These variables provide us with some (but only some) of what a student is *presently* doing, academically, cognitively, and behaviorally. Because they are normally easy to measure, they fit comfortably within education's discrepancy model. Now we will look at the variables that speak to what the student is *expected* or predicted to do. The variables involved—intellectual capacity, mental processing, and how a student should behave—present a more difficult assignment.

INTELLECTUAL CAPACITY

It is probably safe to say that no child has ever completed schooling without once being described as "bright" or "dull," "quick" or "slow." In educational circles, few variables occupy as much interest and speculation as a student's "intelligence." In parental circles, few educational instruments are as well known as the "intelligence" test. Few instruments have as much power as the ever-present tests, the results of which often lead people to speak of the presence or absence of intellectual capacity. As a direct result of an obtained score, students may be colored "gifted," "retarded," "disabled," or "normal." Indeed, their curricula, teachers, school, classrooms, and classmates may change shortly after a psychologist has concluded testing, evaluated answers, checked provided norms, compared relationships among subscales, and totaled a score referred to as an "intelligence quotient" (IQ). Other measures are used to help estimate a child's functioning ability, but "IQ" tests occupy center-stage.

While not all educators or psychologists adhere to the following, many interpret measured "intelligence" as the barometer of a individual's capacity to perform academically. An IQ score is seen as an indicator of a youngster's native or inherent intelligence. From that viewpoint, IQ represents an index of "brain power," of *organic*, neurological/electrochemical intellectual ability—in other words, the "nuts and bolts" of his brain. Such a view can lead one to believe that a student doesn't have the "intelligence" to perform a task, and mean that the youngster's "nuts and bolts" are insufficient to successfully complete an assignment. This view can also lead a professional to say:

> "I am concerned that the child is working *above* his *maximum* capacity."

The statement was made by a teacher at a conference, and when pushed to explain his position, he stated, "The child is making A's in my class yet his IQ is only average, about 100. I am concerned that the child is an 'overachiever.'" In other words, the unique professional didn't believe the student had the necessary "nuts and bolts" (read: "intelligence") to be doing so well.

OUR IQs: A MAGICAL, MYSTICAL SUBSTANCE

For years we've been talking about IQ as though it stands for some singular, all encompassing dimension that one either has, has a little of, or doesn't have.

A professional allows the calculated IQ number to roll past his lips, and the number somehow indicates how much "intelligence" and ability the student possesses. Despite effort spent attempting to show that functional, nonorganic "intelligence" must be more than a singular dimension, some professionals still view the construct as some magical, singular substance.

A FIXED SUBSTANCE?

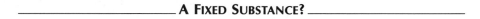

Further, some authorities view the substance of "intelligence" as being *fixed*—you get what you get, and that's it. Putting aside the fact that we don't know what the "it" is, the "fixed" view is easy to dispell. Not too many years ago, a noted boxer had a measured IQ well below "normal." Shortly *after* winning the heavyweight championship of the world, his IQ score, measured by the same "intelligence" test, zoomed into the comfortable "normal" range. Would anyone wish to conclude that being beaten around the head somehow increased the boxer's organic "nuts and bolts?" While there are data showing that the *measured IQ number* is often quite stable over time (meaning that what you score the first time you will likely score the second), does that mean that "intelligence" is equally stable? Or might it mean that "intelligence" and the IQ number are not one and the same? Or that what "intelligence" tests measure has little or nothing to do with "intelligence?"

> We must conclude that whatever it is that IQ tests measure, it is measured reliably [consistently] . . . But exactly what are we tapping? This brings us to a discussion of . . . validity. Opponents of IQ testing have argued that whatever we are measuring, even if it is measured reliably, is measured with little or no validity. . . . At this time there is no consensus on the kinds of traits and abilities being tapped by IQ tests. Do such tests reflect more or less innate intelligence, the ability to use facts and skills that were previously learned, or just a general adeptness at coping with tests like this?[16]

INTELLIGENCE TESTS

Technically, one cannot show that intelligence tests measure or fail to measure "intelligence." We won't be able to show that until we discover all the parameters of "intelligence." The fact that a test has a name doesn't mean that it measures what the name says. (More than a few in my field define "intelligence" as "That which an 'intelligence' test tests!" Such circularity helps no one.)

What do we know about "intelligence" tests? In a variety of ways, *they sample behavior.* They ask factual questions, require problems to be solved, and puzzles to be completed. Some use colored blocks, cards with pictures, and elaborate mazes. They all request that the student answer questions and solve problems provided by an examiner.

Before the instruments are marketed, they are tried and tested with many thousands of individuals. Care is taken to make the instructions clear, the employed stimuli accurate, and to add and delete material that may or may not be valuable as perceived by the tests' developers. Perhaps most important, the years of development concentrate on selecting the best questions, the best problems, and the determination of the best answers, along with the amount of time allotted for the answers and solutions to be given. Further, the questions and problems sample wide varieties of situations that are appropriate for individuals of equally varied ages. These latter purposes are most critical: From the answers and time spent at solving the problems, the developers compile the barometers (norms) by which future tested individuals will be compared.

NO FAULT WITH THE TESTS

Up to this point, it may appear that I have said nothing that would diminish the value of these instruments. That is as intended, for up to this point, assuming the researchers have abided by the rules of good test development, one can comfortably conclude that the finished product will provide educators with *highly usable information.* What then is the problem? There must be one, for many states do not allow "intelligence" tests to be used with some of their students; some psychologists refuse to administer them; and many educational researchers and practitioners believe the tests do not benefit children—that the conclusions often drawn from the produced scores are little more than poppycock.

Six-year-old Charles was a gregarious youngster, preferring to fool around with his classmates rather than attend to his teacher's instructions. By the sixth week of school, his affinity for playing and not working was well known and had become a burdensome thorn for the teacher responsible for his education. When threatened with the loss of valued activities—recess and class movies—Charles would pull himself together and perform adequately, but rarely at the level the teacher desired, or the level of her more-achieving pupils. His teacher, however, had grown tired of the need for coercion and believed that Charles had a problem that prevented him from doing what she wanted. Upon her urging, a referral was made to the special education teacher, and after the necessary forms were filled out, Charles' parents were told of the teacher's desire for psychological testing. They agreed to allow the testing, and within a few weeks, the school psychologist administered, among other instruments, an "intelligence" test.

When the testing was completed, a meeting was held. Those in attendance were the school psychologist, the regular and special education teacher, the speech therapist, the school's principal, and the child's parents. The psychologist indicated that Charles' "IQ" score was in the low 70s; the term "retardation" was used, and the suggestion was made that Charles be placed in a class for children who also had "limited intellectual capabilities." The placement, it was said, would make it easier for Charles to work at a level commensurate with his lower intelligence. The principal remained silent until after the parents had left the meeting. Once alone, his response to the group was firm: "I can't support your conclusions. You have not visited him at home or observed him with neighbors and friends to see how he functions in nonschool surroundings. The 'intelligence' test only taps a few skills under very controlled conditions. The IQ figure does not tell you how well he adapts to everyday situations. I remind you that if the child tests out 'retarded' in school, but does not function 'retarded' at home, then he's not 'retarded.'"

Steven had always been a delight to his teachers. He followed directions, was prepared for assignments, and attentive to the requests that helped his classroom run smoothly. He enjoyed school, always greeting his teachers with a bright smile and an outlook that suggested he was happy with himself and his surroundings. His vocabulary and reading ability were a cut above his fourth grade classmates, and due in part to those skills, he would often find himself in the front of the room reading orally and leading discussions on the specifics of the material. Recently, however, his fourth grade teacher had become concerned about two persistent behaviors. Occasionally, Steven would write numbers backwards when solving math problems, something he had been doing since first grade. More serious was the child's manifested difficulty with mathematical word problems. He could read the problems with ease, solve the problems once his teacher translated the sentences into numerical values, but without the teacher's assistance, he would struggle to derive the concrete numbers from the abstract words. The difficulty had become a source of frustration for both the child and his mentor, and the teacher had found herself at a loss as to what would help. "I think he has a 'specific learning disability,'" one of the teacher's colleagues indicated after hearing of the child's difficulties. "Have you seen his IQ? It is over 120. A child that *intelligent* shouldn't be having those problems. He may be neurologically impaired."

IF IT'S NOT THE TESTS, ____ THEN WHAT IS THE PROBLEM? ____

There's nothing wrong with the tests that have the term "intelligence" within their names. *They just sample behavior.* Although we aren't always certain what the tests measure, they, and most any other instrument developed by educators and psychologists, provide a professional with an opportunity to observe how an individual responds to a variety of situations. That, of course, is worthwhile. But we must keep the value of their products in perspective.

Conventional intelligence tests: CANNOT reveal the capacity or potential of a student.

• • •

Conventional intelligence tests: CAN provide fair predictions of school success, assuming we do nothing exceptional to help or hinder certain students and thus destroy the prediction.[17]

(W)e should remember that (the scores) do not imply that an individual with a high IQ will necessarily be a good learner, or that one with a low IQ will be a poor learner.[18]

INTERPRETATIONS/EVALUATIONS

Problems? Not with the tests. In relation to the breadth and quality of their questions and exercises, they tell us something about students' experiences; their cognitive, motoric, and language strengths and weaknesses; their *acquired* knowledge that may or may *not* relate to what the tested individuals are doing in school. *They are performance measures,* measures of performance regarding the materials specifically included *within* the tests. They indicate some of what individuals *have* acquired and experienced, some of what they choose to show us they have acquired and experienced. The tests certainly do *not* indicate what they are capable of acquiring and experiencing. They only sample behavior—and only the behavior that is sampled given the tests' items. The sampled behavior, then, is limited to the items the tests present. Problems? They rest with *our interpretations* of what the sampled behaviors indicate.

Past abuses of intelligence testing have most likely resulted from user error, not test error.[19]

INTERPRETATIVE ERRORS

As examples of "user" abuse, let's return briefly to the two scenarios involving Charles and Steven. In those instances, the tests were assumed to measure "intelligence"—the "nuts and bolts" kind. The professionals involved assumed, erroneously, that the scores reflected capacity; as such they believed the scores to be an appropriate part of the discrepancy model. There's *no* scientific (much less "common sense") evidence to support the notion that the tests should be a part of education's discrepancy model to determine the presence of a disability.

The Council for Learning Disabilities has recently stated that discrepancy formulas should *not* be used to determine LD because: (a) current instruments are technically inadequate; (b) students who need LD services are denied access because of the improper use of formulas; and (c) discrepancy formulas create a false sense of objectivity and simplistic decision making.[20]

The professionals in the scenario, however, chose to ignore (or were unaware of) the Council's conclusions, and interpreted the test results to suggest that a discrepancy between capacity and performance existed, and the two boys had a disorder that somehow accounted for their academic difficulties.

THE VERBAL COMPONENT OF IQ TESTS

Ironically, the same behavior of the students in the aforementioned cases—verbal skills—set the stage for the professionals' inaccurate interpretations. "Intelligence" tests favor students who possess highly developed vocabularies, more specifically, vocabularies that are used within the tests' questions, problems, and instructions. Children who know the words, know the meaning and conceptualizations of the words, will do better than children who don't. Even the purported "nonverbal" components of the tests favor children with good language skills, for while children may say nothing to the examiner, they can use their *acquired, private* cognitive skills and ask themselves various questions that may clarify both the instructions and exercises. Charles didn't stand much of a chance to show his "nuts and bolts," and the principal, fortunately, recognized that. In his own environment, his own cultural surroundings, Charles did just fine. The test he took didn't sample that culture or its required skills. Steven, on the other hand, was in equal jeopardy, but for different reasons. He was a whiz with words, and his IQ score reflected that skill. But the test he took didn't require the solution to mathematical word problems; he would have "bombed out" in that activity. The test also didn't score him on number reversals; that exercise wasn't included.

HAD THE IQ TEST INCLUDED THOSE TOPICS, NO DISCREPANCY WOULD HAVE BEEN PERCEIVED

Interestingly, had Steven's "intelligence" test measured math word problems and number reversals, his total IQ score would have been *lower*. The lower score would have *reduced* the perceived discrepancy between "intelligence" and class performance; the discrepancy might have been interpreted as "insignificant." The authority who suggested "learning disability" might have altered her conclusion after seeing the lowered IQ score—"He's just an average kid, not overly bright," she might have stated, unaware that an IQ score doesn't provide for that conclusion either.

NOTES

1. Smith, R.M., & Neisworth, J.T. (1975). *The exceptional child: A functional approach.* New York: McGraw-Hill.

2. Kirk, S.A. (1975). Behavioral diagnosis and remediation of learning disabilities. In *Proceedings of the conference on exploration into the problems of the perceptually handicapped child.* Evanston, IL. Fund for perceptually handicapped children, 1963. (Reprinted in S.A. Kirk, & J. McCarthy, [Eds.], *Learning disabilities: Selected ACLD papers.* Boston: Houghton Mifflin.)

3. ————(1987). The learning disabled preschool child. *Teaching exceptional children* (Winter 1987), 78–80.

4. Weill, M.P. (1987). Gifted/learning disabled students. *The Clearing House,* vol. 60, no. 8 (April). Washington, DC: Heldref.

5. Smith, R.M., & Neisworth, J.T. (1975). *The exceptional child: A functional approach.* New York: McGraw-Hill.

6. Reynolds, M.C., Wang, M.C., & Walberg, H. (1988). The necessary restructuring of special and regular education. *Educating exceptional children,* 4th Ed. Guilford, CT: Dushkin.

7. Ibid., p. 6–12.

8. Ibid., p. 6–12.

9. Hobbs, N. (1980). An ecologically oriented based system for classification of handicapped children. In E. Salzmeyer, J. Antrobus, & J. Gliak (Eds.), *The ecosystem of the "risk" child* (p. 274). New York: Academic Press.

10. Hallahan, D.P., & Kauffman, J.M. (1988). *Exceptional children: Introduction to special education* (p. 100). Englewood Cliffs, NJ: Prentice-Hall.

11. Kirk, S.A., & Chalfant, J.C. (1984). *Academic and developmental learning disabilities,* (p. 34). Denver: Love.

12. Keogh, B.A. (1987). Learning disabilities: In defense of a construct (pp. 4–9). *Learning Disabilities Research, 3* (1).

13. Reynolds, M.C., Wang, M.C., & Walberg, H. (1988). The necessary restructuring of special and regular education. *Educating exceptional children,* 4th Ed. Guilford, CT: Dushkin.

14. Hammill, D.D., & Bartel, N.R. (1982). *Teaching children with learning and behavior problems* (p. v). Boston: Allyn and Bacon.

15. Skinner, B.F. (1953). *Science and human behavior.* New York: Free Press.

16. Ibid., p. 53.

17. Smith, R.M. (1969). *Teacher diagnosis of educational difficulties* (p. 45). Columbus, OH: Charles E. Merrill.

18. Levin, J. (1977). *Learner differences: Diagnosis and prescription* (p. 54). New York: Holt, Rinehart and Winston.

19. Taylor, R.L. (1984). *Assessment of exceptional students: Educational and psychological procedures.* Englewood Cliffs, NJ: Prentice-Hall.

20. Brown, A., & Campione, J.C. (1986). Psychological theory and the study of learning disabilities. *American Psychologist, 41,* 1059–1068.

SUMMARY

KEEP IN MIND

1. Observed differences in behavior and performance of students have always raised questions: Why do the differences exist? Why does one student perform differently from another? While many professionals suggest that differences among individuals in the general population are guaranteed, and are not, in and of themselves, cause for alarm, other professionals, when looking at the general population of school children, often assume that differences are synonymous with disabilities. Such a position has proved controversial.

2. A most cursory consideration of the total composition of the natural environment assures us that among students, from every geographic locale, every socioeconomic level, every conceivable culture, regardless of genetic endowments or environmental experience, differences are guaranteed. Differences, in and of themselves, are not synonymous with disabilities.

3. Some professionals believe it is necessary, even beneficial, to use educational labels to both describe and "explain" student differences. Other professionals believe the practice of using labels is not only worthless, but harmful.

4. A child's behavior is the only barometer available to indicate how well the child is performing in school. All professionals use a child's behavior to gain some insight into how the child and system are working. Some professionals use the behavior, specifically the absence of desired behavior, as in indication that a problem exists within the child. Some professionals use the behavior, the same absence of desired behavior, as in indication that a problem exists within the system. Both groups of professionals use a "discrepancy model" as they attempt to assess what is happening.

5. The term "discrepancy" means that an observation is inconsistent with an expectation. In schools, the expectation is that students will perform well. If the students fail to do so, a discrepancy is said to exist. The proposed "cause" of the discrepancy will be dependent on the

professional's view through the window. Some will use the discrepancy as evidence the child in question is disabled. Others will object to such logic.

6. When a discrepancy is observed, the question Why? logically follows. Many of us need to know why an unexpected observation has occurred. We are curious. Indeed we have never gotten ourselves into trouble when asking the question Why. (Often we've gotten into trouble when we haven't asked the question!) Problems do not come from the question. Problems do, however, come from the answers man has determined, developed, or, on occasion, invented to account for vagaries of life.

7. In education, "dragons" represent the answers professionals have developed to account for student differences. Sometimes the dragons represent accurate answers. Sometimes the dragons represent false answers. You will have to draw your own conclusion as to the veracity of our invented dragons.

8. In education, discrepancies are derived by:
   a. Comparing one student's behavior with that of another. Both may be similar in age and grade level.
   b. Comparing one student's behavior with developmental norms indicating what the student should do. The norms may or may not be valid.
   c. Comparing a student's academic performance with his or her measured "intelligence." The "intelligence" measure allegedly indicates how well the student should be performing academically.

   Many authorities believe the above comparisons, used for purposes of determining whether a particular student has a disability, are invalid. Such authorities adhere to the following:
   a. They do not compare two individuals for the purpose of determining what either should be doing academically or socially.
   b. They are cautious about predicting what any particular individual should do. (The term "should" is used predominantly with behaviors that have a strong physiological base.)
   c. The do not use "intelligence" tests as a measure of capacity or ability. They do not contrast a student's classroom performance with a score from a so-called IQ test.
   d. They see behaviors as adaptive; as purposive. They know that two children, the same age, from the same grade, can be significantly different. They know that both children, despite their differences, can be just fine.

9. "Intelligence" tests provide samples of behavior. From that viewpoint, they are valuable instruments. However, they appear to have little or nothing to do with the measuring of ability and capacity. They are, at

best, measures of experience. As such, they do not belong within education's discrepancy model. They are performance tests. They can be compared with other performance tests. They, however, should not be used to judge whether a student is or isn't disabled.

Everybody, Page 27

| 11.1 | In today's schools, in a typical classroom, how productive would a teacher be if he or she said, "Everyone open your books to p. 27 and we will begin"? Question: What problems might arise from such an approach?

Which Name Will You Call Them?

| 11.2 | Why would a consultant suggest that it was necessary to call dissimilar students by some categorical name? What might be his or her justification for doing so? Question: Would knowing what to call the students help the teacher determine how best to serve them? Teach them?

Doing Their Best

| 11.3 | What did the teacher mean when she indicated that the children were doing the best they could given what they had? What does the phrase "what they had" represent? (Hint: Think of the "person" in the formula of the natural environment. Remember there's an environment within the individual as well as one that exists outside.)

Labels on Top of Labels

| 11.4 | I tell you I have a "gifted–learning disabled" student in my classroom. Exercise: You tell me what the student does! Compare your answer with your colleagues. Did you all come to the same conclusion regarding the student's actions? No way!

The Pain from Confusion

| 11.5 | Please reread the section "The Pain from Confusion." I'm going to list a few points the parent made. React to them now. How do you feel about them? Do they bother you? Is there anything wrong with the positions the professionals took? Would you have wanted them to say different things? Say less?

Say more? Say nothing? (While you read the passage, did you get the feeling deep within that you wanted the professionals to simply shut up and begin helping the child?) Points:

a. "We received notes indicating that our son was not living up to his capabilities."
b. "He was considered bright . . . they had given him several tests that indicated he was quite capable, but he wasn't working up to his capacity."
c. "At the first conference, we were told (by the educators) that he might have some neurological problem that might be interfering with his work."
d. "The psychologist kept talking about 'soft' signs of brain dysfunction. He used the term brain dysfunction so casually. . . . He then talked about 'learning disabilities,' 'hyperactivity,' about deficiencies."

(Besides the problems with handwriting, what else seemed to be a problem? the parent was asked.)

e. "[The teacher] brought out a few of his class papers. He was supposed to have written something on one and he hadn't; he was supposed to have answered certain questions she had asked, but he hadn't done them all correctly. Was that so terrible?"
f. "They kept talking about 'normal' this and 'normal' that; about developmental ages and the fact that our son was below the average age; about how he *should* be doing better; about how he was capable of doing better."

You Can't Have "LD"

| 11.6 | In a sentence or two, explain why it is theoretically impossible for a student to "have" a learning disability.

Comparisons: Do Cautiously

| 11.7 | This requires a lengthy answer. Explain what may be wrong with the following comparisons:

a. Compare an individual's behavior with the behaviors of other individuals of similar age/grade level (to determine whether a discrepancy exists).
b. Compare an individual's behavior with developmental norms that suggest what individuals *should* do at particular ages.

    c. Compare an individual's academic performance with his or her measured intellectual ability or capacity, by using an IQ test (for purposes of determining whether the student is academically "slow," "normal," or "LD").

CONSIDER AS WE LOOK AHEAD

1. What should we do with students whose academic performance is less than what we desire? Should we say they are deficient? Should we label them "learning disabled"?
2. What does the term "learning disabled" represent? How will we define it? Indeed, is it something that can be defined?
3. Is it possible that student differences are not indicative of internal deficiencies?
4. Is it possible that student differences are reflective of adaptive differences to a multifaceted environment?

12

Learning Disabilities and Other Dragons

As you recall, the purpose for a discrepancy model, whether it be one with numerical parameters that result from formal testing, or one that we instinctively derive from our experiences in daily living, is to signal the presence of a problem. When a problem is noted, the subsequent task is to determine its "cause," which we hope will lead to a solution. In educational circles, the "problem" almost always refers to an individual's behavior, academic or social, that fails to reach expected standards. Predictably, we will want to know why the problem has occurred.

Traditionally, to determine the "cause" of an individual's absence of desired behavior, we have relied on all manner of developed educational and psychological instruments to help us identify what may be wrong with the individual who has failed to perform according to our expectations. One of our steadfast beliefs has been that the absence of desired performance is a direct result of something being wrong with the individual's physiology or mental processing abilities. The belief sets the stage for a battery of assessments designed to locate, define, and make public that which may be wrong.

The diagnostic process is always a consequence of somebody saying that someone has something wrong with him. We put it this way because frequently it is not the individual who decides to initiate the process. This is the case with children, but there are also times when adults are forced by pressure from others or by legal action to participate in the process. In all of those instances people individually or society in general communicate four ideas: something may be wrong with someone; our lives are being affected; we should find out the source of the trouble; and we should come up with solutions to alter the individual's status and allow us to experience our lives in the way we wish.[1]

Unfortunately, the battery of assessments used to locate, define and thus identify what is wrong with the individual student has not been given, after careful review, the highest marks. It has been concluded that:

[M]ost standardized tests used in special education evaluations do not have adequate validity and reliability and thus do not meet the technical standards published by the profession using the tests.[2]

Further,

There is little question that eventually the tests [used in a learning disabilities test battery] . . . will be discarded; the evidence against them is mounting. The central question is really whether recognition of the invalidity of these tests will result in abandonment of an untenable professional dogma, or whether it will merely result in the test battery being replaced by other equally questionable instruments.[3]

Barbara Keogh, when analyzing the role of testing for learning disabilities, indicated the following.

Let us consider the infamous ability-achievement discrepancy as a criterion for identification as LD. . . . The problems come when we attempt to operationalize and measure this difference; that is, when we attempt to determine what constitutes a discrepancy and to identify who has one. Clearly, we have not done this well . . . In addition to inconsistencies in the particular discrepancy formula applied, the ability-discrepancy criterion is threatened by unreliable, invalid, and inappropriate tests, often administered and interpreted improperly. The vagaries of measurement and assessment in LD have been extensively discussed and should give us real concern.[4]

"What does all that mean?" the parent asked, her mind spinning dizzily.

"It means that the tests we use to determine what is wrong educationally with an individual aren't able to do the job many professionals had hoped or suggested," I answered.

"But they are used all the time," the parent responded. "The professionals who use them speak as if they are valid, reliable instruments; they report results as if they are also valid and reliable."

I nodded, agreeing with her observations. "Many professionals are not aware of the questionable value of the instruments."

> Although the professionals using the tests have published expected test standards, they do not apparently know that the tests they use do not meet those standards.[5]

> The majority of professionals hold incorrect judgments on the reliability and validity of currently used assessment devices. . . . Professionals apparently support the tests they use based on 'cash validity'—if a test is used widely, it must be valid; and 'typographical validity'—if a test is printed, it must be good.[6]

"They use them because they're provided, required, or chosen," I explained.

"Now I'm really confused," she stated. "If you're suggesting that intelligence tests, since they don't measure capacity, shouldn't be used to determine the existence of a discrepancy between ability and performance, and you're saying that the instruments used in the test battery fail to show what is wrong with a student, how then have you decided that nearly 2 million students in the United States are learning disabled?"

"As you remember, I don't use that term; I don't believe it is necessary. In my judgment, it has outlived its usefulness."

Her eyes widened and her back straightened. "Well, some people use it. My child was said to *have* a learning disability!" she responded curtly.

TO DESCRIBE OR EXPLAIN BEHAVIOR: A CRITICAL DISTINCTION

Few educational services have grown as rapidly, have served as many children, and have generated as much controversy as learning disabilities (LD). Despite the fact that, or because, more than one and a half million pupils are currently identified as LD and provided professional services, the LD field is under serious and continuing attack. . . . Criticisms have been directed at the validity and reliability of methods of identification, at the efficacy of intervention programs, and at the confusion and overlaps of LD with other special education categories. Critics have argued that LD is really a political category, that it is racially or economically inspired, and that it discriminates against large numbers of pupils. Indeed, it has also been suggested that there is no such thing as LD and that pupils with learning problems are really victims of poor pedagogy, of inadequate instructional programs, or of limited educational opportunity.[7]

According to researchers at the Minnesota Institute of Learning Disabilities:

> After five years of trying, we cannot describe, except with considerable lack of precision, students called LD. We think LD can best be defined as 'whatever society wants it to be, needs it to be, or will let it be at any point in time.[8]

ADJECTIVES AND NOUNS

Perhaps I've been taken over by a rush of naivete; perhaps my graduate years in the beautiful desert of Arizona tinged more than my skin; or perhaps my role as consultant to schools and parents has provided a different perspective than that of some of my associates; whatever the "cause," I don't see the problems associated with the term "LD" as being extraordinarily difficult either to understand or rectify. To the contrary, they're quite simple. Initially, what is necessary is to realize that we're talking about *two* terms: "learning disabled" and "learning disability." The first is an *adjective;* the second a *noun.* An insignificant difference? Not by a long shot. The first is intended to *describe* something that is observed; the second is intended to *explain* the observation. The first colors, shades, and portrays in the same fashion that "happy" and "sad" and "warm" and "distant" color, shade, and portray. The second goes far beyond characterizing: it is something said to be *had* in the same fashion that one has a defect in hearing or seeing or ambulating. The differences are critical.

"FOR WANT OF A BETTER TERM"

During that original business meeting in 1963, when Samuel Kirk spoke with the concerned group of parents, dissatisfaction was expressed over several areas: The parents were concerned about their children's lack of academic progress; the previous educational terms such as mental retardation and minimal brain dysfunction were not viewed as acceptable; the parents needed a new *descriptive* name that would refer to their children, a name that would not carry the stigma associated with mental retardation or be aligned with the unruly, amorphous term of "minimal brain disorder." *For want of another term,* they decided upon LD as their standard.

TO DESCRIBE OR EXPLAIN BEHAVIOR: A CRITICAL DISTINCTION

——————————— A NEUTRAL TERM NEEDED ———————————

Initially, the term was intended to *describe* a group of children who did not appear to fit or match with any other group of school-age youngsters who were not succeeding as expected or hoped. While I can only speculate, I would assume they were "bright" children; no doubt highly verbal children; nice kids who were struggling with some of their school assignments. Like many other children, outside of school, they were experiencing much success with many everyday, nonacademic activities they enjoyed. During that parents' meeting in 1963, or certainly shortly thereafter, the decision was made to describe and name the children "learning disabled"—an innocent enough term, a new term, unstigmatized, without excessive baggage or negative connotations, an adjective included among the many other adjectives used when characterizing children seemed necessary or purposeful. It was a "handle," something the parents, given their concern and desperation, could hold onto. None of us who love our children, who are witness to something about them that we do not understand, tolerate well the darkness that comes from not knowing what is happening. A term, even though it is only a term, is at least something.

But an adjective is only a construct, a term used to represent other terms. It does not tell us what individuals do, it doesn't tell us how they think or what they think about, it doesn't tell us what individuals see as important or hold of importance about themselves. It can only describe, and often without specificity. Two individuals, described by the same term, can be, and usually will be, different.

——————————— ADJECTIVES CAN SAY ONLY SO MUCH ———————————

As an adjective, the descriptive "learning disabled" doesn't shed much light. Describing someone as a Republican or Protestant or American, someone as a Yippie or Yuppie or Yappie is no more illuminating than a 10-watt bulb used to guide the footpaths of a crowd in a 20,000 seat auditorium. Granted there's light, but not enough to know what is in front of one's nose. Not all Republicans, Yuppies, "learning disabled" or any of us wear the same uniquenesses. To discover those uniquenesses, we must separate individuals from the crowd, we must look at each of them as he or she is: as his or her own self. Adjectives do not afford such scrutiny. Just as beauty must be left to the mind of the beholder, so it is with all manner of words designed to portray. Knowing individuals can, in large measure, only come from knowing what they do, how they think, the way they show us how they feel. Knowing what they do can only come from noting their behaviors within the context in which they occur.

Thus when we describe a child as "learning disabled" we have *not* described much. Such is not a fault of the term—recall that the term, for lack of one that was seen as better, was decided on at a meeting. The fault lies with us: We, knowingly or otherwise, have used the term to represent so much that it now represents next to nothing. The outcome of our failures has produced the following: When a child is described as "learning disabled" we must ask, "What does the child do?" Once that information is forthcoming, we will then know something of the individual child that will enable us to be of help. Interestingly, and not to be passed over lightly, once we know what the individual child does and does not do, we will *no longer need* the descriptive term "learning disabled." It will be redundant and unnecessary, unless of course all individuals described as "learning disabled" do the precise, *literally the precise,* same things, in the same manner, under the same conditions. I would imagine that even the most zealous proponent of the term will hesitate to assert that *that* will ever be a reality.

ASSESSING ADJECTIVES

As with determining whether an individual is or is not possessed of beauty, determining whether an individual should (or should not) be described as "learning disabled" is a function of the mind of the examiner/beholder. It is no longer a secret that school districts, psychologists, and teachers hold different criteria to be necessary before the descriptive term is used. It is not unusual for two professionals, after looking at the *same* student, to espouse different judgments. The same divergence is evident when two people try to judge whether a third person is happy or successful. Adjectives, unless their specific criteria are agreed on by all who use the term, are difficult to assess.

On the other hand, adjectives can be relatively easy to measure if all of us agree on what the term will represent, if that which is agreed to is directly observable, and if we have available the means to measure the observations. If we wished to describe someone as "happy," all we have to do is to agree on what "happy" people do and don't do. The same is true for the term "successful." All that is needed is for us to state what "successful" people do, and then we can see whether the individual in question does it! Such a process, you may recall, is referred to as "operationalizing" terms. We use that process when faced with such difficult adjectives as "depressed," "anxious," or "angry" and the like. We simply decide on what "depressed, anxious, or angry" individuals *do.* That, then, becomes our operational definition of the term. As you might also remember, reaching a consensus on what and how much of the "doing" is necessary before the term represents what we had in mind, isn't always easy. If you'd like to experience the dilemma, try to decide what a child would have to *do* before you would describe him as "hyperactive." Then check to see how many of your friends or colleagues would agree with your determination. I attended a lecture a while back where the speaker indicated that whether or not a child is or is not judged "hyperactive" is solely a function of the "frustration" level of the individual doing the judging: again, the eyes of the beholder!

PRESENT-DAY CONFUSION GUARANTEED

Since the adjective "learning disabled" does not presently stand for any easily identified, measurable, agreed-upon set of responses, actions, or behaviors because we do not know what it is that we are attempting to identify, measure, or agree upon, the term, as a descriptive, is of little or no value. A teacher of "learning disabled" students, is, in fact, *a teacher of students,* all of whom possess different characters, styles, manners, and uniquenesses. The term does *not* stand for any discernible, *homogeneous* (alike) set of particulars. The term *does* stand for a remarkable number of *heterogeneous* (unalike) sets of particulars. As such, when looking at the individuals who compose the so-called "learning disabled" class, we're going to have to ask of each, "what does the individual do?" Only then will we know a part (a very small part) of him or her. The adjective doesn't tell us that. If we are interested in the individual, the adjective-term serves no purpose other than to confuse.

A GNAWING EMPTINESS STILL FELT

As helpful as it was to finally decide on what name would best describe the original small number of pupils who were having problems with their school work, and yet appeared "intelligent" enough to do better, an equally, if not more important, question was yet to be answered: *Why* were the children experiencing their difficulties? A discrepancy was noted; an answer was wanted. *Naming* the children was one thing; *explaining* their absence of desired behavior was another. The moment the question "Why" surfaced, the search (and accompanying pressure) to find a "cause" was on.

PERFORMANCE DIFFERENCES EXPECTED AND OBSERVED

It is hardly a profound statement to suggest that we have always had children (and adults) who have experienced difficulty with school work; that there have always been students who have accomplished more, who have performed better, than others. Nearly any of us could take a step back into our past and recall, fondly or otherwise, a teacher who drove us "nuts," or an academic subject area so entangled with mysterious subtleties and flat-out difficulties as to be just beyond (or far beyond) our cognitive reach. It was a rare bird, a fellow classmate, who excelled, or just performed with ease, across the board. For some of us, at a given point in educational time, learning to read quickly and accurately, while understanding and remembering what often appeared to be Greek filling the printed page, was, in a word, tough. For some, learning to solve arithmetic problems, those with plain numbers or those with formless, obscure terms, was as arduous as climbing Mount Everest barefoot. Despite our academic confusion and the accompanying partial absence of success, promotion to the next point in educational time (grade level) occurred automatically: Our youthful optimism and ignorance never allowed the converse to enter the realm of possibility. Somehow, come September (or late August), we found ourselves in a new class with a new teacher who introduced some new English while reviewing some of the old Greek that was destined to always remained Greek. Fortunately for many of us (or unfortunately, depending on perspectives), promotion was based on time, *not* performance. Had academic performance been the barometer used to determine where we would be in September, some of us would still be in third grade: a nightmarish thought for many of our teachers! The "benevolent" system allowed us to go forward whether or not we were ready for the new frontiers.

"Were your parents told you were 'learning disabled'?" the parent asked.

"The term wouldn't have been used because the time was prior to 1963, prior to the parent/business meeting where the adjective was chosen."

Our "middle-class" parents, more frustrated than we (we thought everything was fine), badgered supportively:

"Why can't you do better? You want to grow up to be a nothing?"

"Come on, Ma," one of us perhaps answered. "The teacher is terrible, the work is no fun, the books are stupid; besides . . . I'm never goin' to need that stuff anyway. Can I go outside and play baseball?"

"What are we going to do with him, Harry?" Ma asked Pa, as one of us made our way into the sunshine.

"Lighten up, Martha, he's just a kid. He'll do okay. I had the same teachers and the same books. Look at me. I came out all right."

Most of us, it seems, did okay despite the *falsely* accused "terrible" teachers, "stupid" books, and the ever-present, equally false, supposition that we wouldn't need the stuff anyway. Some of us (or at least one of us) shiver with fright at the mere possibility that in the 1940s and 50s "LD" could have been around, that medication to alter our neurology could have been prescribed, that segregated rooms or schools where all the "specials" would be gathered could have been the treatment of choice, that hours of "mental-processing" testing could have been initiated to verify the frightening and ignorant belief that we had a squeaky wheel in our craniums, that we were somehow horribly different from the few rare birds. In those days, we were just kids, hanging in, hanging out, hanging on happily, not realizing the gray hairs and wrinkles we were giving our parents. In those days, we had teachers (most marvelous beyond description) who hung in there with us.

THE SIGNAL THAT BROUGHT CHANGE

Soon however, and unknown to anyone who lived in the neighborhood, a spherical, blinking, blanking hunk of metal would produce changes that would affect us all—for better or for worse.

Americans reacted to Sputnik [1957] by charging schools with failing to produce scientists and technicians needed for the U.S. to remain ahead internationally in technological development. . . . American schools were compared with Russian schools and found deficient. The chief problems, critics believed, was lax standards. . . . *Life* magazine compared the schooling of two boys; one in Moscow and one in Chicago. It reported that in the Soviet Union, 'The laggards are forced out [of school] by tough periodic examinations and shunted to less demanding trade schools and apprenticeships. Only a third—1.4 million in 1957—survive all 10 years and finish the course. . . . In contrast, American students lounge in classrooms that are 'relaxed and enlivened by banter,' and in which the 'intellectual application expected of [students] is moderate.'[9]

The satellite, reaching heights far surpassing our birthday balloons and homemade kites, signaled the need for change. And change came. Textbooks were made more difficult; achievement tests were renormed; more work was required and expected. There would be less relaxation; less lively bantering. Quite suddenly, it was time for studious work, for academic acumen, even if you didn't know what the term meant. Benevolence was out; hardnosed discipline was in. No more cruising down the main strip to goggle over one another and test out those new feelings that made you tingle. It was time to hit the books. Of course, few of the students or their parents were aware of the changes and the yet-to-be-stated justifications for them. Most stared in awe at the "flying machine" that seemingly had touched the stars.

"Many of the children were unable to keep up, but few blamed the raising of standards"[10] for the absence of desired academic progress. "Instead, students who scored low on reading achievement tests were blamed personally for their failure. By the early 1960s, children who failed in reading were divided into five categories, differentiated by whether the cause of the problem was presumed to be organic, emotional, or environmental, and whether the child was deemed intellectually normal or subnormal. *They were called* [emphasis mine] slow learners, mentally retarded, emotionally disturbed, culturally deprived, and learning disabled."[11] There *were* new standards, new textbooks, new demands made on teachers whether they were prepared or trained for them or not. There were new expectations for everyone in part because the ubiquitous "they" (who were well beyond their school years and couldn't remember what it was like being a kid) thought we had more "laggards" than Moscow.

THE NEED TO BE BETTER

The raising of standards, the toughening of textbooks, the heightened expectations: all well and good. What fault can one find in wanting us banterers to become better? That's the cherished American way. But a sizable portion of us kids were still relaxing; after all, that's what we had been purportedly doing all this time. Some of us weren't quite academically ready for either the new textbooks or the new expectations, and our work, or its absence, reflected our unpreparedness—*not* our inability or incapability. I doubt too many of us realized how suddenly important it was (to people we didn't even know) to be more prepared.

THE DETERMINATION OF FAULT CAME EASY

For reasons beyond my understanding, some wise folks concluded that the absence of desired performance was the same as the inability to perform desirably: The *absence* of behavior became equated with the *inability* to behave. These wise folks decided that we were deficient, not just that our work was deficient, but that *we* were deficient. We were "slow," "retarded," "disturbed," "deprived," and "disabled."

It was "pin-the-tail-on-the-donkey" time. With blindfold in place, after being spun into a dizzy state they proclaimed that *we* were the problem. Talk about unproductive expediency! Were there any alternative explanations available to account for the observed discrepancy? No. It would have been politically unwise for the wise to have suggested that the *absence* of our desired behavior may have been related to the *presence* of their arbitrary changes within the schools. The names were named; the problem was ours. Neat and tidy. And *wrong*.

_____ FROM ADJECTIVE TO NOUN: ENTER THE DRAGONS _____

To fortify the position that we were the problem, it became necessary for the wise folks to find a *cause* for both the adjectives that were said to describe our deficiencies, as well as the deficiencies themselves. The "cause," of course, would have to be located somewhere within our bodies. It would serve no purpose to suggest that the administrative changes within the schools were somehow related to the observed academic difficulties and discrepancies.

> The cause . . . was believed to be organic. Hypothesized causes included minimal brain damage, a maturational lag in general neurological development, a failure of the brain to establish cerebral dominance, or a failure to achieve certain stages of neurological development.[12]

When *our* new work failed to meet *their* new expectations, our parents, conveniently, were informed that we had "brain damage" of one sort or another. The discrepancy between what we did and what we were expected to do was explained (away) by some cerebral discordance, by organic wiring that wasn't connected correctly, by an inability of our own brain to control its own impulses, or by our left brain and right brain refusing to coexist within the same skull. Something had to be responsible for our unexpected and unwanted underachievement, and the wise folks only knew one place to look for the cause of our failures: inefficient brain tissue. They probably never expected anyone to challenge their opinions and "solid" research findings.

> The evidence from studies using formal neurological examinations . . . is especially damaging to the neurological impairment explanation. Surely, if the neurological thesis were to find support anywhere, it would find it in the techniques and science available to neurologists. Unfortunately for those who have held this thesis, studies of borderline symptoms, soft signs, have uniformly failed to contribute to the diagnosis of academic underachievement.[13]

And nine years later, in 1987, the author of this statement, an associate professor of clinical psychiatry at the Robert Wood Johnson (formerly Rutgers) Medical School, indicated the following.

> No matter whether brain structure and activity were inferred, pictured, or mapped; whether the brain was directly examined; or whether drugs were used to influence brain activity, no body of evidence has confirmed—and much of it has repudiated—the many neurological-deficit interpretations.[14]

Not everyone believed that "brain damage" was an acceptable explanation for performance discrepancies even prior to this evaluation of its validity. Indeed, the parents at the 1963 business meeting, the parents who were directly affected by the Russian "flying machine," the parents who were deeply concerned about their children's discrepant performances, the parents who voted to adopt the adjective "learning disabled," were told that concluding their children had somehow become or been all along "brain injured [had] little educational significance."[15]

> Parents as well as teachers knew that the label 'brain injured' was virtually useless because brain damage is difficult to determine. And even when it was proved, the diagnosis offered little real help in planning and implementing treatment.[16]

In a strange twist of events, every parent who had one of "those" children who somehow didn't fit with their classmates, were back to point zero. They had a name, but nothing more.

THE MIGHTY PEN

A stranger twist of events, however, "solved" the problem. Some infamous, anonymous individual, with or without credentials, by plan or caprice, with or without the knowledge of what he or she was about to accomplish, conveniently changed the adjective "learning disabled" into a noun. It now became a "learning disability." It now became more than a descriptive term. It now became *something* that someone could *have*. It now became a "condition." As a result of nothing more than a slip of the tongue or a scratch of a pen, the parents were given an *explanation* for their children's failures to live up to the new norms, the new textbooks, the new expectations. It satisfied the wise folks: A "learning disability" was somewhere inside the body.

Like its adjective-cousin, the contrived noun was innocent enough in the beginning. The numbers of children said to be suffering from "learning disabilities" was so small that little attention was drawn to the timely grammatical shift, or to the acceptance that a discrepancy in performance now had an *explanation*. Most teachers went about their business trying to educate all their pupils. Soon, however, word began to seep into the portals of school buildings that if a teacher had a "bright" child who wasn't responding to "open your books to page 27 and we'll begin," the student could be removed from the classroom and placed in a special class or a far away special school with other children who also weren't responding to page 27. Ten bucks to a penny there was a teacher in the beginning who asked,

"How come Johnny is being removed from the class?"

"Don't you know, he *has* a learning disability," a colleague informed.

"A what?" the teacher had to have asked.

"A learning disability! He's going to be with other children who also *have* learning disabilities."

"That doesn't make any sense. All of the students are different," the teacher must have said.

"No they're not. They all *have* LD," was the less-than-wise response.

Innocence, sadly, is often inversely related to the passing of time. So it was with the new-found explanation. Soon all sorts of children, exclusively those who were creating academic problems in the classroom, were said to have this perplexing problem that made them no longer kids, but puzzles. In no time flat, their numbers went from near zero to near 2 million. That which was *never intended* to be a "thing," rather a descriptive term, had become a "thing" of enormous proportions. At the first sign of discrepancy, the "thing" was assigned. A prodigious excuse not to teach was in place.

IDENTIFYING THE ADJECTIVE TURNED NOUN

Why should it surprise anyone that we are having difficulty verifying the presence of what doesn't exist, that which has no identifiable parameters, that which was intended as a descriptive term? We have many tests that purport to identify the adjective turned noun. The tests do not accomplish that. All they can do is sample behavior, some not very accurately. We have professionals, bent on echoing the wise folks' view that all discrepancies are a function of some problem within the child. They cannot do that. All they can do is observe behavior, some not very reliably. We have some authorities whose entire logic and advice to the rest of us is based on the assumption that the "thing" that they term "LD" exists in some manner, form, shape, or size. They do not know that. All they know is that some students aren't doing what people expect of them. They, like their predecessors, have a tough time looking at alternatives ways of explaining discrepancies. They're going to maintain the notion of LD (as adjective or noun) come hell or high water. Representing many of her colleagues, a leading authority has stated:

> I am not uncomfortable that a "mixed bag" of pupils is found in LD programs. This does not negate the concept of LD.[17]

But it certainly doesn't verify it either. Indeed, the fact that youngsters find themselves in an LD program doesn't mean they are LD. (Remember, we haven't figured out or agreed on what it means to be LD—a fact some professionals bypass with relative ease.) Suggesting that a youngster who is placed in an LD classroom is "LD" is akin to accepting that all people who find themselves in "mental" institutions are "mentally ill," that all people who find themselves in jail are "sociopaths," or that all people who find themselves in the army are patriots. It doesn't work that way. The name of a classroom program (or institution) is not defined by the students who sit in its seats. The name of the program is determined while the seats are still *empty.* The seats are then filled and the occupants are then named by the previously determined "call-letters." Unhappily, once the occupants are seated and named, they are said to *be* or *have* whatever name appears on the front door. For the army guys and gals, it's not a big issue. They're getting paid for what they do and eventually, if they choose, they can leave. The boys and girls who are escorted through the front door of "special" classrooms aren't always that fortunate.

THE ADAPTIVE STUDENT

We do have children who are not doing well in school. We have children whose less-than-hoped-for efforts and actions are a function of identifiable physical problems with hearing, speech, vision, motor-impairments, and cognition. Consultants, teachers, therapists, and parents are well aware of those potentially debilitating, inhibiting attributes that we all wish would one day no longer be present, but that at the moment are responsible for observed discrepancies in actual performance and hoped-for performance. While this may be of no comfort to the parents and teachers of those children, their numbers are small in comparison to the total population of school-aged students. But since the 1960s, we have an enormous number of students whose discrepancies between actual and desired performance are related to identifiable school inadequacies and *not* student disabilities. Although denied vociferously by those educators and physicians who refuse to look at themselves and their beliefs, the fact is that schools, in large measure, produce, exacerbate and exaggerate the discrepancies said to point to the problems (e.g., "learning disabilities") that exist within students. The discrepancies manifested by all those "intelligent," adaptive youngsters are no more a result of a malfunctioning brain than of the wanderings of a vagrant uterus or a glob of congested blood.

Healthy, Adaptive Differences
That Lead to Discrepancies

One of the major objectives and pursuits of youngsters as they first test their legs, thoughts, and feelings is to love and be loved: a marvelous way to spend one's time. Another is to smell every flower that blooms, watch every bird that flies, touch every worm that wriggles, explore and taste everything that is new, everything that has and has not been explored and tasted before. Childhood, when all goes well, is unencumbered, intrinsically exciting, full, or nearly full of unconditional positive regard. In a word: beautiful. Of course, there are times for words and numbers and colors and music and images while sitting on someone's comfortable lap; this makes what is beautiful even more so. And, on a few occasions, there are times when one has to eat and go to sleep and visit that kindly man or woman who has the cold stethoscope, but whose warm fingers and smiling face and cherry-flavored lollipop make the cold instrument more tolerable. And we can't forget the rules. They are there, but only a few in the beginning: Stay away from this and be careful of that. For the most part it's a time almost exclusively for hugging and being hugged, for finding out about one's developing self.

During that cherished period, few tasks that aren't geared toward survival and safety are required. Those that are, are brief, to the point, and accomplished (when they are accomplished) quickly, without much effort: Eating takes twenty minutes; a bath (if it's fun) maybe thirty; putting on socks perhaps three; brushing teeth, one. These moments come, they go, then it's back to exploring and tasting. There aren't any wooden chairs with flat, wooden desks attached that must be sat in, no rectangular tables that must be sat around with hands folded until a signal to begin is provided, no pencils that must be held correctly, few, if any, papers with marked, thin, straight lines intended to guide the traces of pencil and ink and paint, no assignments that *must* be completed, no books that *must* be read, few, if any, questions that *must* be answered *now*, few, if any, answers that are noted, logged, and graded. Words misused or mispronounced, letters omitted or incorrectly duplicated or written upside down and backwards are observed, maybe corrected, maybe not. Effort, more times than not, is seen as more important than exactness. When the effort turns tiring, or boring, or near exhausting, it is no longer requested. Instead, it's "PB and J," a glass of milk, and off to experiences more intrinsically desired. There are things that can be done, if one chooses; things that need not be done, if one chooses. It is a time when one moves toward that which is interesting, exciting, perhaps challenging. It is a time when it is *acceptable* to move away from that which holds neither interest, excitement, or challenge. Things are clear and understandable, for the child's mind is allowed to produce its own interpretation of clarity and understandability. And everything is right, for even when it isn't, it still is. Outlandish explanations and hysterical conclusions about the way the world operates elicit smiles; mistakes evoke embracing arms; flubs, minor and sometimes major, are responded to with a supporting arm that softly redirects. Wrongs are nearly nonexistent.

SCHOOL: A STUDENT'S NEW AND DIFFERENT WORLD

It is impossible to say what the child, once having reached a prescribed age, steps into. The institution is called "school," but there are so many schools, so many types of schools, so many different philosophies of schools, that saying that children go to school doesn't tell us what they will experience. There are so many teachers, so many types of teachers, so many different philosophies held by teachers, that saying that children will be guided by their teachers doesn't tell us what type of guidance they will receive. What, however, can be said is that children will take with them all the previous cherished years: Whatever knowledge was gained, whatever attitudes were assimilated, all the unconditional acceptance, all the support for effort regardless of outcome, and (if not told otherwise) the belief that it's okay to turn away from that which holds no interest.

SCHOOLS HAVE REQUIREMENTS: SOME FAMILIAR, SOME NOT

Schools, because of their charter, do not foster the notion that effort alone, *regardless* of outcome, is acceptable. Nor do they allow for the option of avoiding that which has no perceived value. On the contrary, there is a curriculum, a series of lessons that must be accomplished in a given period of time, and there is the expectation that each child, regardless of background and experience, will successfully accomplish that which is presented. Effort is applauded, but accurate outcomes are required; partaking in what is seen as fun is understood, but learning to tolerate and participate in skills that are a necessity for development, enjoyable or not, must be acquired. Where, for a brief time, there were no desks with tops, no rectangular tables with chairs, no papers with lines, no books that were a must, the new situation, known as school, contains them all. Quite suddenly, and perhaps inexplicably to the child who may believe that school is an extension of home, certain answers may be wrong; ways of writing may be wrong; ways of reading may be wrong. Where, for a brief time, wrong was rarely an issue, now its possibilities proliferate. Where, for a brief time, leaving an activity that was boring was acceptable, now such a luxury fades away.

ADAPTATION DESPITE RULES

Because students are human beings, they will adapt to this new environment and its new requirements. Not all will adapt in the same manner, of course, but they all will do so nevertheless: Regardless of what the school demands, the students will work hard to obtain what they value; the students will work hard to avoid that which they perceive as aversive. If they experience success (and enjoyment) from their labors, the labors will continue. If, however, their efforts provide them with little or no success (and enjoyment), they will draw upon their previous experiences in the hope of finding something that will bring them their own defined success.

12.1

So much of what will begin to happen as the first school day turns toward the hundredth day depends on an extraordinary number of factors: children's acquired (or predisposed) values; their previous experiences with activities similar or dissimilar to those that occur within the classroom; the knowledge gained prior to school as compared with the knowledge they are expected to have; their acquired (or predisposed) learning style; how comfortable they feel being with many other children; how well they tolerate having to do things; how well they handle not always being right; and any number of other variables the children bring with them that are a unique part of each one of them. But the factors do not end there. Indeed, they just begin there. Teachers will play a crucial role: what they do and how they do it; their preferences, sensitivities, and tolerances; how they feel about their work; how they feel about their pupils, along with many other issues. Then there is the curriculum: It can be as different as the teachers, as varied as the pupils. The principal: strong or weak. The students' parents: active or inactive. I've no doubt left out a hundred variables that might, in some fashion, play a role in this kaleidoscopic experience known as "schooling." I believe, however, that the following point has been made: Lots of stuff, unique to the individual, unique to the "system," goes on from day one to the last day. Differences abound: The natural environment assures that. The same environment assures something else: Individuals will find a means to obtain what they value. Their behavior is adaptive, purposive, functional, and appropriate.

It, however, may not always be desirable to those responsible for their education or upbringing.

MANY DIFFERENCES, ONE SYSTEM

It should not surprise anyone who has spent time with a group of children that differences across the widest possible areas will be observed. It thus should not be any surprise that the children will differ when they enter and proceed through school. To think otherwise is naive. Yet the educational system, because of its own self-determined restraints, often begins and continues to present its programs as though the children are nearly (if not exactly) the same, based on the observation that the children are nearly the same age. Age has always been a key barometer used to predict what children should be able to do: Age has often been held synonymous with "readiness"; age is often equated with acquired experiences.

As evidenced by their performance, age aside, some of the children will have few problems as they make their way through their school's requirements. Thanks, in part, to what they have experienced during their early years and their present developmental levels, they will take whatever the "system" throws at them in stride. They and the system will not be at odds: Sitting in chairs, doing work that may or may not be of interest, and handling the newly imposed lessons and responsibilities will create few, if any, hurdles. Others, however, will have problems, again due in part to the fact that what the schools present doesn't quite mesh with the youngsters' earlier experiences and present developmental levels. The work may, in varying degrees, appear alien; the requirements and responsibilities may be equally foreign. Observing the differences among the children, professionals, if they are not knowledgeable, if they hold to the notion that since the children are the same age they should be prepared for the same things, may come to conclusion that the first group of children is fine, while the second group is having a problem with more than merely adjusting to the new rules and expectations: They may have a problem *within* themselves. How else, the professionals may ponder, can we account for the differences in performance? The children receive the same lessons; they are all being taught by a certified teacher; indeed, since the children are experiencing the same things within their classrooms, they should perform in the same "appropriate" fashion.

If, in fact

1. *All* the children had the same experiences prior to entering school;
2. *All* the children were at the same cognitive and physiological developmental levels once having taken their seats;
3. Their learning styles were the *same* thereby allowing them to

benefit equally from their teacher's teaching style;

4. They were *all* ready for the same material presented by the teacher, and were ready to proceed at the same speed;

5. *All* the children were equally motivated; if they found the presented material of equal interest; and

6. The teachers were equally competent, and all teachers taught in the same manner with equal effectiveness,

then the professional might have some legitimate grounds to assume that those children who were not meeting the "system's" expectations had some anomaly *within* themselves that was interfering with their efforts. Although the logic, given the above assumptions, would appear sound, the assumptions, as we all know, are absurd. All children are not the same in terms of readiness, development, and motivation; all teachers aren't the same, all are not competent; and employed curricula do not always match students' learning styles or degree of preparedness. While the professional might think that everything within the system is the same, that the only thing that varies is the "intellectual capacity and ability" of the students, that if a student doesn't "make it" it means something is wrong with *his* or *her* "system," nothing could be farther from the truth. The only "sameness" that exists within the school system and its charges is the presence of a building. Beyond that, the variability is mind-boggling and, perhaps, incalculable. It happens that when things become too mind-boggling, the easiest approach to take is to ignore them, and replace that which is too much to handle with something simple. What is simple, as we have said, does not always translate into being correct.

CONTROLLING FOR CONFOUNDING (CONTAMINATING) VARIABLES

One does not need formal test results (regardless of their validity or lack of it) to *recognize* the existence of discrepancies between *desired* performance and *expected* performance. And one need not have an advanced degree to wonder *why* the discrepancies are occurring. On the other hand, special training is required to be able to accurately answer the question "why" that is raised when an unexpected discrepancy has surfaced, for the answer is often elusive and may be difficult, if not impossible, to identify.

When researchers attempt to investigate why a discrepancy has been observed, or what influence, if any, one variable might be having on another, they must control for confounding or contaminating **variables**—variables that unwittingly might be influencing (or be respon-

| 12.2 |

sible for) whatever has been observed that has raised concern. While the phrase may sound technical, it represents a simple concept. An example should help clarify the concept.

―――――――――― ALTERNATIVE EXPLANATIONS: A GLANCE ――――――――――

Suppose a youngster is having difficulty following his teacher's expressed directions (in other words, he doesn't do it!), and suppose the teacher wishes to find out *why* the child is not following the directions. For a moment, think of any or "all" the factors that might be responsible for, or involved with, the child's difficulties. I'll list a few possibilities that separately or in combination might be playing a role in the observed discrepancy. There may be many others. The possibilities might become "mind-boggling."

1. The child has a hearing problem: He can't hear the teacher's words.
2. The child has a vision problem: He can't see the directions when they are written on the chalkboard.
3. The child is not familiar with the written or spoken words used by the teacher.
4. The child has heard and/or seen the words, but he doesn't understand their meaning.
5. The child has no interest in following the directions: He can hear, see, and understand what is being requested, but he does not wish to do as his teacher has asked.
6. He can see, hear, and understand the requests; he wants to do as his teacher has asked, but he knows that if he does comply his friends will call him a "sissy"—something he doesn't wish to experience.
7. The child's parents have told him not to do as the teacher desires. They have told him only to do what he desires.
8. The child has a neurological problem that interferes with or prevents him from interpreting the directions and thus he can't follow them whether he wishes to or not.

The above eight variables represent hypotheses ("educated guesses") as to what might be responsible for the student's difficulties with following directions. Loosely, any one, or their combination, might be an accurate answer to the question "why." Any one, or their combination, might be a "confounding" variable—one that is an accurate answer to the question "why" but its influence goes *unnoticed* and thus is not considered to be an influential variable. As indicated, there could be other "confounding" variables not listed above that might be a part of the puzzle. The child's ability, or lack thereof, to follow directions might be directly related to whether he eats anchovies on pizza or to whether he gets a good night's sleep. Trying to figure out why something is happening is often a very difficult assignment. Expedient answers are all too easy.

Before the researcher offers a tentative explanation to account for the child's difficulties, he or she, if well-trained, will make every effort to look at each variable separately, systematically ruling out those that appear to be having no influence. Usually, the physical variables are looked at first, but *each* variable is given equal possibility of being the ultimate culprit. Most assuredly, the researcher will not conclude that any one variable is the most likely source of the difficulties until *all* have been carefully analyzed. He or she will always be guided by the principle that all the variables considered to be likely sources will need to be well-defined, observable, and measurable. Further, the researcher/practitioner will realize the importance of his or her investigation: Treatment decisions are usually made on the basis of which variable or variables are said to be responsible for the observed difficulties. The researcher knows that if an error in determination is made, suggesting, for example, that "motivation" is the problem when, in fact, the child has a hearing deficiency, the results could be disastrous for the youngster; that stating that a neurological problem exists when, in fact, the student has experienced inferior teaching, will lead to suggestions or solutions that are of little help to the youngster.

CONFOUNDING VARIABLES IN SCHOOLS

The number of variables involved with any individual pupil's school behavior are sizeable. The list would include all the subtleties involved in the classroom, those characteristic of the teacher, and those that are a part of the child. Thus, whenever a child's behavior is less than desired (as in the case of not following directions, or being two years behind in school work, or writing letters and numbers backwards, or having difficulty reading), and whenever a professional is interested in determining why the undesired behavior is occurring, the list of possible answers is staggering. So staggering, in fact, that most aren't considered. Instead, an easy name, an adjective turned noun, a word that was intended to describe but now, incorrectly, is used to explain, is named. Such poor research methodology would not be too much of a problem if treatment decisions weren't based on the findings. Unfortunately, treatment decisions are often a direct result of the findings, producing the possibility that an answer is offered to account for a child's absence of desired behavior when, indeed, many possible alternative answers might be equally, if not more, plausible. Then, of course, if one doesn't consider the alternative explanations, or if one doesn't look at them (or for them), the prospects for an erroneous answer increase rapidly. The conclusion that some error within the child is responsible for his or her less than desired performance, when few other variables have been carefully examined, represents the height of expediency. Deciding that an observed discrepancy between performance and ability is due to a "learning disability" or an "attention-deficit-disorder" will take everyone, except the child, off the hook. All other possible variables will be seen as inconsequential. The child will be viewed in isolation; be diagnosed in isolation. If the child is fortunate he or she will be moved to a new teacher in a new situation who will provide the child with experiences that will enhance his or her growth, experiences that should have occurred prior to any move, any diagnosis, or any supposition that the child was disabled—that is only if the child is fortunate; for the move itself will guarantee little.

> [W]e try to sort children into categories so that we can assign those children to a variety of treatments or interventions that we have no evidence make any difference in their academic or social development. And then we teach children in the same ways regardless of what we call them or wherever we put them.[18]

NEUROLOGICAL DEFECTS: AN UNSTABLE CRUTCH

"A part of me wants you to be wrong, very wrong," the parent said shaking her head quietly. "But another part wants to believe you are right," she added as she clasped her hands together in an effort to control her trembling fingers. "I've held to the notion that something was wrong with my child for so long that relinquishing that possibility is difficult. It has become a part of my thinking, a part of my very being. In fact, although I feel uneasy admitting this, I have found an ironic comfort in the belief that his problems in school were due to circumstances that neither he nor I, nor his teachers, had any control over. I've never considered other possible explanations for what he's been doing; I doubt his teachers did either. Do you understand what I mean when I tell you that after a long period of denial, of struggling with the anger that it could happen to my child, I gradually became comfortable with acceptance? I could tell myself that nothing was his fault, that nothing was my fault. Now you're suggesting that the concept of a learning disability and its implied neurological defects is, at best, suspect and more a result of semantic confusion than fact. That gives me reason to be thankful, relieved. But it also gives me cause for pain for you are saying that the schools, because of a host of variables that they rarely look at, may have been partially responsible for the discrepancy that resulted in my being told that my son had a learning disability. That is not fair."

"Not fair, perhaps, but very real," I responded.

"Then things have to change," she stated. "I would have preferred hearing of their ignorance rather than receiving a safe, expedient answer that does nothing but create despair. Things have to change," she said, her voice trailing off.

"They are," I answered. "Slowly, they are."

NOTES

1. Sarason, S.B., & Doris, J. (1979). *Educational handicap, public policy, and social history* (p. 16). New York: Free Press.

2. Shepard, L. (1983). The role of measurement in educational policy: Lessons from the identification of learning disabilities. *Educational measurement: Ideas and practices.*

3. Coles, G. (1978). The learning disabilities test battery: Empirical and social issues. *Harvard Educational Review*, Vol. 48, 3 (August), pp. 313–340.

4. Keogh, B.A. (1987). Learning disabilities: In defense of a construct. *Learning Disabilities Research, 3* (1), p. 4–9.

5. Elam, N. (1988). Curriculum Based Assessment and Remediation. Dissertaton.

6. Attributed to J. Ysseldyke in Elam (1988).

7. Keogh, B.A. (1987). Learning disabilities: In defense of a construct. *Learning Disabilities Research, 3* (1), p. 4.

8. Ysseldyke, J., Thurlow, M.J., Graden, J., Wesson, C., Deno, S., & Algozzine, B. (1983). Generalizations from five years of research on assessment and decision making: The University of Minnesota Institute. *Exceptional Children Quarterly, 4* (1), 75–93.

9. Sleeter, C.E. (1986). Learning disabilities: The social construction of a special education category. *Exceptional Children*, Vol. 53, *1*, 46–64.

10. Ibid., p. 49.

11. Ibid., p. 49.

12. Ibid., p. 49.

13. Coles, G. (1978). The learning disabilties test battery: Empirical and social issues. *Harvard Educational Review*, Vol. 48, 3 (August), pp. 313–340.

14. Coles,G. (1987). *The learning mystique.* New York: Pantheon.

15. Kirk, S.A., & Chalfant, J.C. (1984). *Academic and developmental learning disabilities* (p. 34). Denver: Love.

16. Hallahan, D.P., & Kauffman, J.M. (1988). *Exceptional children; Introduction to special education* (p. 100). Englewood Cliffs, NJ: Prentice-Hall.
17. Keogh, B.A. (1987). Learning disabilities: In defense of a construct. *Learning Disabilities Research, 3* (1), 4–9.
18. Ysseldyke, J. (October 1987). An interview with James Ysseldyke. *Communiqué.*

SUMMARY

KEEP IN MIND

1. The term "learning disabled" was always intended to be an adjective: to describe. The term was never intended to be transformed into a noun, capable of explaining. A student cannot have a "learning disability." A student cannot have an adjective.
2. There are many reasons why a student's academic performance may be less than hoped for, less than someone might expect. The absence of the desired behavior, however, does not have to be interpreted as meaning the student is the one who is deficient.
3. As said many times, "causes" are elusive. In education, they are, for all purposes, nonexistent. Categorical labels, incorrectly used as nouns, become explanations. They are seen by some as being "causes." Such a position, besides being terribly naive, is wrong. There exist a nearly endless number of variables that influence a student's classroom behavior: Any ten (or their combination) can exercise enormous influence on a student's performance. Suggesting a label is responsible for the absence of desired performance is ludicrous. Moreover, it is the essence of viewing the student in isolation. It denies the system in which the student lives and studies.

Adaptive Discrepancies

| 12.1 | Given an youngster's unique life space and "person," explain how a student's life-long adaptation to his or her environment can produce behavioral discrepancies when he or she goes to school.

Confounding Variables

| 12.2 | This one's fun. Listen to TV or radio, or check the local newspaper. Bring to class two articles or examples where some authorities suggested that a certain variable "caused" another variable to happen (like, drinking soda pop causes juvenile

delinquency, or watching TV lowers your self-esteem). Exercise: Offer an alternative explanation that might have accounted for the findings you brought to class—in other words, identify a confounding variable or two the original researchers overlooked that might have influenced the findings.

CONSIDER AS WE LOOK AHEAD

1. There are many teaching ideas that work well with all students regardless of how others describe them.
2. You as teacher can take students from wherever they are and move them beyond that point. You can introduce success to all students no matter what their differences or similarities.
3. As you will see, helping students accomplish success will require time and effort. The teaching profession is, and always has been, a difficult challenge.
4. The tools for helping students are available. They await your commitment.

13

The Consultant Model: Unencumbered by the Dragons

When my services are requested to assist students with their academic or social difficulties, I never ask about individuals' "intelligence quotient," and I never ask what label has been awarded to the individuals for whom my services have been sought. Many of my colleagues, teachers, therapists, and other psychologists likewise find "IQ" numbers and educational labels of *no* value. This is not to suggest that the numbers and names aren't offered for indeed they are. There are many professionals in education who have been taught to place considerable stock in categories and estimates of an individual's "capacity"; many who have been taught that knowing (or believing) an individual has a "neurological impairment" is necessary. It generally takes little effort to convince those professionals that such information will not help them assist the individual; that such information may only provide them with excuses not to offer their assistance.

We all understand the advantages for the "LD" label: It produces money for services; it provides many students with smaller classes and additional one-on-one contact with a teacher. Occasionally, "benevolently," we say that children are or have "LD" just so we can get them into a smaller learning unit that can deal with their academic difficulties. We recognize, however, that such methods and outcomes speak to a deficiency within a system and not to the children. The Assistant Secretary for Special Education and Rehabilitative Services, Madeleine Will, U.S. Government:

Some students who may need help, but who are not handicapped, are sometimes misclassified and placed in programs for mildly disabled students in order to get help."[1]

SUCCESS FOR ALL STUDENTS

One day, and it is beginning to happen now, schools (as they were designed to do, but which they sometimes have failed to do) will provide services based on need, not on the existence of a label, category, or a "condition" that is not one.

What is called for is expressed by the "Rights Without Labels" concept put forward by the National Coalition of Advocates for Students, National Association of School Psychologists, and National Association of Social Workers, which states that "it would be desirable at this time to conduct programs wherein efforts are made to serve children who have special needs without labelling them or removing them from regular education programs.[2]

The Assistant Secretary, once again, states that it is her desire:

to assemble appropriate professional and other resources for delivering effective, coordinated, comprehensive services, for all students based on individual needs rather than eligibility for categorical programs.[3]

Quite frankly, many of us having been doing this for as long as we can remember. We have held with the belief that

it is time to move on to the struggle of changing the educational system to make it both one and special for all students. In doing so, we will affirm the belief that all children are full-fledged human beings, capable of achievement and worthy of respect.[4]

Indeed, it is time to rid ourselves once and for all of the convenient "dragons" that have far outlived their usefulness. We know there are many individuals who need our assistance. Never again will they be locked away behind doors that were kept shut by ignorance and prejudice. The doors are open; the time has come to offer each individual the best chance at achieving the most life can offer.

We can whenever and wherever we choose successfully teach all children whose schooling is of interest to us. We already know more than we need in order to do this. Whether we do it must finally depend on how we feel about the fact that we haven't so far.[5]

CAN WE ASSIST STUDENTS WITHOUT USING
THE FAMILIAR TERMS?

Is it possible to effectively provide remedial services to individuals if one turns a deaf ear to such constructs as "intelligence, capacity, learning disabilities, attention-deficit-disorders, mental retardation" and the like? The answer is, first, yes, and second, the delivery of remedial services will be *better* if we will drop those constructs from our thinking and conversation.

"Hold on, Sonny," the wise, old Emeritus blurted out, his white moustache that spread beyond his ears moving rapidly with his lips. "Do away with those ideas and you do away with the discrepancy model. Without the discrepancy model, how do you intend for us to know which of our students needs help?" he asked, his southern voice undulating like soft ocean waves.

"A discrepancy model will still exist, sir," I answered respectfully.

"How's that, Son?"

"Teachers and parents will tell us, sir."

"My boy, what will they tell you?"

"They will tell us if a child needs extra help."

"That's a skampy excuse for a discrepancy model, Son. I've always been fond of tests, and test scores, and test norms, and test manuals. Been using my own for many years."

"Skimpy, sir. The word is skimpy," I cautiously corrected. "We still use some tests, sir, some are good. Some, you'll pardon the expression, stink."

"Stink's okay, Son. I can tell when something stinks," he said, looking directly at me. "Still can't see what good teachers and parents can do when it comes to figuring discrepancies."

"Well, sir, the model that I'm about to present," I explained, noticing that my speech began to mirror his drawl, "concerns itself with the individual, his unique academic and behavioral problems and the ways he attempts to adapt to them. All that matters is the individual. With few exceptions, I'm not concerned with how the individual compares with his classmates or with others of his same age. I'm more concerned with how he compares now with what he has been doing in the past. Who better to know of the present and past than his teachers and parents. They see the individual everyday. They know when he is having problems. They know, therefore, when he needs extra assistance."

"You're putting lots of faith in them, boy."

"I think it is justified," I responded. "They have constant access to the individual's performance. If they see something that appears off target, a problem that can't be solved, a word that can't be read or spelled, they know a discrepancy exists. They can seek or offer assistance at that moment. They don't have to wait weeks or months for someone to suggest the individual has a problem. They already know it, and they can get to work on it immediately."

"Sounds pretty good, son, on paper that is. But what do you intend to do with the 'slow learners' and the 'under-achievers' and . . . you know, those 'LD' ones," he asked, either smiling or smirking.

"They're just kids, sir."

"How about the other ones, the severe ones, bless their little hearts."

"They're also just kids, sir. They will be worked with as intensely as those you probably call 'gifted.'"

"Radical."

"I beg your pardon, sir?"

"I said 'radical,' son. It won't fly, I'll tell you."

"And why is that?"

"Too many differences. Can't handle too many differences. You think teachers are going to deal with all those different kinds of students? Come on, son. You're too idealistic. Be realistic."

"I can afford to be both."

"You're cute son, naive but cute," he said as he stood to leave the office. "Now let me get this straight. No IQ's to segregate students; no labels to categorize them; ask teachers to treat all the students as if they can learn; ask teachers to believe that all the students can succeed. Son, you're asking teachers to work harder, to individualize their lessons, to forgo the advantages that the special education empire has provided them—fancy sounding reasons for not having to work with those students who make their working lives tough. Heck, Sonny, you need your eyes and ears checked. Wouldn't hurt you to take one of my tests so we could see what's wrong with you. Need to do your homework, too, my boy. Why way back in '24 the 'system' already knew it wasn't a good idea to have all the students sittin' side by side."

> Great relief was and still is afforded the normal pupils and regular teachers by the removal of the flotsam and jetsam, the hold backs and drags, who retarded the progress of the class and often created difficult problems of discipline.[6]

"Next thing I expect you to tell me is that you've found a way to stop teachers from bad-mouthing the students when they sit in the teachers' lounge. You don't intend to close the lounge, now do you, son?'' he asked laughing. ''The teacher's union would have your hide.'' He turned toward the door. ''You young pups. You cause more trouble than you're worth. Why don't you just leave well-enough alone and let us who know what we're doing take care of the students, bless their little hearts. No 'IQ's.' No categories. No labels. Pie in the sky, sonny. Wake up, my boy. It won't fly,'' he snickered as he walked from the office.

''Wait, sir!'' I exclaimed before he had taken his second step. ''I have something for you.'' I fumbled through my desk drawer, looking furiously for the picture one of my graduate students had given me after she had met with a principal who had told her it would be to her advantage to be less concerned with her students and more protective of her job. I had made several copies of the ''mouse and the owl'' and it seemed a perfect gift for this aged authority. The man grew impatient as he watched me tossing out from the desk drawer old notes, book-seller's business cards, and forgotten memos from my university boss informing me of the dates of the year's faculty meetings. Finally, I found what I was looking for. Before handing it to him, I gazed at it fondly. There are on the paper was the . . .

> . . . picture of the owl. Its wings were spread. Its eyes were opened to their limits. Sharp claws protruded, glared menacingly. It hovered a fraction of an inch above the frail, naked mouse. The mouse was standing its ground. His little head was held high despite the hot breath of the preying [owl]. His small chest remained motionless and his tail calm. An imperceptible smile came to his narrow lips. He waited. He watched. Then when a tip of one of the owl's outstretched claws grazed his unperturbed forehead, he calmly, without fanfare, lifted his right hand into the face of the screeching owl and politely shot him a most pronounced *bird*. Not believing what he saw, the owl blinked his eyes. The finger was there. No doubt about it. The meaning of the finger was also there. No doubt about that either. The shock was too great. Immediately the owl dissolved into a gentle puff of helpless feathers and glided the remaining two inches to the ground. He looked once more at the mouse, then he rolled over and fainted. The little mouse took a natural breath, turned his back to the unconscious owl, and went on his merry way.[7]

''Here, sir, I think you know where to place this,'' I suggested casually.

A UNIVERSAL MODEL, INCORPORATING ATTITUDES FROM THE PAST

The following model builds on what individuals *can* do. It takes them from wherever they are in relation to a goal, and helps them move toward the goal. It is an accountable system, for it provides a means to evaluate the effectiveness of teaching methods. It is a model that works effectively with all students regardless of labels or burdens placed on them by a natural environment that failed to provide adequate endowments. Indeed, the model stands apart from the debating over what individuals will be called by people who have a need to call them something, for the model is "disability-blind, culture-blind, and color-blind"; a model equally at home with every conceivable variation that enters a classroom or special facility. It is a no-fault model, for the culprit responsible for the *absence of growth* toward the goal is always the *method* employed.

It will be recognized quickly that the model, or more precisely, its basic foundations, are not new, but rather a restatement of foundations (with "up-to-date" terminology) whose underpinnings were developed countless years ago when many a dedicated teacher chose to accept responsibility for all students, regardless of differences; a teacher who envisioned that all students were capable of learning and growing more successfully; teachers who believed that time was less important than performance; that worth and integrity were at least as important as performance.

It will also be recognized quickly, thankfully, that the model, once it reaches the point where it is ready to provide practical services, can comfortably accommodate and employ any manner of exercises: be they reflective of a "back-to-basics" philosophy, or a philosophy limited only by its own creativity. This allows us to use exercises that we have found to be productive and valuable. Thus, whether we have "camped" ourselves as "developmentalists," "cognitivists," "behaviorists," whether we have deluded ourselves (or been taught to delude ourselves) into thinking that our students represent some homogeneous class of adjective, be the name "LD" or "mentally retarded" or "autistic" or "gifted" or "mildly, moderately, or severely involved," the model will provide us with an opportunity to try a wide variety of remedial exercises with any students who find themselves in our class.

The method includes seven related components, all of which speak to issues that are intimately involved in any academic subject (or daily living experience) an individual will be introduced to. For clarification, I will first list the components, then look at each one separately. After discussing the components, I will provide examples of the model in action. Before doing so, however, a "disclaimer" is necessary.

The model is only as good as the professionals who employ it. As is true of much of what we've discussed, it contains no magic. In itself, it is a bare-bones-skeleton. Without someone's warm hand, energetic mind, and avowed dedication, it will accomplish little. Its worst enemies are ignorance, mediocrity, satisfaction with the status quo, and resignation that nothing can be done. Professionals who are "brain-dead," who are anticipating only a pension, who have embraced expediency, will find no use in the model's tenets. With those folks, as the moustached Emeritus said, nothing will fly.

THE LIST

1. General Goal
2. Present Performance Level
3. Error Analysis
4. Specific Goal
5. Small Steps and Large Creative Exercises
6. Cues
7. Feedback

As you will see, the crux of the method lies with steps 5, 6, and 7. Those steps represent the remediation that will be undertaken. However, before remediation can occur, specific goals must be determined. Before those specific goals can be identified, the student's errors must be noted and evaluated. Before the identification and evaluation process can begin, the student's present level of accomplishment must be measured. And, before that measurement can occur, we need to know the general area where the initial problems are occurring. Thus, each step provides information for the next. The steps within the model, therefore, are interrelated.

13.1 GENERAL GOAL

The general goal states what academic subject area the task involves; it indicates what general academic activity warrants, in your (or someone else's) judgment, a closer look. Occasionally, the general goal will refer to some activity an individual's parents would like seen worked on during a school year. Most frequently, the general goal will speak to an issue that is presently occurring in your classroom or special setting: A discrepancy between something the individual is doing and what someone desires him or her to do. Whenever I receive a call for assistance, one of my first efforts is to determine the description of the problem or what difficulties appear to exist. Often the question: "How can I help you?" will lead to a statement describing, in *general* terms, some observable activity that needs remediating. It can refer to completing addition problems with regrouping, writing a complete sentence, improving reading comprehension, discriminating shapes, following directions, communicating, attending, or holding a spoon—any endeavor that is creating difficulty for the individual. General goals can be established or initiated any time you wish: Simply determine an area of difficulty or a desired activity, and state what you would like the individual to do. That will be the general goal. For the most part, the only purpose for the general goal is to describe the area of concern: math versus reading, answering questions versus following directions. There, of course, can be several general goals, and whatever is stated provides some structure as to the nature of the presently observed difficulty. Invariably, the area involved that will lead to the general goal will be readily apparent to you. As a teacher, you will know from the student's work and efforts where he or she appears to be stumbling. The general goal will refer to that area, be it math, reading, creative writing, or what have you, and it will refer to that area in the most general of terms. Initially, you need not be concerned about establishing a general goal that is "too high" or "too low." What will follow will help you determine the precise, specific goal that will be the focus of your remediation.

PRESENT PERFORMANCE LEVEL (PPL) | 13.2 |

Once the general goal has been identified, our attention turns to a measure I refer to as Present Performance Level (PPL).[8] As the words imply, the PPL tells us the *level* at which individuals are *presently performing*. When measured, it will provide us with information regarding *how much of the general goal individuals presently have within their repertoire*. Said slightly differently, it will tell us what part, component, or percentage of the general goal individuals *can now do* with relative ease. It represents, among other important issues, individuals' acquired cognitive, motor and communicative developmental level, what they have learned from their experiences within their environment; what they are prepared to handle. Once measured, it will:

1. Show where individuals are in reference to what the teacher hopes to accomplish. It will let the teacher know whether youngsters have already attained the goal, whether they are close to it, or whether they are nowhere near it.
2. Tell the teacher where to begin his or her teaching or remediation program.
3. Tell the teacher that a program's present methodology is (or is not) suitable for a given child at the present time.
4. Give a teacher an accurate way of avoiding comparing Child A with Child B. It will tell the teacher where each individual stands, and what strengths each individual possesses.

Before any professional can begin working with the difficulties an individual is experiencing, he or she must determine, as precisely as possible, at what level, regarding the general goal, the individual will experience success.

The PPL will tell us where individuals are, rather than where someone thinks they are, regarding their skill levels. It is a far superior measure of preparedness than age, grade level, or stated "intelligence." These three indices offer, at best, "ball park" estimates of what a group, or *nonexistent* "average" individual, is prepared to handle. With the most limited exceptions, those measures do little to specify what the student, sitting across from us, is prepared to handle. The best way to view the purpose for the PPL is to consider the following, somewhat farfetched, scenario.

Suppose you accepted the responsibility for caring for a child—you have become the child's "adopted" teacher or parent. After being with the child for a brief period of time, you decide you would like to help the child with three *general* goals: playing a violin, solving subtraction problems, and stacking a set of six blocks. (On the surface, an unusual set of goals for the same child. For our purposes, however, the goals are fine.) Now, suppose the child, whose language is the same as yours, came to you from a distant land. Unfortunately, all records of the youngster were destroyed by a catastrophic volcano: there were no birth certificates, no school records, no reports on "intelligence" testing. The bright-eyed, curly-haired child can't recall her age, and she has no knowledge of her parents' whereabouts. What would you do? Given your general goals, you'd give her a violin, a set of math problems, a box of blocks, and say, "Let me see you play, solve, and stack. Do the best you can. I just want to see how much you've learned and what you can do. There are no 'grades,' no rights or wrongs, no pass or fail. Just take a shot at each activity."

You would measure the child's (or student's) *present level of performance* as it relates to the goals you had in mind. You would sample the child's behavior *before* beginning your teaching program because you would not want to ask her to do something for which she lacked the necessary prerequisite skills or have her do something she had successfully completed a hundred times before. Once completing the PPL measurement, you would have an idea of what the child's natural environment had provided and taught her. You, in turn, would have a better notion of where your remediation efforts would have to begin in order for both of you to experience success.

PPL AND SUCCESS

The measured PPL indicates more than just the instructional level that best suits the individual's prerequisite skills and developmental preparedness. It offers you a means of determining the *effectiveness* of *your* teaching efforts. If the individual does *not* advance beyond his or her PPL after your teaching approach has been in place for even a brief period of time, then you would need to refine the method being used. Conversely, if the individual's performance showed progress beyond the PPL, then you would have evidence suggesting that your methods and the individual are on the right track. As might be apparent, the present model offers a different perspective regarding the concept of success: *Success is defined as growth beyond present performance level.* This "redefinition" of success is essential for several reasons:

1. While attainment of a determined goal is important, *movement* in the direction of that goal is also important.
2. Since success is defined as any movement toward the goal, individuals will experience the joy of success early on. To the degree that success is valued by them, they will receive both intrinsic (from their efforts) and external positive feedback (from your recognition) immediately.
3. The redefinition allows *you* to experience success equally quickly; and that feeling will increase the chances that you will continue with your efforts.
4. The model and experienced success will focus your attitude toward what it must be: concentration on what individuals are presently doing—not what you hope they can do, or what someone tells you they "can't" do. As a result, you will be able to rethink the concept of "goal." No longer will it represent a global, amorphous, long range endeavor that has created confusion and presented problems. The goal will become something specific, short-term, capable of being accomplished. It will give rise to a second and third short-term, accomplishable minigoal. Each accomplishment will move individuals closer to what you desire for them—as well as what they might desire for themselves.

PPL AND "EXCEPTIONALITY"

Up to this point, there's likely to be little I've said that could be grounds for controversy: We decide what, in general, we'd like an individual to do, then we find out where he or she is in relation to what we've decided. The following is also likely to be void of controversy: All individuals, children or adults, regardless of the classroom or special facility within which they find themselves, regardless of what name or term is used to describe them, regardless of personal attributes, regardless of what is said to be responsible for their strengths and weaknesses, have the potential for growth, the potential to move toward goals that are established for them and by them. More important than our arguments over "LD," or any other terms, our speculations over neurological dysfunction or its absence, individuals who sit before us in their entirety, can, if we are willing to step into the arena, better themselves. That is fact.

If we want to, we can look at individuals as adaptive, functional beings, extensions of ourselves, people who may not be all they or we might desire, but people who can move in that direction. As a consultant, I enjoy the luxury of being able to avoid the academic debates so common to our profession. I am asked to see an individual, to try to help that individual move beyond where he is. When I sit with him, he is neither disabled, retarded, hyper, or autistic. I do not see his brain-deficiency or its opposite. Whether he is like others or unlike others, matters little from the standpoint of remediation. The same is true regarding which classroom he has been assigned to or which classificatory term has been typed into his personal file. What matters is what he is presently doing, the hopes and expectations we have for him, and what we can do to bring the two closer.

PPL: THE STARTING POINT

Recently, I received a call from the mother of a 4-year-old child I, and many others, have been working with for some six months. The youngster, (nonverbal and very active when first seen—he had been placed on attention-altering medication when he was 2 years old), has made considerable progress over his initially measured PPL during that time period. Without the use of medication, he has begun to attend quite well to the tasks his "early-childhood-team" has designed for him, and his vocalizations and articulated words have increased from a few, randomly uttered sounds, to clearly naming dozens of objects, and spontaneously making his needs known. Still, the youngster is significantly behind other youngsters his own age, and that observation has been a nearly constant source of dispair for his parents and grandparents. The mother had mailed me an article entitled: "A Parental Dilemma: The Child with a Marginal Handicap,"[9] a paper directed toward social workers who provide assistance to parents of handicapped children. The mother was deeply affected by the article because it touched so many of the feelings she, and her family, had experienced while caring for their young child. She and I talked at length about the article, her son, and her concerns for his future. Understandably, she was frightened about his prospects, expressing her fears that he would always be dependent upon others, that he would never be "normal," that eventually he would be a "4-year-old in a 20-year-old body." Predictably, she asked me if that was what she had to look forward to. I had heard her painful questions, expressed by others, many times before.

I haven't met too many professionals who haven't privately wished they had the ability to look into the future and either confirm or dispel the wrenching concerns expressed by those who love the child, who, for any number of reasons, has found the developmental years to be difficult. We, of course, have no such device that affords a look at what will be. What we do have, however, is technology for the present, technology that is perhaps not as complete as we would desire, and not always as successful as we would pray. But what we presently have is what we must rely on.

Eventually, concerns over the future turn (or must be turned) to the realities of what exists. While we need to hope for all we wish, we must spend our energies on what can be done now, for what is done now will help us move toward what we hope will be. Of little comfort to us when fear and dispair overwhelm us like a giant wave, the present level of performance is our best ally. It provides us with a place to start, a platform from which we can propel ourselves and our child forward. The mother of the 4-year-old had heard the "lecture" before, but it seemed as though she wished to hear it again. For her, and perhaps for others, growth beyond present performance levels provide a grain of optimism, for when the growth occurs, it tells us something about the power and drive children carry within themselves. While the growth rarely allays our fears and concerns, it does offer us reason to maintain our hopes. In a field where honest ignorance and uncertainty abound, a child's progress, regardless of size, represents an identifiable, certain rallying point for all our efforts.

MEASURING THE PPL

Although measuring the PPL is relatively easy, *what* is to be measured has points controversial enough to briefly look at in a moment. For now, as the above fictional scenario suggested, goal-related "academic" material is presented to the individual, she is asked to take a shot at it, and we watch her efforts carefully. She is to do what she can, and what she does will provide us with information regarding her present performance level as it relates to the offered material. Frequently, our PPL measures involve tasks for which there are no "academic" materials: sounds made, words spoken, bites of food consumed (or willingness to tolerate the presence of a spoon), questions asked, answers offered, time at a task (or time sitting in a chair), occurrences of screaming or biting, participating in an activity, along with any number of other nonacademic, behaviors. Whatever the "task," our objective is to obtain an accurate and reliable sample of the individual's behavior as it relates to the general goal. We attend to the individual's manifested level of success, as well as whatever errors she makes. (As we will discuss shortly, her errors are critically important pieces of information.) In all, her performance, no matter its manner, frequency, or state of sophistication, is accepted and precisely documented.

DATA COLLECTION: A GLANCE

MEASURING ACADEMIC PPLs

It is almost humorous how often the past (when it offers something of value) is revisted. So it seems is the case with measuring academic PPLs. A long time ago, when a student was having difficulty with reading or math (or spelling or writing or you name it), the "old-fashioned" teacher sat with the student, handed him a reading book or a bunch of math problems and requested, no doubt pleasantly, that he "do his stuff" while he or she watched and made notes. The teacher's intent was to see what specific problems the student was having. (At the conclusion of this masterful method of assessment that had yet to acquire a "fancy" name, the teacher had in hand a measured PPL!) The teacher, then, knew where the student faltered and where the student succeeded. The teacher could, then, alter the instructional approach to meet the student's identified academic needs. From a practical standpoint, not a bad approach: It helped both the teacher and the student for both progressed in their interactive endeavors. But "old days," because of their apparent or interpreted simplicity, often are dismissed with the spoken: "Well, they did what they could with what they had, but they didn't have a whole lot, etc."; simplicity somehow gets translated into inadequacy. Progress does that sometimes, especially progress that produces "flying machines" that make everyone wonder where everyone went wrong. In this instance, the latter "everyone," as I have not too hesitantly implied, referred to students—they were the ones whose academic progress went wrong. Again, as suggested, what went wrong were their brains, not the new books and the new expectations that likely ran counter to the "old" ways of teaching. It certainly didn't take a wise person to figure out that if a brain dysfunction was suspected, you didn't hand a student a bunch of math problems and expect to find a brain problem. (All you might find would be a math problem, and that wouldn't do—it was too simple.) So, the wise folks came up with a different idea: Develop tests, *not* teacher-made math or reading tests that use mathematics exercises or reading passages to see both where the student "was" and where the teacher's lessons "should be," but "brain-processing" tests to measure "brain-processing" problems. The wise folks also decided that it would be helpful (for someone) if they could develop tests that would enable teachers and parents to *compare* the academic performance of a Colorado child vis-à-vis a California child. Given all the confounding variables involved in such comparisons, many of which having nothing to do with the true performance of the two children or the true performance of their teachers, I've never been able to figure out why such information was considered important—other than it made lots of money for some-body. Such only goes to show that I, apparently, am missing something that others see in the clearest light. As "fortune" would have it, I picked up *this* morning's newspaper during a break from writing and found the following.

> The Denver Post, *May 26, 1988:* For the first time ever, Colorado is going to have an ongoing program to keep tabs on the academic performance of public school students across the state.

For a second, I became excited. Finally, I thought our state was going to see what the kids knew when they entered school in late August and monitor academic growth many times throughout the school year to see what individual progress had been achieved. I was wrong.

> Now, for the first time, parents will be able to monitor the academic progress of their children and compare their performance with that of other children nationally.

Then in a statement that both defies understanding, and reflects a keen sense of pedagogical imagination, the Colorado State Board Chairman informed the public that

> We should get a darn good picture of what's happening in kindergarten through twelfth grade.

In an effort to have someone "splain" to me how that information would be realized by using standardized tests that may or may not sample the diverse curriculum being covered in any classroom, that compare what is sizeably more diverse than oranges and apples, I called the State Board of Education and spoke with the very helpful gentleman who holds a very high position. Hopefully not misrepresenting his views, I was told that the tests' results would provide a small piece of information that would be helpful in seeing how Colorado children compare with others; that the tests were being used because the state had few other options to try to monitor academic achievement; that he, personally, would have preferred another assessment approach (to be described shortly) that would have provided more information about individual students; that "typical" parents want such comparative information—knowing how Colorado kids compare with California kids. Okay, I said to myself as I drove away from home to see an individual child who was having individual academic difficulties in an individual school, who soon would be compared with averages and percentages of computer-counted numbers, I'll grant him all his interpretations and justifications. Yet I was bothered by what I had read and heard, and while trying to stay within the highway's white lines, I began to converse with myself and the imagined people who occupied the seats of my car. "Why would you want that type of comparative information?" I asked the fictional parent and teacher who, if they had been with me, would have told me to keep my mind on my driving. "I mean, why would you want to know how Johnny from colorful Colorado compares with Mary from sunny California? Wouldn't you rather know how John and Mary, respectively, *are* doing in comparison to what each *had been* doing—with each of their teachers, in each of their subject areas? Wouldn't you like to know how each was doing in September and October and November? Wouldn't you like to know how each was doing every week (every day) of September and October and November? Wouldn't you like to know what specific difficulties each child was having; not to mention what their teachers should do to help the two?." . . .

"Well, yes, of course," they both "said" in unison. "Certainly we want to know how well the children are doing, what problems they are having, and what can be done to help them, but we want to know also how our state is doing relative to other states."

"State is doing?" I asked. "State is doing in regard to what!" I screamed loudly as an 18-wheeler sped by me.

"State is doing in regard to educating our children!" they replied with equal volume.

I turned toward the back seat: "Do you think that by comparing the scores from all the states that you will know how well schools and teachers from any one state from any one district from any one neighborhood are educating their children? Do you think the tests will tell you what needs to be done if John and Mary are having a problem, tests that are administered once every three years? Holy tuna fish sandwich," I lightly cursed. "Think about your priorities, guys. What's more important: knowing that John is in the 50th percentile in math, or knowing that young John hasn't the foggiest notion of long division?"

"But if we discover that John is in the 50th percentile, that will tell us he's having a problem," they both answered.

"Holy grilled cheese sandwich. Don't you think his teacher already knows that? Don't you think his parents already know that?" I asked with teeth clenched. "The kid's been in school for years! Doesn't anyone look at his class assignments, his homework. Doesn't anyone watch what he's doing?! Holy Kaphlunkenhimmer. Did everybody take an extended holiday? I mean . . . Oh, forget it!" I spat, turning on the radio, whisking the passengers from my mind.

The interests in "brain-processing" and geographic comparisons had their effects: The "old-fashioned" teacher's approach went down the tubes. Looking at the individual student became less important than measuring the correlation between climatic location and percentile scores. Determining what needed to be done with each student became less important than noting whose brains were not functioning properly. Now, when the question: "How's young John doing in school?" was asked, the answer: "Beats me, but he's in the 50th percentile," could be offered. Heaven forbid someone should ask: "But what does that mean?"

Typically, the educational pendulum has begun to swing another way. The "old fashion" teacher's approach is making a comeback, or as one author put it, has been "reincarnated."

I say "reincarnated" because the skills have largely died out and are no longer in common practice in classroom instruction. I believe that the demise of these skills was aided significantly—if not caused by—the dramatic rise in the use of standardized tests to measure student achievement. Little by little, educators (including teachers, of course) lost contact with the direct relationship that exists between what a student knows and doesn't know and how the student is to be taught.[10]

Yes, happily, the "old fashion" is once again available—for those who wish to use it. In the true sense of the phrase, we are "back-to-*the*-basics" of assessment and measuring what we should have been measuring all along—a student's level of present academic performance as it relates to what his or her teachers happen to be doing, academically, for roughly 183 days a year: cloudy averages left to those who love to crunch numbers and draw bell-shaped curves; brain problems rightfully left to those individuals who spent mega-years in medical school looking at brains and not paper/pencil "capacity" tests. Enough said about the controversy.

"OLD-FASHIONED" REVISITED

Academic PPLs are measured by nearly any approach that determines

> the instructional needs of a student based upon the student's ongoing performance within existing course content."[11]

Depending on the general goals, the materials to be used in the PPL assessment process can be students' textbooks, their home newspapers, your magazines, your creative classroom assignments, or any other similar items that can generate words, numbers, ideas, or concepts. The materials, be they from school or what is available at home, again depending on the types of problems the individual is having, should be somewhat familiar to the individual. After the individual has tried what has been presented, the materials' level of complexity is adjusted until the individual achieves total success at whatever we are requesting. As the individual works, we note as specifically as possible how he or she approaches the task, what he or she does, what he or she doesn't do, and anything that seems important. A quick PPL can be taken anytime individuals are working at a task. Asking them the meaning of a particular word, or having them try a specific problem, will provide you with information as to their understanding of various terms, or what difficulties a certain type of problem may be presenting. Sometimes, you can find out more about individuals' readiness in ten seconds than after they have completed a one-hour exam.

"In other words, you sit with the individual, provide various curriculum levels from his books or assignments, and ask him to try his hand at whatever the task?" the parent asked.

"The beginning part is no more complicated than that," I responded.

"Is there an easy way to know where to start?"

"The individual's previously observed efforts and accompanying difficulties will offer a general idea of where to begin the assessment process," I told her. "What he is presently doing in school is often the best indicator of where to begin looking for success and errors."

"Should you correct his errors during the assessment?"

"No. All you want to do is sample his work with a wide variety of materials and note what he does. Correcting will come later, after you've figured out what needs to be corrected."

"But suppose the individual refuses to look at the materials, you know, not even try?"

"If he so chooses, that would be fine. It tells us something very important. His absence of any effort would represent his PPL. That choice can be worked with."

"Suppose you give him materials and he doesn't know anything about what has been presented?"

"Then you go backwards in the curriculum sequence until you discover what he does know," I suggested. "If, for example, you're interested in determining what he knows about subtraction, and he demonstrates that his knowledge in the subject area is zilch, then try addition. Zilch again? Try one-to-one correspondence. If you look hard enough, you'll find an area where he can succeed."

"How much information do you need before you have a good idea of the PPL?" the parent asked.

"Without knowing of a specific student, that is a somewhat difficult question to answer. Ten math problems might be enough, 10 words, a 3-minute reading exercise, or having him write a few sentences may be all that is needed. You may need more or less. What you are looking for is a reliable sample of his work so you can see where he succeeds and when he begins to have difficulty."

"You seem so relaxed about this," the parent suggested.

"There's no reason to be otherwise," I said. "If we place this assessment process in perspective, pressure need not enter the picture. Our intention is to see where the individual is in relation to where we'd like (or expect) him to be. Whatever we find, we find; whatever we find will be very helpful. Pressure may cloud our judgment and it certainly won't change the individual's level of readiness. So, we relax and sample and note what the individual presents to us. His efforts and products, no matter their extent, are invaluable. They will tell us what we must do next."

ERROR ANALYSIS

| 13.3 |

Now the fun starts. The measured PPL leads you to the next phase: analyzing the type, quantity, and quality of *errors* the individual makes. A quick word on errors. Without exaggeration, they are nothing short of gold! When they occur *consistently,* they become the most prized academic gold. Pursued correctly, they can tell you a great deal about what's going on *inside* the individual's head. You can learn much more about the workings of individuals' cognitive processes from the errors they make than from their correct answers. Unfortunately, more often than not, when children make errors on an exercise or during an activity, the errors are noted, a score is reduced, then the matter is dropped. In school, an exam is given, children answer a question incorrectly, and again the matter is dropped. The children learn only that they did something wrong. It is rare that they learn what is right. If they do, it is often from their own efforts, through the help of their "peers" and not from the adults responsible for facilitating their growth. Succinctly, if teachers (and parents) would explore individuals' errors, they'd see fewer errors and more successful work.

TYPES OF ERRORS

Once you have noted individuals' work during the PPL exercise, you need to determine the following:

1. How close individuals are to reaching the goal; how much of what the goal requires can they successfully complete?
2. At what level of difficulty does the successful behavior break down; *where do the errors first begin?*
3. What type of errors do the individuals make?

Take individuals' work, the impressions you have noted, and find yourself a quiet five minutes. You need to determine what may be *responsible* for any observed errors.

"Or observed discrepancies," the parent spoke rapidly. "This is the moment of truth, isn't it? This is where you and others differ so dramatically, isn't it?"

"Help me a little," I asked her, uncertain of her perceptions.

Excitedly, she stated, "You just said we need to determine what may be responsible for individuals' errors. You're talking about the absence of desired behavior, why it isn't occurring; why there is a discrepancy between what a student is doing and what is expected of him! I know you're talking about those 'intelligent' kids in schools; those who people refer to as 'puzzles'; those kids who have difficulty accomplishing what their teachers desire." She paused suddenly, groping for her next words.

"A professional notes the discrepancy and begins to consider *why* it is occurring," the young teacher said to her.

"Right, thank you," the parent remarked. "Why has the discrepancy surfaced?" she asked rhetorically. "Why?" she repeated. "Some professionals would offer the answer 'learning disability.' They will suggest the individual's absence of desired academic behavior is due to some neurological problem tucked away within his physiological system: that problems with reading and math and printing letters are caused by an anomaly within the brain, like a lesion. That's how they account for failure of a student to meet the expectations someone has for him."

"Excuse, me," the teacher interrupted, "but if you wish, you can include other problems that are not related to 'pure' academics. The same views, or physiological explanations, are often expressed when a student fails to attend to his work, sit in his chair, remember a previous day's assignment, or follow directions. The list is extensive," the young professional added.

"That's when they use the term 'attention-deficit-disorder'?" the woman asked.

"Yes," the teacher responded. "That is the explanation they offer."

"But neither of you go along with that way of thinking?" the parent asked us both.

"No," the teacher answered after looking toward me. "While the physiological answers, if I were to accept them, would make my professional life easier, they, in fact, serve no functional purpose for either my students or myself. When I observe an academic discrepancy, I believe the disparity is related to an error directly involved in the interaction between myself and the student. Something is assuredly responsible for the observed discrepancy, but I don't look at the student's physiology for the answer. Although," she added as an afterthought, "there are days so exhausting, so frustrating, that I'd love to take the easy way out and run and hide within the student's central nervous system."

"So you see, I'm right!" the parent exclaimed. "When the discrepancies are observed, you face the moment of truth. What was that term you used earlier?" she said as her eyes found mine. "'Arena,' that's what it was. You either step into the arena or you find sanctuary in the wasteland," the woman concluded.

"May I butt in here for a moment?" the well-dressed consultant from the big city asked, his briefcase held in hand. "There's only so much of this I can take," he said, his face lined with professional anguish.

"Please do," I responded.

"You guys have surpassed idealism. You're dead in the middle of fantasy land. I'm familiar with this 'error analysis' business, and I know it takes time. You expect teachers to spend the time with all their students? You expect them to evaluate their students' work, one by one, daily, to see the types of errors they're making?"

"That's part of what teaching is about," I answered. "No one ever said it was an easy profession."

"Take your sun glasses off, buddy, and look at the real world: thirty different kids in a class with one teacher; an administration that tells the teacher what lessons must be presented and accomplished in a given period of time regardless of the differences of the students; parents who are only interested in how their own kids compare with others, who are interested more in numbers than knowledge; government agencies that pass down edicts but fail to back up their good intentions with money; local districts that can't get needed bond issues passed so they can pay their expenses; good teachers saddled with bad ones. Take all of those 'positives,' and put them within a system that provides an easy way out. You expect everyone to give up the easy solutions? Man, you must be eating some funny mushrooms."

"Funny mushrooms?" the parent questioned.

"Don't ask," I said to her. "He means we're a little daft."

"Daft, eh!" she blurted as she stood from her chair. "I'll give you a daft up your . . . Sorry. Tell you something mister: Say something can't be done and it won't be done. Say it's impossible and people will begin to believe it. Well, I for one say its possible to change a system that is not doing all it can for the children, their teachers, their parents, or their administrators. Change the sucker," she exclaimed uncharacteristically. "Educate parents and watch the results of our grass-roots efforts. Look at what some of us have already accomplished," she said proudly. "Have you ever seen a parent with fire in her eyes when her child's educational future is on the line! Look at the changes we've brought about. Push us further, get us more involved. Tell us what needs to be done. These are our kids you're talking about. Then, find those teachers who are tireless and dedicated, those who refuse to be a part of the expedient. They're easy to spot. Get their ideas and implement them. Then, find the dead-weight: They're also easy to spot. If you can't retrain them or fire them, give 'em a broom. Buy them out. Give them their sought-after pensions, anything, only keep them away from the kids. As for the principals who won't support the strong teachers, let them hold the dust pan. Maybe they'll quit and sell rocks in the desert." She reached for a glass of water, took a sip, then stared at the man who was now dripping with perspiration: "What you can't see is that this stuff makes good sense: you've got a student who is having problems; find out what errors he's making; find out, in *his* judgment or by looking at what he's doing, why the errors are occurring; then teach him! What else is there?" she asked with a threatening posture.

"Right," the perspiring and no longer well dressed consultant muttered, as he put his dark glasses on and left the room.

ERROR ANALYSIS

_____ IDENTIFIED ERRORS HELP EVERYONE _____

Your determinations of what errors are occurring will help you develop the *specific goals* that will become your target and the instructional methods you will use to help move individuals beyond their PPL. While there are many types of errors, I'm going to concentrate on three major variations: mechanical, conceptual and motivational. There is definitely overlap between the first two, and it could be argued that mechanical and conceptual errors are really one and the same. Further, there are types of errors that are field-specific, and you will no doubt need help from field-specifically trained professionals to uncover them. For the moment, however, be less concerned with the semantics and *my* errors of omission, and instead notice the explanations and examples that can serve as guidelines within which to view the following general classifications of errors all of us experience (and have experienced) at various points in our educational careers.

_____ DATA COLLECTION: TYPES OF ERRORS _____

MECHANICAL ERRORS

Not knowing how to connect cursive letters is an example of a "mechanical" error. Holding a pencil like a lollipop instead of like a pencil, writing the letter "b" or the number "7" backwards, omitting the "p" when spelling pneumonia, not being able to tie a bow with shoe laces, keeping peas on a fork are also examples of "mechanical" errors. Memorizing math facts, or the rule " 'i' before 'e' " are further examples. The distinction is that "mechanical" errors have little to do with cognitive operations involved in understanding. Rather, mechanical errors are due to the absence of a relatively minor, specific subskill necessary to complete a task. To rectify the error, the individual must learn the specific subskill: silent "p's" happen, and they must be memorized; writing the number "7" requires initial movement from left to right; and one cursive letter has a "squiggle" that needs to touch, not lay on top of, another letter's "squiggle." "B's" and "d's" are very much alike, and very different—one faces one way; one faces another way. No big deal, just memorize which way they face. The Atlantic Ocean is on the East side of the USA, and the Pacific is on the West. "I's" come before "e's" except when they don't, and that's just the way it is. Sometimes a letter at the end of a word is pronounced, sometimes not. Sometimes a letter has different sounds, sometimes it has no sound. Don't worry about why, just learn when. A rigid tongue that interferes with swallowing and articulating, spastic muscles that interfere with a smooth gait, and weak eye muscles that interfere with tracking, are further examples of mechanical errors. In most cases, and representing one of the few exceptions, mechanical problems can be "fixed" in isolation. The subskill must be practiced until acquired, or compensated for if practice proves unsuccessful. Again, mechanical problems rarely involve extensive thinking. Often, they are "little" things that get in the way of "big" things. They must be identified and, when possible, altered. I worked recently with a third grader whose teacher wanted all of her students to experience the pleasure that can come from writing creative stories. The teacher had informed the students that she was not concerned with spelling errors or punctuation (invented spelling was acceptable): for the moment, all that was necessary was to write down thoughts and ideas that seemed important to the students. The third grader's written ideas were marvelous. Unfortunately, the student's words and sentences ran on top of one another and the child could not read, with any degree of ease, what she had expressed. Since the teacher wanted her students to decipher their own work, it was necessary to resolve a simple mechanical problem: spacing. The child was requested to draw a circle around each of her invented (often misspelled) words. Once accomplished, the child was shown how to place a small space in between the circled words. In a matter of minutes, the youngster learned how to space her words so she could more easily read what she had written. Again, mechanical problems rarely have much to do with important cognitive functions. They just get in the way and need to be altered, most often by modeling and practice.

CONCEPTUAL ERRORS

Adding 23 and 18 and arriving at 311 involves more than a simple mechanical error. Now there's a problem with concepts, making remediation more complex. You could teach an individual to answer "41" when he sees the problem "23+18=" but if he doesn't understand the concept of "ones" and "tens," along with the basic operations in addition, the problem "23+19=" will create difficulty. Errors made when telling time, when figuring out the difference between a horse and a cow, when explaining the conceptual differences of words like "same" and "different," when failing to write a "complete" sentence, are rarely a result of simple mechanical deficiencies. More often, the individual has yet to acquire an understanding of several concepts involved in the exercises. One student I met consistently missed problems that requested her to "find the missing addend." She also had difficulty when requested to determine "the sum of the problem." After sitting with her for less than a minute, it became apparent that the student had no conceptual understanding of either the term "addend" or "sum." As soon as those concepts were explained and defined, the student did just fine. Another student had been told by her teacher that when she came upon a word in a story that she could not pronounce, she was to try "sounding out the word." Unfortunately, the phrase, "sounding out" was not something the child understood. She had heard the phrase many times, but its conceptual meaning eluded her. Again, clarification of the concept helped the student understand what her teacher wanted her to try. All concepts have special characteristics, or what are called "attributes." These attributes help all of us understand and discriminate one concept from another. Take a piece of paper and pencil and try this exercise: Write down how you tell a "bay" from a "lake," or a "cat" from a "dog." To do the exercise correctly, you'll need to know what makes a "bay" a "bay," and a "dog" a "dog." You also need to know what there is about a "bay" that makes it *different* from a "lake," what there is about a "dog" that *differentiates* it from a "cat." In professional language, you need to know what is *relevant* for one concept that is *irrelevant* for another. The task can be far from easy, and there is little wonder why children have difficulty with various concepts. If you answered that a "bay" is a body of water, you'd be right; but then so is a "lake." If you said that a "dog" has four legs, again you'd be correct; but so does a "cat." Since the offered attributes are relevant for both respective concepts, they won't help you discriminate one from another. If, on the other hand, you noted that a "lake" is most often completely surrounded by land while a "bay" is connected to a larger body of water, then you have identified a key attribute that will make "understanding" and "discriminating" easier. If you said that a dog "talks" with a "bark" and a cat does the same with a "meow," then you have, again, found an attribute that will facilitate discrimination. Try this one: Conceptually, what similarities and differences are there between "addition" and "subtraction?" You may notice that your answer says something about "more" and "less." If so, recognize that you've brought *two* additional concepts into play. Try figuring out the attributes for the concepts of "more" and "less" *without* introducing new concepts. Try naming and explaining all the concepts involved with dividing fractions. Try just naming all the concepts that are involved in telling time. Don't try explaining all of them; it will drive you nuts.

The fact that individuals answer a question correctly does not always mean that they understand the concepts involved, understand the purpose of the concepts, or understand how one concept interfaces with another. There are many ways to obtain correct answers! Individuals' errors in any subject area, however, can suggest that a conceptual deficiency exists. Frequently, concept errors are often masked by individuals' prowess with the spoken word. We often mistakenly believe that because individuals can say a word, perhaps use it in correct context, that they understand what they are saying. Such is not always the case. Recently I had taken my younger son to get his "learner's permit" that would enable him to practice driving. Seated next to me, as I waited, were two lovely children, one 6 years old, the other, almost "four," she told me many times. She was a nonstop talker, and our "conversation" helped pass the time. I noticed that she used the word "dozen" at least a dozen times, and on occasion, she used the word correctly within one of her sentences. Eventually, curiosity got the best of me and I asked her what the word "dozen" meant. With a look of utter exasperation, as though I was some old squirrel, she stretched her arms as far as they would extend, curled her beautiful face into a "are you kidding me!" expression, and stated emphatically, "a dozen means a dozen!" "Is that a lot?" I asked her playfully. "Dozens," she answered, moving her hands rapidly up and down. "I eat dozen cereals, dozen pancakes, and dozen milks." "That is a lot," I responded smiling. (It reminded me of my colleagues when they try to explain the concept of "intelligence.")

MOTIVATIONAL ERRORS

Some errors appear to have little to do with the absence of mechanics or concepts. Rather, individuals may see no reason to put forth any effort. They may know or have the skills to use the mechanics, they may understand the concepts, but they may perceive the required activity to have no personal value. They may say, "It's dumb," and end the discussion. They may add, "Besides, it's too hard!" If the latter declaration shows its interesting "head," there's likely a mechanical or conceptual problem hidden somewhere. Putting aside that possibility for a moment, it shouldn't come as any shock that some of our educational requirements are not overly interesting. They can be boring and irrelevant, in the eyes of the student. Good teachers spend considerable time and effort changing the "boring" and "irrelevant" into something interesting and important.

As you recall, I have suggested that we may need to provide

individuals with a reason to put out effort. I have met many youngsters who've perceived an activity to be valueless until they became involved in it! That's one of the reasons why we use artificial reinforcement: Get the behavior going so the individual has a chance to see what the exercise may offer. I have met many youngsters who might have seen the value in an activity if only they could have succeeded just a bit.

It is very important to avoid assuming that a "mechanical" or "motivational" error exists when, in fact, an individual is missing a critical concept. Additionally, it is critical to avoid concluding that a "motivational" error is responsible for the absence of progress when, in fact, the individual is experiencing a "mechanical" deficiency. Asking a youngster to tie his shoes when his fingers are insufficiently nimble, or swallow a liquid when his tongue lacks the necessary flexibility and control, are as detrimental to all concerned as asking a student to solve her regrouping problems if she has yet to understand that the number "6" represents 6 objects, that 23 represents 2 "tens" and 3 "ones," or that the words "sum" and "some" do not mean the same thing.

DATA COLLECTION: FINDING THE ERROR

How do you ascertain what type of error you and the student are facing? Sometimes it is difficult to determine the real basis. Asking a 9-month-old why she doesn't want to eat rarely results in meaningful information, but when it comes to spelling, tying shoes, reading books, doing math, writing names or sentences or paragraphs, answering questions about horses and cows, you have two methods of inquiry. You can look at the individual's work or his behavior and try to figure out what is going on. You can watch him add from left to right, start writing a "7" from right to left, or recognize that he has yet to figure out which way is left, which is right. You can watch a student spell the word "there" for "their" and realize, without much strain, that "sound-alikes" like "two, too, and to" are easy to confuse and require practice and context. You can watch him as he reads and notice what type of words create difficulties; you can watch him solve his math problems and notice when the difficulties surface. After watching his efforts, you can try the second approach, one that seems most natural: *Ask the individual for his opinion of the difficulty.* His words may tell you what his mind and eyes are seeing.

—————————— LET THE STUDENT HELP YOU FIND THE ERROR ——————————

I came home in the afternoon to find my young daughter sitting, distressed, on the couch. When I asked her how things were, she quietly pulled a paper from her backpack and handed it to me. I saw the two large "Xs" on the bottom of the page, the "−2" that had been painted in red ink on the top of the page, and the *stamped* "sad face" in the upper right corner. It was apparent that school had not been the most pleasant experience that day. The assignment appeared to have something to do with using vocabulary words in sentences. Ten words were listed at the top of the page, and ten incomplete sentences, each with a blank space, covered the remainder of the paper. My youngster was to look at the ten words and use each to fill in the blanks, thereby completing the sentences. The "Xs," the "−2," and the "sad face" were loud proclamations that errors were made on the two final sentences. A quick check disclosed the following: The youngster had difficulty with the words "zebra" and "bait." The 9th sentence read—"The fisherman uses the___to help him catch fish." For reasons known only to the child, the word "zebra" had filled the blank. I sat down next to her, caught her eyes, and asked, "What were you thinking about when you answered the question? What thoughts or ideas did you use?"

"Well, Dad," she began, "I didn't know what the word 'bait' meant. I'd never heard of it. So, I thought maybe the fisherman took the zebra down to the river, and the zebra looked for the fish and showed the fisherman where they were." Wrong answer, good logic. (Unknown to the teacher, my child had watched a National Geographic special on Alaska a few weeks earlier. For certain, you *can't* have a documentary on Alaska without having bears show up on the screen; invariably, one of those bears will be positioned by a river catching salmon! From the child's viewpoint, there wasn't much difference between zebras and bears.) Before the week ended, I took her to a sporting goods shop and showed her a bottle of bait. That summer we went fishing. The word "bait" was no longer a problem.

"How did you arrive at your answer?" "What were you thinking about?" "What thoughts or ideas helped you with what you did?" Ask individuals these and similar types of questions. They allow them the opportunity to share their own views of where and why success breaks down, where errors begin. You need to discover the types of cognitive operations individuals use to arrive at their answers; know whether their errors are conceptual, mechanical, motivational or a combination. Individuals' perceptions will aid you in developing activities and practice exercises to help them with their errors.

A quick summary—let's see what we have to this point:

1. An accurately measured PPL will tell you at what level individuals can succeed.
2. Error analysis will tell you where the successful behavior breaks down.
3. Together, they provide you with a wealth of usable information that can make individuals' "private" difficulties more public, and more amenable to remediation.

Think about the above three points for just a moment. Picture yourself with any individual for whom you have accepted responsibility, regardless of age, gender, or uniqueness. If you know where the individual is in relation to a general goal established for him, if you know where he can succeed, know where his difficulties begin, know the subtleties involved with the difficulties, you have within your hands enormous remedial power. That power supersedes any name, label, or category used to describe the individual. It supersedes the suspected, proposed, or confirmed explanations for the absence of desired behavior of neurological dysfunction, genetic predisposition, or environmental deprivation. It renders those explanations, unless they are, in themselves, reversible, nearly worthless. That power brings the individual into sharp focus. It provides you with something to *do*, something that will take the individual from where he is, no matter where he is, and move him beyond that point. It can provide the individual's parents with reason for optimism; provide the professional with a means to demonstrate professional worth.

_____ SPECIFIC GOAL _____ 13.4

By analyzing the PPL, and determining the type(s) of errors the individuals are making, you will be able to ascertain what specific components require remediation. Frequently, this specific goal is referred to as a "minigoal" that, once accomplished, moves individuals closer to the original, general goal.

Successful completion of a minigoal gives rise to a new PPL that is slightly advanced from the original. The new PPL, in turn, will suggest a new minigoal, and the accomplishment of that one sets the stage for yet another. The ongoing process requires further error analysis and exploration.

Keep in mind that time is not an essential component. Some individuals take more time to accomplish a new minigoal than others. So long as the goal is stated in observable terms, and you are willing to look carefully at your part in the teaching process—analyzing whether you have moved too rapidly or too slowly, determining whether your methods have considered the individual's PPL, checking to make certain you have identified which errors (mechanical, conceptual, motivational) need practicing—you and individuals can enjoy learning together.

<table>
<tr><td>13.5</td></tr>
</table>

SMALL STEPS AND
LARGE CREATIVE EXERCISES

Here's where your genius enters the picture, where the excitement of brainstorming, hypotheses testing, and problem-solving can set your brain firing with ideas. It doesn't take much "gray matter" to determine general goals or measure PPLs—the former requiring only your interest, the latter requiring your willingness to spend time with individuals, watching them play, solve, or stack. While error analysis does require an expenditure of "mental" energy, the outlay is often minuscule compared to what is now needed. Whenever I am asked to offer assistance with a problem, be the scope relatively simple or highly complex, I always envision the following diagram before beginning remediation. It offers me the structure I need to develop a plan of action:

Specific Goal

```
5-
  -
4 -
  -
3    - small steps
  -
2 -
  -
1-
PPL
```

The specific goal is the target; the PPL represents how much of the target individuals have in their repertoire. The issue remaining is: how to help individuals progress from where they are to where you would like them to be. While many of us have our own preferred "schemas," I find it helpful to picture the above diagram in my mind as I'm listening to colleagues as they describe the presenting problem. I "see" the goal, the PPL, and then I try to imagine what I call the "small steps" I can use to bridge the "gap" between the goal and PPL. In actuality, the small steps are the creative exercises we use to help individuals move beyond their PPL. For purposes of example only, the above diagram pictures 5 small steps. The total number depends on individuals' strengths, the task, and the methods we intend to use. I see step 1 as being an activity that will present exercises commensurate with, or very nearly commensurate with, the individual's PPL, whereas the diagram's fifth step closely mirrors the accomplishment of the specific goal.

DEVELOPING THE SMALL STEPS

There are several ways to determine the steps, but I use one method fairly often. I take a piece of paper and write, on the top, the specific goal. At the bottom of the paper, I describe individuals' measured PPL. Then I return to the top and ask myself "What does the individual need to do or understand in order to accomplish the goal?" I am attempting to determine the skills and experiences needed to accomplish the final small step (step 5 above) before reaching the goal. Once that is discovered, I ask myself what might be needed to reach the next-to-last-step (step 4). I continue the process until I have reached the measured PPL. The exercise helps me to see students' difficulties and potential ways of helping them in a concrete fashion. That represents my preference (likely due to my own "learning style"), but you may require a less concrete means of envisioning how best to help students. Frequently, the best flow of steps is difficult to discover, and it becomes necessary for me to seek the advice of an expert in a related field to assure the accuracy of the flow. If I am asked to help a youngster who is having difficulty with school work, I will check with various teachers to gain their opinions as to the flow. I rarely work with an eating problem without first consulting a physician and therapist familiar with the child's swallowing skills.

While it is beneficial to predetermine the correct flow, nothing catastrophic happens if an error in judgment is made. The individual's behavior (absence of progress) will tell me that I have moved too quickly or slowly. When such happens, and it does, I add or delete exercises.

The beauty of the model is that it gives you things to try, ideas to consider for *all* individuals, not just for those whom some feel compelled to label as handicapped. It also provides you with a vehicle that allows you to use any number of different approaches that might best suit the individual. Discovery learning, small groups incorporating heterogeneous members whose students help each other, warm-up exercises, group discussions, along with modeling, practicing, and specific lecturing all fit equally comfortably into the model's format. Again, the model is suitable for all individuals; what will be necessary is for you to suit your preferred teaching approaches to the identified needs of the students regardless of the categorical labels assigned.

EXAMPLES OF THE WHOLE MODEL

Let's look at three examples that will allow me to describe the process I, and many of my colleagues, use when attempting to put the model into operation. Turn your attention to the flow and sequence presented rather than only the specifics. Hopefully, you will be able to generalize from the following to circumstances you will be personally involved with. I do not remember ever working with an individual, no matter the presenting difficulties, without envisioning the components we have discussed. The following problems were brought to me by parents who had been told by school personnel that their youngsters' work was not satisfactory. The professionals had suggested that the children might have some form of "learning disability" that was interfering with their efforts. Frankly, had the professionals indicated the children were "retarded," "hyperactive," or "gifted," I suspect little would have changed in my approach.

GENERAL GOAL: WRITING NAME IN CURSIVE

The child was brought to my office at the university, and once the general goal had been established (providing the area of concern), the youngster was seated comfortably at a table and given a standard pencil along with several pieces of lined paper. We talked briefly about writing, what purpose it served, and how enjoyable it could be. I shared some of the reasons I write, and asked him if he could think of something he would like to write once it became a little easier for him to do so. He indicated he wanted to write a letter to his mother.

He was asked to write his name in cursive five times using five separate lines. When completed, he was asked to print his name five times using five separate lines. Finally, he was asked to draw various size circles and curved and straight lines. While he wrote, the position of his hand and elbow, how he held the pencil, what he seemed to be looking at, his overall attitude toward the task, were all noted. The initial observation showed that his name, written in cursive, was, as his teacher had indicated, illegible: the first letter of his name was written perfectly, but the remainder of the letters, some that appeared to have been written backwards, were nearly piled on top of one another. The printed letters of his name were accurate and legible; the letters were well-spaced; and he wrote between the lines. The PPL disclosed the following: He knew what a pencil was; knew the purpose for the paper; knew how to "write" in between the lines; knew how to correctly hold the pencil; knew how to comfortably rest his hand, arm, and elbow on the table; knew how to write circles and curved lines in a "soft," flowing manner; knew how to print all the letters in his name; knew how to write the first letter of his name in cursive; knew that somehow the remaining cursive letters had to be close to one another; and he seemed genuinely interested in improving his performance. By all accounts, the child knew a great deal! Error analysis disclosed the following: The child had yet to learn how to write separately the cursive letters; how to attach one cursive letter to the following letter; how to space the letters.

The first specific goal (minigoal) involved the correct reproduction of each cursive letter found in the child's name. The child's teacher provided the parents with a cursive letter board that depicted each letter separately. The parents selected the appropriate letters and drew them, roughly three times their normal size, on a large piece of white poster board. The drawn letters were colored in blue; the "squiggles" (used to attach the letters) were colored red for easy discrimination. The child practiced each letter in correct sequence until they were written legibly. He could write the letters as large as he wished. The second specific goal was attaching the "squiggles." Initially, the youngster was allowed to color the attached "squiggles" in red, while writing the "body" of the letter in blue. He chose to write all the letters and "squiggles" in blue, then he colored the "squiggles" in red. Throughout the practice sessions, the youngster was reminded of what to look for with each letter, and feedback for his efforts and reproductions were frequently offered. By his choice, all his reproductions were taped to his bedroom wall.

Once the letters were reproduced, attached, and spaced correctly, the third specific goal—writing the letters smaller using a standard pencil thus eliminating the cues—was undertaken. The latter, final, goal was accomplished in short-order.

Generalization of cursive name writing to the classroom occurred immediately. Before the passage of a month, with the guidance of his teacher, the efforts of his parents, the familiar cues, and a little feedback, the youngster correctly wrote in cursive all the letters of the alphabet. He wrote me a thank-you note.

_____ General Goal: "Listening" to Instructions _____

Repeated notes to the parents indicated that their first grader continually refused to listen to his teacher's directions, and that he seemed more interested in "fooling around" than attending to the classroom guidelines. During the first conference with the parents, it was suggested that since "listening" was not an observable behavior, the general goal would need to be changed to *"following* teacher instructions." It was pointed out that the teacher would likely only know if the youngster was listening by noting the presence and absence of compliance to her requests. A visit to the classroom revealed the following: The teacher stood before her pupils, wrote specific instructions on the chalkboard regarding a work assignment, then verbally described the instructions to the seated students. Nearly all the youngsters, after being given the "go-ahead," began their work. The child in question looked around the room at his classmates, appearing to watch what they were doing. Several times, he turned to the child next to him, and they whispered to one another. The teacher, in turn, admonished the two children for talking and not working, escorted the child in question to the front of the room and seated him by her desk. After a few minutes, he was told to return to his seat and work.

At the parents' request, the teacher provided a complete list of the various instructions that were both written on the chalkboard and verbally described to the children, and the parents brought them, and their child, to my office. Prior to the meeting, the parents were requested to obtain information from the child's pediatrician describing the youngster's visual and auditory acuities—the *first* component of the PPL measurement. When it was determined that the child's visual and auditory abilities fell within normal limits, PPL measurement continued. The teacher's instructions were written on a chalkboard in the office, and the child was asked to describe what the instructions told him to do. Once completed, the instructions were verbally described to the child, and again he was asked to tell what the instructions told him to do. The PPL measurements disclosed the following: Within the confines of the office, the child's hearing and visual discrimination abilities were acceptable; he could identify the letters of all the words written on the chalkboard; he could read several of the written words; he could repeat the verbally stated instructions; and when the teacher's work assignments were modeled, the child could complete them with reasonable accuracy.

Error analysis disclosed the following: He was *not* able to conceptually explain many of the words that were either written or verbally expressed—he didn't know what the words meant; he didn't know what the words told him to do. When asked why he talked with his classmate after the teacher had delivered the instructions, he said he tried to find out *what* he was supposed to do. When asked why he didn't ask the teacher to repeat her instructions, he said he was afraid to do so. When asked if he thought it was important to follow the teacher's requests, he shrugged his shoulders as though uncertain. When asked if he thought it was important to follow his *parents'* requests he answered immediately, "Yes."

The first specific goal involved the learning of the conceptual meaning of the words the teacher had used—both written and oral. Attributes the youngster could understand were used to help him discriminate the meaning of the words involved in the teacher's instructions. The second specific goal involved the generalization of the importance of compliance. Since he believed it was important to follow his parents' requests, it took little time to explain why it would be helpful if he followed the directions of his teacher.

Prior to working on the specific goals, the child's teacher was informed of the youngster's conceptual deficiencies. Surprised by the PPL's findings, she gave the parents a list of assignments that would be forthcoming, along with the instructions she intended to provide. She stated she would contact the school's speech therapist and request an examination of the child's conceptual skills, along with suggestions for its improvement.

Remediation involved the use of the teacher's provided concepts, their explanation, and how they translated into work requirements. The teacher's terms were modeled, defined and practiced, first orally, then written on the chalkboard. When the child acquired understanding of the words and their meaning, the academic requirements conveyed through the teacher's words were modeled and practiced. Once the parents were assured the child understood what he was to do when his teacher provided the instructions, they developed a "soft" reinforcement system to increase the child's efforts at compliance. The parents' employed social reinforcement for compliance was needed sparingly. When the child began to work more effectively in class, his own progress, along with his teacher's positive feedback, was more than sufficient to maintain his efforts.

_____ GENERAL GOAL: MATH _____

The youngster was experiencing considerable difficulty solving addition problems with regrouping. His teacher indicated that the child had a "high intelligence quotient." A quick look at his work assignments showed that he would come up with correct answers for the regrouping problems less than 10 percent of the time. He was seated at a desk and given a work sheet that contained 26 problems that presented single-digit (2+5=) and double-digit (23+12=) addition problems that did not require regrouping. He was then given a work sheet that contained 26 new problems, half of which were single- and double-digit, nonregrouping problems, and half that presented double-digit addition problems where the "ones" column would exceed 9 (25+17=), thus requiring regrouping. PPL measurement disclosed the following: The child recognized all numbers from 1 to 100; he understood one-to-one correspondence (the number 5 represents 5 objects); all single digit problems were successfully solved quickly; all double-digit problems, without regrouping, were successfully solved without difficulty; all but one of the double-digit problems that required regrouping were missed. Error analysis disclosed the following: *Whenever* the child was presented with double-digit addition problems, with or without the requirement of regrouping, *he worked from left to right,* adding the "tens" column *first,* then adding the "ones" column. The result: The child's answer to the problem "25+17=" was 312. Close, but not quite right!

The first specific goal involved exercises that would explain over again the concepts of "ones" and "tens," along with place value for all written numbers from 1 to 100. (The child indicated that he had been taught "ones" and "tens" but had forgotten what they meant.) The second specific goal involved exercises to explain again "carrying" from the "ones" column to the "tens" column. The third specific goal involved practicing adding from right to left. Remediation of the latter included the use of a small written cue placed next to the first number in the one's column to alert the child to a possible regrouping requirement. Initially, the cues were used only when regrouping was necessary. Soon, "bogus" cues were placed next to the one's column requiring the child to look carefully at the sum of the "ones" column and indicate whether regrouping was required. Further, the child was presented with double-digit addition problems and was taught and later requested to estimate the answer without using pencil/paper computation. By learning to estimate answers, the problem "25+17=" would be less likely to produce the sum of 312. The child resolved his regrouping problem within days. The problem had existed for months. It was not called to the attention of the parents until the school year had nearly ended.

THE MODEL IN OPERATION

Recently, through the support of a grant provided by Colorado's State Department of Education, the aforementioned model was put into operation at a representative suburban elementary school with nearly 600 pupils. The school was selected as a result of its principal's dissatisfaction with an unusually high number of referrals being made to the school's special education committee, and the faculty's interest in trying some "new" assessment methods to better understand the pupils and their specific curricula needs. There had been widespread dissatisfaction voiced about the traditional normative tests used to evaluate the students, and the staff was interested in exploring alternative ways of viewing each student on an individualized basis. After a brief inservice was held explaining the basic components of the model, an evaluation committee, composed of the school's psychologist, resource teachers, and speech and language specialist, was established. The principal's role was to oversee the committee's actions. Each of the school's working faculty members were met with individually to explain what services were being provided, what process was involved, and what role they were expected to take. Once the staff understood what was to occur, and felt comfortable with the particulars, the "assessment/remediation" process began. A sign-up sheet was made available to the faculty in order for each of them, if they desired, to meet with the committee to discuss a particular child. The only prerequisite necessary for a student to be reviewed by the committee was his or her teacher's determination that the student was experiencing some academic difficulty with any of the exercises presently occurring within the student's class. The teacher's initial responsibility was to bring the student (along with a general goal established for the student) to the meeting room. Prior to doing so, care was taken to share with the child the purpose for everyone getting together. It was important for the student to feel comfortable and relaxed since his or her assistance in the assessment process was essential. (All of the students seen appeared quite excited about the get-together.) After greetings, the committee set about to determine the child's present performance level as it related to the teacher's general goal. This was accomplished by having the student answer questions, solve problems, read passages, or write sentences, any or all, of course, depending on the teacher's general goal. More often than not, students brought the classroom assignments they had been working on that had set the stage for the observed difficulties. (On more than one occasion, a teacher wanted an exceptionally successful child reviewed by the committee. The purpose for the evaluation, rather than being remediation, was to gain ideas as to the best way to further challenge the youngster.) When the general goal referred to reading, students had the opportunity of bringing whichever books they thought were there favorites. Occasionally, the teacher supplemented their choices. The present performance evaluation continued until the students began to produce the errors the teacher had noted. When the errors began to occur consistently, the committee, with the help of the students, evaluated the errors to determine both their type and what exercises might be beneficial. Throughout the evaluation process, generally lasting no more than fifteen minutes (often considerably less), the students were supported and encouraged to take a shot at whatever questions were posed. Incorrect answers or solutions were not only accepted, they were applauded: The committee's members wanted the students to feel comfortable making whatever errors occurred. A few of the students appeared quite surprised that it was more than acceptable to make their errors; a few of the teachers were surprised not only at the extent of the errors but even more at the student's shared explanations for why the errors were occurring. After the assessment process was completed, the children returned to the classroom, and the committee, along with the teacher, explored remedial ideas intended to help the students with the manifested difficulties. If requested, one of the group's members was assigned to the teacher to both assist in the remediation as well as taking data to determine the remediation's effectiveness. Future meetings, if needed, were scheduled.

Since the overall goal of the committee was to help the teacher build the assessment/remediation model into his or her daily activities within the classroom, future assessment and remediation, when possible, occurred within the confines of the classroom. Occasionally, because of class size, teacher preference, or uniqueness of the presenting academic difficulties, a particular student was returned to the committee for additional assessments and brain-storming sessions. Within a relatively short period of time, the teachers who chose to become a part of the process discovered the benefits of looking at each student's work independent of how other students in the classroom were performing. They also appeared to appreciate the immediate help they received; many had been accustomed to waiting weeks (sometimes months) before being assisted with a particular student's difficulties. While the process is still in its beginnings, all parties, including the students, seem pleased with their own progress. No one, including the school psychologist, has voiced any objection to either the absence of "intelligence" testing or the absence of categorical labels.

_____ THOUGHTS, IMPRESSIONS, REFLECTIONS _____

As can be seen, the model requires that you identify an area where individuals are having difficulty. It requires that you identify what there is about that area that is creating the difficulty. It requires you discover how far individuals succeed and where their success falters. Then it requires *your* brain power and your willingness to discover effective methods to help the children move beyond their present level of performance. It is not a particularly fancy approach that uses an enticing acronym to trumpet its presence. Instead, its a get-your-hands-dirty affair, where you get down on the floor, figure out what's going on, what's missing, and what needs to be done.

The model's drawback, if such a term is applicable, is that it requires time to explore the uniqueness of each individual; it requires the creative use of tutors, parents, professionals, and adjunct staff who are willing to help individuals. Students are not seen as members of groups, be the groups 10-year-olds or third-graders. Students are not exposed to a blanket approach where all are told to open their books to page 27 unless, of course, all the students' present performance levels place them at that level of instruction. Individuals are not required to vie solely against one another. Competition includes "self-competition," where individuals endeavor to advance beyond their previous performances rather than being "first" in a group which, ironically, may require much less effort.

Taken to its logical end, this model redefines both success and failure. Success refers to growth beyond past performance, not the attainment of a dictated goal designed by a curriculum committee or national norm. "Failure" refers always to employed methods, regardless of the uniqueness of the individual. The system is one where no one loses so long as we do not settle for the expediency. It represents a starting point; a point at which we dig in and see what can be done. If a particular approach doesn't work, we try something else. Once we step into the arena, the door leading to alternatives is always open.

_____ MY VIEW _____

Disagreements and ensuing debates are healthy. They force us to look at issues that might otherwise be ignored if agreement and acceptance were the order of the day. All of us must constantly monitor the systems and beliefs that guide our actions. In an area so important, so complex as educating individuals, continual evaluation is essential. The following represents one consultant's point of view.

1. When the issues of "intelligence" and performance are broached, center your questions around the latter. Interpret an IQ score as an indication of the number of questions and exercises correctly solved on an instrument. Since we have no measure of "intelligence," much less a thorough definition, the concept of "intellectual capacity" must be placed on hold until we obtain such a measure. Inevitable terms such as "bright," "slow," and the like, should be a reflection of a child's classroom work in all subject areas and extracurricular endeavors, not a score on an "intelligence" instrument. Regardless of what you have heard, IQ tests do not measure "retardation," "brain damage," or "learning disabilities." The tests sample behavior! Professional interpretations of the tests' scores will tell you more about the professionals' training and biases than an individual's capacity to accomplish sought-after goals.

2. Obtain a large, representative sample and description of the individual's classroom efforts—both written and oral. Always evaluate performance rather than potential. The provided information should be interpreted as representing the individual's present performance level. Observe and note the youngster's errors, as well as successes. Try to determine the types of errors—mechanical, conceptual, or motivational. Once accomplished, visually set up the model.

Goal

Small Steps

PPL

Brainstorm what steps, exercises, and experiences will be used to move the individual toward the goal. Keep in mind that the goal should refer to an academically related area that has been identified as a problem. The discrepancy can involve any activity, from the solution to math problems, completing work, attending to a instructions, asking questions, handing in assignments, to identifying attributes of concepts. Focus your attention on the individual's actual performance, the types of academic experiences he or she has had, and the types of experiences and exercises he or she will need to grow beyond his or her PPL. Determine how much time the proposed remediation will require, where the remediation will take place, and *who* within the school will assume responsibility for providing the needed experiences and exercises.

3. Always remember that individuals' performance is only a reflection of what they *are* doing, not what they *can* do. Individuals may see little value in either the exercises or experiences. Motivation is an

integral part of performance—some kids have it, some kids need it. Some are highly motivated to "work," but what they see as "work" has little to do with school activities. If there is the slightest doubt that individuals' classroom performance is affected by an absence of interest, develop a means to heighten their interest. Promising sports cars for correct spelling is not advisable.

4. While at present it may be necessary to accept the labeling of individuals, do not conclude (or allow it to be concluded) that the labeling means the individuals' *absence* of desired academic behavior (the likely basis for the label) is an indication that the individuals *have* an internal educational or psychological problem. Convenient dragons, no matter their names, do not tell anyone else what individuals need. There are many reasons why a child's academic performance might be less than desired, and none of the reasons suggest the child is the one with the problem.

   Coloring a child "LD" is theoretically untenable and *nearly* useless. The only semijustifiable reason for "its" use is to allow an individual's school to obtain funding for lower teacher–pupil ratios. So long as State Departments of Education continue their insistence that schools use the inadequate discrepancy model for funding purposes, rather than looking at the PPLs and error analyses of each child to determine what youngsters need and funding schools on the basis of the identified needs, you and the schools should use every trick possible to gain access to as much educational money as possible. Labeling a child "LD" is such a trick—*it reflects the inadequacy of the system, not the child!*

5. Never be satisfied with measurements of individuals' performance that occur once every three years! Since instruction occurs daily, consider recording individuals' progress daily. While this may not be feasible, due to the numbers of individuals in a class or special setting, some approximation of repeated measurements is necessary. Repeated measures is the best way for us to determine the effectiveness of our methods. If growth beyond PPL does not occur, our methods need to be altered.

NOTES

1. Government Document U.S. G.P.O. 1987-201-668: 60222, p. 5.
2. Rights without labels. (1987, May 27). *Education Week*, p. 22.
3. Will, M.C. (1986). Educating children with learning problems. A shared responsibility. *Exceptional Children, 52,* 411–415.
4. Lipsky, D.K., & Gartner, A. (1987). Capable of achievement and

worthy of respect: Education for handicapped students as if they were full-fledged human beings. *Exceptional Children, 54* (1), 73. This paper is one of the finest I have read in many years. I urge you to read it in its entirety.

5. Edmonds, R. (1979). Some schools work and more can. *Social Policy, 9*(2), 28–32.
6. Wallin, J.E.W. (1924). Classification of mentally deficient and retarded children for instruction. *Journal of Psycho-Aesthenics, 29*, 166.
7. Macht, J. (1980). *The slaying of the dragon within: A question of educational/psychological diseases of school children* (p. 128). Littleton, CO: Jem.
8. ———(1975). *Teacher/teachim: The toughest game in town.* New York: Wiley.
9. Willner, S.K., & Crane, R. (1979). A parental dilemma: The child with a marginal handicap (p. 30–35). *The Journal of contemporary Social Work, Family Service Association of America.*
10. Tucker, J.A. (1987). Curriculum-based assessment is not fad. *The Collaborative Educator* (Fall), 4.
11. Gickling, E.E., & Havertape, J.F. (1981). Curriculum based assessment. In J.A. Tucker (Ed.), *Non-test based assessment.* Minneapolis: The National School Psychology Inservice Network. University of Minnesota.

SUMMARY

KEEP IN MIND

1. All students, regardless of endowments and experiences, can be assisted to grow and develop, to taste success, to be better today than yesterday, without anyone, at anytime, ever using any categorical label other than "human being."
2. To help individuals taste academic success, consider the following:
    a. General Goal: Determine the academic area creating difficulty.
    b. Present Performance Level: Find out how much of the general goal the students now know. The PPL will tell you where the students succeed at or near 100 percent; it will tell you where to begin your program. It will provide you with much more usable information than the students' ages or grade levels. Use your classroom materials to develop your test, then sample your students' behavior.
    c. Error Analysis: Assess the individuals until they begin to make reliable errors. Support them through this process: explain that

their errors are important. Evaluate the errors: are they mechanical, conceptual, or motivational?

  d. Specific Goal: Develop a goal based on the errors the students made. The goal should be related to those errors and the successful steps beyond the errors.

  e. Small Steps/Creative Exercises: Help the students overcome the errors: find out what they need to experience in order to solve the problems you have uncovered.

3. Do not allow any categorical label to interfere with your efforts to help students with their academic difficulties. Labels will not tell you what to do for students. Labels will not tell you what the children need. Labels only provide money. That, again, is a systems problem. Only your acquired skills and willingness to use them will benefit the youngsters.

General Goal

| 13.1 | Make contact with a teacher and ask if you can practice a few things with some of his or her classmates. If the teacher agrees, select one student and, with the teacher and child, determine an academic area creating problems. Develop a general goal for the student.

Present Performance Level

| 13.2 | With the teacher's permission, do a present performance level test with the child. If possible, try a couple PPL exams with several of the children. Determine where the child is in relation to the general goal. At what level does he or she succeed at or near 100 percent?

Error Analysis

| 13.3 | Keep testing the child until he or she begins to produce reliable errors. (Support students: tell them their errors are what you want!) Talk to the child about his or her errors. Determine whether they are mechanical, conceptual, or motivational.

Specific Goal

| 13.4 | Develop a specific goal for the youngster. Make certain it is related to the types of errors the child made during your examination.

Creative Exercises

| **13.5** | Put your creative hat on, and with the permission of the child's teacher, develop some ingenious ways of helping the child overcome his or her measured errors. Try several things; keep track of precisely what you did. Bring your ideas to class and discuss them with your classmates.

CONSIDER AS WE LOOK AHEAD

1. Academic difficulties are not the only problems teachers face in their classrooms. Social/emotional concerns may also be prevalent.
2. There are ways of helping students learn to be more responsible for their activities. For this to occur, you may need to be more sensitive to the role you play regarding the students' behaviors.
3. There exists little need for such terms as "attention-deficit-disorder," "hyperactivity," or the like. As will be evident, such terms do not tell you how to help the child. Acceptance of the terms increases the chances the child and his or her behavior will be treated in isolation.

14

SOCIAL BEHAVIORAL DISCREPANCIES AND THE CONSULTANT MODEL

There is little question that students occasionally behave in ways that interfere with their growth and development, and drive our patience thin. In schools, some do not attend to their work, some appear very active, some aggressive. The same behaviors, of course, can be, and often are, observed at home. The vast majority of calls I receive requesting assistance involve behaviors that are creating stress for adults who are having a difficult time dealing with the individuals' actions. The range of unacceptable behaviors is extensive. The names used to describe (or explain) the behaviors are equally varied. Before looking at some ideas that can be of assistance, a few words to help put the topic into perspective is advisable.

"ADD," "ADHD," "EBD," AND OTHER LETTERS PINNED TO THE DART BOARD

Social behavioral dragons surface only when a professional believes children are not behaving as they *should*. The descriptive terms "hyperactive," "attention-deficit-disorder," (ADD) and "emotionally disturbed" (EBD—sometimes referred to as "educationally, behaviorally disturbed," or "emotional, behavior disorder" or . . .) indicate that a behavioral discrepancy exists. (The American Psychiatric Association has conveniently combined "attention-deficit-disorder" and "hyperactivity" into its own classification with its own "call" letters: "ADHD." If you have the APA's "diagnostic" manual close at hand, you'll find it under number

314.01.) Succinctly put, from a *remediation* point of view, the terms (or similar ones) do *not* provide any usable information. (Their only practical reason for existing is for purposes of money—again, a system defect—or for providing a few professionals with a convenient and confusing set of terms and descriptions.) As adjectives—"he's a hyperactive or disturbed child"—they do not represent any clear, operationally defined class of actions; the authority will have to describe what the child *does* before anyone will know what is being said. When used as nouns—"she does those things because of her emotional disturbance or hyperactivity"—the authority has erred by suggesting first that a "condition" exists, and second, that the "condition" has caused something. Since the terms are adjectives turned nouns, they can't be the *cause* of anything other than the all-too-quick conclusion that something is wrong with the individual, and, on occasion, the all-too-quick use of drugs, where alterations within the child's natural environment might be much more effective. When behaviors are said to be symptomatic of a "condition," fixing in isolation most often becomes the treatment of choice. Such a choice, as noted, reflects the essence of tunnel vision.

A REMINDER: SEEING BEHAVIOR WITHIN THE CONTEXT IN WHICH IT OCCURS

It is essential that you continually remind yourself that undesired social/ emotional behavior is nearly always associated with the tasks and activities being requested of an individual. As said many times, **you must view the behavior as being only one part of the student, not the whole student, and further, you must see the behavior as it relates to the academic and daily living assignments presently facing the individual. Only by doing so, can you hope to see both the individual and his or her actions within the context in which these actions are occurring.** Remediating the behavior outside of that context will rarely benefit either you or the one you are assisting.

14.1

> [T]he ecological model implies that it is meaningless to discuss problems of behavior in isolation from the contexts in which these behaviors arise, since it is these very contexts that define the behavior as a problem. . . . One must accept that ecosystems rather than children are disturbed, and that ecosystems are directly influenced by the culture in which they exist.[1]

> Every child is an inseparable part of a complex web of interrelated systems. For "normal" children, these mini-social-systems function appropriately and may be defined as congruent or balanced. When the system breaks down, we term them incongruent or unbalanced. We also tend to place the blame for such incongruence on the child, rationalize our actions by labeling

the child as emotionally disturbed, and plan our interventions to focus on remediating the identified child's emotional disturbance while neglecting the other aspects of the system.[2]

We cannot hope to provide effective intervention if we "pluck" a child from a context of disturbance, attempt to fix or change him, and then place the child back into the unchanged environment from which he came.[3]

It is critical to recognize that a child's external environment can influence when (and if) a behavior is manifested. Once more: behavior never occurs in isolation. Thus, the presence of behavior (undesired or desired) tells us much about the child's external environment: it tells us about the cues that surround the child; the feedback that influences his or her behavior; and the perceptions the child holds of both. It reminds us that to help the child acquire alternative behaviors, the child's entire ecological system must be investigated. Suggesting that a disturbed physiology or psychology is the root of a problem, when little else has first been examined, represents tunnel vision at an extreme. Such a view ignores the adaptability, indeed the integrity, of the child.

"ADD": A BLIND CASE STUDY

The first-grader seemed to be having extraordinary difficulty focusing on his teacher's lessons and assignment. He was a constant talker, frequently interrupting his teacher during a lesson so as to have a "burning" question answered immediately. When the class began to exit for lunch or an outdoor activity, he would charge recklessly to the front of the line, seemingly not hearing that another child had been appointed "line leader." His attention to detail was minimal, and while he could successfully print his name, the letters would be strewn over the top of the page rather than be written in the upper right-hand corner as requested. His game playing was equally without boundaries: He'd start a game, stop long before he had completed it, then begin another with the same impulsivity. He rarely sat quietly during "story time," requiring that his teacher remind him many times to sit still so others could hear what was being said. His compliance was brief, and he often was made to sit by himself so as not to further disrupt the class. Even then, away from the others, he'd fidget in his chair and turn and toss as though desperate to return to the group. Invariably, his teacher would admonish him from a distance, and while he would sit quietly once being warned to do so, his calm would evaporate within minutes.

After exhausting her ideas on how to help the youngster, the teacher conferred with his parents, suggesting that the family physician be contacted for an evaluation. The parents were not surprised by the request for they had been in constant contact with the teacher for the past month. While they believed their son was not quite as active at home, and indeed capable at times of attending to many of his favorite activities, they understood the teacher's plight and agreed, although somewhat reluctantly, that perhaps the child was not able to control his own actions while at school. It was plain to the physician that the child was experiencing considerable difficulty, and after being told that the teacher was insisting that something be done to calm the child and help him become more focused, a small, trial dosage of Ritalin was prescribed, and "attention-deficit-disorder" was diagnosed.

After the regime had been in effect for five days, and the child's behavior had not changed appreciably, the dosage was increased. Positive effects were noticed, although the teacher described them as being only moderately significant. After the physician had received several phone calls from the boy's parents, each one expressing their ambivalence over what was happening, he contacted me. I visited the child at his home and noticed, as the parents had suggested, that the youngster, on occasion, was quite capable of maintaining his attention to various activities. I asked the parents if they had altered their approach to their child since the medication had begun, and they both believed that other than a few conversations regarding his activities at school, little had changed. Once permission was granted by the school officials, I went to the class both to speak with the teacher and observe the child. Initial observations indicated that he was the most active and least attentive youngster in the class, even under the influence of the medication.

The teacher and I spent several hours discussing her programs and approaches. She seemed almost apologetic when the topic of medication was broached, stating that she felt bad both for having to admit that her teaching methods had not been sufficient to help the child attend more successfully to his work, and for having to recommend that medication be tried. After sharing my understanding of the difficult situation she was facing, we began to make some changes in his program. Data were taken over several days to ascertain how the teacher and classmates were responding to the child's actions. Behavior-pairs were established and a baseline of the behaviors' frequency under their cuing conditions was documented. Present performance levels and the child's manifested academic errors were evaluated. With the assistance of the youngster, a reinforcement menu was developed, and a clear continency system, incorporating many "When . . . then" quickies were put into operation by the teacher.

Within a week, the child's behavior had changed appreciably. He sat more quietly with his classmates while stories were read. He listened to the teacher to find out who could be "line-leader" (a privilege he earned on several occasions). His interrupting had decreased, and was replaced with a waving, raised hand when he wished to ask a question (an alternative behavior chosen by the teacher). While his game playing was less impulsive, it continued to be highly varied (a behavior his teacher agreed to accept). He still moved around the class, during transition times, more energetically than some of his classmates, but the movements' "flavors" were less phrenetic than they had been. His teacher expressed that she felt more comfortable with him, and was better able to guide him effectively. Predictably, the teacher/parent conference produced the critical question: Was the change in the child's behavior due to the medication or to the teacher's new approach to the child? Everyone agreed the question was worthy of experimentation. Everyone also agreed that a "blind" study would be more illuminating.

With the physician's approval, the child's parents were given the responsibility of deciding when the medication would be administered. The guidelines were as follows: No one other than the parents and myself would know when the child was on the medication; the medication, if it was to be administered, would have to be taken by the child for a minimum of a three-week period; if it was to be withheld, it would be withheld for the same period of time; the parents were not to contact the teacher to see how the child was doing—the teacher accepted the responsibility of providing the parents with daily reports describing the child's behavior, its progress or the lack thereof; the child would be seen briefly by the physician once a month; I would visit the school and speak with the teacher once a week at a designated day and time, to evaluate the continually documented baseline; the teacher was to go about her daily business, educating all the students while continuing to incorporate the procedural alterations designed for the child.

Two "medication-on" and one "medication-off" conditions occurred prior to Thanksgiving vacation. An additional "two-off" and "one-on" occurred after the child returned from his Christmas/New Year's school break. The teacher was uncertain, from the child's behaviors, whether he was "on" or "off" the medication. Unknown to the teacher, the decision was made to reduce the medication to its earlier low dosage. By her own admission, the teacher was still unable to tell whether the child was medicated or not. During one particularly "good" week, the records showed the child had been without medication. The decision was eventually made to completely remove the Ritalin. The child continued to progress; the teacher, once being informed, readily agreed with the decision. She shared with me the feeling of pride she had knowing what she was doing was making a difference.

THE ARENA

For the consultant who works directly with individuals whose behaviors are perceived as less than desirable, the major concern is to help the individual and those significant people within his or her immediate environment find solutions to the troubling circumstances. This tenet holds true whether the terms "emotionally disturbed," "attention-deficit-disorder," or any similar term enters the discussion. Getting started requires that we go back to the beginning of the manuscript. Everything we have covered now comes into play. We must:

1. See individuals as they exist within their natural environment, not as isolated in a vacuum.
2. Be aware of what they are doing that has been deemed undesired, and determine, carefully, what behavior will serve as an alternatively more desired response.
3. Recognize that individuals' behavior, no matter how distasteful or disruptive, *is* adaptive; it *is* serving some purpose; it *is* functional and appropriate, given how their natural environment responds to what they do.
4. Note the conditions under which the desired and undesired behaviors occur and fail to occur. Frequently, the cues that set the stage for undesired behaviors will be related to school work or daily work assignments: All individuals, not just those labeled or considered "special," experience difficulties during their education, and those difficulties can easily carry over into everyday behaviors.
5. Determine how the immediate environment responds to what individuals do. How does the environment react to the individuals' behaviors? What payoffs are being provided for both sides of the behavior-pairs?
6. Discover what is of value to individuals; discover if they know how to access that which they perceive as positive.

7. Recognize that the undesired behaviors may be allowing individuals to avoid what they would prefer not to experience. Find out what there is about the activities the individuals perceive as aversive.
8. See individuals as doing the best they can given their experiences and endowments. Jump into the arena and help individuals move beyond where they are. Be less overwhelmed by what they're not doing; be more attentive to what they can do. Show them how they can do more.

DATA COLLECTION: TEACHER-MADE FORMS

Throughout this volume you have been introduced to varied glances at the collection of data. My purpose in presenting the topic in "bits and pieces" was to show you how data collection can fit comfortably into your daily activities. Data collection is very important, for it is from the documented evidence that we can determine, among other things, the effectiveness of our programs. Let me share a few instances where collecting data is essential.

1. All present performance and error analysis investigations
2. All academic programs designed to help students work through the errors that were determined and evaluated through error analysis
3. Any time an artificial reinforcement system is used to help increase the occurrence of desired behavior
4. Any time any "aversive" intervention is used to help redirect undesired behavior
5. Whenever cues are being investigated to see what part they are playing within the natural environment
6. Whenever the influence of environmental feedback, as it occurs within the natural environment, is being monitored to determine its effects on behavior
7. Whenever a student's behavior has been called into question and there is a need to know the behavior's frequency, intensity, and duration

This sample represents only a few instances where data collection is important. Speech and language therapists, occupational and physical therapists, school psychologists, and many other professionals will be able to share with you occasions where additional data collection is warranted. Of particular concern is how best to record the needed information. The overall rule of thumb is that you should develop a record-keeping system that will "feel" comfortable to you. You need to be able to look at what you have recorded and understand the presented data without difficulty. I prefer a "diary" approach (to be described shortly) where I can envision the target behaviors as they are occurring and being influenced within the natural environment. Other consultants use charts and graphs that depict frequencies, change over time, and the outcomes resulting from interventions. Still others use a combination of something similar to a diary format along with charts and graphs. Regardless of style, nearly all data-keeping measures are concerned with documenting behavior as it occurs during (and over) a period of time. The time period can refer to class sessions, minutes, hours, days, etc. The behavior will most often be recorded with slashes or marks that indicate how often the activity has occurred. A piece of paper with the student's name, the date, the description of the target behavior, and space to mark the frequency with which the behavior occurs is often sufficient. You would simply keep track of the behavior as it occurs over the determined time period (class sessions or days, as examples), and then compare the recorded frequencies to monitor how often the behavior is occurring. If more than one behavior is being monitored simultaneously, the behaviors can be coded with squares and circles (circle=in-seat behavior; square=asking questions), and the like. Sometimes, every incident of a targeted behavior is recorded; other times, only a sample of the behavior over a determined period of time is documented. In the latter instance, you might want to know how often a student is doing something, but rather than watch the child continuously, you might look in his or her direction ten times an hour (or three times every minute) and record whether the behavior in question is occurring. Again, you would have a frequency count of the behavior and could thus compare the frequency over a period of several days. Perhaps you might want to know whether your remediation had some influence over the targeted behavior. To keep things simple, you could take one piece of paper, date it, describe the behavior, and count its frequency prior to your intervention. After you had obtained a reliable (consistent) sample of the behavior, a second piece of paper (with name, date, etc.) could be used to keep track of the behavior during your remediation process. By comparing the total frequencies, you'd have a pretty good notion whether the targeted behavior had changed in conjunction with your remediation efforts.

The types of forms you develop (or purchase) are not, obviously, as important as the information you obtain. Try to determine what you wish to find out as a result of monitoring a student's (and your) behavior. Keep your data collection methods simple, clear, and comprehensible. No doubt many of your colleagues will have a wealth of ideas (and sample forms they have developed) to share with you. Remember the overall purpose for data collection: It helps you know how well you and the student are doing.

THE DIARY

I know that each person I assist is unique; each circumstance within which he or she finds himself or herself is equally varied—the individual will be far more than merely a certain age or category. I know he or she is going to be a complex individual adapting to a complex situation. Because I see the person as an adaptive being, I must know something of the natural environment that both surrounds and influences him or her. Labeling the individual according to whatever "handicap" he or she is said to have provides little if anything to build on. For me to be able to help people, I must know them, including their values and adaptive strengths. I must also have a brain that will enable me to remember everything important about individuals and the circumstances in which they find themselves. If I am going to develop programs that will help individuals progress beyond their present circumstances, I must know what those circumstances are and how they are influencing what the individuals are doing. Unfortunately, I don't have the sort of brain that allows me to take multiple pictures and recall, with any degree of accuracy, what has been "shot." I, as is true of most of my colleagues, have to write things down. I have compromised from the zealousness of my earlier days and have adopted a "semiformal" means of keeping track of what is going on. While no more sophisticated than some of the forms I described above, it nevertheless can provide valuable information regarding what is happening and what needs to be done to find solutions. This is the format I use.

Cues	Behaviors	Feedback	Individual's Reaction

I take several pieces of paper and write these headings on the top of each. Since I, and those I work with, will be writing in columns, I space the headings to allow enough room under each for observations and notes. In order to capture all that is happening, my colleagues and I record the events immediately after their occurrence. (The folder in which we keep all the papers is brightly colored. We'd lose it otherwise.) Often this moment-by-moment task of record keeping is difficult (because of additional responsibilities), so when necessary we jot down our observations as quickly as is feasible. We are as objective as possible and write down everything we believe to be important. If we are going to make an error, we make the error of writing too much. It is much easier to throw something away than to recall that it happened. (I have been handed a 20-page diary taken by parents over a four-day period of time. It was a fabulous effort. Teachers, I have discovered, are a drop more stingy.)

Ideally, we carry the notebook/folder with us. Pragmatically, we leave it at a location where we can retrieve it quickly. If the individuals we are working with, having seen our note taking, ask what we are doing, we tell them. Nothing is hidden; everything is placed on the table. We calmly (!) explain that we are trying to find out what we're doing so we can help them learn some new things.

Oftentimes, a four- or five-day period is generally sufficient for the initial note taking. That time period is an approximation. We may get a handle on what's happening in less time. Our goal is to obtain a good sample of the natural environment's components. Time is not the key issue. A reliable, consistent sample of the behavior and the surrounding environment's reactions are the goal. We write down what we see: what individuals are doing, when they're doing it, and how the environment responds to them. What do we get from all our efforts? The following is probably familiar:

1. How often, and under what conditions, individuals are behaving desirably
2. How often, and under what conditions, individuals are behaving undesirably
3. How individuals' natural environment is responding to what they are doing
4. What effect, if any, the natural environment's reactions are having on individuals' behaviors
5. What purpose individuals' behavior might be serving
6. What components of the natural environment need to be changed to help individuals acquire the behaviors deemed desirable.

We take the above information and put it to the side for a moment. The next task is to review both the academic and daily living skill exercises required of individuals. Again, this will be familiar to you:

1. The accurately measured PPL that indicates at what level individuals can succeed
2. The carefully evaluated error analysis that indicates where the successful behavior begins to break down.

Once accomplished, the gathered material is scrutinized before any plan of action is initiated. Among other things, the evaluation is intended to determine what effect the natural environment is having on individuals' actions, what components of the environment need to be changed, what creative exercises and motivational systems will best serve individuals, who will take the responsibility for the remediation, what additional information will be collected to measure the effectiveness of the plan, and how that information will be disseminated to teachers, therapists, and parents who will also be working with the individuals. When the plan is put into action, progress-data that refer to what individuals are doing are continually recorded and reported. The only comparisons made are those that indicate how each individual is advancing (or failing to advance) beyond his or her own PPL.

While all of the collected material is important, the most critical component is the individual's reaction (the last column) to the environment's feedback that is being used to influence and redirect behaviors.

Cues   Behaviors   Feedback   *Individual's Reaction*

The individual's reactions will indicate whether the program is effective. If, for example, the purpose of the remediation plan is to help an individual attend more frequently, consistently, and accurately to assignments, the last column will indicate whether that goal is being achieved. If it is, the plan is working. If not, the plan must be altered. The same holds for any problem that has become the target for remediation. Whether I'm attempting to help an individual consume more calories, become more involved with classwork, comply more frequently to requests that are made, or come out from under a table and discover what the world can offer, I watch and measure carefully the individual's reactions and responses to the remediation program. The assumption is always made that if the method is effective, success (as defined by growth beyond PPL) will be achieved. If success is not achieved, the culprit is not the individual, but the program I have developed. Without the "diary," without continual *repeated measurements* of the individual's performance, I'm left to guess whether the remediation is effective. I haven't worked with too many teachers or parents who are satisfied with such a position. Guessing incorrectly places everyone in a precarious position. Even if I guess correctly but fail to record what is happening, I may change what should remain or maintain what should be changed.

WORKING FROM THE IDEAL TO THE REAL: INFORMATION DERIVED FROM THE DIARY

As you no doubt recall from earlier discussions, it is rare that individuals manifest disruptive behaviors continually. Even those seriously involved appear to have the ability to find for themselves circumstances that, for any number of reasons, allow them to feel comfortable enough to be relaxed, satisfied, and in some degree of control of their actions. Frequently, individuals who are labeled "disturbed," "hyper," or are said to have "attention-deficit-disorders," spend a sizeable portion of their day doing precisely what nondisturbed, nonhyper, and highly attentive individuals do. Many of the "failure-to-thrive" youngsters I've seen over the past few years do, in fact, eat, although their selections are often very limited. I've seen combative children and adults who, when things are right, are productive, compliant, cooperative, and easy to be with. I've seen students who have difficulty listening and attending to what their teachers are saying, but have no difficulty listening and attending to their favorite TV shows or stories. I've seen many youngsters who can be "hell-on-wheels" at home, but angelic when they are seated in my office or playing with friends. Frankly, if youngsters could survive on only potato chips and soda pop, if they could become great teachers, scientists, and poets by only watching the "boob" tube, if they could adapt socially to the world by only sitting on someone's lap, receiving everything they wanted, when they wanted, the ranks of those described as difficult would be slimmed to a near handful. As we all know, however, reaching the desired plateau of "full potential" requires the individuals to go beyond their momentarily perceived "ideal" situation.

There is a brain-storming exercise I rely on heavily when first starting to develop remediation approaches intended to help teachers and parents who are experiencing difficulty with their charges. It is suitable, and can be successful, for all individuals regardless of the degree of their disruptiveness or physical involvement. It builds on the "ideal" and works backwards to that which is real and administratively feasible.

CUES REVISITED

After the diary has been run and the aforementioned data have been collected and carefully reviewed, I ask the professionals I work with the following: "Speculate on the ideal situation where the disruptive, nonattentive, or general *undesired* behaviors would be at zero, or near-zero frequency." What I am asking the professionals to do is to figure out, from the data, the conditions (cues) under which the undesired behaviors would be virtually *nonexistent.* They are to think purely in terms of the "ideal" situation: a situation where time, costs, resources, personnel, location, or what have you, are *not* a concern. I request them to consider: If they could develop or manufacture *any* scenario where the undesired behaviors would not occur, and the desired alternatives would take their place, what would that scenario entail? The "sky" is the limit.

The purpose for such an endeavor is to begin identifying what conditions seem to set the stage for an individual's *desired* behaviors. When is the individual calm and satisfied? What type and quantity of "academics" (regardless of their nature) produces attending and effort? What conditions need to be present before the individual does what we believe will serve him or her best? Once we determine those conditions, we can try tailoring a program that will approximate what seems to facilitate the individual's desired behaviors.

More times than not, we won't be able to (or won't believe it wise to) replicate the ideal situation. The fact is that time, costs, resources, and the like are limited. A student might perform beautifully if she could but share her teacher with only a few others. A child might be attentive and calm if his parents were to spend an entire day sitting by his side or walking with him in a sunlit park. An adult might coexist with staff and peers if no demands were placed upon him. Such conditions are rarely realistic or, with the exception of the first, productive. By identifying them, however, we will be able to compare the "ideal" with the "real," think about what the "ideal" offers the individual, consider what he or she derives from that "ideal" situation, and then speculate on how to incorporate the payoffs into a realistic program.

The exercise affords a glimpse of the individual's preferences, as well as what he or she is prepared to handle. In a sense, the exercise tells us something of the individual's PPL: at what level, and under what conditions, he or she experiences success. We need to evaluate carefully the components of those conditions to see, again, what they offer the individual. We ask ourselves: why does the individual do so well under those conditions; why does he or she experience difficulty under other conditions? What is there about the "ideal" situation that helps the individual behave desirably? The answers, sometimes very obvious, will tell us something of the individual's perceptions of what we are requiring, as well as something of the individual's private motivational system. It will tell us what he or she feels comfortable moving toward, as well as what he or she wishes to avoid. It will tell us which of the analyzed components will need to be incorporated into our behavioral program. It will give us some insight into what we will have to do to gradually help individuals go beyond where they are, moving, gradually and successfully, toward where we would like them to be.

MY VIEWS

There are, of course, different theories that attempt to account for the "misbehavior" of individuals. Likewise, there are different remediation orientations that are employed to help individuals and those who are responsible for their welfare. Consultants bring with them their own views and biases, some that are shared by their colleagues, and some that evoke disagreement. I offer the following ideas that reflect my thinking for your consideration.

1. Recognize that the individual in question is different from any other individual; his or her endowments and experiences guarantee uniqueness. Be concerned, therefore, with his or her behaviors and ways of reacting. Do not focus entirely on how the individual might compare with other children or adults, be they in his or her class, or program, or living on the same street. While the temptation will be great to see the individual as a member of a group of individuals the same age or grade level or "diagnostic" category, none of those variables are sufficient to insure that he or she will, or should be, like the others.

14.2

2. **It is important to see individuals as adaptive, healthy individuals, whose behaviors are appropriate given the circumstances within which they find themselves, purposive given their own perceptions and values, and functional given the fact that their behaviors work: they bring them what they want.** Spending time debating over which category or label best fits an individual is a poor use of time. The conclusion, after many hours of discussion, often is that he or she doesn't fit comfortably within any group. That decision should have been reached before the discussion started.

3. When judgments are made about the individual, it is necessary to determine whether the views are based on well-established norms or personal opinion. While opinions are important, they maybe wrong. If the judgments are based on test scores, it is essential to determine if the tests measure what their authors intended. Tests that purportedly measure such constructs as "self-concept," "insecurity," as well as varying grades of "disturbance," in fact only measure an individual's responses to presented questions and scenarios. The constructs offer little assistance in developing programs. The individual's responses, if they are analyzed carefully, however, can provide information about perceptions and preferences as they relate to the tests' materials. Often that information can be very helpful.

   It is also important that judgments made about individuals reflect their behaviors under all conditions, not just those that occur within one classroom or setting. Individuals do behave differently depending on where they find themselves; thus it is necessary to see individuals under many different conditions before they are said to be a certain way.

4. Whenever an individual is characterized by any adjective, be it "hyperactive," "behaviorally disturbed," or the like,

determine what specific, observable behaviors are being represented by the term(s). Never assume that you and other professionals are thinking of the same behaviors. Do not hesitate to ask for clarification, and make certain that the clarification "clears the water" rather than adding more mud to it.

I have observed hundreds of meetings where professionals have described individuals with enough adjectives to chronicle the hardships faced by the Plymouth Rock Pilgrims. Some parents and teachers remained quiet, attempting to absorb what was being said. Others voiced objections to the negative characterizations almost before they were spoken. Amazingly, few in attendance asked for definitions. Sadly, few who were providing the characterizations offered them.

5. Once the problem behaviors have been identified, begin the process that will produce ideas for remediation. Start with an attitude that encompasses the belief that individuals are doing the best they can given their endowments and experiences. Then begin to consider the following:

  a. Behavior-pairs: We know what individuals are doing that is creating difficulty. What would we prefer they do? When possible, avoid placing the term "not" in front of the undesired behavior. Identify an active, positive, forward-moving behavior; something individuals can do that will lead them to what is valued.

  b. Cues: Identify when the desired and undesired behaviors occur. Look specifically for the conditions under which the undesired behaviors do *not* occur, as well as the conditions under which the desired behavior does occur.

  c. Feedback: Have everyone involved with the individuals note how they are responding to both sides of the behavior-pair. Avoid terms like "positive" and "negative;" instead, have everyone write down what they are doing.

  d. Purpose: Behavior does not occur whimsically. It serves some purpose; it provides individuals with something of value, or it enables them to avoid what they perceive as aversive. If, for example, you believe an individual is doing something for "attention," then speculate on what might happen if the attention was provided for the desired side of the behavior-pair. If you believe that the individual is working hard to avoid something, determine what aversive component is operating and see what can be done to alter its aversive characteristics. If you find yourself using the term "manipulate" in a negative way, recognize that manipulating the environment is an essential component of adaptive behavior. Find out what the manipulative behavior produces; it will tell you something of what the individual values.

e. Value/reinforcement Menu: Compile a list of all the activities and objects the individual perceives as valuable. Once the menu has been determined, ask yourself if the individual knows how to gain access to what is valued. It is not at all uncommon for the natural environment to have taught the individual "undesired" ways of producing what is valued. Until the natural environment alters its approach, showing the individual alternatively more desirable ways of obtaining what is valued, the undesired behavior is assuredly appropriate: It works!

f. Tasks: Look carefully at what the individual is being requested to do regarding academics and daily living exercises. Consider the relation between what is expected of the individual, his or her PPL, and the types of errors he or she is making. "Attention-deficit-disorders" are most common when an individual is asked to do something that either holds no personal value or produces no personal success. Such a "deficit" speaks more to the "system" than to the individual.

g. Convenient Dragons: If an "educational/psychological" malady must be named, either for purposes of funding or because a professional won't be able to get a good night's sleep unless some diagnosis is made, give the "dragon" its due: two seconds; then move on to what needs to be done. Suggesting that an individual has a problem is an example of expediency. Suggesting we are all having a problem with the individual's behavior is a much more productive beginning.

h. Our Part: Think about how we might provide the individual with a reason to behave desirably. Aversive discipline programs, alone, are nearly worthless. We need for the desired behavior to produce its own positive feedback, preferably what is referred to as "intrinsic" motivation. Give the "instrinsic" a chance to occur through the use of an "artificial" system: "When . . . then quickies," "token systems," and

"non-freebie" reinforcement. Such interim programs
will help the desired behavior get started; they can begin
to show the individual how to access what is valued. If
compliance is an issue, look carefully at the "type-one"
and "type-two" requests that are being made, and the
willingness of all involved to assure that "type-ones" are
carried out.

i. Self-Directed Behavior: All of us benefit from knowing
how the natural environment intends to respond to our
behavior. Being able to predict that "A" produces "B,"
and "C" produces "D" will help individuals gain control
over their own behavior. For that to occur, individuals
must know the components; for them to know the
components, we must help them recognize they exist.

"This part isn't easy, is it? An individual's undesired behavior can
push us to our limits," the parent reflected as she closed her note
book and placed her pencil on the table.

I smiled at her. "Writing advice on paper is the easy part.
Putting it into practice, determining what to do, is somewhat more
difficult."

"I can appreciate that," she responded. "I remember receiving
reports from professionals who had seen my son. Ninety percent
told me what was wrong; the remaining 10 percent was devoted to
what should be done. My sense is that you would like those
numbers reversed."

"You couldn't be more right. We've created a system that honors
'dragon' hunting and naming rather than 'dragon' slaying. I've
watched countless professionals become (or be required to become)
so entangled with tasks that have little to do with the problems at
hand, that they have little direct time for those who are
experiencing the problems."

"Will that change?" she asked.

"Only if we want it to change," I answered. "We are the system.
If we wish, we can alter it. If not, it will remain as it is. Each of us
has the opportunity and ability to see the individual for what he is:
unique and in need of assistance rather than someone colored by
our ignorance into obscurity. It is up to us, each of us."

"You have made changes," she said more as a question.

"In a quiet way, I suspect you could say that."

"Somehow I don't see you as doing anything quietly," she joked.

I hesitated for a moment as my mind carried me back to a most
glorious professional time. "Well, a couple of my colleagues and I,
several years ago, did decide to disregard some of the system's

inane requirements and function in ways we believed were more beneficial to the children. We took the initiative to change things.''

She waited briefly before prodding. "You'll tell me what you did?''

"I shouldn't,'' I responded. "The group involved promised each other to keep it a secret.''

"I won't tell anyone,'' she stated with anticipation. "It will not pass my lips.'' I smiled as more memories drifted into my consciousness. "Come on now,'' she said, "let's not over dramatize this last story.''

"All right,'' I answered knowing that I could not keep the story to myself. "Many years ago, I served as a consultant to a very special school that was mandated to care for a sizeable number of children who were sent to us from some six different school districts in the Denver area. We had a team composed of the sharpest professionals one could ever hope to work with. Together, the teachers, speech therapists, physical therapists, occupational therapists, aides, principal, nurse, worked very hard to help the children who were enrolled in the facility. I think we did some good work with many of the youngsters. Some, however, were very difficult and, frankly, we weren't able to do all we wished. Many of the youngsters were easy to work with: They were kids who were having problems in reading or math or writing or attention/social behavioral difficulties, but they had no identifiable physical problems. They were simply experiencing difficulty meeting their home-school teachers' expectations. We were able to get them to 'grade level' within a very short period of time. Some only needed individualized approaches; then they took off on their own.

"When the children would first come to the building, each would be seen by a representative from our multidisciplines. The observation period would generally last about four hours, which would give all of us a chance to interact with the child and determine his PPL. After the PPL was measured, we could assign the child to a class and a teacher prepared to handle the measured uniquenesses.

"Our biggest problem, however, was not with the children. We possessed the skills to help most of them. The major difficulty had to do with a form that needed completion. The form was purely for funding purposes: it had nothing to do with any remedial approach. In those days, we were required to identify *two* handicapping conditions before the school could be reimbursed for servicing the children.''

"Two?'' she said with disbelief.

"Yes. We had to identify two areas of difficulty that would be listed on the form and returned to the district that, in turn, would submit it to the state for funding. For a brief period, we did what the form required: We tried to identify two areas that perhaps were interfering with an individual child's progress. The more we tried, however, the more we realized the futility of the requirement. Our concern was with the children: what they needed; what we could do for them. The time spent debating the 'handicapping conditions' was absurd. We all knew it made no difference what we called the children or what we said were the two conditions. Each of the children were as different as day and night, and clumping them into a common category was more than foolish: It was wrong."

"What did you do?" the wide-eyed parent asked.

"At first, we tried to talk with the officials who had stated that the form had to be filled out. We tried to explain that the 'conditions' were purposeless; that all that mattered were the programs developed for the students. No one seemed to listen; everyone was quite content with the status quo. 'Name the names,' they said. 'Fill out the forms,' they insisted. So we did."

"You did?"

"Yes, we sure did. My office was located in the back of the school building. It was a very small office, which was fine because I was out with the kids most of the time. It had a window that you could not see out of unless you played center for the Los Angeles Lakers. One of the walls was covered with books and supplies. A dart board was nailed to one of the other walls."

"No!" she exclaimed, anticipating what was to follow.

"I had covered the dart board with the endless letters that abbreviated the 'handicapping conditions:' LD, PCD, MR, EBD, SLI, SIEBD, and the like. ADD wasn't in vogue then, and we didn't get any kids who were labeled 'gifted.' When the time came to fill in the two terms on the form, I would go into my office, pick up a dart, and. . . ."

"You didn't," she interrupted.

"You're right; let's say I didn't."

"You did?"

"Anything for the kids," I responded as I stood up and took all the characters in this book out for a drink.

NOTES

1.   Coleman, M.C. (1986). *Behavior disorders: Theory and practice* (pp. 102–103). Englewood Cliffs, NJ: Prentice-Hall.

2. Apter, S.J. (1982). *Troubled children/troubled systems* (p. 139). Elmsford, NY: Pergamon Press.
3. Rhodes, W.C. (1970). A community participation analysis of emotional disturbance (pp. 309–314). *Exceptional Children, 36.*

_____ SUMMARY _____

KEEP IN MIND

1. Always remember:
    a. Behaviors do not occur in isolation. Taking behavior out of the context in which it occurs is fruitless. Children are part of a complex world. To understand individual children, you must see each within his or her own world.
    b. Behaviors are influenced by their surrounding cues and environmental feedback.
    c. Behaviors, despite the fact you might find them highly undesirable, are, nevertheless, adaptive, functional, appropriate, and purposive. Children, through their behaviors, are telling you something. You must interpret their message and the purpose behind their actions.
2. Regardless of the labels used to describe the student, we're still talking about what the individual is doing. Go beyond the labels; go beyond the assertions that the student has some emotional or cerebral dysfunction. See what the student is doing. See what he or she is doing within the context of his or her life space.
3. More often than not, social/behavioral discrepancies are directly associated with academic tasks and assignments. More than a few "emotionally disturbed" children behave beautifully when their academic requirements are to their liking. An equal number of children purportedly "suffering" from "attention-deficit-disorder" attend just fine when what they are asked to become involved in has meaning and value; when what they are asked to do is within their prerequisite skill level. Perhaps, as some have suggested, the "disturbed" and "disordered" behavior represent the students' way of telling everyone else that something is wrong with the system in which we all operate. Perhaps the students are asking us to change something.
4. When discussing students' behavioral discrepancy, be particularly alerted to the degree to which the natural environment can (and does) influence what the students are doing. If the environment can influence what students are doing, then the observed problems manifested by the children are not solely theirs—they do not "own" them. The

environment, because it can influence, shares a sizeable portion of the ownership. Treatment, therefore, must begin with the environment.

5. Whenever your students are having behavioral difficulties:
    a. See individuals as they exist within their natural environment.
    b. Recognize the undesired behavior as being adaptive, purposive.
    c. Determine behavior-pairs.
    d. Note the conditions under which the behaviors occur and do not occur.
    e. Determine the type of feedback the behavior-pairs are receiving from the environment.
    f. Identify what is of value to the students. Find a way to provide students with payoffs for their desired behaviors.
    g. Check students' academic present performance level. Analyze their errors. Find their strengths; what they succeed at academically. Have them experience that success as you help them with their social behaviors.
    h. Jump into the arena. Ask those who have nothing else to offer but "what is wrong with the student" to leave. Be the children's advocate. Become a controlled gambler. Find something students value; find something they can succeed at; show them how good they are; how much value they already possess. Discard the dragons. Embrace the children. Take them and yourself forward.

A Classroom without Dragons

| 14.1 | Visit a classroom that works with "special" children, children labeled "emotionally, behaviorally disturbed" (EBD) or something similar. (Each school district has their own letters, and their own criteria and definitions for the labels!) Forget the labels. Watch the children closely as they interact with each other and their teacher(s). Take a piece of paper and describe, in great deal:
    a. The undesired behaviors. (Speculate on what might serve as desired alternative behaviors.)
    b. The conditions underwhich the undesired behaviors occur and fail to occur.
    c. Note carefully the feedback the teachers provide the child when he behaves undesirably. Remember, keep your descriptions neutral—no "positive" or "negative." You'd have to ask the child about the feedback to get that information.
    d. What do the teachers do when the child behaves acceptably? What feedback occurs?

e. See if you can determine what purpose the undesired behavior may be serving. If possible, ask the child?

f. Does the child's undesired behavior appear to have any relationship to the assignments his teachers have provided? Are there any assignments? Did the teacher do a PPL? Does the child appear interested in the assignment?

g. Most important: if you were the child's teacher, what would you do differently, if anything. Bring your ideas (and justifications) to your class. Discuss with your classmates.

Your View through the Window

| 14.2 | Some professionals would see these EBD children as being driven by their disturbance. Think about your own theoretical view: How do you see the children? What moves them? How do you explain the children's behaviors?

Appendix

SOME SPECIAL VOCABULARY

As with other technical professions, speciality areas, devoted either to particular populations (adolescent versus child) or problems (emotional or academic), have evolved within the general fields of education and psychology. While most of us, through our academic preparations, are guided toward experiencing components of each of the speciality areas, few of us consider ourselves "generalists": equally at home and confident in all aspects of the profession. Instead, we find ourselves drawn toward an identifiable area with its own, often unique, elements. One of those elements, nearly always unique, is language: Each area of specialty has its own jargon; each professional within the area adopts the jargon as part of his or her everyday speech. Problems with the terms singularly associated with a speciality area rarely arise so long as the conversationalists belong to the same "fraternity." Occasionally, however, "outsiders" and "insiders" are required to communicate with each other; often a most enlightening experience: they discover that despite the fact that each group has its own proudly guarded jargon, they're both actually talking about the same things!

The following brief section is intended more as a discussion than an orthodox glossary of a few popular terms often employed by "ecological/behavioral" consultants. As such, my interest is less toward offering formal definitions (which, by the way, often vary among those who attempt to speak the same language), and more toward looking at the functional purposes for the few entries. Several of the terms selected will be familiar: They were mentioned and briefly discussed in the body of the text. Other terms will be new in that I purposely avoided using them when presenting the dialogues and prose. I found that attempts at adding the following thoughts and explanations within the major body often broke the "flow" that I was attempting to create. Since that outcome was not desired, I chose to reserve this discussion for an "appendix" section. The terms to be discussed will be:

1. Backward Chaining
2. Baseline
3. From Continuous to Intermittent to Natural Reinforcement
4. Antecedents (S^D, S^Δ)
5. Curriculum Based Assessment/Measurement
6. Differential Reinforcement
7. Extinction
8. Consequences
9. Negative Reinforcement
10. Shaping

BACKWARD CHAINING

When using this approach, a student is provided nearly all of what he or she needs to know or do in order to accomplish a task. A very helpful idea, if a math problem contains five separate steps, the teacher might provide the student with the first four, requiring only that the student complete the fifth and final component. Once a success is accomplished, the teacher will begin to reduce the number of provided supports: The teacher will provide three components, requiring the student to complete the final two. Spelling words that are particularly troublesome can be presented with all but one letter produced in their correct order. Once the student masters the "all but one," the next practice period might include "all but two" letters. Those of us who work with children who have difficulty self-feeding most often use the "backward chaining" approach by first helping the youngster hold the spoon very close to his or her lips (or perhaps touching them) as the initial step in the self-feeding sequence. Once the child masters the "small" move with the spoon, the next step might involve the spoon being held an inch or so from the mouth. This "backward" approach gradually continues until the child learns to scoop food off the plate, which may be considered the first component of the self-feeding sequence. The approach is very much at home with a wide variety of academic and motor activities.

"Backward chaining," provides the student with a greater chance for experiencing success immediately. Such success, of course, can facilitate a student's willingness to become more involved in the activity. If you are having difficulty assisting a youngster with a fairly complex academic or motoric task, consider developing a sequence of steps that you believe make up the total task, and then having the student complete the last of the steps to see what the total product will look like. By gradually moving "down" the developed steps, the student may gain more understanding of what the task requires.

BASELINE

This term, also used within the text, represents a measure taken of any sort of behavior *prior* to your teaching or therapeutic intervention. In a sense, it represents a "pretest" of the student's skills or behaviors as they relate to a general goal or concern. The measure will provide you with a "base" upon which you will be able to assess the effects of your methods. You can "baseline" academic skills—the number of words read; the number of math problems solved; or you can "baseline" social skills— how often a child raises his hand; how often he calls out; how many minutes he stays on task, etc.

The measure is taken by allowing the behavior to occur, unencumbered, and noting how often it occurs, under what conditions it occurs, and what it looks like (its unique characteristics) as it occurs. (When "baselining" a social behavior, it is necessary to note how the "natural" environment responds—if indeed it does—to the behavior during its occurrences.) As may be apparent, it is similar to a present performance level measure in that it lets you know where the student is in relation to a general academic or behavioral goal. When I am called into a case where a child purportedly manifests a high or low frequency of a particular behavior, I will watch the child (inconspicuously) and document the occurrences of the behavior (when it happens, what it looks like, etc.). I prefer to take baseline observations for several periods of time in order to gain a reliable sample of what the child is doing. The baseline measurement will provide you with an accurate statement of the child's behavior: From it, you will know precisely what the youngster is doing. Often, such information is the key first step to knowing how best to help the individual.

FROM CONTINUOUS TO INTERMITTENT
TO NATURAL REINFORCEMENT

Nearly all newly implemented positive reinforcement programs have the following in common: They start out by providing the student with a rich amount of artificial reinforcement, then they gradually reduce the amount of positive feedback offered, until eventually, if all goes as planned, natural reinforcement takes over and maintains the originally targeted behavior. Said slightly more formally, new programs often begin with *continuous* reinforcement that gives way to *intermittent* reinforcement that, in turn, gives way to natural reinforcement. In all likelihood, the two italicized terms are familiar to you. Still, let me briefly run through them as they relate to educational programs.

As the name implies, *continuous* reinforcement provides valued feedback each time a specifically targeted, desired behavior occurs. From a practical standpoint, its purpose is twofold: (1) its "rich" schedule of artificial reinforcement helps maintain students' interest in the task at hand; and (2) its continuous application helps students recognize precisely which of their behaviors has produced the desired feedback. For example, if a teacher wishes to help a youngster be more considerate of other classmates, and thus learn to raise his hand rather than calling out an answer, the teacher might recognize the child the first few times he raises his hand to be called on. Assuming "being recognized" is valued by the child, the repeated (or "continuous") recognition will help the child learn the lesson his teacher believes is important.

As is evident, employing continuous reinforcement with 30 students in one classroom is cumbersome, not administratively feasible (and not likely possible), and, most importantly, it rarely teaches children to persist with an activity when, inevitably, artificial reinforcement fails to come their way. Therefore, once it is believed that students understand fully which of their behaviors has produced the desired feedback, the "schedule" of reinforcement changes from continuous to *intermittent.* The term "intermittent," whether it refers to rain or reinforcement, means that sometimes it comes and sometimes it doesn't. It is administratively feasible, and it does produce behavior that persists when reinforcement doesn't come. Nearly all of our everyday behaviors are provided with feedback on an intermittent or occasional basis: We aren't always called on when our hands are raised; we don't always reach a person by phone when first trying.

When working with your students, you will undoubtedly introduce them to many new tasks. During their first few experiences with the new components, try providing valued feedback each time students move in the direction you desire. Once the behavior is established, gradually introduce the students to intermittent feedback. One final word: You have earlier been cautioned to avoid using any reinforcement with "undesired" behaviors. The reason is obvious: Undesired behavior that is reinforced will likely occur more often in the future. However, undesired behavior that is reinforced "intermittently" will not only occur more often in the future, it will become highly persistent, highly resistant to change. As always, watch carefully the behaviors gaining your attention and recognition.

ANTECEDENTS, "S-DEES" (S^D), AND "S-DELTAS" (S$^\Delta$)

Throughout the text, I used the term "cues" to represent conditions that both occur prior to behavior and, perhaps, *set the stage* for the behavior to occur. Other authors and practitioners prefer the term "antecedents." Still others use a set of "short hand" notations, referred to as S^D (pronounced s-dee) and S$^\Delta$ (pronounced s-delta) to represent the cues, or antecedents, or conditions under which behaviors are most and least likely to occur. (S-dees are cuing conditions in the presence of which a particular behavior is *most likely* to occur—putting your foot on your car's brake in the presence of a red traffic light, for example; S-deltas are cuing conditions in the presence of which behaviors are *least likely* to occur—putting your foot on your car's gas pedal in the presence of a red traffic light.)

Some of us, frankly, combine all of the above terms. While we use them interchangeably, the meaning and importance behind all of them remain the same: We do not see behavior occurring in isolation; we attempt to identify "antecedent" conditions that appear to be associated with the behaviors; we try to determine the conditions under which the behaviors, from the behavior-pairs, occur and do not occur. We know that finding the associative cuing conditions often provides us with the information we need to obtain in order to provide the most beneficial services to an individual. Whether you choose to use "cues," "antecedents," or S^D/S$^\Delta$, your purpose is the same: Locate the active components of the environment that appear to be providing an individual with information. Part of those components will be occurring prior to the individual's behaviors: They will be helping the individual know what to do and what not to do.

CURRICULUM-BASED ASSESSMENT (CBA)/ CURRICULUM-BASED MEASUREMENT (CBM)

This is the "new" stuff that is a lot older than you and I combined. It first entered the teaching profession when a teacher decided to find out what an individual knew about a subject area before beginning any formal teaching endeavor. The teacher's logic was something like: "Better not introduce the material until I make sure the student will benefit from it!" Smart teacher.

The process is not very complicated; never has been very complicated. It involves sampling a student's academic skills as they relate to the *curriculum* being used in the classroom. The materials are most often the student's books and printed exercises. The idea is to gain an accurate measure of the student's *present performance level*. From that, the teacher can determine, more accurately, which book and which exercises will best teach the child. Students learn a lot more that way! Teachers have more fun that way!

Much of the educational delivery system discussed in the book is based on the model often referred to as a curriculum-based assessment and remediation format. I chose not to use the terms "CBA" or "CBM" because they, like so many other terms, have acquired multiple meanings and accompanying baggage. What's behind the terms is, obviously, more important than their "call-letters." A quick check in your university library will provide a rapidly growing list of sources describing the many uses for the curriculum-based approach.

DIFFERENTIAL REINFORCEMENT

This term has found its way in nearly all professions that provide services to children and adults. Basically, it represents the selective reinforcing of one response while not reinforcing another. It is most often spoken of when working with behavior-pairs: One of the behaviors, being viewed as desired, receives reinforcement, another behavior, viewed as undesired, does not receive the same feedback. The behaviors, then, are said to be "differentially reinforced." Quite possibly, you may run into the following abbreviations, each of which stands for a form of differential reinforcement.

1. DRI—differential reinforcement of an *incompatible* behavior. A student receives attention and recognition (assuming they are valued) when sitting; the child does not receive the recognition when standing. The main idea behind this approach is to *decrease the undesired behavior* (standing, at a time the teacher determines is not acceptable) *by increasing an incompatible behavior*—obviously, you can't be sitting and standing at the same time.

2. DRA—differential reinforcement of an *alternative* behavior. In this instance, the behavior to be reinforced does not need to be incompatible with the undesired behavior. Rather, it can be nearly anything else but the undesired behavior. If, for example, a teacher wishes to decrease a student's excessive talking in class, the talking would receive no attention or recognition, while some alternative behavior, such as listening, reading, writing, studying, or what have you, would receive some sign of appreciation.

EXTINCTION

Originally at home in animal laboratories, where an animal's responses were said to be "placed on extinction," the term has found its way into special settings where there is a need to reduce the frequency of certain undesired behaviors. In such settings, the term represents a procedure: The withholding of all social attention and recognition when the undesired behavior occurs. While it is a very effective way of reducing certain behaviors, it can be a difficult procedure to administer: As suggested in the book when discussing the withholding of attention and recognition, our inclination, when a problem presents itself, is to jump in and do something. Extinction doesn't work that way. The procedure requires that you leave the behavior alone—completely, totally, no exceptions. As is likely obvious, it is used alone with differential reinforcement: You place the undesired behavior "on extinction," while reinforcing an incompatible or alternative behavior.

One small note regarding the use of the term: It must always refer to behavior. You (we) do not place individuals "on extinction," nor do we withhold reinforcement until an individual becomes "extinct"! Such uses of the term carry a slightly different, and unintended, meaning.

CONSEQUENCES

While I used the term "consequences" on several occasions throughout the manuscript, my preference for the term "feedback" was based on one major factor: Many people carry the mistaken notion that "consequences" refer to something negative. The old TV show, "Truth or Consequences," along with such statements as, "You must pay the consequences," has no doubt helped produce this incorrect interpretation. The terms, of course, can be used interchangeably. Just remember that both must, initially, be viewed as neutral: A consequence or form of feedback is not, ipso facto, positive or negative. The individual who is experiencing the consequence makes that decision.

NEGATIVE REINFORCEMENT

This term, for many of us, is most confusing: It is difficult to reconcile something "negative" being associated with the term "reinforcement." The most common problem with the term is the belief that it and "punishment" are synonymous. There are, indeed, several differences between the two technical words. First, the procedure referred to as punishment *decreases* behavior; the procedure known as negative reinforcement *increases* behavior. While both procedures employ "aversive" stimuli, punishment *applies* the stimulus; negative reinforcement *withdraws* the aversive component. Confusing, yes. No harm is done by dropping the term completely.

SHAPING

This term represents an approach where we attempt to help individuals move from their present performance level to our determined objectives and goals. Progress occurs across what are referred to as "small steps" or "successive approximations." In a true sense, these small steps or approximations "bridge" the gap between where students are and where you would like them to be. Shaping is a technique used by all of us at one point or another when helping someone accomplish a complex task, be the task related to reading or riding a bike. In my judgment, shaping represents the genius part of our efforts. It is where you will call upon all your brain power to determine how best to resolve errors you uncovered during error analysis, or how to help a student hurdle an academic impasse, or assist a child in understanding a most complex concept. The process requires that you provide assistance to students as they gradually progress toward the goal: Practice exercises and accompanying positive feedback are provided along the way; anything students do (involving behavior or thinking or problem-solving skills) that moves them closer to resolving errors or understanding the concept or accomplishing a complex task is supported through your encouragement and valued appreciation. In the absence of assistance provided through shaping, students may either not reach a desired goal, or may experience such frustration as they attempt to reach it that when it is finally within grasp, they may not appreciate their own accomplishment. Shaping, on the other hand, often provides students with just what they need to continue with their efforts: your helping hand, and a taste of success as they gradually accomplish what is perceived to be important and necessary.

INDEX

INDEX